BRITISH POLITICS AND FOREIGN POLICY
1744–57

For

Stephen and Dorothée Perring

British Politics and Foreign Policy, 1744–57

Mid-Century Crisis

JEREMY BLACK
University of Exeter, UK

Routledge
Taylor & Francis Group

LONDON AND NEW YORK

First published in paperback 2024

First published 2015 by Ashgate Publishing

Published 2016 by Routledge
4 Park Square, Milton Park, Abingdon, Oxon OX14 4RN

and by Routledge
605 Third Avenue, New York, NY 10158

Routledge is an imprint of the Taylor & Francis Group, an informa business

Copyright © 2015, 2016, 2024 Jeremy Black

Publisher's Note
The publisher has gone to great lengths to ensure the quality of this reprint but points out that some imperfections in the original copies may be apparent.

British Library Cataloguing in Publication Data
A catalogue record for this book is available from the British Library

The Library of Congress has cataloged the printed edition as follows:
Black, Jeremy, 1955-
  British politics and foreign policy, 1744-57 : mid-century crisis / by Jeremy Black.
    pages cm
  Includes bibliographical references and index.
  ISBN 978-1-4724-2369-6 (hardcover : alk. paper)
  1. Great Britain--Foreign relations--1727-1760. 2. Great Britain-
-Politics and government--1727-1760. 3. Seven Years' War, 1756-1763--Causes. I. Title.
  DA500.B535 2015
  327.41009'033--dc23
                                                                    2015007104

ISBN: 978-1-4724-2369-6 (hbk)
ISBN: 978-1-03-292381-9 (pbk)
ISBN: 978-1-315-57024-2 (ebk)

DOI: 10.4324/9781315570242

Contents

Preface

A mid-eighteenth century crisis is not the usual way in which the rise of Britain to imperial greatness, and unprecedented global power by 1763, is approached. However, the period from 1744 to 1757 is important and instructive, because there was indeed both a crisis and a strong sense of crisis. For Britain, these were years of repeated failure and of serious anxiety, both of which were important in their own way and were to affect subsequent attitudes and policies. A focus on these problems, and on the resulting search for solutions, provides a key subject and theme in this book, and a way to examine foreign power and to consider its relationship with domestic politics.

Imperial greatness was to be amply displayed in the terms of the Peace of Paris of 1763, terms that arose from a series of triumphs, most obviously in 1759, 'the Year of Victories'. In that year, British forces captured Quebec as well as Guadeloupe in the West Indies, a French army was defeated at Minden in modern Germany, and the French fleet was heavily defeated in two dramatic battles, Lagos and Quiberon Bay. In 1763, Britain made major territorial gains in North America, the West Indies and West Africa, bringing the war to a triumphant conclusion. It is all too easy, therefore, to write an account of the eighteenth century, or, more narrowly, of the mid-eighteenth century, in which the structural reasons for British success, ones that explain the victories, are emphasised, while Britain's success appears well nigh inevitable. That was not, however, how the earlier situation struck most contemporaries, both British and foreign. Instead, crisis was to the fore.

This crisis was given dramatic force from the outset. In 1744, Britain was nearly invaded by the French, being saved by spring storms in the Channel from a major naval expedition designed to help the Jacobites, the supporters of the Stuart claimants on the throne. To Whigs, those who supported the tendency, movement or inclination that captured the political alignment and heritage of the government and, in addition, those of some of the opposition, this French backing for the Jacobites represented a fundamental threat and:

gives a flat lie to the boasted moderation and innocence of her [French] views; and must convince every subject of the [Dutch] republic, as well as of England, that not only the possessions of the House of Austria, and the Balance of Power, but even our own liberties, and religion, are struck at by that ambitious power.[1]

The following year, the Hanoverian regime, that established in 1714 as a result of the Act of Settlement in 1701, and headed from 1727 to 1760 by George II, was nearly overthrown by a Jacobite rising. Under Charles Edward Stuart, 'Bonnie Prince Charlie', the elder son of the Jacobite claimant 'James III' (and 'VIII' of Scotland), the Jacobites overran much of Scotland, before marching south in England as far as Derby in the East Midlands. Whether they would march on to London as Charles Edward wanted, and whether, if so, it would be possible to stop it, became a key issue. Despite victory at Culloden on 16 April (os) 1746, invasion fears persisted.[2]

Abroad, and over a longer time span, Britain found the War of the Austrian Succession far more difficult than had been anticipated when British troops were sent to the Continent in 1742. These forces began fighting the French the following year, famously and victoriously so at the battle of Dettingen. However, this victory did not have the anticipated outcome, while the 1744 campaign proved a serious disappointment. In addition, repeatedly defeated from 1745, the year of the battle of Fontenoy, British forces were driven from the Austrian Netherlands (Belgium). Moreover, in 1747, the United Provinces (Netherlands), Britain's key ally, were invaded by the French, with the major fortress of Bergen-op-Zoom falling. Britain's alliance system could not deliver the anticipated results, either militarily or diplomatically, a major failure for foreign policy. The war ended, in 1748, with serious anxiety about the ability to defend the United Provinces, where the major fortress of Maastricht fell, which it had last done to the French in 1673. There was concern over what France and its sometime ally Prussia could, and would, go on to do.

In the event, after war panics, notably involving the possibility of a Prussian attack on Hanover in 1753, Britain began hostilities with France in 1754 and, on a greater scale, 1755, but without an alliance system able to deliver support. This continued to be the situation in 1756 when war was formally declared by both powers. In addition, in 1756, Britain's flawed alliance system, with Austria, the United Provinces [modern Netherlands] and Russia, collapsed. As a result of unexpected diplomatic changes that year, Britain was left linked to the weakest

---

[1]   Robert Trevor, envoy in The Hague, to John, Lord Carteret, Secretary of State, 14 Feb. 1744, NA. SP. 84/402 fol. 90.

[2]   *General Evening Post*, 6 May (os) 1746.

of the trio of Austria, Prussia and Russia: Prussia under Frederick II, the Great (r. 1740–86). The Russian alliance that had been eagerly sought by successive ministries from the early 1730s was no more, and this was perceived as a major diplomatic and strategic failure.

The subsequent war initially went badly for Britain. The Mediterranean island of Minorca was lost in 1756, with a British fleet failing to relieve the British garrison, a cause of great humiliation. There were fears of a French invasion of Britain, fears that greatly affected government policy. Claims that Britain had lost its historical vigour – 'the Breed of our Britons is changed from what it was when we conquered France under our Edwards and Henrys', a reference to Edward III and Henry V – were matched by suggestions of ethnic, indeed racial, degradation as a consequence of the arrival of Hanoverian troops and Jews.[3] Critics looked back, to the glories of the victorious reign of Queen Anne (1702–14),[4] rather than forward. *Old England* printed the terms of the 1670 treaty with Spain in order to throw critical light on the present situation.[5]

The ministry fell in 1756, despite its very strong showing in the latest general election, that of 1754. In 1757, Robert, 4th Earl of Holdernesse, one of the two Secretaries of State, discerned a fundamental threat, with France and Austria 'upon the point of subverting the System of Europe, and of Submitting the World to their Arbitrary Will and Pleasure'.[6] There were fresh blows in North America. Moreover, on the Continent, a British amphibious attack on the French port of Rochefort was unsuccessful, French forces overran George II's Electorate of Hanover, and Prussia was in great peril. Its King, Frederick, referred to the need to 'give a spirit to the English nation, who have, hitherto, been frightened with vain terrors of invasion'.[7]

Thus, this period needs to be considered in its own right, and not as a prelude to eventual British triumph (and Prussian survival) in the Seven Years' War (1756–63). In part, the book will take us back to the uncertainties of the period, uncertainties that involve us in the counterfactuals of what might have happened, counterfactuals that were of great weight to contemporaries. It will therefore show the importance of the period, both in itself and as a means to consider the broader question of Britain's success in the Seven Years' War, which

---

[3]   Anon., *A Serious Defence of some late Measures of the Administration* (London, 1756), pp. 8, 10, 14–17, 50.

[4]   *Old England*, 1 Aug. (os) 1752; Orrery to Thomas Carte, 5 Aug. (os) 1752, *Orrery Papers* II, 116.

[5]   *Old England*, 14 Oct. 1752.

[6]   Holdernesse to Onslow Burrish, envoy in Munich, 26 Aug. 1757, NA. SP. 81/106.

[7]   Andrew Mitchell, envoy in Berlin, to Holdernesse, 2 July 1757, NA. SP. 90/69.

turned out to be a key episode in global history. If the focus is on the latter, then the emphasis is on trans-oceanic expansion. That, however, captures neither the anxiety of Britain's position at the outset of the conflict, nor the extent to which there was support for peace. Linked to this consideration of success in terms of earlier crisis, a prime intention, in a book that necessarily involves much detail, is to ask about the importance of politics and foreign policy to the central narratives and questions of eighteenth-century British development. The key ones in this case are those of imperial expansion, governmental capability, political strength and economic growth.

This approach involves an analytical narrative, supported by thematic chapters, on the relationship between politics and foreign policy. This is for a period not hitherto treated as a unit, not least as it is carved in part from sections of two wars, each of which it is all too easy to treat as a coherent unit. There is excellent scholarship covering much of this period, but no adequate recent account of the interaction of politics and foreign policy, one that is written from both perspectives, and treating each as independent spheres as well as interacting. This book will show that ministerial change and political fortunes were closely linked to foreign policy, and will discuss the consequences. The relationship worked both ways, with foreign policy repeatedly affecting, and being affected by, political developments, in a relationship that was both structural and a matter of agency, both reactive and dynamic. As a result, this is a study both of 'aussen' and of 'innen' politics: of foreign policy dominated by both foreign and domestic pressures. It will provide important guidance to both foreign policy and political history. Because the relationship worked both ways, it is necessary to study diplomatic sources, both British and foreign, alongside material on British politics and on the debate over foreign policy. To consider only part of the material risks offering a seriously flawed account of the subject.

Far from being simply a study of a number of episodes, my book will include the structural aspects of the relationship between foreign policy and politics. This original approach is taken in order to examine questions about political stability, motivation and effectiveness. In particular, the role of monarch (George II, r. 1727–60), Court and ministers will be considered, alongside those of Parliament, parliamentary politics, and the public sphere of discussion, notably, but not only, the press. The book will therefore offer a guided narrative that both uses and builds on the analysis that would have been offered by contemporary commentators, British and foreign. The analysis of the content and tone of political discussion about foreign policy will provide an informed assessment of the significance of the ideas, terms and language employed by contemporaries.

The use of the nation as a key concept in the discussion about foreign policy was particularly important.

In looking through a different lens and asking new questions about a period I have considered before, notably in a book on foreign policy in 1739–63, published in 1998, that adopts a different methodological approach,[8] I have benefited from work done, by others and myself, over the last seventeen years. I would first like to pay tribute to the excellent studies produced by other scholars. Key figures include Stephen Conway, Richard Harding, Hamish Scott, Brendan Simms and Andrew Thompson, each of whom has greatly advanced the subject. Contrasts in approach and interpretation with my work will emerge, but these indicate the extent to which the period is one that is full of issues and questions, as well as significance. I recommend reading the contrasting accounts now available as a result of this book in order both to understand the eighteenth century and to ask broader questions about how best to approach and present the study of foreign policy.

Secondly, I have benefited from fresh archival research on my own part. Part has been in archives in which I had already done much work, but material new to me has been a priority. The major sources employed in this book are the diplomatic series in the National Archives, the private papers of key ministers, the parliamentary debates, and the culture of print, especially newspapers and pamphlets. In addition to British sources, there is also due consideration to foreign material. This focuses on Britain's prime opponent, France, with manuscript material from a range of archives there, but there is also the use of material from other states. The close connections between the envoys of the kingdom of Sardinia (rulers of Savoy-Piedmont) and the British minsters ensure particular attention to their reports.

I would like to thank Her Majesty the Queen for permission to use material in the Royal Archives, as well as the Trustees of the Bedford Estate, the Trustees of the Wentworth Woodhouse Estate, the Earl of Harrowby, Lady Lucas, and John Weston Underwood for permission to use private papers. Private papers repeatedly provide information that supplements and clarifies what is in the official correspondence. Thus, in 1756, at a time of international tension, Holdernesse, the Secretary of State, wrote to Charles Hanbury Williams, the envoy in St Petersburg:

> Do you think it quite impossible to gain the Favourite [of Czarina Elisabeth]. If that could be done, I think I can answer that anything in reason would be

---

[8]   J. Black, *Europe or America? British Foreign Policy 1739–1763* (London, 1998).

complied with. I write this absolutely without orders; and beg that in your answer you would not take notice of my having wrote to you.[9]

This book is part of a sequence that is intended to cover the politics of foreign policy from 1713 to 1783, and can be profitably read alongside *Debating Foreign Policy* (2011) and after *Politics and Foreign Policy, 1727–44* (2014). However, the book is also designed to stand on its own. This study benefits from the opportunity to work on the subject for many years. I would like to thank all those who have supported my research, not least by offering encouragement and hospitality. I have profited from the comments of Bill Gibson on an earlier draft. Tom Gray has proved a most helpful editor. The book is dedicated to Stephen and Dorothée Perring with thanks for good friendship, excellent company and wonderful meals.

---

[9]   Holdernesse to Hanbury Williams, 6 Aug. 1756, HW.

Abbreviations

Add	Additional Manuscripts
AE	Paris, Archives du Ministère des Relations Extérieures
AM	Archives de la Marine
AN	Paris, Archives Nationales
Ang	Angleterre
AST	Turin, Archivio di Stato
Aut	Autriche
BL	London, British Library, Department of Manuscripts
Bod	Oxford, Bodleian Library, Department of Manuscripts
Br.-Han.	Brunswick-Hanovre
Cobbett	*Parliamentary History of England*
CP	Correspondance Politique
CRO	County Record Office
Cumb.P.	Cumberland Papers
Darmstadt	Staatsarchiv Darmstadt
Farmington	Farmington, Connecticut, Lewis Walpole Library
Goodwood	The papers of the Dukes of Richmond
Hanover	Hanover, Niedersächsisches Hauptstaatsarchiv
HHStA	Vienna, Haus-, Hof-, und Staatsarchiv
HL	San Marino, California, Huntington Library
HMC	Historical Manuscripts Commission
HP	London, History of Parliament, Transcripts
HW	Newport, Public Library, Hanbury Williams papers
Ing	Inghilterra
LM	Lettere Ministri
MD	Mémoires et Documents
Marburg	Marburg, Staatsarchiv, Politische Akten nach Philipp d. Gr.
Munich	Munich, Bayerisches Hauptstaatsarchiv, Bayr. Gesandtschaft
NA	London, National Archives

NAS	Edinburgh, National Archives of Scotland
NeC.	Nottingham, University Library, Clumber Papers
Polit. Corr.	R. Köser (ed.), *Politische Correspondenz Friedrichs des Grossen* (46 vols, Berlin, 1879–1939)
Polwarth	Polwarth Manuscripts
RA	Windsor, Royal Archives
Sandon	Sandon Hall, Harrowby papers
SP	State Papers
UL	University Library
Weston Underwood	Iden Green, Weston Underwood papers

Unless otherwise stated, all dates are given in new style, which became the British calendar on 14 September 1752. Old- style dates which were eleven days earlier are marked (os).

Chapter 1

Introduction: Mid-century Crisis

In Dorchester, the county town of Dorset, the news was bleak in December 1757. An express from Bridport, a coastal port in west Dorset, brought the news that French troops had landed there and were marching inland on the nearby county capital. The West Country, the invasion route unsuccessfully pursued by James, Duke of Monmouth in 1685, but eventually chosen and successfully used by William of Orange in 1688, apparently lay open. William had pressed on to take London and become king as William III.

Now, a far more terrifying French invasion was on. In fact, a French privateer had driven a British coaster ashore and, determined to enjoy the benefits, had sent some of its hands to pillage the ship.[1] However, the news of alleged invasion captured the strong sense of vulnerability that marked Britain at this juncture. Indeed, there were other false reports of French invasions, especially, but not only, on the south coast of England. This was notably so in December 1745 when the news briefly delayed the pursuit of the Jacobite forces under Bonnie Prince Charlie (Charles Edward Stuart) retreating into Scotland which helped ensure that the campaign lasted into 1746. Similarly, in April 1755, as full-scale war with France neared, Dublin 'was alarmed' with reports that the French had invaded western Ireland.[2]

A mid-century crisis is a term and thesis frequently applied by Western scholars to describe Britain, Europe and, indeed, the world in the mid-seventeenth century. For Britain, however, the term is also very applicable for other periods, including the 1060s, 1140s, 1260s, late 1340s, 1450s, 1540s–50s, and the 1940s. The term crisis is also acceptable for the mid-eighteenth century, definitely for the 1740s and possibly also for the early stages of the Seven Years' War in the 1750s. The crisis of the 1740s had a number of dimensions and peaks. At the outset, there was a demographic crisis linked to terrible weather, disease and dearth (shortage of food). The relationship between these and the political crisis of the early 1740s, notably the unpopularity of the government

---

[1]   *London Chronicle*, 1 Jan. 1757.
[2]   Henry Meredyth to Sir Robert Wilmot, 19 Apr. 1755, Matlock, Derbyshire CRO, Catton Collection, WH 3448.

of Sir Robert Walpole (1721–42), is unclear, but these problems appear to have contributed to an atmosphere of malaise, if not general crisis. Furthermore, in 1741, military failure against Spain and the results of the general election in which the government had done badly led to a strong sense of the need for a political change. In terms of ministerial stability, this sense helped produce a very difficult situation that lasted until 1746. However, the immediate 1741 crisis appeared largely assuaged by Walpole's enforced resignation in February 1742 and by the subsequent reconstitution of the ministry to take in some of the opposition, notably William Pulteney (made Earl of Bath in 1742) and John, Lord Carteret (Earl Granville from 1744), the key leaders of the opposition Whigs.

A more serious crisis arose from the move to war with France. British troops were rapidly sent to the Continent by the new government in 1742, and conflict with France began in 1743 as a result of the movement of the army into the Empire (Germany). In February–March 1744, in response, the French made a large-scale attempt to invade England on behalf of the Jacobites, an attempt, however, thwarted by a serious storm in the Channel.[3] In 1745–6, there was the most serious Jacobite rebellion of the eighteenth century, while, in 1744–8, France made major conquests in the Low Countries, overrunning the Austrian Netherlands (Belgium), capturing Bergen-op-Zoom (1747) and Maastricht (1748), two of the major Dutch fortresses, and doing far better than when fighting British and allied armies in this region in the Nine Years' War (1688–97) and the War of the Spanish Succession (1701–14).[4] This was a contrast drawn by contemporaries.

This outcome appeared a clear demonstration that Britain could no longer achieve the success of the past. As a result, the Revolution Settlement, the political and constitutional changes following the Glorious Revolution of 1688–9, was apparently being overthrown, or at least endangered, by the inadequacies of what had come since. Such a point, that of structural failure and grave mistakes in policy and implementation, was made by contemporaries, and thus contributed to the sense of serious crisis, giving it greater depth. The impact of these challenges was increased by their apparently cumulative, interacting and self-sustaining nature. Together, they created the impression of a fundamental threat to Britain and its political system. The combination, of war with a successful France and a resurgence in Jacobitism, brought together the anxieties

---

[3]   J. Colin, *Louis XV et les Jacobites. Le projet de débarquement en Angleterre 1743–44* (Paris, 1901).

[4]   The years given are for the wars and not for British participation in them.

of the age, both political and religious, and thus contributed greatly to a sense of existential challenge for Britain.

It is easy to overlook this sense when discussing the period as is conventionally done, notably in terms of the pursuit of political power, by means of the struggles of parliamentary advantage and ministerial position, or of an accessible culture apparently offered by Henry Fielding's novels, notably *Tom Jones* (1749). However, anxiety, indeed foreboding, were important aspects of the 1740s, and Fielding's journalism will be employed in this book to make this point. Some of the political language of the period, such as the reiterated references to corruption and to factionalism, was for specific partisan purposes, but such language also spoke to wider concerns. Moreover, these concerns took on much of their bite because of the anxieties about Britain's international position, as well as the related but deeper anxieties centred on Jacobitism and the challenge it really and apparently posed to the entire existing British system.[5]

As a consequence, any account of the decade, of the reign of George II (1727–60), or of the eighteenth century, in terms of a smooth progression toward national greatness has to be seriously qualified. If there is to be a narrative, indeed a teleology, of Whig success, it should not ignore repeated problems. The 1740s deserve discussion in terms of a series of crises that greatly challenged Britain. Others occurred in 1756–7, more obviously in 1781–3, as America was lost, and again in 1795–8 as the French Revolutionary War, in which Britain had become involved from 1793, became a disaster for it. In all four cases, external challenges were accompanied by serious internal problems, with ministerial crises in 1744, 1746, 1756–7, and 1782–3, and insurrection in the empire – in Scotland, America and Ireland respectively – in 1745–6, 1775–83 and 1798. There were also serious problems with harvests and food supplies, especially, but not only, in the early 1740s and the late 1790s.

Rivalry with France and Spain drew on potent ideological elements, notably affirmations of liberty in the shape of anti-Catholicism and opposition to autocracy, as well as on the historic and present fears these themes represented, and on a legacy of war. France was a formidable military power, with a far larger army, and with the world's second-largest navy after Britain. This rivalry with France was that of state and society, economy and ideology, culture and religion. France was seen as becoming an enemy that had to be constantly checked and held back.

Rivalry with France created pressures and debate in Britain, each looking toward stronger remedies and new solutions, to calls for revival and to warnings

---

[5]   J. Black, 'British Intelligence and the Mid-Eighteenth Century Crisis', *Intelligence and National Security*, 22 (1987), pp. 209–29.

about failure. For mid-century, there is no epic warning work of British decline comparable to Edward Gibbon's *Decline and Fall of the Roman Empire* (1776–88), the resonance of which was affected by the crisis caused by the American War of Independence. However, the warning theme of challenge was present in much of the political and historical writing produced in the 1740s and 1750s.

An awareness of problems directs attention to the significance of countervailing factors contributing to national strength and resilience, both in these crises and at other times. These factors included the economy, the fiscal system, the absence of rebellion in the key territory, England, and the nature of leadership, both royal and ministerial, whether individual or collective. For all their limitations, George II (r. 1727–60) and George III (r. 1760–1820) proved impressive figures in a crisis. In particular, alongside his customary impatience, George II displayed considerable fortitude. His views over ministerial composition caused serious political problems in Britain in 1744, 1746 and 1757, but he finally accepted the exigencies of parliamentary monarchy in each case. Failure over America and domestic governance led George III to contemplate abdication in 1782, but he also adapted to circumstances.

Some of their ministers, whether in 1745–6, in 1756–7 or in 1775–83, were less impressive, notably showing less unity or resolution, or both; although, under William Pitt the Younger, the ministry proved effective in 1795–8. The essential support of England and Wales, as well as of the key groups in Scotland and Ireland, was crucial in all four crises. More Scots fought in William, Duke of Cumberland's army than against it in suppressing the Jacobite rising in 1746; although modern Scottish nationalists are particularly apt to forget or underplay the point. The harsh consequences of William III's defeat of the Irish Jacobites in 1690–92 helped ensure that there was no rebellion in Ireland during the mid-eighteenth century (unlike in the mid-seventeenth), despite or, perhaps, because of an appalling Irish famine in 1740–1.[6]

In the 1740s, the equation of public support for the system in England was a matter not only of only limited backing for Jacobitism, but also of the absence of serious radical political pressure from the lower and middling orders when the political nation was divided and the state vulnerable. Had there been such a challenge from below, it is possible that the non-Jacobite élite would have sought to avoid the bitter political disputes that occurred in 1741–2 and 1744–6; although anxiety might well have led to a greater determination to transform an apparently failing domestic situation. It is also possible that the government

---

6   J. Kelly, 'Coping with Crisis: The Response to the Famine of 1740–1', *Eighteenth-Century Ireland*, 27 (2012), pp. 99–122.

would not have risked the confrontations with France from 1742 and 1754, not least due to the likely balance between populist pressure to act against France and the risks of division affecting the capacity to do so. Looked at differently, such a challenge might have encouraged political disputes, as strategies to address it were contested. As another threat, Jacobitism might have sought a broader constituency of support as, indeed, James II and VII had attempted to do with the Dissenters in 1685–8.

Instead, the absence of a wide-ranging national Jacobite activism, certainly in England, was matched by the lack of a social challenge on the part of the unpropertied, a lack which allowed the elite to pursue their divisions and policies. There was a degree of social tension in England in 1745, when there was some opposition to the idea that peers receive government pay for the volunteer regiments they were raising and commanding against the Jacobites; but there was nothing serious. The situation did not change appreciably until the 1790s; although the American War of Independence (1775–83) saw a major rise in social challenge, not only in the American colonies but also in Ireland and Britain.

Whatever the social context, it was necessary to secure political advantage. The 'Old Corps' Whigs was the name given to the group that constituted the ministry and its supporters under Walpole, a group that, led by Thomas, Duke of Newcastle and his brother, Henry Pelham, was also the largest parliamentary interest thereafter. In the 1740s, the leadership of the 'Old Corps' helped ensure the continued operation of a parliamentary monarchy that successfully resisted external crises, internal challenges, and the less certain hazard of excessive commitments, commitments that posed both external and internal problems. This achievement had not seemed obvious at the beginning of the decade, not least because, then and for several years, it was unclear to all what the replacement of the Walpole ministry would lead to. Certainly, the incessant attack on the Walpole system as corrupt scarcely appeared to admit of compromise or continuity. *Common Sense*, a leading London opposition newspaper, in its issue of 10 May (os) 1740, offered a prognosis of civil strife:

When one servant of the Crown usurps to himself the whole power of the state, without admitting any person of the least share, a practice inconsistent with the nature of a free government, he may, no doubt, in a little time, fill all employments with spirits like his own. Rapine within, and ignorant measures without, will beget a dislike in the people towards those in the administration, and this dislike (if the same measures are continued) must proceed at last to an invincible hatred. When it comes to this, the man in power will naturally think, that he is not safe till liberty is subdued.

However, civil conflict only occurred in the very different circumstances of a Jacobite rising in 1745–6, and then with very few English rebelling, and notably not in southern England. That the latter situation would be the case, however, was unclear prior to 1745.

Instead of Walpole's ministry being replaced in 1742 by one drawing on a united opposition, the latter fractured. Indeed, most of the opposition Whig leaders, notably William Pulteney and John, Lord Carteret, abandoned their Tory allies and, instead, joined the bulk of the 'Old Corps' Whigs in a new government. The ministry, therefore, remained Whig, as George II very much wanted if he could not keep Walpole. The disillusioned and bitter Tories continued in opposition, some, in their anger, saying they would have preferred Walpole back.[7] They were joined, at least in parliamentary divisions, by a group of opposition Whigs who were not involved in the new system, a group among whom the young William Pitt (later Pitt the Elder) was making his name as a vigorous speaker with a penchant for causing offence.

Although an important member of the new political order, Pulteney, previously the leader of the opposition Whigs in the House of Commons, did not actually take office. Instead, Spencer, 1st Earl of Wilmington became First Lord of the Treasury, but without the directing power over patronage and government Walpole had wielded. This was not only because Wilmington, although a long-standing politician who had been Speaker of the House of Commons, lacked the relevant ability to manage Parliament on behalf of the ministry, but also because he sat in the House of Lords whereas the Commons was the key political cockpit. There was a significant policy change in 1742 under the dynamic and autocratic leadership of Carteret, who became Secretary of State of the Northern Department: the ministry abandoned Walpole's long-standing policy of peace with France. War on the Continent appeared more necessary to Carteret than the trans-oceanic conflict with Spain (the War of Jenkins' Ear) that had begun in 1739 and that continued until 1748. This focus on France reflected the fact that it was a more major power than Spain. Moreover, large-scale French advances across the Rhine in 1741 had threatened Hanover and seriously challenged Austria. As a diplomat at a key posting and, then, an active Secretary of State (1721–4) under George I, Carteret had participated in a situation in which Britain could act as a major power on the Continent. This capability had appeared lost under Walpole in the 1730s. Now, the very foundations of any revival were seemingly under grave threat from French power and ambitions, which apparently demonstrated the need for urgent action.

---

7   Matthew Decker to the Earl of Morton, 16 Dec. (os) 1742, NAS. GD. 150/3485/46.

Aside from the French challenge in Europe, Spain's overseas empire had not collapsed as had been widely hoped in 1739. The Walpole government had felt it necessary to respond to the national mood, the demand for action, and a large force had been sent to the West Indies in 1741. However, the ability of Spain, assisted by tropical diseases, to defend its empire had been gravely underestimated, and by the ministry as well as public opinion. Cartagena, a fortified port-city on the Caribbean coast of modern Colombia, successfully resisted siege, helped by an effective defence and by inadequate co-operation between the British army and navy. Yellow fever and malaria were also significant. In 1740–2, largely due to disease, the British forces in the West Indies lost over 70 per cent of their strength. The outcome helped discredit the Walpole government, which was in a far more difficult domestic political position than the Pitt the Younger government was to be in the mid-1790s when its Caribbean expeditions faced heavy death tolls. Failure at Cartagena in 1741 marked the effective end of bold plans for expansion at the expense of Spain, in part because concern about French expansionism in Europe was becoming more pronounced. British forces did not take a major position in the Spanish New World until, in 1762, they captured Havana, in an expedition again made very costly by disease, but at least successful.

In contrast to Cartagena, conflict with France in Europe resulted in great glory for George II. Under his command, an army that had moved into the Empire (Germany) to thwart the French army was victorious at Dettingen on 27 June 1743. George was severely criticised by the opposition for overly identifying with his Hanoverian troops rather than their British counterparts, but the battle brought a welcome prestige to the monarch as well as greatly altering the strategic situation in the Empire.

When Wilmington died in office on 2 July (os) 1743, Pulteney, with the support of Carteret, tried to succeed him as First Lord of the Treasury. However, still greatly affected by the rivalries of the Walpole ministry, George preferred Newcastle's brother, Henry Pelham, a vital victory for the 'Old Corps' as this position was crucial to government patronage. In turn, George had to part with Carteret in November 1744 because of opposition by key political figures, notably Newcastle, the Secretary of State for the Southern Department from 1724 to 1748, to what was presented as Carteret's excessive commitment to George's wishes as Elector of Hanover. Support for George's wishes had played a central part in Carteret's foreign policy, although the vigorous pursuit of the war with France was his main objective. Carteret's neglect for his colleagues was significant and had destroyed the always weak coherence of the ministry.[8]

In response to this neglect, the Pelhams – Newcastle and his brother Henry – forced George to part with Carteret and some of his allies, and to take in other former opposition Whigs in their place. The latter measure brought strength to the ministry, notably in the House of Commons, wrecked the cohesion of the opposition Whigs, and left Carteret and his allies without options as those Whigs who remained in opposition were not going to co-operate with them. The ministerial crisis in 1744 led to speculation about the political system, speculation in which George's support for Carteret produced serious criticism. *Old England*, a leading opposition London newspaper, in its issue of 26 May (os) 1744, stated:

> Governments are subject to diseases, consequently dissolutions. The disease of a free government is disunion, therefore infirmity in counsel ... the fault not of the constitution but of the administration.

In the issue of 16 February (os) 1745, this paper also emphasised the role of popular pressure, describing the ministerial alteration accordingly: 'the People, by whose voice alone that change was effected'. Concerned that the King could protect a minister who did not enjoy Parliament's confidence, the paper pressed for a limitation of the royal prerogative in this respect. In the event, in accordance with the characteristic nuances of the constitution, and with the related, and successful, imprecision of the political system, the relationship between Crown, ministers and Parliament resolved itself in 1744, as repeatedly, in favour of those ministers able to lead Parliament. As this study will show, this was to be a key aspect of the politics of foreign policy, one that was necessary in order to provide the finance essential to implement policy, as well as the impression of stability and continuity important in winning foreign support.

Divided by the contest over the legacy of Walpolean politics, and, more specifically, over ministerial office, the political order was to be challenged by an upsurge in Jacobite activity. This upsurge was made possible by French support for the cause of the exiled Stuarts. Indeed, the French response in 1744 to British intervention on the Continent in 1743 was serious. Their invasion attempt in 1744 was thwarted by a major storm in the Channel, but it indicated the

---

8   R. Lodge, 'The Hanau Controversy in 1744 and the Fall of Carteret', *English Historical Review*, 38 (1923), pp. 509–31; B. Williams, *Carteret and Newcastle: A Contrast in Contemporaries* (Cambridge, 1943).

challenge posed by the French navy until it could be defeated. In successive wars, this defeat did not decisively occur until 1747 (two battles off Cape Finisterre), 1759 (the battles of Lagos and Quiberon Bay), 1781 (the Saints),[9] and 1805 (Trafalgar). Prior to these, the very existence of the French navy, the second-largest in the world after that of Britain, and one supported by nearby naval bases, notably Brest, posed an acute strategic challenge to nearby Britain in each war, including the serious threat of invasion.

However, the failure of the French invasion attempt in 1744 was followed in 1745 not by another, but only by a small-scale initiative on the part of Charles Edward Stuart (Bonnie Prince Charlie), the elder son of the Pretender. He evaded British warships and, on 23 July (os), with a few followers, landed on Eriskay in the Western Isles of Scotland. Raising his standard at Glenfinnan on the mainland on 19 August (os), Charles Edward quickly overran much of Scotland, despite the reluctance of some Jacobite clans to rise for a prince who had brought no soldiers, and, more seriously, the hostility of the many Scots, notably Presbyterian Scots, who were not Jacobites.

The Jacobites did not only want a Stuart Scotland, not least because a Hanoverian England would not allow its existence: coexistence between Scotland and England was not an option for either party. In part, this was because of the parliamentary Union of 1707, but a sense of ideological struggle was also to the fore. Archbishop Herring of York, one of the few grandees to remain in the North, told a meeting there on 24 September (os) that the Jacobite rising was only 'part of a great plan concerted for our ruin' to establish 'popery and arbitrary power' under the direction of France and Spain. Contemporaries were in no doubt that domestic politics and the international system were closely linked, as indeed they were in both war and peace. From London, the *General Evening Post* of 3 May (os) 1746 referred to the 'quadruple league of France, Scotland, Hell and Spain'. At the same time, there were concerns in Britain about 'the indifferency and lukewarmness of the many'.[10] The poor performance of some of the militia units that deployed against the Jacobites was not encouraging.

Crossing into England on 8 November (os) 1745, Charles Edward took Carlisle after a brief siege (10–15 November (os)). Then, without any resistance, he advanced across Cumbria into Lancashire and captured Lancaster, Preston, Manchester and Derby, the last of which was entered on 4 December (os). Carlisle

---

[9]   However, a large French fleet remained in existence in the West Indies until the end of that war in 1783.

[10]   Robert Trevor, envoy in The Hague, to Robinson, 30 Sept. 1745, BL. Add. 23821 fol. 107.

had a castle, but the rapid fall of the other cities revealed the consequences of the unfortified nature of a country that was less militarised domestically than Continental states. Although the Hanoverian regime re-established control in Edinburgh after the departure of the Jacobite army for England, its armies were totally outmanoeuvred in England. In particular, based in Newcastle, the army in northern England under Field Marshal George Wade was bypassed because the Jacobites advanced south to the west of the Pennines. Wade sought to relieve Carlisle, but did not move fast enough to engage Charles Edward who, as a result, moved closer than Wade to London.

Subsequently, a successful feint towards Wales enabled Charles Edward to pass the army assembled in the Midlands under William, Duke of Cumberland, younger son of George II, opening the way to Derby and ensuring that he was closer than Cumberland to London. While few English Jacobites had risen to help Charles Edward, many of his opponents were hit by panic, although not George II. Dudley Ryder noted in his diary on 3 December (os) 1745: 'people in great pain for the City [of London] ... Papists suspected of an intended rising as soon as the rebels are near London.'[11] By any standards, this was crisis.

---

[11]   Diary of Dudley Ryder, 3 Dec. (os) 1745, Sandon. See also, W. Gibson, 'Edward Weston's Ecclesiastical Correspondence, 1729–61', *Archives*, 39, no. 125 (Apr. 2012), pp. 22–31.

Chapter 2
The Means of Policy

The texts of weekly sermons seem not so much observed of late as those prefixed to periodical papers: the former are, too often, remembered only by idle old women; but the latter, I with great pleasure remark are carefully attended, to, even by young men.

Crab-Tree, 5 July 1757

The themes and goals of policy cannot be separated from the means without creating a misleading impression. This is as true of foreign policy as of other branches of policy. In part, such a misleading impression is somewhat akin to that of trying to separate policy from strategy or implementation, with the means of policy presented as the way to implement and secure policy. This approach risks confusion, because, differently understood and defined, the means were also the context within which themes and goals were established. Moreover, the very same people were involved in discussing, planning and handling both goals and means, which encouraged the process by which means influenced goals. This confusion, or, looked at differently and more accurately, overlap, reflects not only conceptual points, institutional conduct, and the character of foreign policy, but also the ambiguous nature of the British constitution and the complex and varied practice of politics in this period. A quest for precision, therefore, is inappropriate today, as it was inappropriate at the time, because this overlap captured the different elements of the formulation and execution of policy.

The nature of the political and governmental system is a key element when discussing the means of policy. So also is the relationship between domestic and external factors on foreign policy. In assessing both these issues, it is necessary to devote due attention to perception, namely the perceptions, both within Britain and abroad, of how, why, and with what consequences, British policy operated. These perceptions constituted key elements of reality. This was because these perceptions were crucial, both to the deterrent aspect of British power and to Britain's relations with its allies, whether effective or limited. These perceptions were unfixed, indeed, dynamic, in that they changed with reference to the nuances of argument and the views and prejudices of commentators, to British politics, and also in response to developments in the international system.

Throughout, first, in both this chapter and the next, and, second, in the subsequent, narrative, section of the book, there is a need to understand that the elements of reality and perception were not separate. Instead, they were both aspects of a more complex and interactive situation, one, moreover, that, in its context and consequences, covered both Britain and the wider world. In part, this situation rested on the ambiguities of British parliamentary monarchy. These ambiguities were not due to a failure by contemporaries to appreciate how Britain was governed, although that element played a role. Instead, the ambiguities arose, first, from the inherent nature and dynamic character of parliamentary monarchy in this period. This was a system newly created from 1689. Second, the ambiguities arose from the complexities of what this monarchy represented in terms of Britain as a political system and society to both Britons and foreigners.

Throughout, for the years 1744–57, there are the added complications, in the operation of parliamentary monarchy, that stemmed from the fact that Britain was at war. It was formally at war from 1739 with Spain and 1744 with France until 1748, and again, from 1756 to 1763 with France and in 1762–3 with Spain. There were also hostilities in the interwar period of 1748–56, notably with France from 1754. At times, conflict was not central to the politics and foreign policy of Britain, let alone the experience of its public. This was certainly true of the wars in India waged by, and on behalf of, the East India Company: in part, conflict in India was an aspect of the formal wars with France, but there was a separate, and more serious, strand of conflict with France and its local allies in the 1750s. Initially, although to a far lesser extent, this marginality also appeared to be the case for the frontier clash with the French in the Ohio River country in 1754. At that moment, it appeared unclear that there would be major conflict as a result, let alone full-scale and formal war. Nevertheless, in a context driven primarily by British fear and the British response, the crisis very rapidly escalated even though neither power wanted war, as opposed to frontier clashes. Large-scale hostilities with France in North America and at sea began in 1755, and war was declared in 1756; although only after hostilities began in Europe with the rapidly successful French invasion of the British Mediterranean colony of Minorca.

The first years of the period 1744–57, as well as the close of the period, therefore, were years of a difficult and apparently intractable war. As a consequence, there was, and is, in the case of the response to reality and to perceptions, the added factor of the need to consider how the British state and (linked, but separate) its politics actually operated both in peacetime and in war. In the case of 1744–57, part of the contemporary perception of peacetime

Britain was affected by wartime circumstances, both recent and anticipatory. The converse could also be true, not least in the argument, made by both British and more commonly foreign commentators, that British constitutionalism made the state less effective in wartime. However, while the anxieties of, and about, wartime greatly affected the peacetime years, there was no comparable reverse tendency.

The Royal Family

The presiding figure in the state, its government and its politics, in both war and peace, was George II (1683–1760), King since 1727 and one of the most experienced and generally underrated figures in the politics and military affairs of the realm.[1] Throughout the book he will be of significance, but aside from being seen in, and affected by, specific conjunctures, this significance was of varied character. In part, this was a matter of his different roles as a ruler: as King of Great Britain, King of Ireland, and Elector of Hanover, a major German principality. More specifically, the first and the last were of importance. George's position as King of Ireland was not of particular note for the conduct or politics of foreign policy. Nevertheless, setting aside diplomats' speculations about a future wish for independence,[2] there is still room for a scholarly study of Irish views on eighteenth-century foreign policy, and for consideration of whether Anglo-Irish politicians had distinctive views.

As a ruler, there was a major governmental function for the King as far as foreign policy was concerned. This significance is masked because, unlike George III, George II was not an active correspondent. Indeed, no royal bureaucrat, he left very few letters, and notably so for his last two decades. There is a striking contrast in this respect between George and Frederick II of Prussia (r. 1740–86), his nephew. Instead, George worked, as most monarchs did, through conversation and the resulting correspondence and discussion of others, the latter notably formal bureaucratic instructions to British diplomats. As a result of their formulaic style and institutional character, this official correspondence did not always make the King's distinctive role apparent. However, it is evident from the private correspondence of ministers. This correspondence makes it apparent

---

[1] See J. Black, *George II* (Exeter, 2007) and A. Thompson, *George II* (New Haven, Connecticut, 2011).

[2] Perrone to Charles Emmanuel III, 27 Dec. 1753, AST. LM. Ing. 57. For forwarding a French translation of material from the Irish Parliament, Alt, Hesse-Cassel envoy, to William VIII of Hesse-Cassel, Marburg, 4f England, 255.

that George was principally interested in foreign policy.[3] It was expected, by both British and foreign diplomats, that he would be kept informed, and British diplomats returning home or meeting George in, or en route to or from Hanover, were instructed to analyse the situation in order to report to George in person.[4] He also saw and commented on important dispatches,[5] including deciding which the Council was to discuss,[6] and read intercepted correspondence from, or to, foreign diplomats, whether intercepted in London or in Hanover.[7] George's audiences with foreign envoys were not restricted to pleasantries, but covered policy, and often in detail.[8]

At times, as a result of the frequent anxieties and suspicions that arose from George's determination to pursue his interests as Elector of Hanover, the King was deliberately kept in the dark by British ministers, but, in such cases, diplomats had to be both trusted and carefully instructed by the ministers. Keeping rulers, ministers or diplomats in the dark was not unique to Britain, but was a common pattern,[9] albeit one complicated in the case of Britain by the degree of public accountability posed by Parliament. Moreover, George's visits to Hanover created significant managerial and diplomatic problems for his British ministers (and practical issues of governance) as well as being a political issue in Britain. This was notably in 1745 and 1755 when he was abroad at a time of serious, major and rapidly developing crises.

Although George demonstrated his awareness of the significance of national affairs, as when defending British policy in the North American crisis of 1755,[10] ministers could be put on the defensive by George's views on foreign policy, and even more by his wish to give effect to them. The position over foreign policy was affected by the more general situation relating to the King: foreign policy was not separate from the politics and constitutionalism involved in this situation. In 1752, accompanying George to Hanover (for only the second time, the first was in 1750), Thomas, Duke of Newcastle, the senior Secretary of State, noted that the King had commented about an acquittal in London of a disaffected

---

3   Newcastle to Hardwicke, 6 Sept. (os) 1751, BL. Add. 35412 fol. 3.
4   Newcastle to Holdernesse, 2 Apr. (os) 1751, NA. SP. 84/457.
5   Bedford to Joseph Yorke, 4 Apr. (os), Newcastle to Bedford, 26 Sept. (os) 1749, Bedford to Keene, Feb. (os) 1751, 1749, in John Russell (ed.), *Correspondence of John, Fourth Duke of Bedford*, II (London, 1843), pp. 23–4, 46, 70.
6   Russell (ed.), *Bedford*, II, 51.
7   HMC., *Polwarth*, V, 272.
8   Ossorio to Charles Emmanuel III, 23 Feb. 1748, AST. LM. Ing. 54.
9   Guy Dickens, envoy in Moscow, to Newcastle, 18 July 1753, *Sbornik*, 148 (1916), p. 437.
10   Bussy to Rouillé, 29 July 1755, AE. CP. Br.-Han. 52 fol. 19.

printer. The printer was linked to the controversy over Parliament's decision to support the ministry in the contested return for the Westminster by-election of 1750: 'he ran into one of the usual, but strongest declamations against our laws, that punished nobody'. Newcastle's comment linked this anger to George's wish to be as independent as possible of his ministers:

> This spirit in the juries and the City [of London] which the King had flattered himself was almost entirely spent, and at an end; and indeed there were great appearances of it. From thence, His Majesty fears that that quiet which he thought himself sure of, is not so certain, and that he may still be more obliged to follow the advice of his ministers, than he has of late thought himself.[11]

The government's sole remedy, according to Newcastle, was 'to get better juries'. Philip, 1st Earl of Hardwicke, the Lord Chancellor from 1737 to 1756, replied that the jurymen: 'were in general well-affected; but … that a strange run of unpopularity had been raised in the City against the proceedings of the House of Commons in that affair',[12] with opposition to what was seen as the use of arbitrary power by the Commons. This attitude, which was focused because the situation in London was at issue, looked toward the views of the American colonists in the Stamp Act Crisis of 1765–6.

The official correspondence of ministers could be highly instructive about George's opinions. His forceful views and competitive attitudes were often to the fore, standing forth from the documents, as in 1752 when Newcastle reported from Hanover that the King:

> extremely approves the directions for fitting out, with the greatest expedition, a stronger squadron for the coast of [West] Africa, than the French will have there. In the present circumstances, there is no other certain way of doing with them, but by being stronger where we can.[13]

This was very much an approach to Anglo-French relations that was reliant on force, intimidation, and deterrence as a key background for negotiations, an approach also seen with his second son, William, Duke of Cumberland.

George was indeed sensitive to the tone of negotiations, the aspect that is frequently most difficult to recover. In May 1756, Robert, 4th Earl of

---

[11]　Newcastle to Pelham, 26 July 1752, BL. Add. 35412 fol. 209.
[12]　Newcastle to Hardwicke, 26 July 1752, BL. Add. 35412 fol. 185.
[13]　Newcastle to Holdernesse, 26 July 1752, NA. SP. 36/119 fol. 143.

Holdernesse, the Secretary of State for the Northern Department, informed Andrew Mitchell, envoy in Berlin: 'His Majesty was particularly pleased to observe the frank and confidential manner in which His Prussian Majesty had thought proper to open himself to you, upon the several points of business now depending'.[14] This comment reflected George's view of the behaviour he ought to adopt, as well as his awareness of what was required in order to assuage Frederick's concerns about George, his uncle and Electoral rival.

George's significance was greatly enhanced by his international role as Elector of Hanover, a role accentuated when he visited Hanover.[15] He was repeatedly greatly anxious about Hanover's vulnerability to attack,[16] particularly from neighbouring Prussia and from France. This vulnerability had been demonstrated in a series of invasion panics from 1727, notably from Prussia in 1727, 1729 and 1738, and from France in 1734 and 1741. Vulnerability from Prussia owed much to it having dominions to the west as well as east of Hanover. This was a situation that was exacerbated when Prussia acquired East Friesland in 1744, ensuring that it also had a territory to the north. Moreover, East Friesland's port of Emden gave Prussia a port on the North Sea. In competition, George sought to emulate his father and grandfather and to further Hanoverian expansion. This was notably so at the expense of neighbouring prince-bishoprics, particularly Hildesheim and Osnabruck, and, even when allied from 1756, he wished to ensure that Prussian territorial gains were matched by Hanover.[17] George was repeatedly tempted by Frederick with territorial gains for Hanover.[18] However, George's attitude to Frederick, one of rivalry and envy, was a serious cause of concern to the British ministers, notably in 1747–8 and 1752–3.[19] Policy toward Prussia was a sphere in which, because of his interests as Elector of Hanover, the royal role was central, as in the mid-1740s when he pursued a secret anti-Prussian foreign policy, operating through the Hanoverian government and the British envoy in St Petersburg, John, 3rd Earl of Hyndford, in a way that contradicted the anti-French emphasis of the British ministry. This compromised the wish of the ministry to focus Russian attention on opposing France, rather than, as George wished, Prussia, and also thwarted the hope of winning over Frederick II after his Second Silesian War with Austria ended at the close of

---

14   Holdernesse to Mitchell, 28 May 1756, NA. SP. 90/65.
15   Rouillé to Aubeterre, 17 July 1755, AE. CP. Aut. 254 fol. 225.
16   Mirepoix to Saint-Contest, 10 Jan. 1754, AE. CP. Ang. 437 fols 17–18.
17   Newcastle to Hardwicke, 11 Oct. 1756, BL. Add. 35416 fol. 89.
18   Frederick II to George II, 25 Dec. 1756, *Polit. Corr.*, XIV, 168.
19   Holdernesse to Newcastle, 29 Dec. 1756, BL. Add. 32869 fol. 422.

1745. Largely thanks to George, the attempt to improve relations with Prussia in the aftermath of the War of the Austrian Succession miscarried.[20]

Hanoverian diplomats and couriers could play a role in supplementing those of Britain. At times, any attempt to supplement such activity could be secret due to the sensitivities of some British ministers,[21] the concerns of British politicians and public opinion, and the conventions of the British constitution. Although modest in size, the Hanoverian diplomatic network provided George with a source of information separate to that of his British diplomats, which gave him a greater room for manoeuvre, vis-à-vis both of his governments, than he would otherwise have had. The Hanoverian postal interception and deciphering system brought many benefits and George claimed that it was not only better than its British counterpart, which itself was highly impressive, but also an essential source of information for the British ministry. Indeed, in July 1745, writing from Hanover, William, 1st Earl of Harrington, the Secretary of State for the Northern Department, sent Newcastle Danish and Prussian diplomatic intercepts about the possibility of French support for the Jacobites.[22] Moreover, separately to George, the Hanoverian government was capable of its own initiatives, as in 1756 when it pressed for Prussian help against a threatened French invasion,[23] and in 1757 when, against the wishes of Frederick II and the British ministry, it very much supported a neutrality for the Electorate and, indeed, debated the value of the maintenance of the personal union with Britain.[24]

British ministers were well aware of George's concern for Hanover, its interests, security and potential for expansion. In 1756, Holdernesse remarked 'every appearance of an alarm from the French towards the Empire touches the King nearly':[25] and efforts were made to coordinate policy between the British and Hanoverian governments. It was believed that the head of the Hanoverian

---

[20] U. Dann, *Hanover and Great Britain 1740–1760* (Leicester, 1991).

[21] Michell to Frederick II, 25 June 1756, *Polit. Corr.*, XIII, 31.

[22] NA. SP. 43/36; Newcastle to Pelham, 26 July 1752, BL. Add. 35412 fol. 209. For the use of intercepts at Hanover, Plesman, Prussian envoy in Dresden, to Frederick, 21 July 1753, *Polit. Corr.* X, 28.

[23] Podewils and Finckenstein to Frederick II, 15 July 1756, *Polit. Corr.*, XIII, 78.

[24] W. Mediger 'Hastenbeck und Zeven. Der Eintritt Hannovers in den Siebenjährigen Krieg', *Niedersächsisches Jahrbuch für Landesgeschichte*, 56 (1984), pp. 137–66; H. Wellenreuther, 'Die Bedeutung des Siebenjährigen Krieges für die englisch-hannoveranischen Beziehungen', in A.M. Birke and K. Kluxen (eds), *England und Hannover* (Munich, 1986), pp. 170–2.

[25] Holdernesse to Mitchell, 27 July 1756, BL. Add. 6832 fol. 80.

Chancery in London saw the dispatches of British diplomats.[26] Nevertheless, the legacy of earlier politics left foreigners with a strong sense of difference between Britain and Hanover.[27] These differences appeared to challenge the consistency of British policy or, at least, the ability of British ministers to pursue their goals.

George's importance in foreign policy was accentuated because he was also the leading figure in military affairs. His role in this derived from his royal position but was underlined by his prominence in command during the Dettingen campaign of 1743; although he never took to the field again. In 1748, as the war with France headed for a crisis, there were unfounded suggestions that George would go to the Low Countries to head the army.[28] George delighted in reviewing troops, and did so in particular in Hanover.[29] The contrast between the opportunities to do so in Britain and Hanover was striking. The major military role of his second son, William, Duke of Cumberland, as Captain General from 1745 to 1757, put the royal family into greater prominence, in both military and political terms, which in 1757 created a serious political crisis. In contrast, the King prevented his young eldest grandson, the future George III, from having a military role during the Seven Years' War.

War and the possibility of war thus pushed George's governmental role in foreign policy to the fore. The same was true in the politics of foreign policy. This was the case for the confidential politics of ministerial combinations and governmental tensions. It was also the case for public politics. These were institutional, notably parliamentary; printed, particularly in newspapers, pamphlets and caricatures; and diffused, especially in conversation and correspondence. The real, or supposed, views and role of George were discussed in all these milieux. He was already one of the most experienced political figures in the state, if not the most. As a result, the fact that despite a few episodes of poor health[30] he was essentially alert, fit and active throughout the period[31] added cumulative significance to the King. The succession to George was a

---

[26]   Holdernesse to Mitchell, 7 Dec. 1756, NA. SP. 90/67; Perrone to Charles Emmanuel III, 19 Dec. 1754, AST. LM. Ing. 58.

[27]   Duke of Brunswick to Frederick II, 2 Aug. 1756, *Polit. Corr.*, XIII, 184.

[28]   Zamboni to Landgrave Ludwig VIII of Hesse-Darmstadt, 19 Jan. 1748, Darmstadt, E1 M10/6.

[29]   Newcastle to Holdernesse, 1 June 1752, NA. SP. 36/118 fol. 343.

[30]   Ossorio to Charles Emmanuel III, 20 Dec. 1746, Perrone to Charles Emmanuel, 2 May 1754, AST. LM. Ing. 52, 58; Bedford to Joseph Yorke, 4 Apr. (os) 1749 re ague, Richard Wall to Don Joseph de Carvajal, 11 Mar. 1751, Russell (ed.), *Bedford*, II, 25, 74–5; Henry Fox to Devonshire, 27 Mar. 1756, History of Parliament, Chatsworth transcripts.

[31]   Newcastle to Holdernesse, 1 June 1752, NA. SP. 36/118 fol. 343; William Murray to Rockingham, 21 July 1752, Sheffield, Wentworth Woodhouse Papers R1–15.

topic throughout, particularly in light of the probable changes to policy that would follow, and his advanced years and likely longevity were more frequently mentioned in the 1750s.[32] However, as with George I, this topic was very much secondary to George's continuing role in directing foreign policy. He could not be forced out as Walpole had been in 1742. Nor was George going to abdicate, as Victor Amadeus II of Sardinia had done in favour of his son in 1730, only to fall out with Charles Emmanuel III and be imprisoned.

As a consequence of this situation, ministers and foreign diplomats anxiously noted and speculated about George's views and reported any conversations with him.[33] These were carefully recounted whatever their subject. The individuals whom George saw were a significant matter of report.[34] Just as opportunities such as hunting were taken for confidential discussions with foreign rulers,[35] so efforts were made to talk with George.

In 1749, George told Perrone, the Sardinian envoy, that he had a low view of Saxony and regarded it as in no position to do good or bad.[36] This comment throws light on the governmental pressure for a subsidy treaty with Saxony, emphasising the role of Newcastle in pushing this policy. The Duke felt that he was greatly restricted by George's more cautious view on subsidies to German princes.[37] The following year, George complained to Perrone about the impertinence of the Austrian government and, urging patience on Sardinia, gave his word that he would try to get Austria to be reasonable[38] The kingdom of Sardinia centred on Savoy-Piedmont which had disputes with neighbouring Austrian-ruled Lombardy. The King's comments were in line with British diplomatic efforts to preserve good relations between the two powers, and thus give Britain the option of an Italian policy.[39] These comments also provided guidance on George's views on how Britain should react to its most troublesome ally, Austria. In 1753, George not only complained to Perrone about Austria, but also spoke much about the bad state of France, which led him to conclude that its weak

---

[32]   Frederick II to Michell, 6 Mar. 1753, *Polit. Corr.* IX, 363; Mirepoix to Saint-Contest, 10 Jan. 1754, AE. CP. Ang. 437 fol. 21.

[33]   Haslang to Preysing, 11 June 1756, Munich, Bayr. Ges., London 231.

[34]   Viry to Charles Emmanuel III, 16, 23 July 1756, AST. LM. Ing. 60.

[35]   Aubeterre to Rouillé, 9 Aug. 1755, AE. CP. Aut. 254 fols 249–50

[36]   Perrone to Charles Emmanuel III, 19 June 1749, AST. LM. Ing. 55.

[37]   Reporting Newcastle, Perrone to Charles Emmanuel III, 14 June 1751, AST. LM. Ing. 56; Newcastle to Pelham, 18 Sept. 1750, BL. Add. 35411 fol. 126.

[38]   Perrone to Charles Emmanuel III, 15 Jan., 5 Mar. 1750, AST. LM. Ing. 56. For other comments, 22 July, 19 Aug., 2, 9 Sept. 1751, Ing. 56.

[39]   Bedford to Rochford, 22 Jan. (os) 1750, NA. SP. 92/58 fol. 264.

ministry would not want war and would not back Frederick II if he did.[40] In 1756, responding to a very different international situation, and notably to the transformation in Anglo-Prussian relations, George justified Prussian actions to the Bavarian envoy and attacked what he presented as Austria's despotic conduct within the Empire.[41]

As an aspect of the role of the Crown, Frederick, Prince of Wales discussed foreign policy with diplomats.[42] He was regarded by foreign powers as worth cultivating.[43] Similarly, Cumberland's views were reported.[44] The political significance in Britain of Princess Amelia, an unmarried daughter of George, received some attention.

The major role of the King was made more controversial by his repeated attempts to create a ministry on which he felt he could rely. This entailed both supporting certain ministers, notably John, Earl Granville (formerly Lord Carteret), whose ability he greatly respected, and seeking to thwart others, particularly William Pitt (the Elder). There was also royal support for specific policies, especially on behalf of Hanover. The net consequence was to make George, his position and views, a more problematic factor in the politics of the period, both as the driver (or obstructer) of policy and as the key individual in the political landscape.

To explain this situation, Britain in this period was not a parliamentary monarchy in which the monarch was subsumed within established conventions of Parliament's role and the attendant parliamentary politics. Nor was the extent to which these conventions would constrain the monarch fixed or obvious to contemporaries; although they were far more set than those affecting the Princes of Orange in the United Provinces. Part of the significance of the period constitutionally and politically is that it saw a working through of the results of the Glorious Revolution of 1688–9 as far as the monarch was concerned. Moreover, this working through, in the aftermath of the long Walpole ministry (1721–42), and the establishment, then and subsequently, of an effective system of compromise around Whig rule that drew on a range of experience, created a context within which, from his succession in 1760, George III's real and apparent intentions were subsequently to be considered as innovative.

---

[40]   Perrone to Charles Emmanuel III, 25 Jan. 1753, AST. LM. Ing. 57.

[41]   Haslang to Preysing, 10 Oct. 1756, Munich, Bayr. Ges., London, 231.

[42]   Perrone to Charles Emmanuel III, 6 Feb. 1750, AST. LM. Ing. 56; re that June, A.N. Newman (ed.), 'Leicester House Politics, 1756–60', *Royal Historical Society, Camden Miscellany* (London, 1969), p. 176.

[43]   Frederick II to Andrié, 13 Dec. 1746, *Polit. Corr.*, V, 265.

[44]   Boutel to Rouillé, 22 Aug. 1754, AE. CP. Ang. 437 fols 283–4.

Within Britain, George II's position was in part a matter of his relationship with his ministers; a relationship that was frequently difficult. Ministers freely gave unwelcome advice, albeit advice generally expressed in polite terms. For example, in 1745, the Lords Justices, a Regency Council (Queen Caroline had died in 1737), was left in London when George went to Hanover; a Regency Council in practice run by the ministers of the Cabinet Council. As the Secretary of State remaining in London, Newcastle accordingly delivered its views to George in Hanover, noting that suggestions came: 'from a sense of our duty to His Majesty, and a just concern for his service, and that of our country'. Again

> with the utmost submission ... lay our thoughts ... before His Majesty, in a manner, which nothing but our duty to the King could have engaged us to have done; that we might not reproach ourselves, or be reproached by others, with the ill consequences of neglecting this opportunity of detaching the King of Prussia from France.[45]

As was to be expected in a parliamentary monarchy, each was in need of the other. George was dependent on his ministers in order to ensure parliamentary support, and thus the financing of government. However, anxious for 'a lucky moment, when *we* [George] are in good humour',[46] the ministers needed the peevish[47] King not only in order to receive their positions, but also to maintain them. This was in the face of competition between ministers, as well as would-be ministers, a competition that lacked the cohesion of the organisation and discipline of more modern political parties. As a consequence, diplomats, anxious to ascertain the real basis of authority, reported that ministers, notably Newcastle, flattered George in order to try to conserve their position[48] and to deploy patronage.

Alongside this instrumentalist account of ministerial support for the Crown, there was a significant cultural dynamic. Ministers felt personally involved in supporting the royal family. In 1753 Henry Pelham, the First Lord of the Treasury since 1743 and a marked critic of peacetime subsidy treaties, told George that he needed four or five years to regulate the affairs of the nation, but that, if the royal honour demanded war, he would find the necessary resources.[49] This cultural factor is underplayed in most modern accounts of eighteenth-century British

---

[45] Newcastle to Harrington, 4 June (os), 19 July (os) 1745, NA. SP. 43/37.
[46] Newcastle to Holdernesse, 11 July 1755, BL. Add. 32857 fol. 54.
[47] Reporting Henry Pelham, Ryder diary, 2 Dec. 1753, Sandon.
[48] Haslang to Preysing, 19 Jan. 1748, Munich, Bayr. Ges., London 220.
[49] Perrone to Charles Emmanuel III, 19 July 1753, AST. LM. Ing. 57.

politics, in part because the language of respect receives scant attention, but it was significant, not least because it touched on a range of responses, from the constitutional to the psychological, and the intellectual to the social. The Court provided the milieu for this interaction.

As the head of the government, the King played a crucial role in the composition of the ministry. His favour or, even more, lack of favour, for example his persistent dislike for Pitt, were highly significant in political manoeuvres, as were changes in his attitude, notably toward an acceptance of Pitt in 1746, 1756 and, most significantly, 1757. After the defeated Cumberland agreed a neutrality convention for Hanover with the victorious invading French army in 1757, George treated him as a disgrace, and, most damagingly for the Duke, made this clear in public. This change in attitude greatly affected the ministers close to Cumberland, such as Henry Fox, and also lessened the chance of effective resistance at Court to the Newcastle–Pitt ministry.

In the role of the ruler, British politics was not totally different from the Continent. In France, Louis XV interacted with royal favourites and Court factions, and in a fashion similar to George. Foreign observers speculated on Court and ministerial changes including the credit of Louis' lover, Madame de Pompadour, who was believed influenced by bribes.[50] George's relative importance, however, was greatly lessened by the role of Parliament. At the same time, far from France being, as some British commentators claimed, a placid society, readily controlled by and for an autocratic monarch, there was much criticism of government there. In 1749, Joseph Yorke, a British diplomat in Paris, noted:

> I confess nothing since my coming into this country has surprised me more than to find the French King spoke of with so little regard which is so contrary to the notion one generally has conceived, of their outward at least affection for their monarch; but it is certainly much otherwise at present.[51]

In 1754, the visiting Count of Gisors, an observant French aristocrat, was told by Joshua Vanneck, a prominent Dutch-born merchant who was politically well-connected in London, notably to the government, that the House of Hanover was very popular. Significantly, he said that this was because the Hanoverians did not try to change the British constitution. Like his father, but not his grandson, George II took great delight in reviewing troops, both in Britain and in Hanover,

---

[50]   Lord Marshal to Frederick II, 25 May 1753, *Polit. Corr.* IX, 444.
[51]   Yorke to Cumberland, 1 Mar. 1749, RA. Cumb. P. 43/122.

but did not then use them to try to transform politics.[52] Nor was there any suggestion that he would. The army served to defend the constitution, political world and society, most prominently in 1745–6, and not to overturn them.

As a reminder of the significance of the royal family, the key British political family, the Pelhams – Newcastle and his brother Henry – having publically seen off George's plans for the ministry in 1746, were to be challenged by another member of the royal family. In 1747 Frederick, Prince of Wales moved again into opposition, as he had earlier done to Sir Robert Walpole in 1737, only becoming reconciled with his father after Walpole was forced out of office in 1742: 'fell' is not a helpful term. Frederick was frustrated with his inconsequential position, which was accentuated and darkened by his father's animosity, albeit an animosity that was restrained and did not show the violence displayed by Peter the Great and Frederick William I of Prussia, George's brother-in-law, toward their sons. Frederick's challenge was beaten off, at least in so far as the election of 1747 was concerned. After the contested returns had been settled, the ministry had a majority of 144, a major achievement.

The role of the royal family emerged in a different light in 1748 in the shape of dynastic links. There were rumours that a marriage might be negotiated between Cumberland and a Prussian princess in order to improve relations between Britain and Prussia.[53] However, there was no active search for marital partners in this period. In addition, there was no basis for Frederick II's concern in 1749 about Cumberland being intended for the Swedish throne. Frederick saw George's Hessian son-in-law as an alternative.[54] Possibly a homosexual, and certainly preferring the company of men, Cumberland remained unmarried. Indeed, that was the most important aspect of marital diplomacy, its absence compared to the active search for Prussian marriages for Frederick, Prince of Wales and Princess Amelia in the 1720s. Nevertheless, the legacy of the 1730s, in the shape of the marriage of Anne, the Princess Royal, and William IV of Orange in 1734, played a major role in encouraging British support for William gaining power in the United Provinces in 1747, support that played a major role. Dynasticism, constitutional change and the international system were linked, the interventionist British envoy, John, 4th Earl of Sandwich, remarking:

---

[52]   Gisors, Journal of Visit to England, 7 Feb. 1754, AE. MD. Ang. 1 fol. 28.

[53]   Alt to William VIII, Regent of Hesse-Cassel, 12 Jan. 1748, Marburg, 4f England, 241. William was regent 1730–51 for his brother Frederick I of Sweden, and Landgrave from 1751 to 1760.

[54]   Frederick II to Chambrier and Frederick II to Princess Royal of Sweden, 25 Jan., 1749, *Polit. Corr.* VI, 351, 372.

> I think the settling the office of Stadtholder for ever upon the Prince of Orange's posterity will be for ever securing the union and connection between England and the Republic, and consequently an immense addition to His Majesty's weight in the balance of Europe.[55]

However, William IV proved a serious disappointment for Britain, with the Dutch unable in 1748 to deploy the forces promised against France. Moreover, after he died young in 1750, Anne was not seen as pursuing British interests, nor those of her father, George; and this perception was indeed correct. Dynasticism, however, was not a key theme for British foreign policy, nor even for that of Hanover. The major exception, the Imperial Election Scheme of the early 1750s, did not involve the House of Hanover, but was rather considered as a means to secure Austria's future in the balance of power and the European international system. At best, this was an indirect dynasticism, one seen as a means of power politics. In contrast to the lack of ambition for the British royal family, the marital prospects of Louis XV's daughters were regarded as of considerable significance in the politics of Italy and Poland.[56] George's mistress, the Countess of Yarmouth (formerly Madame Wallmoden), attracted the attention of diplomats (as well as British ministers), and they discussed matters with her, seeing this as a way to understand George's views,[57] but it was claimed that she had no influence.[58]

Ministers

There were many parallels with Continental monarchies, but Parliament created an utterly different dynamic in British politics to that in France, Austria, Prussia and Russia. This was a difference very much highlighted by foreign envoys. Thus, in 1748, with the ministry seriously divided over whether to continue the war with France, there was a suggestion that Parliament's advice might be sought on the matter, this was presented as a way to free ministers from the political onus of negotiating an unsatisfactory peace. However, this proposal was allegedly opposed by Newcastle on the grounds that it would infringe the royal prerogative

---

[55]   Sandwich to Newcastle, 3 Oct. 1747, BL. Add. 32810 fol. 62.

[56]   Chesterfield to Burrish, 10 Nov. (os) 1747, NA. SP. 81/96.

[57]   Haslang to Preysing, 19 Jan. 1748, Munich, Bayr. Ges., London 220; HMC, *Polwarth*, vol. 5, 272.

[58]   Perrone to Charles Emmanuel III, 17 July 1754, AST. LM. Ing. 58.

(which would have been the case), and was rejected.[59] Ministers, indeed, had to manoeuvre not only with regard to the monarch and his succession, but also with reference to a system in which Parliament was a powerful consideration, one, moreover, made more unpredictable by the absence of any reliable party unity. Unlike the situation today, there were no official leaders for parties, no parliamentary whips, no membership, and no manifesto. Instead, there was a sense of party identity that, however, did not preclude opportunistic co-operation with those in opposition from the other party: Tories and opposition Whigs. Pitt was to take this further by being able, while in office from 1756, to elicit a significant degree of Tory support for the ministry, and in doing so trying to formulate a wartime strategy that would appeal to them.

Keenly aware of the importance of the House of Commons, Pelham, then Paymaster General and the leader of the 'Old Corps' of Whigs in the Commons, declared there on 9 March (os) 1742:

> the voice of this House is the voice of the people, the voice of the British nation.
> It must always be understood to be so; for there is no other way of determining
> what is the voice of the nation. If we were to form a judgement of this from what
> we heard without doors, every man's judgement would be according to the sort of
> company he usually conversed with.

In the aftermath of the fall of Walpole the previous month, this speech by a major Walpole protégé represented a rejection of being directed by opinion 'out of doors'. This view was central to the thought of the 'Old Corps', even if their practice could be different as, eventually and under strong pressure, over war with Spain in 1739, Jewish naturalisation in 1753, and the continuation of the ministry in 1756. Indeed, the contrary view to that of Pelham was clear and frequently expressed. The *Craftsman*, an opposition newspaper, declared on 12 November (os) 1748:

> We should enforce the necessity of popular enquiry into the conduct of men
> in trust and power, and of such an unpardonable contempt of the Voice of the
> People, which cried out aloud against their schemes on the Continent, and for a
> vigorous war by sea.

Pelham, from 1743 until his unexpected death in March 1754 the First Lord of the Treasury, was the impressive manager of the Commons and the finances.

---

[59]   Ossorio to Charles Emmanuel III, 2 Feb. 1748, AST. LM. Ing. 54.

However, his elder brother, Newcastle, was definitely not subordinate to him. The hard-working Duke was the effective foreign minister, the most influential politician in the House of Lords, and the wielder of much government and Church patronage. His presence in London, or absence from it, usually in order to visit his Sussex seat and political stronghold, were very important for the activity of the diplomatic corps.[60] However, Newcastle's febrile, insecure and over-anxious personality posed major problems for ministerial coherence and calm. Besides his habit of speaking without reflecting first,[61] he lacked the stable personality and the governmental position to sustain the political structure that his paranoia dictated: a concentration of decision-making and power on his own person.

Irrespective of not being in the Commons, important as that was, Newcastle could not be a second Walpole. His personality was not strong enough and, more crucially, he was loath to take responsibility for decisions. Newcastle was anxious, petulant and indecisive, lacking the character for the easy retention of high office. In the face of his anxieties and, more practically, of the problems of managing the Commons, Newcastle wanted strong colleagues able to take responsibility, and, for that reason, worked best with Pelham and, later, Pitt. Yet, Newcastle wanted his colleagues subordinate and could not accept his own dependence on them nor, indeed, criticism; he was weak, but did not wish to acknowledge it. Similar factors affected Newcastle's response to the King and, in particular, to George's favour for other ministers. George's ability to handle Newcastle was not the least of his political abilities. This ability emerges indirectly in Newcastle's reports on their meetings and ironically so as Newcastle tended to present himself as more prescient. However, the letters can be read differently.[62]

The correspondence of Newcastle and his brother survives, as do the letters with Philip, 1st Earl of Hardwicke, Lord Chancellor from 1737 to 1756, to whom each brother frequently complained about the other and who, as they clearly wanted, sought to mediate between them.[63] It is clear that each brother was frustrated by the difficulty of managing the other. In particular, Pelham, who was very much governed by a 'spirit of economy',[64] thought Newcastle

---

[60]   Alt to William VIII, Landgrave of Hesse-Cassel, 22 June 1753, Marburg, 4f England, 254.

[61]   Perrone to Charles Emmanuel III, 6 Sept. 1753, AST. LM. Ing. 57.

[62]   R. Browning, *The Duke of Newcastle* (New Haven, Connecticut, 1975); D.G. Barnes, 'Henry Pelham and the Duke of Newcastle', *Journal of British Studies*, 2 (1962), pp. 62–77.

[63]   Newcastle to Hardwicke, 21 Sept. 1753, BL. Add. 32732 fols 699–701.

[64]   Perrone to Charles Emmanuel III, 21 June 1753, AST. LM. Ing. 57.

insufficiently mindful of financial issues[65] and, regarding his commitments to would-be allies as too expensive, sought to limit them. This attitude proved particularly significant at the time of the Imperial Election Scheme. Pelham also had views on the desirable configuration of the European system:

> I have always wished for a strict union between Spain and Great Britain; which joined with the House of Austria is in my mind a real balance of power against any of the most aspiring governments.[66]

As a reminder of the extent to which specific views of international relations were held across the political spectrum, the need to detach Spain from France was also emphasised by the opposition newspaper *Old England* two months later.[67] Spain tends to be underplayed in the literature on British foreign policy in the period. Nevertheless, Spain remained of considerable importance, in part a legacy of its earlier significance, and of the extent to which Mediterranean politics and trade excited the interest of British ministers. Spain also added the trans-Atlantic dimension, and was a key and growing naval power. Because Ferdinand VI (r. 1746–59) did not adopt the revisionist attitudes and expansionist policies of his father, Philip V (r. 1700–46), and was not as active and anti-British as his half-brother, Charles III (r. 1759–88), Spain's role is underrated. However, part of the reason why British ministers and commentators could focus on other questions, notably the Imperial Election Scheme and relations with France in North America, rested on Ferdinand's search for peace and stability, a search very much seen with his ministers.

Newcastle's enthusiasm, in peace and war, for a diplomacy of alliances and mutual guarantees reflected his continued concern about the international situation, specifically with regard to French power and intentions. Newcastle's political significance, the great scale and long accessibility of his surviving correspondence, and the extent to which foreign envoys focused on the Duke, ensure that his views bulk large in the scholarship, both British and American, on the period. Although negotiations were, primarily, generally verbal, rather than by memoranda,[68] the nature of the sources certainly gives a flavour of

---

[65] Pelham, note on letter from Newcastle, 13 July 1753, BL. Add. 33201 fol. 162.

[66] Pelham to John, 1st Earl Gower, 10 Oct. (os) 1751, NA. PRO. 30/29/1/11 fols 327–8.

[67] *Old England*, 21 Dec. (os) 1751.

[68] Joseph to Philip Yorke, 12 Feb. 1754, BL. Add. 35364 fol. 4; Mitchell to Newcastle, 11 July 1755, BL. Add. 32857 fol. 64, reporting views of former Russian envoy in London; Holdernesse to Hanbury Williams, 24 July 1755, HW.

discussions between ministers and senior members of the élite. For example, in 1748, in what was a characteristic approach, Newcastle sent Sandwich, then abroad as a diplomat, a private letter in which he commented on the views of John, 4th Duke of Bedford, an ally of the Earl. Bedford was an opposition Whig until 1744, when he became First Lord of the Admiralty on Carteret's fall, thus becoming a 'New Whig' in the language of the time. Recounting their conversation, Newcastle made it clear that Bedford had definite views on the process of obtaining peace, opposing Newcastle's view that the best way to achieve this was through a separate peace with Spain that would divide Ferdinand VI from France. Bedford pressed the need for peace with reference to 'the inconvenience of increasing the debt of the nation' if war continued.[69] His view was not to change significantly when he became Secretary of State later that year, replacing Chesterfield.

Newcastle's anxiety in the late 1740s and early 1750s over ministerial colleagues, and more generally, demonstrates the extent to which surviving the crises of 1744–6 did not bring an end to all, or, indeed, most, political problems and diplomatic concerns. In part, this situation was a product of what was a pessimistic and sceptical context for the response to developments. In particular, the War of the Austrian Succession (Britain was a combatant from 1743–8) had angered the Tories and disillusioned not only the Patriots and other opposition Whigs, but also the 'Old Corps' Walpolean/Pelhamite Whigs. This disillusionment, and its varied consequences, provides an important unity to the period in addition to that of crisis.

At the close of the 1740s, nevertheless, despite a lack of confidence, there had been solid achievements. In contrast to the start of the decade, Jacobitism had been crushed, ministerial cohesion established and, with the 1747 election contrasting greatly with that of 1741, a solid and apparently stable parliamentary majority achieved. The Pelhams were in a far stronger position in 1750 than Walpole had been in 1739–42 and, indeed, this was the case from after their triumph in the election in 1747, until the death of Henry Pelham in 1754 and arguably until the fall of Minorca in 1756. Moreover, religious enthusiasm in the shape of Methodism had proved, not highly disruptive, as had been suggested by critics, but, instead, compatible with the political and social order. The most prominent Methodist, John Wesley, condemned some aspects of society and was unusually critical of the social élite, while Methodism was particularly popular among artisans and servants, and was responsive to the religious needs of such groups. However, Wesley was loyal to the Hanoverian dynasty and to the political

---

[69]   Newcastle to Sandwich, 19 Jan. (os) 1748, BL. Add. 32811 fol. 88.

system, and was concerned about personal and social disorder. Methodism was not revolutionary. The same was true of other aspects of the so-called 'Great Awakening' of Protestant evangelicalism and, in addition, of the Dissenters, the Protestant Nonconformists who looked back to the Puritans. In works such as Samuel Chandler's *Great Britain's Memorial against the Pretender and Popery* (1745), Dissenters responded to the Jacobite rising in 1745 by stressing their loyalty and emphasising a broad, Protestant, patriotism which could include them as well as the established faith. Indeed, Chandler had very good relations with the Archbishop of Canterbury and several senior bishops.

In addition, the opposition to these Protestant movements was contained, which limited tension and, even more, disruption, and thus the possibility of political instability. Methodist meetings sometimes met with a violent response, as in Sheffield (1744), Exeter (1745), Leeds (1745), and York (1747), and individual clerics could be hostile. In his *Enthusiasm of Methodists and Papists Compared* (1749–51), George Lavington, Bishop of Exeter, condemned Methodism by the comparison. However, the degree to which the Church of England did not respond to Methodist activity in an official fashion is striking. Methodism tended to be condemned, as by Lavington, only when it appeared to be too close to Catholicism or disloyal to the state. Wesley was not expelled from the Church, and there was an effective toleration of Methodism at the national level whatever the (varied) situation at the local level.

The cross-currents in the public sphere indicated the need for management, in Church as well as state. That need was a key element in the means of policy. In particular, at the national as well as the local levels, the institutional character of government was not so developed and complex that it could not be greatly affected (and more so than today) by the interplay of individuals, an interplay accentuated by the absence of party structures. This situation was seen, for example, in the respective, greatly varying, role of the two Secretaries of State (for the Northern and Southern Departments) covering diplomacy, and in the influence over foreign policy of the First Lord of the Treasury. While this latter influence was minimal under Walpole's ineffectual successor, Spencer, Earl of Wilmington (1742–3) and limited under Henry Pelham (1743–54), the situation was to be very different when, in 1754, Newcastle, who had overborne his brother, moved from being a longstanding Secretary of State to being First Lord. He held the post until he resigned in October 1756 and, after the brief interlude of the Devonshire–Pitt ministry, then again from 1757 to 1762.

Aside from their competence, the political influence of individual Secretaries was a key and continuing issue. Newcastle, Southern Secretary from 1724 to 1748, and Northern from 1748 to 1754, had far more influence than his counterparts as the other Secretary. This was notably so after the fall of Carteret, the Northern Secretary, in 1744; for Carteret had considerable influence with George even if not, like Newcastle, in Parliament, and notably not (indirectly) in the Commons, as the Duke did. In contrast to Carteret, Newcastle's later colleagues as Secretary, William, 1st Earl of Harrington (1744–6), Philip, 4th Earl of Chesterfield (1746–8), John, 4th Duke of Bedford (1748–51), and Robert, 4th Earl of Holdernesse (1751–61), were less politically powerful than Newcastle at Court, as well as in Parliament and in the ministry. Indeed, Chesterfield was extensively quoted as saying in 1748, when his dismissal was first rumoured and then occurred, 'that he cannot be out, for he was never in'.[70] Neither George nor Newcastle viewed Chesterfield, who had been kept from the same post in 1730, with favour. As Charles, 2nd Viscount Townshend had done toward Newcastle in 1724–30, Newcastle continued to take an interest in the Southern Department after he moved to the Northern from the Southern in 1748. In 1749, he was angry that Bedford had sent what he regarded as absurd instructions about the dispute with France over the Caribbean island of Tobago, a situation he blamed on Bedford failing to consult other ministers, in other words himself.[71] Unlike Newcastle, Bedford, a politician of weight, was a supporter of maritime or 'Blue Water' policies.[72]

With Newcastle in the Treasury from 1754, and wanting to stay there, there were four Secretaries of State in this period, Holdernesse, now the more experienced of the two as Secretary, moving to the Northern Department in 1754, being matched by Thomas Robinson (1754–5), Henry Fox (1755–6), and William Pitt (1756–61) in the Southern. Like Carteret, Harrington, Chesterfield and Robinson, but not Newcastle, Bedford, Fox or Pitt, Holdernesse had diplomatic experience. More significantly, he had had the chance to acquire experience as a Secretary of State, a circumstance even more true of Newcastle and Harrington, but not of Chesterfield, Bedford, Robinson, Fox and Pitt. Although, in the characteristic manner of an envoy from a second-rank court, Perrone thought Holdernesse prone to forget easily what did not strike him as of the greatest consequence, Frederick II, generally a harsh critic, was ready to praise

---

[70] Thomas Secker, Bishop of Salisbury, to Edward Weston, 12 Jan. (os) 1748, Farmington, Lewis Walpole Library, Weston papers vol. 3; Le Man to Duke of Huescar, 19 Jan. 1748, BL. Add. 32812 fol. 21.

[71] Newcastle to Hardwicke, 26 Mar. (os) 1749, BL. Add 35410 fol. 116.

[72] Peronne to Charles Emmanuel III, 28 Aug. 1749, AST. LM. Ing. 55; J.M. Haas, 'The Rise of the Bedfords, 1741–1757: A Study in the Politics of the Reign of George II' (PhD., Illinois, 1960).

Holdernesse's ability.[73] However, Holdernesse lacked political strength and in 1756 he commented 'my opinion is of little consequence' as well as explaining that he dare not expound his views on paper.[74] Irrespective of individuals, and their abilities, the divided system of the British administration of foreign policy did not have the coherence of some of its Continental counterparts.[75]

Although lacking relevant diplomatic experience, Fox and Pitt were key figures of consequence in the politics and management of the House of Commons, and were seen as such, even by opponents. While an experienced former diplomat (who was regarded as conspicuously pro-Austrian), Robinson, in contrast, lacked the relevant ambition, drive, experience and reputation. All three men sat in the Commons, as no previous Secretary of State had done since James Craggs (1718–21). In part, sitting there reflected the significance of the management of that House; but it was also a consequence of the First Lord of the Treasury, Newcastle, being in the Lords, whereas Walpole (First Lord, 1721–42) and Pelham (First Lord, 1743–54) had each long sat in the Commons. The pattern was not to be sustained, as all subsequent Secretaries of State, bar George Grenville (1762) and Henry Seymour Conway (1765–8), sat in the Lords, as Carteret, Harrington, Chesterfield, Bedford and Holdernesse had already done. So to establish a general rule may appear problematic. At the same time, the need for management in the mid-1750s was far greater in the Commons than the Lords, as was the talent there that, if in opposition, had to be tackled, notably Fox and Pitt.

As a reminder of cross-currents and of the variety of factors at play, 1755 was a year in which George II visited Hanover. Alongside parliamentary government as a factor in ministerial politics and the development of Cabinet structures came the need to cope with regular monarchical absence, a factor that did not pertain under the later Hanoverians.[76]

Secretaries of State were political as well as governmental figures. They explained and defended foreign policy in Parliament. They also issued instructions to British diplomats and saw their foreign counterparts. Moreover, Secretaries of State played a central role in defining foreign policy. This role

---

[73]   Perrone to Charles Emmanuel III, 8 Nov. 1753, AST. LM. Ing. 57; Frederick II to Michell, 28 Nov. 1756, *Polit. Corr.* XIV, 81.

[74]   Holdernesse to Yorke, 30 July 1755, BL. Eg. 3446 fol. 182.

[75]   G. Klingenstein, *Institutionelle Aspekte der österreichischen Aussenpolitik in 18. Jahrhundert* (Vienna, 1977), pp. 86–90.

[76]   A.C. Thompson, 'The Development of the Executive and Foreign Policy, 1714–1760', in W. Mulligan and B. Simms (eds), *The Primacy of Foreign Policy in British History, 1660–2000* (Basingstoke, 2010), p. 74.

helped ensure that they were the focus of attention. This attention extended to Secretaries of State being rumoured or believed to follow their own initiatives. Indeed they did, as in 1756, with Fox raising the idea of returning Gibraltar to Spain, in order to win its support, an idea already floated by Chesterfield, Bedford and Sandwich in 1748, and by Stanhope under George I.[77] This idea, which led to public speculation and criticism, testified to the continued conviction of the significance of Spain and the possibility it apparently offered as an alternative, or additional, ally to Austria, and as a way to weaken France.

In 1744, the King told the two Secretaries of State that he wanted issues of foreign policy referred for decision to the Cabinet Council. Newcastle was unenthusiastic on the grounds that such a process would lead to what he presented as confusion (i.e. dissent) and delay[78] In practice, government activity continued to be more ad hoc. Ministers could take steps to keep colleagues in the dark about policy, and this could extend to keeping sensitive information from the Council, as in 1745 when Newcastle sought to keep such information from the large Regency Council which included members favourable to Granville.[79]

Nevertheless, however much discussion was restricted, many ministers had views, and the place of the Secretaries of State in expounding and defending foreign policy was certainly lessened by the part taken by other ministers in these tasks. There was the key and recurrent issue of money, an issue made more significant due to the importance of subsidy treaties. Reliance here was on the Treasury. Foreign envoys emphasised that the Secretaries of State had no Departmental money to disburse.[80]

As a result, the views of Pelham in 1743–54, and of Newcastle thereafter, were correctly regarded as central to foreign policy, its content as well as implementation. In a significant linkage of individual views and government policy, Frederick II initially thought Newcastle more circumspect in granting subsidies as First Lord than when he had been a Secretary of State.[81] As First Lord of the Treasury, and extremely busy on that account, Newcastle read intercepted diplomatic correspondence,[82] frequently continued to discuss foreign policy with

[77]   Sandwich to Newcastle, 16 Mar. 1748, Newcastle to Hardwicke, 12 July 1756, BL. Add. 32811 fols 341–2, 32866 fol. 141; T.W. Riker, *Henry Fox* (2 vols, Oxford, 1911), I, 433–5.

[78]   Newcastle to Hardwicke, 10 Nov. (os) 1744, BL. Add. 35408 fols 88–9.

[79]   Newcastle to Cumberland, 10, 21 May (os) 1745, BL. Add. 32704 fols 223, 301.

[80]   Mirepoix to Puysieulx, 22 Feb., 13 Mar. 1750, AE. CP. Ang. 428 fols 132, 200.

[81]   Frederick to Lord Marshal, 9 Apr. 1754, *Polit. Corr.* X, 292.

[82]   Newcastle to Holdernesse, 11 July 1755, BL. Add. 32857 fol. 43.

diplomats as he had declared he would do,[83] and also corresponded with British diplomats, providing assurance in 1757 about his commitment to the Prussian alliance.[84] He was compared to Walpole, with the significant difference that he had to have others manage the Commons.[85] In practice, comparison between his period as Secretary of State and as First Lord is difficult as the exigencies of approaching war and then war ensured that the situation from 1754, when Newcastle was at the Treasury, was more serious than hitherto while also leading to particular commitments. French Foreign Ministers, such as Puysieulx, could also complain about the difficulties of disbursing money,[86] a situation which offers a significant qualification to the claim for British exceptionalism, in at least this respect. Indeed, fiscal pressures and their implications for the working of government operated for all states whatever their constitution. As First Lord, Newcastle took a more direct role in foreign policy than Pelham had done, but he also had greater experience, as a former and longstanding Secretary of State, indeed the most longstanding ever. Moreover, initially while First Lord, Newcastle had two Secretaries of State (Holdernesse and Robinson) who lacked much political weight, skill or ambition, a situation that changed only when Robinson was replaced by Fox in 1755. Although Newcastle emphasised that he discussed key issues with Robinson 'very fully', Philip, 1st Earl of Hardwicke, was Newcastle's closest confidant and more important to him.[87] In 1756, Newcastle wrote directly to Mitchell, in order to reassure Frederick II about his views.[88]

The role of other ministers and officials was important, but varied. The significance of the Board of Trade for the governmental consideration of most commercial and colonial issues ensured that British envoys could expect to receive instructions that originated in pressure from the Board, as over disputes with the Dutch concerning trade with West Africa, a trade dominated by the acquisition of slaves.[89] With George, 2nd Earl of Halifax, both active and ambitious, playing a key role, the Board of Trade very much pushed America in governmental attention in the early 1750s. Whereas Martin Bladen, the leading

---

[83] Mirepoix to Saint-Contest, 25 Mar. 1754, AE. CP. Ang. 437 fol. 109; re French envoy, Newcastle to Holdernesse, 11 July 1755, BL. Add. 32857 fol. 43; Viry to Charles Emmanuel III, 3 Sept. 1756, AST. LM. Ing. 60; Haslang to Preysing, 22 Mar. 1754, 14 Sept. 1756, Munich, Bayr. Ges., London 229, 231.

[84] Newcastle to Mitchell, 16 July 1757, BL. Add. 6832 fols 25–6.

[85] Alt to William VIII of Hesse-Cassel, 22 Mar. 1754, Marburg, 4f England 255.

[86] Löss, Saxon envoy in Paris, to Bruhl, 25 Mar. 1750, HHStA. StK. Interiora Intercepte, 1.

[87] Newcastle to Holdernesse, 11 July 1755, BL. Add. 32857 fols 5–6, 40.

[88] Newcastle to Mitchell, 28 May 1756, BL. Add. 6832 fol. 1.

[89] Holdernesse to Yorke, 22 Sept. 1752, NA. SP. 84/460.

figure on the Board from the 1710s to the 1740s, had been principally concerned with Europe, notably seeking to improve trade with the Austrian Netherlands, priorities changed thereafter.

In the case of India, the East India Company was the agent for negotiations in India, but negotiations about India, notably with France, were handled by the diplomatic system as well as the East India Company. Moreover, ministers had a view. This was true of Viscount Anson, the First Lord of the Admiralty, when a neutrality agreement between the British and French East India companies was proposed in 1753. He, Newcastle, Hardwicke, Holdernesse, and Granville discussed the proposal. Thus, the two Secretaries of State were joined by other ministers covering a range of competence and expertise, as they also were on other occasions.[90]

In giving advice, there was an overlap between governmental and political functions, but also differences. In part, there were direct interventions in policy debates and, in part, indirect intervention by means of providing informal advice. The latter had policy implications, as with the persistent refusal during the Seven Years' War (1756–63) to heed Prussian pressure to send a squadron to the Baltic, a move that would have compromised British relations with Russia and Sweden. In this case, Holdernesse noted:

> some of the most experienced sea officers have their doubts as to the utility of
> great ships, in the defence of the coasts of the King of Prussia's dominions from an
> invasion, which might be carried on by gallies and vessels that draw little water, in
> spight of a much superior naval strength.

This view reflected an informed understanding of the naval situation, although one that avoided the symbolic implications of such a step. The matter had earlier been discussed on the orders of George II by 'those of his servants who are consulted upon His Majesty's most secret affairs'.[91]

A range of ministers who had no formal Departmental responsibility spoke to foreign envoys. Some had considerable experience of international relations, notably former Secretaries of State. Granville (formerly Carteret) was of particular consequence, as he had been Secretary of State in both Departments (1721–4 Southern, 1742–4 Northern), as well as a diplomat, and knew and used German. As Secretary of State, he had dealt in a confidential manner with some of the

[90]   Newcastle to Yorke, 26 June, Council meeting, 30 May 1753, NA. SP. 84/463; Haslang to Preysing, 6 July 1753, Munich, Bayr. Ges., London, 227; re discussing Anglo-Spanish relations, Bedford to Keene, 30 Aug. (os) 1750, Russell (ed.), *Bedford*, II, 51–3.

[91]   Holdernesse to Mitchell, 5, 9 July 1756, NA. SP. 90/65.

envoys he continued thereafter to speak to, such as the Bavarian, Baron Haslang. Once he returned to office in 1751, as Lord President of the Council, Granville became an important minister and a regular attender of key meetings,[92] but a second-rank minister and, crucially, one whose influence was no longer a public issue, as it had been in 1742–6. In 1754, Granville was very much 'on message' in stressing financial considerations in the case of the Imperial Election Scheme, a project he was believed in particular to support.[93] Most significantly, he was believed, with much reason, to be able to influence Newcastle.[94] Although they had been ministerial rivals, they had been colleagues when Carteret was in office, and, earlier, had been to the same school, Westminster. In the crisis with France in 1755, Granville was presented as more unaccommodating than Newcastle, but, after talking with him, the French envoy was initially more pleased with his views.[95] In a reprise of former views of Granville as a royal confidant, Rouillé, the French Foreign Minister, asked Mirepoix whether the minister's assurances were concerted with Newcastle and Robinson or represented a secret intelligence with the King.[96] Newcastle assured Holdernesse and himself that Granville was 'entirely of opinion with us'.[97]

Closer to Newcastle, both friend and confidant, Hardwicke was more significant politically than Granville, and also spoke with diplomats on international matters.[98] He corresponded with Newcastle on foreign policy and attended key ministerial meetings on foreign policy.[99] Hardwicke's views included uneasiness about going to war with France in 1756.[100] Hardwicke did not serve in the Newcastle-Pitt ministry.

A range of ministers spoke in Parliament on foreign policy. Thus, in 1751, in the debate on the Bavarian subsidy, a key issue, William Murray, the Solicitor

---

[92]   Ministerial meeting, 3, 20 Feb., 3 Apr. 1755, BL. Add. 32996 fols 19–22, 34–5, 69.

[93]   Haslang to Wreden, 12 Jan., 12 July 1754, Munich, Bayr. Ges., London 229.

[94]   Viry to Charles Emmanuel III, 30 July 1756, AST. LM. Ing. 60.

[95]   Reporting Newcastle and Robinson, Mirepoix to Rouillé, 28 Mar., 21 Apr. 1755, AE. CP. Ang. 438 fols 340, 362, 420; Alt to Landgrave William VIII of Hesse-Cassel, 11 Apr. 1755, Marburg, 4f England 258; Van Eyck, Bavarian envoy in Paris, to Preysing, 28 Apr. 1755, Munich, Bayr. Ges., Paris vol. 13.

[96]   Rouillé to Mirepoix, 24 Apr. 1755, AE. CP. Ang. 438 fol. 432. See also, Anon, État actual de la Cour de Londres, 31 Jan. 1754, AE. MD. Ang. 51 fol. 200.

[97]   Newcastle to Holdernesse, 25 July 1755, BL. Add. 32857 fol. 359.

[98]   Viry to Charles Emmanuel III, 13 Aug. 1756, AST. LM. Ing. 60.

[99]   Newcastle to Hardwicke, 18 Sept., Hardwicke to Newcastle, 19 Sept. 1756, meetings 16 Jan., 3, 7, 10, 20 Feb., 3, 17, 21, Apr. 1755, BL. Add. 32867 fols 317, 339, 32996 fols 5–6, 19–22, 25, 29–30, 34–5, 69, 77–80, 87.

[100]   Hardwicke to Newcastle, 29 Aug. 1756, BL. Add. 32867 fol. 143.

General from 1742 to 1754 and subsequently Attorney General, one of the most articulate members of the government, defended government policy. At the time, both Secretaries of State were in the Lords. Murray offered a misleading gloss on the proposed subsidy: 'That this was the first instance in history, that, after an unsuccessful war, the allies remained in perfect union – that this would be a great means of preserving and consolidating that union'.[101] In late 1753 and early 1754, Murray was mentioned as a possible replacement for Holdernesse, and it was alleged that Pelham opposed this scheme of his brother and Granville.[102]

Outside London, the key officials who took a role in foreign policy were diplomats and colonial officials. Diplomats were important, although not responsible for key initiatives. In contrast, initiatives taken by colonial officials played a significant role in overseas relations with France.[103] The same situation was true for France. Indeed, as a result of the tendency for both powers to support their officials, Joseph Yorke, an army officer turned diplomat, was convinced that, despite the French government being willing to settle colonial disputes: 'North America will be an inexhaustible source of quarrels.'[104]

Parliament

The issue, organisation and ethos of management returns attention to Parliament as a key means of foreign policy.[105] The politics of foreign policy in part arose from this means, just as the politics could also affect the means. Parliament provided a vital governmental tool in the shape of financial support for policy as with the vote of credit on 25 March 1755, a necessary step in the crisis with France. Parliamentary backing also offered the crucial political means of validation. In December 1754, Joseph Yorke, who was convinced that the British constitution was generally misunderstood abroad,[106] thought it

---

[101] Stone, report on debate, 22 Feb. (os) 1751, BL. Add. 32724 fol. 131.

[102] Alt to William VIII of Hesse-Cassel, 4 Jan. 1754, Marburg, 4f England 255; Perrone to Charles Emmanuel III, 7 Mar. 1754, AST. LM. Ing. 58.

[103] M. Savelle, *The Diplomatic History of the Canadian Boundary, 1749–63* (New Haven, Connecticut, 1940), p. 148.

[104] Joseph to Philip Yorke, 25 July 1750, BL. Add. 35363 fol. 275. For French concerns about Colonel Edward Cornwallis, Lieutenant-Governor of Nova Scotia, President of the Council of Marine to Marquis de La Jonquière, 11 Sept. 1750, AN. AM. Colonies B, 91.

[105] See more generally, J. Black, *Parliament and Foreign Policy in the Eighteenth Century* (Cambridge, 2004).

[106] Joseph to Philip Yorke, 14 Dec. 1753, BL. Add. 35363 fol. 341.

very agreeable ... to see the supply voted as it is, and it puts a stop to all disadvantageous reports in the foreign world, where it was imagined that some difficulties would be thrown in the way of the administration ... The vigorous measures with the decency observed in taking them will have a better effect in France I am persuaded than the most obstreperous representations from the ablest ministers.[107]

In 1756, Parliament agreed to support Hanover if it was attacked in consequence of measures taken to support British rights. This was not an abstract constitutional issue, but an important declaration in a highly-charged diplomatic and political environment. The question was of Hanover's vulnerability, being exposed to French attack as a consequence of Britain and France clashing in North America.[108] Conversely, the ministry could also avoid the exposition of circumstances and policy if it thought it appropriate. In 1753, Yorke noted from The Hague that the King's speech opening the session was regarded as very guarded and 'particularly admired for the dexterity that is employed to say nothing, and to give hopes of everything'.[109] Then and in November, when the next session opened, commentators suggested that the ministry was putting off difficult issues until after the general election due in 1754.

In providing validation for policy, Parliament offered the opportunity of contesting the policy, and thereby of advancing legitimate opposition. Moreover, as a forum for such action, Parliament ensured that opposition, or the prospect of opposition,[110] gained a publicity and prominence that in part made it an acceptable, or at least more readily understood, element in an international political world that was inherently conservative and uneasy with opposition. The interactions of the British opposition in this role with political circumstances and developments, both at home and abroad, were a prime topic for diplomats. In 1748, Justus Alt, the experienced Hesse-Cassel envoy, reported that public unease, about whether the arrival in Germany of Russian troops would be in time to affect the campaigning against France, had led the heads of the opposition to discuss how to raise the issue in Parliament. Several had proposed an Address to George, but others, correctly arguing that parliamentary arithmetic meant that such a measure would be rejected, had prevailed. As a result, it had been agreed that the subsidy treaty with Russia would simply be criticised when it was

---

[107] Joseph to Philip Yorke, 10 Dec. 1754, BL. Add. 35364 fol. 23.
[108] Holdernesse to Mitchell, 9 July 1756, NA. SP. 90/65.
[109] Yorke to Hardwicke, 19, 23 (quote) Jan. 1753, BL. Add. 35356 fols 115, 118.
[110] Perrone to Charles Emmanuel III, 15 Aug. 1754, AST. LM. Ing. 58.

debated.[111] The sub-text was the belief that the real reason for the British-backed Russian deployment was to put pressure on Frederick II[112] of Prussia, a misuse of British resources to the benefit of Hanover. How best to derive political benefit, however, was unclear.

It was widely believed that good news from abroad made parliamentary sessions go better for the ministry;[113] although, in turn, the exigencies of debate could set the timetable for diplomacy, and in an inconvenient fashion.[114] Foreign envoys kept a close eye on Parliament, notably in periods of international crisis.[115] So also did foreign rulers. In 1753, Frederick II asked his envoy in London if George would be able to get Parliament to pay subsidies to Russia.[116] This question reflected his sensitivity on that point, as well as his awareness that Parliament's role was crucial to the wide-ranging and complex geopolitics of threat and deterrence. Frederick repeatedly kept a close eye on Parliament's position with regard to subsidies for Russia,[117] and also on discussion of other aspects of foreign policy.[118] In turn, when Britain and Prussia were allied, Frederick's desire for praise was regarded as important when preparing for the session, as such preparations included deciding how best to present government policy.[119]

Although foreign policy was not the issue, a parallel set of problems in management was posed by the Parliament in Dublin. There was also the need to win the support of colonial assemblies in North America and the West Indies. The assemblies in North America posed serious issues of management in the early stages of the Seven Years' War.

Within Britain, Parliament's place in the politics of foreign policy overlapped with the wider public debate. In part, this was because this very place encouraged discussion about the character of domestic politics, and notably Parliament's probity and its ability to represent the nation as a whole. Discussion about corruption could therefore play a role in the debate over foreign policy. There was also the place of Parliament as a focus for this debate, notably with regard to Petitions, Instructions and Addresses. Parliament was the focus of a sense

---

[111]   Alt to William VIII of Hesse-Cassel, 16 Jan. 1748, Marburg, 4f England 241.

[112]   Zamboni to Ludwig VIII, Landgrave of Hesse-Darmstadt, 19 Jan. 1748, Darmstadt, Staatsarchiv, E1 M10/6.

[113]   Newcastle to Bedford, 28 Sept. (os) 1749, Russell (ed.), *Bedford*, II, 46.

[114]   Reporting Robinson, Mirepoix to Rouillé, 8 Mar. 1755, AE. CP. Ang. 438 fol. 265.

[115]   Haslang to Preysing, 9 July 1756, Munich, Bayr. Ges., London, 231.

[116]   Frederick II to Michell, 25 Sept. 1753, *Polit. Corr.* X, 112.

[117]   Frederick II to Klinggraeffen, envoy in Vienna, 28 Dec. 1754, Frederick to Michell, 18 Jan. 1755, *Polit. Corr.* X, 507, XI, 26.

[118]   Frederick II to Klinggraeffen, 12 Mar. 1754, *Polit. Corr.* X, 266.

[119]   Mitchell to Holdernesse, 9 Oct. 1756, NA. SP. 90/66.

of accountability by government. This was a sense and practice within which policy could be debated, and action taken, to affect government and political practices, for example limiting corruption.[120] It was believed that parliamentary criticism could help the ministry by justifying its foreign policy.[121] Although the Prussian envoy suggested in 1753 that it was harder for the government to have a favourable Parliament elected in wartime than in peace,[122] in practice both the wartime 1747 and the peacetime 1754 elections went well for it.

Publications

Pamphlets were particularly aimed at the highpoint of political activity around the parliamentary session. They frequently appeared on the eve of the session. There was a similar rhythm with reference to the intensity of press activity. The press also acted to amplify other forms of news. Thus, on 30 March 1757, the front page of the *Citizen*, a London newspaper, declared:

> The desire of many of our readers, whom we are always ready to oblige, occasions the Instructions of the City of London, to their representatives, to be this day again inserted, as not yet unseasonable in the present national situation.

The press also spread news of celebrations. For example, the *Penny London Post* of 11 January (os) 1749 carried an illustration (which was unusual in the newspapers of the period) depicting 'A View of the Public Fireworks to be exhibited on the occasion of the General Peace', fireworks, for which Handel wrote the music, launched on what turned out to be a very damp occasion. The latter underlines the contrast between image and reality that is significant in considering the impression of government in this period.

The nature and role of debate over foreign policy was a matter of particular interest to foreign commentators as it was unique in Europe, with the exception of the United Provinces (Dutch Republic). There were powerful, in some respects more powerful, representative assemblies elsewhere, in Poland and Sweden, but no press there comparable to that of Britain. Moreover, Britain's pamphlets and press were less under governmental influence than its Dutch

---

[120] A. Graham, 'Auditing Leviathan: Corruption and State Formation in Early Eighteenth-century Britain', *English Historical Review*, 128 (2013), p. 838.

[121] Perrone to Charles Emmanuel III, 7 Feb. 1753, AST. LM. Ing. 58.

[122] Michell to Frederick II, 1 May 1753, *Polit. Corr.* IX, 408.

counterpart and often more insolent.[123] The ephemeral character of newspapers and the greater authority of pamphlets ensured that international concern about publications on foreign policy focused on pamphlets rather than newspapers, and led to attempts to influence content and to commission favourable works, as by Frederick II in the United Provinces. The regularity with which newspapers appeared gave them a particular impact. However, pamphlets remained important, notably because they offered an opportunity to deploy arguments at length. They also enjoyed particular status, in part because, on a longstanding pattern, they were sometimes written by prominent individuals and, anyway, seen as more reputable, and in part because of the absence of advertisements. Their tone was not necessarily inaccessible. A homely image in one pamphlet of 1748 discussing foreign affairs is more generally indicative:

> as to his Sardinian Majesty [Charles Emmanuel III], if he be obliged to resign Placentia to Don Philip, and be recompensed nowhere else; shall not we leave him in a worse condition than we found him, considering that his new neighbour will soon spread himself around him, like a drop of oil on a piece of stuff [cloth].[124]

This was a reference to the likely spread of Bourbon influence in northern Italy, as indeed occurred with the establishment in Parma and Piacenza of Philip, son of Philip V of Spain, half-brother of Ferdinand VI of Spain, and son-in-law of Louis XV of France.

There was also considerable foreign interest in the press. British pamphlets and newspapers were acquired by the French government,[125] as well as by other powers. In 1749, Alt sent a translation published in the *Daily Advertiser* of 21 March (os) of a letter from Barbados about France's schemes concerning Tobago. This indicated the potential for trouble posed by this distant issue.[126] Earlier, the issue of 2 February (os) reporting the Baltic crisis was discussed and sent on 14 February. Alt kept a close eye on relevant publications, dispatching in 1753

---

[123] Joseph to Philip Yorke, 11 Jan. 1754, BL. Add. 35364 fol. 1.

[124] Anon., *A Free Comment on the Late Mr W-G-N's Apology for his Conduct* (London, 1748), p. 39.

[125] AE. MD. Ang. 51 fols 171–3. See also *Westminster Journal*, 21 Jan. (os) 1748, AN. AM. B⁷ 359; piece on Jewish Naturalisation Bill from *Public Advertiser*, 25 June 1753, AE. MD. Ang. 51 fol. 184; extract from *London Evening Post* of 13 Dec. 1756 on Franco-Spanish trade, AE. CP. Ang. 400 fols 497–9. For the conviction that books also influenced British opinion, Mirepoix to Rouillé, 23 Jan. 1755, AE. CP. Ang. 438 fol. 49.

[126] Alt to William VIII, Regent of Hesse-Cassel, 28 Mar. 1749, Marburg, 4f England 250, see also 18 May 1753, vol. 254, re items on East Friesland dispute.

a French translation of a pamphlet on Anglo-Prussian differences.[127] In 1753, both the original and a translation of the 'Delenda est Carthago' essay in the *London Evening Post* on 9 January, an essay implying inevitable conflict between Britain and France, was sent to Paris.[128] Perrone, indeed, reported that only this newspaper merited attention. A copy of the *London Evening Post* of 24 June 1756 was translated for Frederick II so that he could see what the British public thought of the new direction in Austrian policy. He referred to press reports from London on other occasions.[129] Surviving copies and references in the archives suggest that the practice of sending published material to foreign courts was widespread. Caricatures were also acquired.[130] The British state papers also contain foreign newspapers. Thus, the *Gazette de Vienne* [Vienna] of 27 April 1757 carried a report from London on opinions about ministerial changes, while that of 11 June 1757 reported on the parliamentary debate about a Vote of Credit.[131]

British diplomats could seek to encourage favourable reports in foreign publications,[132] while they were encouraged to send reports to the *Gazette* 'in order to the obviating and articles discrediting of the many false and often mischievous articles of foreign news which are inserted in other printed papers or otherwise propagated and dispersed'.[133]

The press was of significance as part of a world of report and rumour in which the representation of policy and events was a key aspect of power politics.[134] The accuracy of press reports was a frequent topic of diplomatic comment,[135] alongside claims that some were inserted by rival diplomats.[136] In January 1755, as diplomatic relations deteriorated, Mirepoix, the French envoy, complained to Robinson, a Secretary of State, about the hostile nature of the press. Robinson responded by drawing attention to the nature of the British constitution and by saying that ordinarily the government itself received more press criticism than France, which, indeed, was the case. He added that the ministry had sought to

---

[127] Alt to Landgrave, 11 May 1753, Marburg, 4f England 254.

[128] Perrone to Ossorio, Secretary of State, 25 Jan. 1753, AST. LM. Ing. 57.

[129] Finckenstein to Frederick II, 5 July 1756, Frederick to Michell, 26 Oct. 1753, *Polit. Corr.* XIII, p. 37, X, 138.

[130] For example *A Nurse for the Hess—ns* (1746), AE. CP. Ang. 422 fol. 128.

[131] NA. SP. 80/198.

[132] Yorke to Holdernesse, 3 Oct. 1755, BL. Eg. 3446 fol. 239.

[133] Holdernesse to Keith, 19 Aug. 1755, BL. Add. 35480 fol. 54.

[134] Mitchell to Hanbury Williams, 30 July 1756, HW.

[135] Alt to William VIII Landgrave of Hesse-Cassel, 1 Oct. 1751, Marburg, 4f England 248.

[136] Zamboni to Kaunitz, 31 Dec. 1751, HHStA, England, Varia, 10 fol. 85.

quieten the situation.[137] Holdernesse, facing criticism about the inconsistency between British policy and a British brochure [pamphlet], replied that the latter were of scant value.[138] However, the dispatch of newspapers to Paris continued.

Interest in foreign news had increased in 1744, the year in which war with France was formally declared. That July, John Roberts, a major London printer long close to the 'Old Corps' Whigs, produced the first number of a monthly the title of which emphasised the significance of foreign news: *The Political Cabinet: or, An Impartial Review of the most remarkable Occurrences of the World, Particularly of Europe. Collected from the most Authentic Papers, published by the several Courts (whether Friends or Enemies to Great Britain) as well as from private Intelligence. Containing a great variety of articles not mentioned in the British Newspapers; and interspersed with extracts from the most curious State-Pamphlets published abroad.* As the preface in the opening issue mentioned, there was nothing already like this in Britain.

At the same time, the incessant nature of new developments, and the rapid pace of change, were such that more regular news that what could be provided by monthlies was sought. Here the prime requirements were reliability and punctuality. For Britain, the latter was a particular problem due to its island position, the impact of contrary winds in delaying boats sailing to Britain, and the extent to which the eastward move of the focus of much Continental diplomacy made Britain geographically more marginal for European news. Winds, especially westerlies, were a year-round problem, notably affecting the provision of news from northern Europe via Hamburg and the United Provinces. Mitchell's dispatch from Berlin on 23 July 1756 only reached London on 4 August, due to contrary winds.[139]

The press frequently proclaimed its value. Thus, on 29 March 1757, the *London Evening Post* announced:

> The freedom of speech, and the freedom of writing that at present prevails, and, which in some measure, proceeds from the need that all parties have of the press, will bring lasting advantages to this kingdom. Things have been already so clearly explained, and so fully exposed, that we cannot hereafter be deceived or deluded, though we may be driven into distress.

---

[137] Mirepoix to Rouillé, 16 Jan. 1755, AE. CP. Ang. 438 fol. 22.
[138] Bussy to Rouillé, 29 July 1755, AE. CP. Br.-Han. 52 fol. 23.
[139] Holdernesse to Mitchell, 6 Aug. 1756, NA. SP. 90/65.

The press was significant in terms of the content of policy, the subject of the next chapter. It was also important as a means of policy because the press was the leading way in which policy was discussed and explained, and thereby substantiated, in a public sphere that was broader than that of Parliament. Indeed, there was criticism that the press revealed British military plans, and thus made Britain less effective than France.[140] Newspapers were not simply major components in the information network through which the government and the political world came to understand what was happening abroad. They were also significant in the shaping of this information. This shaping contributed greatly to the politicisation of foreign policy, as positions were fixed, explained and used. In turn, the shaping of information became a topic for the press. Thus, the *Centinel* on 8 October 1757 reported 'a curious political debate between Mr Profound and Mr Superficial' in 'the coffee room' over the strength of France, specifically whether her ships could sail for want of sailors, and whether Lombardy was in Italy. Coffee houses were a prime location for the discussion of politics, the *Test* critically referring on 18 June 1757 to 'the reports of shallow coffee-house graduates in politics'.

There were frequent references to alleged attempts to control this process. Thus, the *Citizen* announced on 29 June 1757: 'I am credibly informed, that the Ministry and their emissaries, threw a certain honest paper lately, called the CRAB-TREE, out of every coffee-house near the Court, or the public offices, because it told home truths.' News circulated around the country. In July 1757, John Tucker, MP for Weymouth, received a letter from his younger brother Richard, who managed the Tucker interest in the constituency:

> We are greatly mortified at the bad news from the King of Prussia and much in pain for our noble Duke [Cumberland] who we conclude must not now expect any succour from the King of Prussia and by the news of today it looks as if the King of Denmark was almost broken with us.[141]

These were perceptive remarks. A different form of episodic comment was provided by ballads, which were described as 'the merriment of the Mob and the

---

[140]   John Thomlinson, London merchant and colonial agent for New Hampshire, to Granville, 13 Dec. 1756. Pargellis (ed.), *Military Affairs in North America 1748–1765* (New York, 1936), pp. 258–9.

[141]   Richard to John Tucker, 4 July 1757, Bod. Ms. Don. C. 112 fol. 53. For reading 'the melancholy account of affairs abroad ... in the newspapers at Carlisle' en route to Edinburgh, Bedford, CRO., Lucas papers L30/9/17/11.

treasury of our hawkers'.[142] Ballads could focus on issues of national humiliation, such as Byng's failure off Minorca in 1756, and gave them greater political weight.

The impact of the press was seen in the transcribing of items into commonplace books.[143] In shaping and reflecting public opinion,[144] the press also provided opportunities for the amplification of issues so that they achieved a national resonance. Thus, in 1748, there was a bitter and sustained controversy over grain exports to France, with which Britain was at war. These exports were presented as an instance of sectional and selfish interests, as opposed to that of the nation as a whole, 'the public good'.[145] This was a juxtaposition that was of great significance in so far as the bridging from wartime concerns to post-war anxieties was concerned. The press spread this account across the country. For example, on 5 January (os) 1748, the first issue of *Aberdeen's Journal* [sic] included an attack on these exports. The *Newcastle Courant* followed suit, reprinting a London item that claimed that, without this grain, France could not support its forces in the Low Countries. Indeed, a shortage of grain in France helped to drive prices there up.

Public Opinion

The issue raised broader questions about the operation of the political system, not least with the report that George II was angry about the grain exports and that a public subscription would seek to purchase the grain.[146] The subject was complicated by claims that, unless they could export, ruin faced farmers,[147] claims which reflected the significance of grain exports for East Anglia and south-east England and the extent of agricultural problems in the second quarter of the

---

[142] Anon., *The Constitution* no. 2 (London, 1757), p. 33.

[143] Anon. commonplace book, BL. Add. 63648, pp. 156, 165, 175, 188, 195.

[144] R.D. Spector, *English Literary Periodicals and the Climate of Opinion during the Seven Years' War* (The Hague, 1966), p. 18; R. Harris, *A Patriot Press: National Politics and the London Press in the 1740s* (Oxford, 1993) and 'The *London Evening Post* and Mid-Eighteenth-Century British Politics', *English Historical Review*, 110 (1995), pp. 1132–56.

[145] Zamboni to Landgrave Ludwig VIII of Hesse-Darmstadt, 19 Jan. 1748, Darmstadt, Staatsarchiv, E1 M10/6.

[146] *Newcastle Courant*, 16 Jan. (os), *General Advertiser*, 1 Feb. (os) 1748. For French sensitivity about Dutch press reports on grain exports from France, Saint-Contest to Bonnac, 18 Feb. 1753, AN. KK. 1400 fol. 75. For Austrian action to stop export to France, Yorke to Newcastle, 27 Apr. 1753, NA. SP. 84/463.

[147] *Jacobite's Journal*, 30 Jan. (os), 13 Feb. (os) 1748.

century. The agricultural interest was also referred to by commentators when they commented on land tax rates.[148]

Related to the controversy over wartime grain exports, the terms used in the press to describe those linked to the export varied. They could be referred to as some major individuals or, more positively, as all the farmers in the country.[149] This point can be amplified by considering the variety of meanings attached to the 'people'. In part, these meanings reflected the extent to which the people were believed important, both in reality and as an aspect of the constitution. There was a widely-expressed view that the people offered a core component of sense. In 1745, *Old England* published a tale of a Sussex fisherman in the 1690s, who told the French admiral Tourville with reference to James II and William III who both then claimed the British thrones: 'God bless them both: As to matters of government, how should he know anything of them, for he could neither read nor write', but that he would not fight against his country with which France was then at war.[150] A variant was the view that the ordinary people were primarily concerned with the immediate issues of livelihood, such that 'the accounts of prices of corn and stocks are to most of our readers of more importance than narratives of greater sound'.[151]

At the same time, there was also the opinion that the people could be misinformed, were overly prone to follow their emotions, and, therefore, could be led astray and stirred up to dangerous ideas.[152] For example, in arguing, in October 1750, that 'all impartial and disinterested persons' would support the Anglo-Spanish treaty and that 'all the nation must agree in the rightness of the measures',[153] Bedford was creating a space for those who lacked these virtues to challenge this national view. However, the political resonance of this opposition 'space' varied. Four years later, William Lorimer commented on the failure of Sir William Calvert, a former Lord Mayor, prominent brewer, and government supporter, to win re-election as an MP for London: 'Calvert came pretty near, and it is certain he had the majority of merchants and substantial people, but the

---

[148] Alt to Landgrave William VIII of Hesse-Cassel, 6 Feb. 1753, Marburg, 4f England 254.

[149] Zamboni to Landgrave Ludwig VIII of Hesse-Darmstadt, 19 Jan., 9 Feb. 1748, Darmstadt, Staatsarchiv, E1 M10/6.

[150] *Old England*, 16 Feb. (os) 1745.

[151] *London Chronicle*, 1 Jan. 1757.

[152] *True Patriot*, 25 Feb. (os), 11 Mar. (os), 3 June (os) 1746; *A Dialogue Between a Gentleman from London ... and an Honest Alderman of the Country Party* (London, 1747).

[153] Bedford to Keene, 26 Oct. (os) 1750, Russell (ed.), *Bedford*, II, 58, 60.

mob could not forgive his joining in the Jewish [Naturalisation] Bill'.[154] When, in 1757, Pitt was described as the minister for the affairs of London, this came with the caveat that he was a bad one to handle foreign affairs.[155]

Doubt about public opinion justified different policies on the part of government, as in March 1756 when Newcastle favoured peace with France even though 'the people are still wild for war'.[156] A pamphleteer writing in 1757 in favour of the militia, addressing 'the People of England', noted of those opposed: 'It is true many of you, my countrymen, who compose the giddy multitude that oppose it are friends to the Constitution – but you think not for yourselves – you take reports for facts, and credit hearsays ... think for yourselves'.[157] The pamphlet included an appeal to economic self-interest, by arguing that any reliance on foreign troops, instead of the militia, to defend Britain would lead to an increase in the cost of bread.[158] One of a number of arguments, this one indicated the significance of social order in the presentation of British goals.

Alongside the emphasis on the need for coherence, there was also the view that public opinion over policy was divided and that contradictory political demands could be generated, such that there was no one national view. In 1756 Josiah Tucker, a conservative commentator, observed of Bristol, a city with a marked level of political partisanship: 'Our city is at present tolerably free from the epidemical madness of addressing, instructing, etc.... if such an attempt shall be made, the government might depend upon a counter address, instructions, etc. if that measure should be thought advisable'.[159] Other commentators argued that the people had a right to address and instruct.[160] The process certainly attracted great attention. In particular, true or forged Instructions were given publicity by the press. Newspapers thereby attracted additional scrutiny, as in October 1756, when Holdernesse, a Secretary of State confronting a very difficult international situation, wrote from London to Rockingham, a fellow Yorkshire peer, about the report in the *Public Advertiser* about a Yorkshire Instruction.[161] More generally, rumour played a key role in both politics and political reporting,

---

[154] Lorimer to Sir Ludovick Grant, 11 May 1754, Edinburgh, Scottish Record Office, GD. 248/182/1/41.

[155] Viry to Charles Emmanuel III, 19 July 1757, AST. LM. Ing. 62.

[156] Newcastle to Devonshire, 7 Mar. 1756, BL. Add. 32863 fols 215–16.

[157] Anon., *A Letter to the People of England*, pp. 7–8.

[158] Anon., *A Letter to the People of England*, p. 6.

[159] G. Shelton, *Dean Tucker and Eighteenth-Century Economic and Political Thought* (New York, 1981), p. 158.

[160] *London Evening Post*, 1 Jan. 1757.

[161] Holdernesse to Rockingham, 28 Oct. 1756, Sheffield, Archives, Wentworth Woodhouse papers, R1–85.

its role in the latter an aspect of public politics. As a consequence, there were repeated attempts to seek more accurate reports. John Hotham, a Cambridge student, wrote in 1755 to his elder brother Charles, a lieutenant in the army and later an MP: 'I should be externally obliged to you for a true account of what you hear in London, for Cambridge intelligence is generally worse than none.' John was clear in his views: 'I do utterly detest the French (for whom I had contracted a kind of sneaky regard), as a double tongued race of people.'[162]

The nation was the usual phrase adopted by foreign commentators, as in May 1753 when Saint-Contest, the French foreign minister, referred to the impatience of the nation about Anglo-Prussian disputes and of Frederick II as thus engaged with the English nation, or in March 1756 when explaining the difficulty of easing Anglo-French relations,[163] or the following month, when Francesco Viry, the Sardinian envoy, who was close to the ministry, reported that the nation was against restoring captured French ships. Françis de Bussy told George II in 1755 that all affairs of state were national affairs in Britain; a remark based on his experience as an envoy there.[164]

Diplomats, British and foreign, commenting on other states believed that their governments were influenced by views about the British nation. Thus, in October 1755, Aubeterre, the French envoy in Vienna, wrote that the Austrian government thought that if the naval and colonial conflict went badly for Britain, the British 'nation' was capable of forcing George II to peace without thinking of Austria, and that this worried the government and made it hesitant of entering into British views against France, even though the British alliance was considered essential.[165] In practice, Aubeterre was wrong and the Prussian issue dominated Austrian policy, but his comments were an instructive guide to attitudes. The contrast between King and nation was very much seen with Frederick II's views of British policy,[166] and Frederick was believed to be trying to use Hanoverian issues to exploit this contrast: 'his view seems evidently to provoke the King, and to alienate as far as in him lies, the affections of the English from their sovereign, by mixing the affairs of the Electorate with those of England'.[167] King and nation

---

[162] John to Charles Hotham, 1, 13 Apr. 1755, Hull, UL., Hotham papers, DDHo 4/6.

[163] Saint-Contest to La Touche, envoy in Berlin, 22 May, 22 June 1753, Van Neck to Wernet, 8 Mar., enclosed in Wernet to Rouillé, 12 Mar. 1756, AE. CP. Prusse 171 fols 260–1, 310, Ang. 440 fols 113–14.

[164] Viry to Charles Emmanuel III, 1 Apr. 1756, AST. LM. Ing. 60; Bussy to Rouillé, 29 July 1755, AE. CP. Br.-Han. 52 fol. 19.

[165] Aubeterre to Rouillé, 15 Oct. 1755, AE. CP. Aut. 254 fols 301–2.

[166] Frederick II to Klinggraeffen, envoy in London, 4 Feb. 1749, *Polit. Corr.* VI, 362.

[167] Joseph Yorke to Hardwicke, 22 Dec. 1752, BL. Add. 35356 fol. 107.

was not the sole vocabulary employed by British and foreign commentators when discussing policy. Thus, on 11 February (os) 1749, the *Remembrancer*, a London opposition paper, contrasted people and ministry.

The interest of the bulk of the population in foreign policy was forcibly asserted by the *Monitor*, a leading London opposition paper, on 6 September 1755:

> The burden of a war must be borne by the people, which gives them a right to complain, when they are neglected ... it is now become a maxim in politics, founded upon experience, that he who had the longest purse will wear the longest sword.

The *Monitor* was particularly keen to discuss constitutional issues as a key aspect of its political engagement with the state of Britain. However, it is important to temper British exceptionalism by noting that similar explanations were offered for other states. Thus, Walter Titley, the long-serving British envoy in Copenhagen, reported that the attempts by France and its Danish supporters to use a subsidy to win over Denmark had not worked as 'contrary to the true interest and general bent of the Danish nation'.[168] This was a convenient as well as complacent argument, and one that indicated the general assumptions about how policy should be conceived and conducted.

Alongside this standard emphasis on the nation as having a single view, came an understanding of a division in views. Considering both Britain and other states, diplomats could refer to such divisions. Mitchell, an MP as well as envoy at the key embassy of Berlin, found his request that he be sent by the government a regular copy of the *London Evening Post* refused. In response, he explained that he had requested the paper because it was 'the source of intelligence for the disaffected', and that he thought it necessary to be informed of their perspective.[169]

Trade and Industry

Turning to particular sectors and themes, grain exports as an issue demonstrated the extent to which trade was far more complex as an interest and a political issue, than as an ideological drive and rhetorical flourish, and an explanation of policy, as used by George II among others.[170] There was a general assumption that the

---

[168]   Titley to Keith, 10 Mar. 1756, BL. Add. 35480 fol. 140.
[169]   Mitchell to Holdernesse, 7 June 1756, BL. Eg. 3460 fol. 18.
[170]   Bussy to Rouillé, 29 July 1755, AE. CP. Br.-Han. 52 fol. 19.

British government would help trade, as for example against Algerine (North African, Barbary) pirates.[171] Merchants were widely, and correctly, regarded as more influential than industrialists, although there was a significant link between the two in the case of export trades. Merchants pressed for protection in foreign markets and for the amelioration of commercial conditions there. In both peace and war, they sought support against unwarranted seizures and privateers. In late 1756, merchants trading with the Mediterranean pressed for an increase in naval strength there.[172] Ministers saw merchants, and foreign envoys commented on this process and on what was said.[173] Financiers were also significant. Sir John Barnard, both a longstanding London MP and alderman and a prominent insurer, was consulted by Newcastle in 1755 about the financial implications of war and how best to raise taxation. Barnard also offered advice on diplomatic and military strategy.[174] The duke did not turn to a younger London MP, William Beckford, who was linked to the Tories and had been linked to the Duke of Bedford.

The opposition also sought advice from merchants. Thus, in 1750, prior to a parliamentary debate on the state of Dunkirk, George Bubb Dodington requested advice from Stephen Janssen,[175] a leading London merchant, Sheriff of London in 1749–50, and an opposition Whig MP for London from 1747 to 1754. Janssen, who also sent Newcastle advice on trade, had backed a bill to prohibit insurance of French ships in wartime, which was debated in the Commons on 18 December (os) 1747.

Pressure from industrialists left fewer traces in the archives, in part because the merchants were far better represented than them in Parliament, dominated the City of London, and played a key role in providing the government with liquidity and credit. Nevertheless, there were references to such industrial pressure. In 1753, Newcastle expressed his concern about protectionism in the Austrian Netherlands (Belgium), adding: 'Our manufacturers in Yorkshire are already full of complaints upon this head; and if they were, by such a Convention, to be precluded from all hopes of readdress, there would be no standing their

---

[171] Lagau, French Consul in Hamburg, to Ministry of Marine, 23 Mar. 1750, AN. B⁷ 375.

[172] Viry to Charles Emmanuel III, 1 Oct. 1756, AST. LM. Ing. 60.

[173] Bedford to Benjamin Keene, envoy in Spain, 13 July (os) 1749, Russell (ed.), *Bedford*, II, 38; Boutel to Rouillé, 7 Nov. 1754, Rouillé to Mirepoix, 19 Feb. 1755, AE. CP. Ang. 437 fol. 362, 438 fol. 186.

[174] Newcastle to Holdernesse, 11 July 1755, BL. Add. 32857 fols 3–4, 45–6.

[175] H.R. Wyndham (ed.), *The Diary of the Late George Bubb Dodington* (3rd edn, London, 1785), p. 34.

importunities.' Newcastle located this issue of social politics in a wider context of the purposes of British foreign policy:

> The power, and influence, of this country depends upon the extent of our trade. It is that consideration, that engages us in the support of the Continent, and it is for that reason, that we are so strictly, and I hope, ever shall be, united to the House of Austria.[176]

The following year, Newcastle told the Sardinian envoy that he would get into trouble with the nation, an instructive comment, if he formally recognised the Sardinian position in a commercial dispute.[177]

The Duke had major electoral interests in Yorkshire, which contained many parliamentary boroughs. Holdernesse and Robinson were also Yorkshire political figures. At the county meeting held in Yorkshire in July 1753 to nominate the candidates for the county seats in the election due in 1754, there were numerous peers and gentry, but also delegations from the manufacturing centres of Halifax and Sheffield, a sign of a rising new political interest. References to industrial interests increased. Describing the Pitt–Devonshire ministry as 'inactive', the *Test* of 30 April 1757 claimed as its sources enquiries made with Birmingham ironworks, the linen and cotton business, the Spitalfields silk trade, and the woollen cloth industry. However, alongside demands from mercantile and industrial interests, there were serious tensions between, and within, trades, as well as the different, but crucial, issue of the gap between policy and implementation. Moreover, references to pressure for action did not mean that action ensued.

Aware of the sensitivity of trade as a political issue, the government sought to demonstrate its support and to discredit suggestions that it would yield commercial interests for political concerns, and notably those of Hanover. Thus, in 1753, Newcastle responded to the suggestion that the 'public' would believe that the ministry had ordered the seizure of Prussian vessels going to the Indies in order to serve Hanoverian goals, by strongly asserting that George had to act against this Prussian trade and that if, as a result, there was harm to Hanover, the British would be ready to fight as a consequence.[178] This was a conscious echo of the controversy in the 1720s over the Ostend Company, an Austrian plan to trade to India which Britain had successfully blocked; and reflected both Newcastle's long experience in office and the sensitivity of commercial issues.

---

[176] Newcastle to Keith, 20 Apr. 1753, NA. SP. 80/191.
[177] Perrone to Charles Emmanuel III, 17 Oct. 1754, AST. LM. Ing. 58.
[178] Perrone to Charles Emmanuel III, 4 Jan. 1753, AST. LM. Ing. 57.

The questions of neutral rights, monopoly commercial claims, and the seizure of ships, proved a major strand in diplomacy and the related public discussion. This was notably so in the United Provinces where there was a large mercantile cadre.[179] Frederick II was seen as trying to persuade Dutch merchants that he was fighting their battles over trade.[180] British envoys habitually sought to foster British trade. Having persuaded Bavaria to accept British tobacco imports, Onslow Burrish moved on to sugar.[181]

Women

Politics engaged women, even though they lacked the vote. The correspondence of women with their husbands reveals knowledge of politics and a willingness to express their views. In May 1744, Martha Mussenden, daughter of one MP and sister to another, wrote to her husband, Hill Mussenden, an opposition Whig MP, from their seat in Suffolk, arguing that Britain needed peace, that the ambitions of Continental powers were no reason for British intervention there, and that the recent rapid loss to the French of fortresses in the Austrian Netherlands that it had taken years to capture during the War of the Spanish Succession (1702–13) was a national disgrace. That war served as a point of reference across the political community.[182] In 1756, Lady Harcourt feared that bribery by France, 'that faithless nation', which, she claimed, only adhered to the most solemn treaties if they served their purposes, was involved in the loss of Minorca.[183] A sexual dimension also played a role: alongside the presentation of French men as effeminate and thus of cultural borrowing as a threat to British masculinity, came a different challenge. Women as potential victims of rape was a theme of calls for a militia to protect against French invasion.[184] This was an aspect of a more general sense of French men as dangerous, being both degenerate and rapacious seducers.

News circulated in a context of sociability and by means of its practices and mediums. In 1755, Viscount Dungarvan wrote from Bath, 'The report of

---

[179]   Bonnac to Saint-Contest, 4 Jan. 1753, AN. KK. 1400 fols 30–1.
[180]   Yorke to Newcastle, 5 Jan. 1753, NA. SP. 84/462.
[181]   Burrish to Holdernesse, 12 Aug. 1755, NA. SP. 81/105.
[182]   Martha to Hill Mussenden, 31 May (os) 1744, Ipswich, East Suffolk Record Office, HA 403/1/10; Pelham, note on letter from Newcastle, 13 July 1753, BL. Add. 33201 fol. 162.
[183]   Lady Harcourt to son, Lord Nuneham, 27 July 1756, *Harcourt Papers*, III, 85–6.
[184]   Anon., *A Letter to the People of England* (London, 1757), p. 7.

a war greatly disturbs the rooms and coffee-houses',[185] while Henrietta, Lady Luxborough, Bolingbroke's half-sister and the wife of a Whig MP, wrote to William Shenstone, a literary figure with whom she had a long correspondence, enclosing a letter from Sir William Meredith, a Tory MP: 'it is a more satisfactory account than printed news affords to those who are attentive to the great affair of peace or war'. Having commented briefly on the current political and military situation, she added: 'it is as natural to an English subject to be a politician, as to a French one to be a courtier'.[186]

Conclusion

The varied uses and diverse roles of the press, and the range of meanings attached to public opinion, underlined the extent to which the different means of considering foreign policy operated, and were seen to operate, as aspects of a system in which government and politics were scarcely separate but, instead, largely coterminous. Moreover, foreign policy was an important theme and expression of social concerns and norms. This helps explain the significance and interest of the subject.

---

[185] Dungarvan to Quick, 25 Jan. 1755, Exeter, Devon Record Office, 64/12/29/1/121.
[186] Luxborough to Shenstone, 29 Mar. 1755, Bod. Ms. Don. C. 56 fols 4–5.

Chapter 3
The Themes of Policy

We wish the circumstances of the nation and the behaviour of our allies made it practicable for us to act as great a part upon the Continent, as we did in Queen Anne's time; but the fact is otherwise.

Newcastle, 1755.[1]

Themes and means overlap in the character and impact of the discussion over foreign policy. To focus on themes is to approach the perennial issue of structure and agency from a new perspective. The themes can take on the character of agency, but it is also possible to note the extent to which there is a structure of themes, a fundamental set of ideas and aspirations. In turn, this set was affected by the pressure of events, both domestic and international, and by the changes in ideas that arose as a consequence.[2]

Europe versus America?

This perspective is made particularly significant due to the role of the ideas of the period in the development of attitudes toward the global geopolitics of British concerns. In particular, there was a shift in Britain, among ministers, politicians and commentators, from an emphasis on Britain's role in European power politics to an account that was broader in geographical scope, more aware of the interactions of Britain's varied regions and themes of concern, and more engaged with the trans-oceanic world. In the case of the last, there was a transition from a concern, economic and strategic, with the Spanish Atlantic[3] to one with the French Atlantic. In some respects, this shift involved the same language and similar ideas, but there were also important differences. Indeed, much of the significance of this period rests not only on Britain's ability to survive its mid-century crisis, but also on the redefinition of its prime imperial concern, certainly

---

[1]   Newcastle to Holdernesse, 11 July 1755, BL. Add. 32857 fol. 53.

[2]   J. Black, *Debating Foreign Policy in Eighteenth-Century Britain* (Farnham, 2011), pp. 127–40.

[3]   S. Satsuma, *Britain and Colonial Maritime War in the Early Eighteenth Century: Silver, Seapower and the Atlantic* (Woodbridge, 2013).

of imperial expansion: from the Caribbean to North America. This redefinition had geopolitical, military, economic and racial consequences.

There is controversy over the timing, indeed nature, of this development because it intercuts with the protracted debate over the prominence of Continental (i.e. European) as opposed to Oceanic (i.e. trans-oceanic) interests and concerns in British foreign policy.[4] These topics, which played a major role in public and political discussion at the time, will be addressed where relevant throughout the book. In considering the shift to a focus on North America, there is a need to assess the respective significance of the capture of Louisbourg from France in 1745 and the outbreak of fighting with France (and its Native American allies) in the Ohio River Valley in 1754, or, rather, the domestic political consequences of both in Britain.

A key element is the politics of the policy issues mentioned in the last paragraph. As was only to be expected, these politics were 'reset' and energised by the course of international developments and by how they played through domestic divisions. The different results of two expeditions in the 1740s were important. Success in capturing the major French fortress of Louisbourg on Cape Breton Island in 1745 contrasted with conspicuous and humiliating failure against its Spanish counterpart of Cartagena, in modern Colombia, in 1741. This success led to hopes of a new imperial geopolitics, hopes that crucially included denying comparable prospects for France. The overlap of public politics and governmental concerns was readily seen in the zeal with which the idea of Canadian gains was propagated and plans accordingly proposed.

In the event, just as the international conjuncture and related events had led to the disillusionment of the earlier hopes of British gains from Spain, so the same was initially true of those from France. Having made significant moves in 1742, 1743 and, to a lesser extent, 1744 in Europe, Britain failed to retain or regain the initiative from 1745. Instead, French conquests in the Low Countries set the dynamic of events in the latter stages of the War of Austrian Succession, 1745–8. More generally, a sense of threat was to the fore, one that drew on longstanding anxiety about French intentions, anxiety comparable to that expressed about the Papacy and international Catholicism during the '45, a crisis that lasted until 1746, and was then given an afterlife in terms of French conquests on the Continent. It was as if history was coming to a height, history as both purpose and drama. In 1748, Sandwich referred to the terms offered

---

    4   R. Pares, 'American versus Continental Warfare 1739–63', *English Historical Review*, 51 (1936), pp. 429–65; M. Peters, 'Early Hanoverian Consciousness: Empire or Europe?', *English Historical Review*, 122 (2007), pp. 632–68; B. Simms, *Three Victories and a Defeat. The Rise and Fall of the First British Empire, 1714–1783* (London, 2007).

'by which France ensures to herself that entire conquest over the Liberties of Europe, which has been her uninterrupted pursuit for so many centuries'. In contrast, Sandwich emphasised 'the independency of Europe'.[5] As an instance of continuities in assumptions and language, the idea of France as in pursuit of universal empire, a theme much expressed in opposition to Louis XIV (r. 1643–1715), was reiterated.[6] In 1755, Joseph Yorke presented Britain as 'the only power that stands in the breach to defend the Liberties of Europe'.[7] This was very much the view among the 'Old Corps' Whigs, although Frederick II was soon to win a short-term addition to this honour.

Both Britain and France focused their military efforts on Europe during the War of the Austrian Succession up to its end in 1748. Earlier, the British had been made cautious in 1744–6 about trans-oceanic possibilities in North America in part by the Jacobite threat to Britain. This was an issue of strategic prioritisation that did not end with victory at Culloden in 1746 but that continued thereafter. For example, the Jacobite challenge and the danger of a supporting French invasion highlighted the importance of naval and land operations in the European theatre in 1756–9 to the war in North America. Moreover, the failure to defeat the French fleet until two battles were won off Cape Finisterre in 1747 was also significant in British prioritisation and planning.

The return of Louisbourg to France as a consequence of the peace of Aix-la-Chapelle (1748) compounded and focused the frustration and anger in Britain caused by the failure, as a result of these concerns and of military commitments in the Low Countries, to send expeditions against Canada in 1746 and 1747. There was much criticism of this return in the opposition press. As a result, empire as a rallying cry for opposition revived, which helped explain its political positioning at the time of Pitt's rise in importance and then to power in the mid-1750s. In a highly political fashion, trans-oceanic imperial expansion was juxtaposed as the national destiny to an alternative, rival and malign focus on Europe, as the politics of factional interest directed attention to the King's ambitions as Elector of Hanover.[8] This contrast was important not so much as an accurate description

---

[5]   Sandwich to Newcastle, 5 Jan. 1748, BL. Add. 32810 fol. 411.

[6]   John Thomlinson, London merchant and colonial agent for New Hampshire, to Granville, 13 Dec. 1756, S. Pargellis (ed.), *Military Affairs in North America 1748–1765* (New York, 1936), p. 258.

[7]   Joseph to Philip Yorke, 31 Jan. 1755, BL. Add. 35364.

[8]   G.C. Gibbs, 'English Attitudes towards Hanover and the Hanoverian Succession in the First Half of the Eighteenth Century', in A.M. Birke and K. Kluxen (eds), *England und Hannover* (Munich, 1986).

(although a case can be made to that effect[9]), but rather as a strengthening of a political impression of lasting importance. Empire was apparently national, necessary and progressive, and its denial allegedly selfish, foolish and retrograde. This point became part of the currency of public discussion and polemic.

At the same time, there was a strategic dimension to the debate, one conducted both in public and in government circles. Alongside discussion related to goals or policy, there was consideration of implementation or strategy, although the separation between policy and strategy could be tenuous. This consideration focused on prioritisation and on the effectiveness of particular operational choices. Thus, part of the opposition to the commitment of British troops to the Continent rested on arguments of cost,[10] as well as on the greater value and safety of their use elsewhere. This issue indicated the character and role of trade-offs in the consideration and presentation of policy. The nature of trade-offs was a repeated theme of political debate, both ministerial and public, and whether the approach was positive or critical. For example, Pitt pressed Newcastle in a private meeting in 1753 on the need 'To make some savings in the army in Scotland and Gibraltar in order to provide for the expense of this subsidy ... without savings made, the new expense with Russia may be difficult, if not impracticable'.[11] Savings in the army were politically sensitive due to the great interest in the army taken by George and Cumberland and because the costs were debated annually in Parliament. Pitt was seeking to make political capital as well as to argue the need to offset the cost of subsidy treaties. It was no wonder that both George and Cumberland disliked and distrusted Pitt. Such a memorandum of a meeting is very rare indeed, which is a situation that obscures the extent to which trade-offs were an important part of the processes by which politics related to government and by which policy was formulated and implemented. The arguments employed in debating trade-offs are also unclear.

Comparable views and trade-offs were also discussed in France. Again, there were contrasts over goals and implementation. Despite the assumptions of most British commentators, French goals did not always, or, indeed, usually, entail a focus on Britain. In so far as they did, which was certainly the case in 1755, there were major differences over implementation. In particular, the view that France should focus on a maritime war in order to prevent a loss of trade and colonies that enabled Britain to make gains and subsidise allies[12] contrasted with the fear

---

[9]   J. Black, *The Continental Commitment. Britain, Hanover and interventionism, 1714–1793* (Abingdon, 2005).

[10]   Anon., *Reflections upon the Present State of Affairs* (London, 1755), pp. 8–9.

[11]   'Mr Pitt's points', 21 Sept. 1753, BL. Add. 32995 fols 29–30.

[12]   Champeaux to Rouillé, 16 Apr. 1755, AE. CP. Ang. 438, fol. 413.

that Britain would win if a war was confined to the sea[13] and that, if France was thereby beaten, it should attack by land,[14] conquering Hanover and the Low Countries, or fearing defeat at sea, should attack by land at the outset.

The French capacity to choose where to attack posed serious problems for Britain. The latter prospect, that of French attacks in Europe, ensured that thwarting France in Europe might be a necessary counterpart to success in America,[15] not least but not only to prevent a humiliating peace of the type of 1748, that of the necessary return of gains. French policy was also significant for British security. In July 1755, as a crisis of choice came to a head, Sir John Barnard told Newcastle that he:

> agreed to that in a national view it would be melancholy to see the French in possession of Flanders, Holland and all that extended coast which might fall a sacrifice to their conquests; but as to Hanover he seemed to think that we might more easily procure a restitution of it by pushing our conquests at sea and in America than preserve it by endeavouring to support a Continental war,

the cost of which frightened Barnard.[16] As a result of the uncertainties of these wider relationships, Newcastle informed Perrone in 1755 that he was unsure whether to be pleased or angry that France would only go to war with Britain,[17] in other words not attacking the Low Countries and thereby denying Britain both Austrian and Dutch support, and the need, on the part of all three, to help defend the Low Countries. The distinction between doing what was possible, as opposed to desirable, was emphasised by Newcastle.[18] This was a distinction that much of the public debate, and notably arguments critical of government policy, did not capture or even attempt. It was easier to conceive of policies than to work out how to implement them or to achieve a domestic and international context that permitted implementation. Moreover, the same policy might be presented and perceived in very different ways. Protecting Hanover as a means to absorb French attention and also to thwart France, by denying it the chance to make gains there in order to counteract British successes in North America,

---

[13]   Rouillé to Marshal Noailles, 21 July 1755, AE. CP. Ang. 439 fols 264–5.

[14]   Rouillé to Aubeterre, 24 May 1755, AE. CP. Aut., 254 fol. 159; Mitchell to Holdernesse, reporting view of Frederick II, 27 May 1757, NA. SP. 90/65.

[15]   Joseph to Philip Yorke, 12 Aug. 1755, BL. Add. 35364 fol. 52.

[16]   Newcastle to Holdernesse, 11 July 1755, BL. Add. 32857 fols 45–6.

[17]   Perrone to Charles Emmanuel III, 7 Aug. 1755, AST. LM. Ing. 59.

[18]   Newcastle to George Lyttleton, 1 Nov. 1755, Sotheby's catalogue, 12 Dec. 1978, catalogue of the Lyttleton Papers at Hagley Hall.

were themes that predated Pitt's advocacy of it from 1758. However, he proved particularly successful in associating himself with this theme and making it appear national, rather than designed to serve Hanoverian interests, and thus of benefit to him with George II.

Religion

With France, there was not only the case of threatening policies. In addition, differences over policy were expressed in a political, strategic and geopolitical environment that contrasted with that of Britain. The ability of British commentators to appreciate the nuances of these differences and contrasts, and their consequences, varied. The political placing of competing policy options, in Britain, France, and elsewhere, was not new, and can be regarded in part as a matter of political expediency and advantage.[19] However, this placing was given greater energy by the sense of existential threat or national destiny that appeared to be the counterpoints in much of the public discussion over policy. There was a rhetorical dimension to this discussion that was particularly striking; and this dimension provided scant opportunity to consider matters in terms of a more cautious and incremental approach to policy. This dimension was seen among ministers as well as in Parliament and the press.

The British were not alone in this. For example, Rouillé, the French Foreign Minister, who was not given to alarmist or bold remarks, feared the war of religion[20] seen as a prospect by some British commentators. The latter did not regard such a conflict as a feature of a past age, one ended by the Peace of Westphalia (1648) or subsequently. Seeking to lessen concern, Rouillé emphasised that France was not planning to support the Jacobite cause nor to change Britain's government and religion.[21] On the other hand, there was frequent talk of Austria forming a Catholic league.[22]

Aware of sensitivities, the British government was cautious not to give offence to Catholic powers,[23] but was under frequent pressure to act on behalf

---

[19]   R.H. Harding, "'A Golden Adventure': Combined Operations in the Caribbean, 1740–2. A Re-examination of the Walpole Ministry's Response to War with Spain' (PhD, London, 1985), pp. 312–17.

[20]   Rouillé to Bonnac, 10 Sept. 1756, AN. K. 1351 no. 111.

[21]   Rouillé to Bonnac, 17 Mar. 1756, AN. KK. 1402, p. 257.

[22]   Keith to Holdernesse, 5 May 1756, NA. SP. 80/197 fol. 95.

[23]   Bristol to Fox, 26 May 1756, NA. SP. 92/64.

of co-religionists.[24] This pressure, which has been underplayed in much of the literature,[25] was both from foreign Protestants and more significantly from British counterparts. The Church of England was one source of pressure, and was able to influence the most senior politicians. Thus, in December 1749, the Archbishop of Canterbury pressed both the Secretary of State (Bedford) and the envoy in Paris (Albemarle), on behalf of Huguenots (French Protestants) who had been sent to the galleys. There was pressure on behalf of the Waldensians in the kingdom of Sardinia, another longstanding issue;[26] while representation at the *Reichstag* in Regensburg was a key aspect of the defence of Protestant interests in the Empire, a matter of considerable concern to George as Elector of Hanover[27] In turn, foreign envoys made representations on behalf of British Catholics, for example in response to concerns that the Clandestine Marriages Act would invalidate Catholic marriages.[28] At the same time, neither the Austrian nor the Sardinian envoy proved as active as the papal Apostolic Vicar wanted.[29]

There was an awareness that popular views in Britain were in part engaged by religion, principally through the widespread use of church briefs to raise funds for foreign Protestants, which meant that people heard accounts of persecutions in their parish churches. In addition, religion played a role in relations with other Protestant powers. A significant instance was that of the discussion of relations between Britain and Prussia, an instance that came to replace that of Britain and the Dutch republic. Henry Legge, envoy in Berlin as well as an MP, wrote thence in 1748: 'We are both Protestants, and I think it is impossible that sooner or later our political interests should not coincide.'[30] Seeking to persuade Frederick to be favourable, Newcastle wrote in 1756: 'The King of Prussia, a great Protestant power, will be supported and adored here, when he acts for the Protestant cause, the Liberties of Europe, the support of the Statholder in Holland, and the Protestant succession in England.'[31] Thus, Prussia could be grafted onto a system of foreign policy designed to protect

[24]   Perrone to Charles Emmanuel III, 30 Aug., 22, 29 Nov., 6 Dec. 1753, AST. LM. Ing. 57.
[25]   For a conspicuous exception, A. Thompson, *Britain, Hanover and the Protestant Interest, 1688–1756* (Woodbridge, 2006).
[26]   Perrone to Charles Emmanuel III, 2 Aug. 1753, AST. LM. Ing. 57.
[27]   E. Schütz, *Die Gesandtschaft Grossbritanniens am Immerwährenden Reichstag zu Regensburg und am kur (Pfalz-) bayerischen Hof zu München 1683–1806* (Munich, 2007).
[28]   Perrone to Charles Emmanuel III, 25 Oct., 1 Nov. 1753, AST. LM. Ing. 57.
[29]   Perrone to Charles Emmanuel III, 6 Dec. 1753, AST. LM. Ing. 57.
[30]   Legge to Henry Pelham, 30 Apr. 1748, Nottingham, UL, NeC 564.
[31]   Newcastle to Mitchell, 28 May 1756, BL. Add. 6832 fol. 4; M. Schlenke, 'England blickt nach Europa: Das konfessionelle Argument in der englischen Politik um die Mitte des

the Revolution Settlement that followed the Glorious Revolution of 1688–9. As part of a situation of confessional–political rivalry, such an alignment was also open to criticism from within Britain on religious grounds. John Barker, a Presbyterian minister, observed of the Treaty of Aix-la-Chapelle that ended the War of the Austrian Succession in 1748: 'The King of Prussia had, it seems, a great hand in this affair – so that the Jacobites, I fear, will call it a Presbyterian peace.'[32] Pietist Prussia was most readily understood in Britain as Presbyterian. Britain was not alone in the circulation of alarmist material about foreign-backed Catholicism. It was also seen in the United Provinces.[33] At the same time, there was understandable scepticism about the extent to which Frederick was motivated by religious considerations.[34]

System and Balance

An emphasis on challenges and on stark choices can be related to the threatening context of the period, but also reflected a more general sense of uncertainty. The sense of uncertainty, indeed chaos, arising from the unpredictable nature of individual actions on the part of rulers, 'quick shifts in the European chessboard',[35] was bad enough. In addition, both dynastic fortune and war introduced multiple uncertainties, each making the situation appear inherently changeable, as, indeed, it was. This apparent chaos clashed with the preference for an understanding of international developments in terms of a European political system[36] and, more specifically, the idea of each state having a 'natural interest'[37] and a 'natural alliance',[38] and of the related mechanistic notions of the balance of power.

System was part of the vocabulary of international relations, not simply a European political system, but also a system of state policy in the sense of consistency and of meaningful purpose, as opposed to individual wilfulness.

---

18. Jahrhunderts', in P. Kluke and P. Alter (eds), *Aspekte der deutsch-britischen Beziehungen im Laufe der Jahrhunderte* (Stuttgart, 1978), pp. 24–45.

[32]   Barker to Philip Doddridge, 5 May (os) 1748, G.F. Nuttall (ed.)¸ *Calendar of the Correspondence of Philip Doddridge* (London, 1979), p. 274.

[33]   Bonnac to Saint-Contest, 3 Jan. 1754, AN. KK. 1400 pp. 2–3.

[34]   *Citizen*, 16 June 1757.

[35]   S. Horowitz, 'Franco-Russian Relations, 1740–1746' (PhD., New York, 1951), p. vi.

[36]   Rouillé to Bonnac, 1 Mar. 1756, AN. KK. 1402, p. 228; Holdernesse to Keith, 23 Mar. 1756, NA. SP. 80/197 fol. 47.

[37]   Holdernesse to Mitchell, 28 May 1756, NA. SP. 90/65.

[38]   Mitchell to Hanbury Williams, 3 June 1756, BL. Add. 6804 fol. 24.

This concept was linked with that of natural interest. In 1748, Sandwich wrote to Robert Keith, a fellow envoy, also accredited to an ally: 'in the sort of scene that you and I are engaged in, fluctuations will frequently happen, but where people mean the same thing at the bottom, and pursue a system, matters generally subside in the end'.[39]

Balance was a key element in the vocabulary, one that continued the previous usage. However, as before, it was unclear how regional balances of power, for example of the 'North' or the Empire (i.e. Germany),[40] were related to that of Europe, while the regions themselves could be variously defined. These relationships, between regional balances of power and the Continental balance, were held to be significant both in wartime and in peace. Thus, in 1745, Britain was pressed by the envoys of Austria and Saxony to devote more attention to Germany than to Italy, on the ground that the former was more important to the European balance of power.[41] As another instance of the same issue, while acknowledging the need for a balance of power in Europe, Frederick II was concerned in 1746 about 'the great weight of Austria', and did not regard French advances in the Low Countries as threatening the balance.[42] This was an assessment that was very much different from that of Britain: British commentators saw France as the threat to Britain, Europe and the general balance of power, and a strong Austria as a key defence against this threat. Whatever the perspective, individual states, and thus their internal political development, could be presented as of significance depending on whether they could contribute to the balance.[43]

A religious dimension could be added to the balance with the reflection that the conversion of a ruler to Catholicism would hit 'the Protestant Interest, and ... the Balance of Power in the Empire'.[44] The more general consequence of such a conversion was less clear and, at least in part, apparently depended on the views taken by and about the key German powers, namely Austria and Prussia. Thus, while also independent, the religious issue was heavily dependent on international alignments.

---

[39]   Sandwich to Keith, 26 Sept. 1748, BL. Add. 35464; H. Kleinschmidt, 'Systeme und Ordnungen in der Geschicht der internationalen Beziehungen', *Archiv für kulturgeschichte*, 82 (2000), pp. 433–54.

[40]   Robinson to Titley, 3 Oct. 1744, Hanbury Williams to Chesterfield, 28 Oct. 1747, Chesterfield to Burrish, 10 Nov. (os) 1747, NA. SP. 80/165, 88/69, 81/96.

[41]   Ossorio to Charles Emmanuel III, 29 Oct. 1745, AST. LM. Ing.

[42]   Villiers to Harrington, 22 Feb., 21 June 1746, NA. SP. 80/68.

[43]   Frederick II to D'Ammon, Prussian envoy in The Hague, 26 Aug. 1749, *Polit. Corr.*, VII, 70; Joseph Yorke to Hardwicke, 6 May 1750, BL. Add. 35355 fol. 239.

[44]   Keith to Holdernesse, 11 Dec. 1754, NA. SP. 80/194.

Whether or not linked to the assessment of the balance, the provision of information about the outer world was an aspect of a concern with the need for self-consciously instructed decision-making. This need was related to the drive for 'political arithmetic' in the shape of scientific processes or, at least, images. The central manifestation in the field of international relations was the 'mathematisation' of power, which proved an aspect, sometimes an integral aspect, of balance-of-power thought and was captured in the idea of an international system. The apparent precision brought by the balance was associated with concepts of perfectibility that drew on neoplatonic ideas of essential character related to the apparent precision of the laws of the natural world. The use of this language, however, could not hide the very different ideas held over what was the national interest of the states that, together, constituted the balance. While employing deductive theoretical language to justify views, commentators in practice used intuitive assumptions to define and advance interests. Intuitive suspicion of France played a significant role in Britain. In all respects, there was also the question, for contemporaries, of whether the balance naturally pertained, requiring therefore modest effort to sustain it; or whether it had to be created, and thus entailed greater effort. For modern commentators, the emphasis can be placed on the balance as a means to encourage restraint or as an aspect of a ruthless pursuit of self-aggrandisement involving often short-term shifts in alliance partner.[45]

Matching its use in domestic politics,[46] the balance of power operated for contemporaries along a continuum from analysis to rhetoric, although, in practice, the two were not invariably separate or seen as such. Rhetoric played a particularly prominent role in the public sphere, but it would be misleading to suggest that it was restricted to that. Britain's opposition to France in terms of Europe was routinely explained, or at least discussed, by ministers, other politicians, and commentators, in terms of the balance, which could serve as a catch-all.[47] What that should mean in practice was often unclear, but there was repeated reference to the balance. However, as Orator Henley, a populist public speaker in London, caustically noted in 1744: 'What this Balance of Power is no Parliament ever yet has explained nor one member ever yet once mentioned it in the House of Commons, although it has cost the nation above 300 millions.'[48] It

---

[45]   J.A. Lynn, 'International Rivalry and Warfare', in T.C.W. Blanning (ed.), *The Eighteenth Century. Europe 1688–1815* (Oxford, 2000), pp. 185, 200.

[46]   *Monitor*, 9 Aug. 1755.

[47]   Carteret to Robinson, 11 Sept. 1744, NA. SP. 80/164.

[48]   Henley's Oratory, 15 Apr. (os) 1744, BL. Add. 33052 fol. 262. How the balance of power is defined today is also a matter of contention.

is significant that Henley covered foreign policy in his soapbox style harangues.[49] Given such views, it is not surprising that the *True Patriot* of 27 May (os) 1746 could recount how a companion on a coach journey said 'that the Balance of Power in Europe was a mere jest'. The circulation of such views is unclear, but the evidence is suggestive. The *Remembrancer*, an opposition newspaper, in its issue of 22 October (os) 1748, used the problem of defining the balance in order to question the recent peace and, thereby, the ministry's claims to success: 'though the latter war was undertaken to preserve the Austrian inheritance entire for preserving the Balance of Power, and preserving the Liberty of Europe; yet Spain is now gratified at the expense of the House of Austria which we undertook to preserve', a reference to the situation in Italy. Other opposition papers claimed that the balance had been lost.[50]

Separate to this, but part of the general theme of criticism of government policy, was the argument that the balance of power indeed existed, but had been misunderstood and misplayed; indeed, that Britain had intervened excessively, and inconsistently, in order to counteract what appeared to be an unwanted preponderance on the part of other states.[51] This was a critique that had been made frequently from the early 1710s, one directed in particular against what was held to be a Whig tendency to intervene and seek to direct European politics.[52] Private correspondence echoed these themes. John, Viscount Tyrconnel, an opposition Whig, wrote:

> if a Nation can ever learn wisdom by past sufferings, we shall never more enter into a consuming land war, we shall leave the balance of power upon the Continent, and the Liberties of Europe, a couple of cant words.[53]

James, 5th Earl of Balcarres, thought the balance 'chimerical'.[54] No alternative European policy, however, indeed no real substitute for British policy in Europe, was offered by these and other critics. Instead, on the part of some of these critics, there was a focus on the maritime and trans-oceanic sphere. This dimension

---

[49] For Henley's blunt critique of interventionism, 19 Feb. (os) 1744, BL. Add. 33052 fol. 266.

[50] *Old England*, 17 Dec. (os) 1748; *Remembrancer*, 15 Oct. (os) 1748.

[51] *Old England*, 28 June (os) 1750; cf. 1 Aug. (os) 1752.

[52] J.A. Downie, 'The Conduct of the Allies: The Question of Influence', in C.T. Probyn (ed.), *The Art of Jonathan Swift* (London, 1978), pp. 108–28.

[53] Tyrconnel to Sir John Cust, 30 Apr. (os) 1748, L. Cust (ed.), *Records of the Cust Family*, series III (London, 1927), p. 129.

[54] Keith to Balcarres, 2 Dec. 1753, G. Smyth (ed.), *Correspondence of Sir Robert Murray Keith* (2 vols, London, 1849), I, 26.

to policy did not appear to suffer ambiguities and qualifications similar to that of Continental interventionism and also offered greater popularity and a clearer image.

Criticism of the balance of power was countered by frequent arguments about its value. The balance was presented as an operative principle, not only in foreign affairs, but also in domestic. In 1748, the oleaginous Samuel Squire became Newcastle's chaplain and published *An Historical Essay upon the Balance of Civil Power in England*. More significantly, in his *The Present State of Europe* (1750), a lengthy, well-considered assessment that offered much to readers, John Campbell saw the balance not simply as a device for political order, but also as an aspect of the commercial system that was particularly necessary for trading powers such as Britain. This was an argument that was to be frequently made in the nineteenth century. Campbell wrote:

> The reciprocal connections resulting from trade, have quite altered the state of things, and produced within these two, or most these three centuries past, a kind of system in Europe, or in the Christian parts of Europe at least, by which every state is led to have a much greater concern than formerly for what may happen to another ... We may therefore safely say that the balance of power ... was created by trade, and must continue to be the object more especially of trading countries, so long as they preserve their commerce and their freedom.[55]

As an historical account of the balance of power, this did not match that which was to be adopted by William Robertson when, in his biography of Charles V, he dated the onset of the modern European system to the outbreak of the Italian Wars in 1494. Nevertheless, the emphasis on trade more readily linked developments in Europe to the wider global situation, and notably its maritime dimension. This emphasis made sense of the role of the Atlantic powers, notably Britain. Campbell's approach, however, left very unclear how the balance could best be preserved, and how far it was necessary to act to do so. As before, the answers offered were refracted through the exigencies of politics, as well as through the pressures of personality. The latter was most obviously the case with Newcastle's concerns.[56] By 1752, the ministry was strongly committed to the view not only that its foreign policy was based on Britain preserving the balance of power, but also that this goal required action, however expensive. Such an approach could be employed to justify the problematic policy of subsidy treaties.

---

[55]   J. Campbell, *The Present State of Europe* (London, 1750), p. 24.
[56]   Perrone to Charles Emmanuel III, 22 Apr. 1751, AST. LM. Ing. 56.

Defending the subsidy to Augustus III of Saxony-Poland, William Murray, the Solicitor General, the ministry's most fluent speaker in the Commons, told the House that:

> the principles upon which this treaty is founded ... evidently appears to be the preservation of peace and a balance of power in Europe ... the peace, as well as the balance of power, depends upon preventing a vacancy in the Imperial throne.[57]

To employ the ministerial language of the period, this approach implied that Britain should hold the balance.[58] At the same time, other powers could be seen as, in combination, separately, or, instead, playing the key role hitherto held by Britain and the Dutch, the most notable of these being Prussia.[59] The theme of the balance was advanced anew during the Seven Years' War, with the *Test*, on 18 June 1757, rejecting the idea it was a 'mere empty unideal sound, for it is in reality a very momentous concern of which it is incumbent on us to be mindful'.

With the British, Frederick II used the language of the balance.[60] In 1757, he emphasised the danger of the French gaining 'the arbitrage of the affairs of Europe ... becoming the arbiters of Europe'.[61] Frederick could also draw attention to the damaging implications for Prussia of organising international relations around opposition to France, implications that British ministers were reluctant to accept and to consider the consequences of: 'acknowledged that a Balance of Power should be maintained in Europe, but is jealous of, and dreads, the great weight of Austria'.[62] Frederick was more perceptive about the difficult consequences of the thesis than British ministers who tended to assume that the model should determine developments. At the same time, politicians understood that self-interest as a motivating force was in large part activated by assumptions and attitudes. Henry Fox, a newly minted Secretary of State and leader of the House, told the Commons on 2 December 1755, in a debate for speedily manning the navy:

> the judgment of nations as well as of private men is pretty much governed by what they take to be their interest; but whilst France takes care to prevent her neighbours conceiving a jealousy of a too great increase of her power, I am afraid

---

[57] 22 Jan. (os) 1752, Cobbett, *Parliamentary History*, XIV, 1151.
[58] Newcastle to Hardwicke, 21 Sept. 1753, BL. Add. 32732 fol. 699.
[59] *Gentleman's Magazine* (London, 1752), p. 142.
[60] Frederick II to Mitchell, 21 Sept. 1756, BL. Add. 6843 fol. 23.
[61] Mitchell to Holdernesse, 9 July 1757, NA. SP. 90/67.
[62] Villiers to Harrington, 22 Feb. 1746, NA. SP. 88/68.

that, in a war between France and us, several of the nations in Europe would think it their interest to join with France, notwithstanding the greatest preparations we could make, because in the chances of war they would look upon the odds to be on the side of France; and therefore in all our disputes with that nation, it is prudential in us, to conduct so as to convince every nation in Europe that, if a war should ensue, it is not owing to injustice on our side, but to ambition on the side of France ... [that] would stir up the jealousy of the other powers of Europe.[63]

The British insistence that their policy amounted to a support for a collective security that would maintain the peace, and in a benign fashion, was matched by France, which, unsurprisingly, claimed a similar commitment.[64] This argument led Puysieulx, the thoughtful French Foreign Minister, to propose in 1749 that Britain and France consult on contested European issues[65] and 'tell the rest of Europe that they would unite their force against whoever should attempt to disturb the peace'.[66] Such views echoed the British position during the alliance with France in 1716–31, notably in response then to the rise of Russia, to Spanish expansionism, and to concerns about Austrian policy within the Empire. However, after the suspicions of France in the 1730s and the conflict of the 1740s, as well as better relations with Russia, Spain and Austria, such views now ran strongly athwart the direction of British policy, the strategic culture of its political establishment, and the contents of public debate.

The Puysieulx approach can be seen as a lost opportunity for Britain and France, prefiguring other such British responses to French approaches in 1772 and 1786. These approaches fell victim of international crises, notably over Sweden in 1772 and the Dutch in 1787, but also lacked traction in British politics. This was also the case in 1749–50. In particular, the specifics of a Baltic crisis, in which Britain and France were linked to opposing powers, Russia and Austria and Sweden and Prussia respectively, were set against the background of suspicion. In June 1756, Holdernesse referred to France as 'the natural enemy of England',[67] a view voiced throughout the period of this book. This view conditioned British attitudes. The same month, Newcastle told Viry that Austrian support for better relations between France and Russia surprised him as that would destroy the balance of power in Europe, and that Austria would be the

---

[63]   Fox, 2 Dec. 1755, Cobbett, XV, col. 594.

[64]   Argenson to Valory, 3 Mar. 1746, NA. SP. 78/331 fol. 439; Puysieulx to Hautefort, 8 Nov. 1750, AE. CP. Aut. 248 fol. 26.

[65]   Puysieulx to Durand, 14 Mar. 1749, AE. CP. Ang. 425 fol. 406.

[66]   Yorke to Hardwicke, 5 Apr. 1749, BL. Add. 35355 fol. 34.

[67]   Holdernesse to Keith, 21 June 1756, NA. SP. 80/197 fol. 175.

first sacrifice.[68] This observation captured Newcastle's assumption that Britain's conception of the balance benefited Austria. This assumption was closely linked to the Duke's difficulty in responding to the change in Austrian policy, which he hoped could be reversed by the overthrow of Count Kaunitz, the Austrian Chancellor,[69] the minister to whom the French alliance was attributed.[70]

Newcastle's observation reflected an inherent hostility to the idea of a lack of a balance of power on the Continent, and, related to this, concerns about what such a lack might lead to. Partly as a result, Newcastle was not alone in finding the change in the international system in 1756 difficult to accept. Aside from the threat to British interests and views, there was the belief that any lack of a balance challenged the order necessary to the international system and the system crucial to this order, the two regarded as linked. There was also a general conviction that, aside from its malign character and consequences, the alliance between Austria and France could not be a strong and lasting basis for a new international system.[71] Instead, this alliance was held to be inherently based on weak foundations, to be threatened by the mutual distrust and clashing interests of Austria and France, and to be threatening to other powers. British commentators put Britain to the fore here, but also saw themselves in this as linked to others.

Separate to that threat, but related to it, there was the challenge (from international developments) to the established view, both of the Atlantic international system and of the balance of power, that was expressed by British commentators in terms of British rivalry with France or Spain. Rivalry with France had been the dominant theme from the origins and presentation of a national foreign policy in the Middle Ages. Parliament had developed and become more significant in England both in opposition to royal power and in order to support conflict with France. This point was as valid for the period from the 1690s as it had been in the thirteenth and fourteenth centuries. However, a new challenge to the international situation, and to the British understanding of it, was posed by the transformative rise in the relative importance within European international relations of Austria, Russia and Prussia. The first had become more significant from the defeat of the Turks outside Vienna in 1683, that of Russia from Peter the Great's defeat of Charles XII of Sweden in Poltava in 1709, and that of Prussia from Frederick II's (the Great) successful invasion

---

68   Viry to Charles Emmanuel III, 4 June 1756, AST. LM. Ing. 60.

69   Newcastle to Mitchell, 28 May 1756, BL. Add. 6832 fol. 2.

70   Keith to Holdernesse, 20 Sept. 1756, NA. SP. 80/198.

71   Haslang to Preysing, 18 June 1756, Munich, Bayr. Ges., London 231; Fox to Bristol, 22 June 1756, NA. SP. 92/64; Mitchell to Holdernesse, 24 June 1756, NA. SP. 90/65.

of Silesia in 1740–1. The attempt to incorporate these powers into a system of rivalry between Britain and France broke down, both because it was difficult to align them with trans-oceanic conflict and because these powers, understandably, followed their own agenda. This was demonstrated in 1745 when Frederick II attacked Austria and Saxony, despite having settled his differences with them in 1742 under the aegis of Britain. In 1756, neither Austria, nor Prussia, nor Russia, behaved as the British ministry thought necessary for their interests, nor that of Britain or the European system.

The Problem of Allies

Britain's relations with Austria, Russia and Prussia, moreover, played a major role in the creation of a new history of international relations that, in turn, became at once a currency of international and domestic political debate. Indeed, this history was an important aspect of the definition and re-definition of national interests, a process crucial to the debate over policy. In an audience with Maria Theresa in May 1756, in which Robert Keith sought to preserve good relations between Britain and Austria, she and he made contradictory reference to the 1748 Peace of Aix-la-Chapelle. Keith echoed British domestic debate by arguing that Britain had 'purchased that peace': helping secure it by returning the British gain of Cape Breton to France, a step necessary in order to persuade France to evacuate the Austrian Netherlands. This, however, was not the Austrian view. The two also differed as they considered British policy in the initial stages of the War of the Austrian Succession, before, in the audience, Maria Theresa put competitive gratitude and ingratitude aside, by arguing that her principal object was the defence of the Habsburg hereditary lands, and, therefore, relations with Russia and Turkey. In contrast, 'remote parts of her dominions', namely the Austrian Netherlands, were presented as of little consequence to her, a view frequently expressed by Austrian ministers. However, it was this region that came foremost in British calculations as far as Austria was concerned. In his report, Keith argued that Austria had left its 'natural channel' due to the malign influence of Kaunitz.[72] Referring to a river, the phrase 'natural channel' captured the extent to which terms readily understood by landowners were used. Moreover, such phrases scarcely invited debate about their definition.

In June 1756, Joseph Yorke remarked that Austria had 'determined to abandon us unless we fought for Silesia, when we should be fighting for

---

[72]   Keith to Holdernesse, NA. SP. 80/197 fols 104–24.

America'.[73] Looked at differently, the re-assessment of Austrian interests in light of the changes in the European system, including, but not only the rise of Prussia, proved a dynamic element in international relations. This was an element to which the British government failed to respond adequately. Furthermore, this was a dynamic factor from the mid-1710s. This issue raises the question of what it was reasonable to anticipate, both on the part of contemporaries and of scholars. Expectations in terms of needs, rather than perceptions, are an aspect of this question. For example, for an alliance, is the issue one of stability in relations between the powers, or of closeness and future development,[74] and, if so, how are the latter to be assessed? Was an alliance to be kept alive by making allies doubt each other's commitment, in order, in turn, to confirm the alliance through fear or need?[75] Moreover, there was the question of whether it was more glorious and certain to settle issues without turning to allies;[76]; or, if the latter, how best to assure or define reciprocity within an alliance.[77] The latter was a constant issue for Britain and for other powers, and an issue that repeatedly joined international and domestic politics, not least for Britain with the continual need for ministers to be mindful of its public politics.

The difficulties of managing the relations with Austria, Prussia and Russia were a major theme in British foreign policy, and also affected the public discussion about Continental power politics which tended to focus on France. Indeed, alongside the Oceanic 'pull', there was the Continental 'push'. This 'push' away from the Continental commitments arose in part from the problems of defining a plausible and acceptable British commitment to Continental power politics. Plausibility and acceptability were at issue both in domestic and in international terms, with the latter in part discussed, if not defined, with regard to the former; a process that did not occur the other way round. These problems helped lead, on the part of some commentators, to mounting opposition not only to existing alliances, but even to any alliances. The latter was a theme seen in public debate from the Tory critique of the latter stages of the War of the Spanish Succession. The theme was particularly associated with the Tories,[78] who, in opposition from

---

[73]   Yorke to Newcastle, 18 June 1756, BL. Add. 32865 fol. 340.

[74]   R.N. Middleton, 'French Policy and Prussia after the Peace of Aix-la-Chapelle' (PhD., Columbia, 1968), p. 310.

[75]   Perrone to Charles Emmanuel III, 7 Mar. 1754, AST. LM. Ing. 58.

[76]   Champeaux to Rouillé, 16 Apr. 1755, AE. CP. Ang. 438 fol. 414.

[77]   Holdernesse to Keith, 31 May 1755, Holdernesse to Mitchell, 9 July 1756, NA. SP. 80/196 fol. 37, 90/65; [S. Martyn], *Deliberate Thoughts on the System of our Late Treaties* (London, 1756), p. 49; *A Sixth Letter to the People of England* (London, 1757), p. 4.

[78]   J. Black, 'Foreign Policy and the Tory World in the Eighteenth Century', *Journal for Eighteenth-Century Studies*, 37 (2014), pp. 285–97.

1714, did not face the exigencies of office; but was also increasingly the case with opposition Whigs from the 1740s.

A commitment to Continental power politics, and its heavy costs, nevertheless appeared viable, indeed necessary, in 1745–8 when this commitment could be presented in terms of defending the Low Countries against French invasion. This defence, both military and diplomatic, attracted former critics of Continental interventionism. Both Pitt and Pelham were able to speak in favour of this policy in the Commons. The sense of a shared challenge from France was increased by French support for the Jacobites, notably in 1744–6. The ability to deploy Hesse-Cassel forces against the Jacobites contributed to the political debate within Britain, and gave concrete form to the benefit to Britain of Continental power politics.

However, the situation changed in the latter stages of the War of the Austrian Succession. Co-operation then with the Austrians and Dutch did not deliver shared victories, as, in contrast, had been the case for much of the War of the Spanish Succession. As a reminder of the range of counterfactuals, it is instructive to consider what might have been the case had Cumberland enjoyed a string of victories in 1745–8, as John Churchill, 1st Duke of Marlborough had done in 1704–9, from Blenheim to Malplaquet. Aside from the specific military consequences, there would have been major results in foreign policy and public debate. The alliance with Austria and the Dutch would probably have been strengthened at the governmental level, while the domestic commitment to such an alignment would have been enhanced. Such a counterfactual is instructive because it throws light on the contemporary debate over policy and on the course that was followed.

Despite considerable anger toward both the Dutch and Austria, the government, after peace was negotiated in 1748, remained committed to the alignment and, indeed, sought to strengthen it. However, the political underpinning for this strengthening amongst the political nation, those interested in politics, was weaker than when British troops had been sent to the Continent in 1742. Fielding noted in the *Jacobite's Journal* on 6 February (os) 1748 that the 'New Whigs', who had come into office in 1744, had found during the war: 'that of our allies, all of whom were weak, some of them indifferent, and those who were most in earnest were pursuing interests separate from that of the common cause'.

The British focus on the war with France ensured disappointment at the hands of allies who had other interests to pursue, as well as limits to their resources. Nathaniel Cole observed of the Dutch and Austrian failure to act decisively in the Low Countries: 'I join in the common opinion that it is impossible in our exhausted state and with allies who do nothing for themselves but receive our money to continue the war any longer.'[79]

The serious decline in political and public support for, or at least confidence in, Britain's alliances was significant for the relationship between politics and foreign policy, and requires consideration in the chapters dealing with the postwar period. In 1756, traditional themes about a French threat to the European system were brought to the fore anew. Holdernesse 'hoped that the cause of Religion, and Liberty' would induce the Dutch 'to oppose the invaders of both'.[80] However, the Dutch did not do so.[81] This failure compounded that of Austria. Moreover, in the case of the Dutch, it was not a failure that could be explained in terms of a problematic individual, as with Kaunitz for Austria. Similarly, with Russia, when it rejected the British link in 1757, there was an attribution of blame to particular individuals in the leadership, and a tendency to underplay the geopolitical dynamic of the determination to reduce Prussian power.

The variable, but persistent, disjuncture between British government policy and public debate, notably over allies, related in part to the implementation of goals. In the public debate, allies appeared unsatisfactory in their response to the need to implement policies. In that, the disjuncture between government and public drew on a longstanding tension focused on the means of interventionism. At the same time, this disjuncture related to the very goals of the policy, and notably to the need for interventionism. To add a further dimension, both the discussion about means and, more consistently, that about ends, were greatly affected by a growing alternative, the rising agenda of interest in the transoceanic world, with the accompanying public and ministerial calls for policy engagement and military commitment accordingly.

This agenda, and the problems of defining acceptable relations with Continental states, interacted with the more general understanding, both in Britain and abroad, of international relations in terms of the inherent pursuit of self-interest and, therefore, a related uncertainty. Thus, the *Herald* argued in 1757 that the Prussian alliance would only last until Frederick II had achieved his goals.[82] This was a reasonable assessment, although, ironically, the alliance was in fact to fail after a new monarch came to the throne in Britain. The stress in Britain was very much on what would subsequently be termed a 'realist' interpretation. Alongside an emphasis on an harmonious and clear international system, there was a stress on national self-sufficiency. Both were discussed in

---

[79] Cole to James Brockman, 9 Apr. (os) 1748, BL. Add. 42591 fol. 56.
[80] Holdernesse to Mitchell, 13 July 1756, NA. SP. 90/65.
[81] A. Carter, *The Dutch Republic in Europe in the Seven Years' War* (London, 1971).
[82] *Herald*, 22 Dec. 1757.

terms of self-interest, but there were differences in content and tone. The linked calculation of the European system, on behalf of Britain and other states, in national terms alone, was stronger by 1757 in the case of British commentators than at any stage since the Glorious Revolution. This was a key element in Britain's 'Diplomatic Revolution'. It was not only a case that the alignment with Austria and the Dutch had gone, but also, to a degree, the commitment to Continental interventionism. This diplomatic revolution lasted until Britain entered the French Revolutionary War in 1793.

The Flow of Information

This range of discussion was set against a background of very varied flows of views and information.[83] This background has received insufficient attention, but it was significant not least because public debate, like government policy, was in large part reactive to developments. The flows of news and opinion, in turn, were received by a political world that was frequently short of reliable information. There were particular problems with reliability in the winter, when the weather was worst, the roads most disrupted, the rivers in spate, and the nights longer, which affected the parameters within which messages were sent. In January 1755, Benjamin Keene, envoy in Spain, gave a messenger permission to wait until daybreak: 'As it is a terrible night, and it will be very difficult for Maddock to pass the mountains near Madrid in the dark.'[84]

At the same time, there could be problems in sending messages rapidly at every season, and in all circumstances. These problems were felt most strongly when ministries and alliances were, or seemed, unsettled. The issue was particularly acute in late 1756, when ministerial instability in Britain harmed its alliance with Prussia. Mitchell wrote on 11 December from Dresden, whither he had accompanied Frederick on campaign: 'I have no letters from England since the 2nd November, except a very short note of the 16th November. Judge then of my present situation.'[85] Reliable news was particularly short in wartime when routes were disrupted by the severance of relations and by conflict. Austria stopped the packet boat link between Ostend and Dover in 1757.[86] Moreover, the need for

---

[83]   J. Black, *British Diplomats and Diplomacy, 1688–1800* (Exeter, 2001), pp. 118–45.

[84]   Keene to Robinson, 12 Jan. 1755, Leeds Archive Office, Vyner papers, no. 11864.

[85]   Mitchell to Hanbury Williams, 11 Dec. 1756, HW.

[86]   Irvine, Vice-Consul in Ostend, to James Wallace, Under Secretary, 17 July 1757, NA. SP. 110/6.

news was more urgent in wartime. Clashing reports about the results of battles were produced by competing governments and diplomats.[87]

Linked to this, rumour was a tool of policy, frequently a significant tool, but also a key element in the general background, both of international relations and of domestic politics. Contrary reports circulated all the time, and the manufacture of news by inserting false reports abroad was referred to frequently. On 30 September 1752, *Old England* directed its caustic eye on Anglo-Spanish relations asking:

> Whether this new Convention is one of those mi-puffs we so frequently see among the foreign news in the common papers.... Who knows but some ignorant understrapper, to curry favour and get a place, has at his own expense and of his own motion, inserted the tale of a NEW CONVENTION in the foreign news papers to amuse the people when translated into our own?.

The *London Evening Post* on 31 March 1757 noted:

> It is some weeks or months since a certain set of people industriously propagated a report that the late Marquis de la Galissonniere [French victor over Byng] did not die of the dropsy, but was secretly poisoned by order of his court, and that four captains of his squadron were shot for cowardice or negligence on the ever-memorable 20th of May; which report some, to this day, believe to be true: But as we have not yet seen the least hint of this in the foreign gazettes, and as we suspect such a report to have been spread with a view to enhance the guilt of the late Admiral Byng, we would humbly advise the authors of it to remit a few pieces to Holland, in order to get the story inserted in the gazettes there, *if they can*, that we may, on the return of the post, have the pleasure of translating it.

The insertion of false news could be directly encouraged by diplomats. In 1757, Mitchell reported that Frederick, being informed that the French were planning to attack Emden, the Prussian North Sea port in East Friesland, had:

> spread a report that English troops are to be sent to defend it. This he knows cannot happen, but he desires that it may be inserted in our newspapers, and that mention may be made of the particular regiments destined for this service, and of the transports, convoys, etc that are to carry them. A puff of this kind properly

---

[87]   Viry to Charles Emmanuel III, 12, 19 Oct. 1756, AST. LM. Ing. 60; *London Chronicle*, 16 June 1757.

inserted, and repeated in our newspapers, he thinks, will make the French cautious of attempting the siege of Emden and may at least serve to gain a little time ... I took the liberty to assure His Prussian Majesty that this should certainly be done, as [one] more lie more or less could not essentially hurt the credit of the English news-writers whose veracity, however, I feared was often suspected by the French.[88]

There was also the more general issue of credibility, a persistent problem. For example, Richard Rigby reported to Bedford in June 1758 that the Prussian siege of the fortress of Olmütz had been raised by the Austrians. He had received the news, while dining at Holland House, from John Calcraft, a key regimental agent as well as a War Office official, and a protégé of Henry Fox. Rigby then went on to Arthur's 'where this news has been heard, but I find is not believed'.[89] Calcraft was to go on to seek a direct news source from The Hague in order to help his stock market speculations and these were held responsible for the publication of inaccurate news.[90] The financial centre, notably 'Change', was a major source of reports.[91]

There was often a lack of a necessary grounding in an understanding of the world. This problem was accentuated by an expansion of Britain's concerns as trans-oceanic interests and speculations became more prominent. Referring to the mid-1750s, a caustic Tobias Smollett had one of the characters in his successful novel *Humphry Clinker* (1771) describe Newcastle, a figure of fun, as follows:

> the best thing he can do, is to sleep on till Christmas; for, when he gets up, he does nothing but expose his own folly.... In the beginning of the war [Seven Years' War], this poor half-witted creature told me, in a great fright, that thirty thousand French had marched from Acadie [Nova Scotia] to Cape Breton – "Where did they find transports?" (said I). "Transports! (cried he) I tell you they marched by land" – "is Cape Breton an island?". "Certainly." "Ha! Are you sure of that?" When I pointed it out in the map, he examined it earnestly with his spectacles; then, taking me in his arms, "My dear C-! (cried he) you always bring us good news – Egad! I'll go directly, and tell the king that Cape Breton is an island."[92]

88   Mitchell to Holdernesse, 12 June 1757, NA. SP. 90/69.
89   Rigby to Bedford, 20 June 1758, Russell (ed.), *Bedford*, II, 339.
90   Anon., *An Inquiry into the Origin and Consequences of the Public Debt* (London, 1754), pp. 21–2.
91   Edward Owen to Edward Weston, 3 May 1757, Weston-Underwood.
92   Smollett, *Humphry Clinker* (London, 1771, London, 1967 edn), p. 143.

The mid-century expansion of Britain's trans-oceanic interests created major issues for the provision of accurate information, and both for government and for the public. The formal process of news acquisition and analysis for these interests was very different to that entailed in Britain's Continental policy. In the latter, diplomats played the key role, although there was an issue as to how far the preference in news was given by British ministers to British diplomats, and how far to their foreign counterparts who could offer more insight on the views of foreign powers. These latter diplomats were present in London, which increased their significance. Moreover, there was the relationship between news from diplomats and that, first, from other official or semi-official sources, and, second, from those not linked to the government.

In contrast, diplomats were able to provide little news about the trans-oceanic world, and that news only indirectly. British envoys in the courts of other oceanic powers provided valuable guidance on the relevant policies of their governments, but they only offered indirect news about developments across the oceans, news, moreover, that was frequently late and uncertain. Instead, the prime source of governmental news was from the relevant officials in British colonies: governors, lieutenant-governors, and army or naval officers. In so far as these officials, like diplomats, went native, they did so in terms of their conception of colonial interests, rather than in fostering bilateral diplomatic links with other powers. Across the oceans, Britain generally had less close links with foreign powers than was the case in Europe.

Moreover, this conception had distinctive characteristics. The officials tended to think in imperial terms, and not with reference just to one colony. Indeed, there was often, on the part of officials, a critical view of the local political interests within individual colonies. Part of the official mind of empire was set by this group of agents on the periphery. They were the protectors and projectors of empire on the ground, those who were more able to initiate, adopt, adapt, and implement action than their counterparts in London, significant as the latter were. This was an aspect of the role of military interests in imperial expansion that has been highlighted by Geoffrey Plank in his important discussion of Cumberland's military clientage and its policy implications.[93] Plank makes the valuable point that these men sought to apply in the colonies the precepts and processes of government-driven development already pursued in Scotland from the suppression of the Jacobite rising in 1746. His work can be supplemented by

---

[93]   G. Plank, *Rebellion and Savagery: The Jacobite Rising of 1745 and the British Empire* (Philadelphia, Pennsylvania, 2006).

looking at other groups of officials, notably naval commanders and also senior figures in some of the North American colonies.

The net effect was that, while suffering from a lack of information,[94] government received reports that ensured, or helped ensure (a significant difference), a theme of imperial expansion. The information was inherently competitive and explicitly confrontational as far as other empires were concerned. Indeed, in the case of trans-oceanic news, there was little of the interwar about the period between the end of the War of the Austrian Succession and the outbreak of the Seven Years' War. Official reports from the colonies tended to lack the equivocation and caution shown in those from Continental Europe, and this characteristic was matched in the press. Providing an apt summary of the standard European view, Yorke observed:

> I am convinced there is no real design to play us foul play, and yet the conduct of governors gives just cause to suspect double dealing; that continent of North America will be an inexhaustible source of quarrels for us with this country [France], every one would be the most powerful, wrongheaded men make inflammatory complaints, as wrongheaded ones make use of inflammatory actions, the respective courts are unwilling to disavow and give up the men they employ, so that insensibly both parties grow warmer.[95]

Indeed, it was not only that a new conflict increasingly appeared imminent, as a result of differences in North America, but also that there was need, in assessing this prospect, to consider the implications for Britain of its existing alliance politics and of the commitment to Hanover. Despite attempts to present benign links, such a consideration helped make the Continental prospectus of policies unpopular politically in Britain. It did so notably by highlighting the cost and difficulty of the implementation of this prospectus. The latter also appeared irrelevant as far as securing Britain's interests were concerned.

Although it provided abundant and generally accurate information,[96] the press faced significant and readily apparent challenges in reporting and commenting on trans-oceanic news.[97] Moreover, colonial officials tended to be less reliable for news about the hinterland, notably trans-Appalachia. These

---

[94]   G.S. Graham, *Empire of the North Atlantic. The Maritime Struggle* (Toronto, 1950), p. 389.

[95]   Joseph to Philip Yorke, 25 July 1760, BL. Add. 35363 fol. 275.

[96]   D.E. Clark, 'News and Opinion Concerning America in English Newspapers, 1754–1763', *Pacific Historical Review*, 10 (1941), p. 75.

[97]   For the inaccuracy of reports from West Africa, *London Chronicle*, 7 May 1757.

challenges contributed to the character of the discussion of this news and related issues. For Continental news, the British press could draw on a network of newspapers there, notably those in the United Provinces, but also newspapers and newsletters produced in other countries. Similarly, Dutch papers contained much material from British counterparts.[98] In a comparable fashion to the items from diplomats, there was frequently a tendency to note different points of view, and also to point out propensities to bias and inaccuracy, as when the *London Chronicle* on 1 January 1757 commented on the Brussels and Paris gazettes.[99] Out of office, Bedford referred to taking news from the 'Dutch Gazettes'.[100]

There was no comparable international press for British newspapers to draw on when reporting trans-oceanic news. Instead, in so far as items were reprinted, they came from British colonial newspapers in North America and the West Indies. These were generally hostile to France and Spain, not least because they took British expansion as normative. The sources of news and comment repay consideration because they were scarcely value-free, but, instead, affected the milieux within which policy was formulated and discussed. Indeed, the sources of news and comment play a role in what has more recently been termed strategic culture. Moreover, the strong demand for news furthered a dynamic for action. This was particularly so when the government could not control the agenda of overseas news as very much happened with the outbreak of hostilities in North America in 1754. The following March, the government assured the French envoy that a press report of fighting in the Ohio country was inaccurate, and the latter suggested that it was inserted by malcontents or stock market speculators.[101] More generally, Rouillé was convinced, with reason, that both London and Paris were affected by inaccurate reports from North America.[102]

Uncertainty and Challenge

The very sense of uncertainty and challenge that was a key characteristic and theme of press reporting, was highly significant for the discussion of policy. This sense encouraged the view that something had to be done in an inherently changeable international environment, indeed that policy entailed doing something. That attitude created pressure on the ministry. In practice, the idea

---

[98]   Bonnac to Rouillé, 1 Apr. 1755, AE. CP. Hollande 488 fol. 166.
[99]   The paper also made use of the *Hague Gazette, London Chronicle*, 4 Jan. 1757.
[100]   Bedford to Gower, 15 Oct. 1755, Russell (ed.), *Bedford*, II, 170.
[101]   Mirepoix to Rouillé, 5 Mar. 1755, AE. CP. Ang. 438 fol. 244.
[102]   Rouillé to Mirepoix, 19 Feb. 1755, AE. CP. Ang. 438 fol. 176.

of doing relatively little in response to the changeable international environment had had only limited purchase among Whig ministers after Sir Robert Walpole lost control of the policy initiative in 1739. In contrast to other Whig leaders, such as James, 1st Viscount Stanhope in the late 1710s, Charles, 2nd Viscount Townshend in the late 1720s, and the hawks during the War of the Polish Succession (1733–5), he had appreciated the value of limited action. From 1739, in contrast, there were different views on what to do, but always a commitment to action during the subsequent war, first with Spain and then with France. In the latter case this commitment appeared necessary, not least because deploying an effective coalition appeared essential for Britain to enjoy security, let alone to secure Continental goals.

At the same time, there was persistent and strong division within the ministry in the shape of a reaction against what was regarded as over-ambitious interventionism. The potent opposition to Carteret in 1744 and the sustained criticism in the early 1750s of the expense of Newcastle's Imperial Election Plan can be seen in this light. This division was linked to deep anxieties about policy within the 'Old Corps' Whig party as a whole, as well as in the wider political world. Thus, Frederick Frankland hoped that, in the event of future war, we shall 'not be principals when we should only be auxiliaries'.[103] A London merchant who was MP for a Yorkshire pocket borough, Frankland also demonstrated the way in which interests overlapped, rather than being rigidly segregated: the classification of MPs has to address this point.

The political problem of foreign policy in part lay in the differences over interventionism and in the related wider resonances of goals and means. A different problem, in 1738–41 and anew from the late 1740s, came to rest on the pressure for action in response to the trans-oceanic agenda, or, rather, what was presented as the trans-oceanic agenda. That is a shorthand reference to an agenda that was broader in character, as well as politically loaded, and, to a degree, partisan. The item that was of particular significance was that of naval primacy. Indeed, trans-oceanic expansion was seen as necessarily dependent on that primacy, as was national security. As a result, there was particular sensitivity on this point. Moreover, naval strength was an issue that could resonate widely throughout society, and could, and frequently did, reach across the political spectrum. Such strength was a significant issue both at the national scale and more locally. Thus, in 1745, the Merchant Adventurers of Bristol encouraged the city MPs to press for a more powerful warship to provide nearby protection

---

[103] Frankland to Robinson, 15 Jan. (os) 1748, Leeds Archive Office, Newby Hall Mss, 2833, no. 71.

against French privateers, not least because the insurers did not think the current one adequate. As an instance of the need for advice in negotiating the routes of lobbying and related politics, the MPs were asked to apply to the Admiralty or, if they thought it more appropriate, to recommend to the Merchant Adventurers that they apply to the government by 'petition or remonstrance'. The MPs acted, and the Lords of the Admiralty responded accordingly, while complaining of the difficulty of raising sailors in Bristol.[104] Foreign diplomats picked up the issue.[105]

Redefining the State

The ability of critics within the government as well as opposition Whigs and Tories to find common ground on naval strength helped ensure that the related trans-oceanic issue was given added traction. It was thanks to the navy that Porto-Bello had been captured in 1739 and Louisbourg in 1745. Were fresh attempts to be made, then naval superiority would be required. This appeared of particular note because a belief in imperial destiny very much came to the fore in this period. So also did the commitment to naval mastery. The Glorious Revolution had been enacted on land, and, alongside the significance of naval power in opposing invasion threats, notably in 1692, 1708, 1744, and 1745–6, successive Jacobite challenges had been defeated on land. A shift to concern about the naval situation gathered pace from the late 1730s, but for a variety of reasons. This variety captured the complexity of concerns, attitudes and policies, a complexity that involved cumulative factors as well as cross-currents. Concern about the naval dimension reflected the greater sensitivity of trans-oceanic issues, the marked rise in Bourbon naval strength, which was a contrast to the situation from the 1700s, and repeated anxieties about invasion. Without British dominance at sea, there was no security for, indeed logic to, the empire. It appeared to be of scant value unless maritime links could be maintained. In 1745, James Nicholson wrote from Maryland to relatives back in Britain that

---

[104] Arthur Hart, Master of Merchant Venturers, to Edward Southwell and Robert Hoblyn, MPs, 10 Feb. (os), Southwell to Hart, 15 Feb. (os) 1746, Bristol, Public Library, Southwell papers, vol. 9; K. Wilson, 'Empire, Trade and Popular Politics in mid-Hanoverian Britain: The Case of Admiral Vernon', *Past and Present*, 121 (1988), pp. 74–109.

[105] Zamboni to Landgrave Ludwig VIII of Hesse-Darmstadt, 25 Feb. 1746, Darmstadt, Staatsarchiv, E1 M10/6.

the war had increased transport charges so much that very little profit was made on tobacco, and that the colony was forced to become more self-reliant.[106]

Themes were not advanced in isolation. That of naval strength was linked to foreign trade and its ability to help British manufacturing; and both to an emphasis on the interests and views of the nation.[107] Over trade, government policy and public opinion were potentially aligned, but could also be seen as opposed if the ministry's search for peace meant that overseas interests were not pursued, or apparently were not pursued. The opposition argued that the ministry consistently neglected the protection and furtherance of British trade, a longstanding theme. On 4 February (os) 1749, the *Craftsman* claimed:

> Our trade has been constantly clogged injudiciously and shamefully neglected. Can there be a more pregnant proof of the latter than the Definitive Treaty [Aix-la-Chapelle], where not a single article is to be seen relative to that trade and navigation which gave rise to the war,

a reference to the failure to secure the interests at stake when Britain had gone to war with Spain in 1739. The protection of trade was also a continual refrain for ministers and diplomats. Thus, in 1749, Bedford insisted that trade with Spain should be on the same footing as pre-war.[108] At the same time, there could be, among contemporaries, a tendency to exaggerate the impact of commercial issues: for Britain, for other states, notably republican ones,[109] and for other powers.[110]

The trans-oceanic and naval themes can be described in 'realist' terms, relating to particular challenges and opportunities, each as part of a more general situation of challenge and opportunity. Yet it would be misleading to separate these elements from the sense (as opposed to 'realist' situation) of challenge and opportunity. This sense ultimately derived from politics in both narrow and broad dimensions. The narrowness was that of the specific political advantages, domestic and international, to be gained by adopting this position. The broader dimension was that the political imagination of Britain, the very conception of the nation, the state, and its place in the world, developed in this period. The opposition rhetoric of the late 1730s, of maritime destiny or, as the opposite, enslavement, was increasingly presented and received as a national mission and

---

[106] James Nicholson to Margaret, Elizabeth and Jean Nicholson, 24 Nov. (os) 1745, Northumbria Record Office, Berwick Office, 1955 A no. 25.

[107] Viry to Charles Emmanuel III, 15 Apr. 1756, AST. LM. Ing. 60.

[108] Bedford to Keene, 19 Jan. (os) 1749, NA. SP. 94/135 fol. 8.

[109] Mitchell to Holdernesse, 30 Aug. 1756, NA. SP. 90/66.

[110] J. Black, *Trade, Empire and British Foreign Policy, 1689–1815* (Abingdon, 2007).

need. Correspondingly, the latter were defined in terms of this destiny. This rhetoric contributed to, and reflected, the degree to which, although sometimes expressed, for example with reference to French expansionism in North America, balance of power ideas were not strongly at play in colonial policy[111] or in naval goals. Instead, there was public support for national primacy in both, with strength in trade a common theme.[112]

This broader culture of politics, one in which international rivalry and national identity interacted,[113] greatly affected the understanding of Britain and its global role, and helped in the transformation from the concerns of the early decades of the century to those of its later decades. The winning of victory in 1758–62 was a key aspect of this transformation. So also was the earlier reconceptualisation and revival of the rhetoric and, indeed, reality of global power. That was important to the relationship between politics and foreign policy that is the theme of this book. The reconceptualisation and revival serve as a reminder that crisis was not the sole element in the years 1744–57. Instead, both this rethinking of global power and the sense of crisis are of greater significance, and were to contemporaries, because of the very cross-currents seen in this period. There was no simple causal relationship to be described in terms of the reconceptualisation of assumptions and policy as a response to the crisis of this period; but, instead, a complex situation that contemporaries struggled to understand, explain and shape.

---

[111] J.R. Sofka, 'The Eighteenth Century International System: Parity or Primacy?', *Review of International Studies*, 27 (2001), p. 157.

[112] G. Niedhart, *Handel und Krieg in der britischen Weltpolitik, 1738–1763* (Mannheim, 1979).

[113] M. Schumann, 'International Rivalry and State Identity in the Seven Years War', in L. Eriksonas and L. Müller (eds), *Statehood Before and Beyond Ethnicity* (Berne, 2005), pp. 159–76.

Chapter 4

The Crisis of 1744–6

French warships in the Channel in 1744 and a Jacobite army in Derby in 1745 might appear to reflect failures of policy and implementation, as well as to make issues of politics and foreign policy redundant. Instead, it is the power and presence of military force that comes to the fore, an element that was bluntly displayed with Cumberland's total victory over the Jacobites at Culloden on 16 April (os) 1746. However, approached differently, it was the consequences of politics and foreign policy that led to these French warships in the Channel and to the Jacobites in Derby. Indeed, politics and foreign policy were both the cause of the crisis that affected Britain and, also, were part of the solution. The determination of the post-Walpole ministry, established in 1742, to broaden the conflict with Spain into a war with France and thus, in its eyes, to rescue the European system, to win glory, and to revive the Whig brand, led both to the French riposte and to an upsurge in Jacobite conspiracy. Separately, the drive by George II and Carteret to use war with France in order to create a more conducive international system, conducive for both Britain and, far more controversially, Hanover, helped divide the ministry and offend public opinion. This outcome gave a new direction to the powerful sense of distrust about government already seen when discussing Walpole's policy towards both France and Spain.

In 1744 these pressures came conspicuously to the fore. George cast about in a bitter and sustained effort to save Carteret from the opposition of the Pelhams. However, he was unable to do so, in large part because other prominent politicians also wanted Carteret gone. Moreover, the fall of Carteret offered an opportunity to bring in support for the ministry from the opposition. Henry, 3rd Viscount Lonsdale linked this possibility to parliamentary calm, writing from London on 8 December (os) 'there is great unanimity in Parliament', and adding, on 21 December (os):

> The unanimity that has hitherto appeared in Parliament is almost unprecedented, and it seems likely to continue, for this day a good number of the Heads of those

who have been lately in opposition have kissed the King's hand for employments about the Court.[1]

A more jaundiced account was offered by John Campbell, an 'Old Corps' MP and a Lord of the Admiralty under Walpole who had lost office in 1742. Campbell was part of the residue factor in politics, the major extent to which those defined by earlier struggles and prominent then continued to have an impact, a process encouraged by their frequently having great influence in individual constituencies, whereas political parties as abstractions and organisations did not. This factor led to a layered character for British politics. Campbell captured the tension involved in forming the ministry, but was unhappy with the specific solution in this case:

> is this what the Duke of Newcastle called to me standing upon the bottom of their old friends and only taking some help from others, is it not rather accepting a partnership with I don't know who and standing upon what bottom they please to set you ... the Old Corps are too numerous to be despised, no minister can in this Parliament do without them.[2]

In practice, despite the 'New Allies' brought in from the opposition in 1744, the 'Old Corps' remained dominant, and notably in the shape of leadership by the Pelhams. The resulting ministry was the one that was to confront the Jacobites in the '45. Ironically, that was not the sole dynastic challenge, because the ministers were also resolved to restrain George's commitment to his native Hanover, and, by extension, to German politics. A British focus of the war on the Low Countries was the political and strategic solution pursued for Britain and its allies in 1745, until, unexpectedly, British troops had to be brought home to confront the Jacobites. Parliament readily accepted this policy.[3] By presenting the war on the Continent as in defence of the Low Countries, a clearly-understood national goal, rather than in support of Hanover, which was not a convincing national goal, nor a strategic end or means, the Pelhams were able to rally backing for the war, and to defuse the issue politically. The protection of the Low Countries was successfully presented as the strategic pivot for Britain, one that was second only to the resistance to Jacobitism and to foreign schemes

---

[1]　Lonsdale to Fleming, 8, 21 Dec. (os) 1744, Carlisle, Cumbria RO. D/Sen/Fleming 14.

[2]　John Campbell to son, Pryse, 18 Dec. (os) 1744, Carmarthen, CRO., Cawdor Muniments, Box 138.

[3]　Harrington to Chesterfield, 25 Jan. (os) 1745, NA. SP. 84/408 fol. 87.

on its behalf. British neutrality when Austria was attacked in the War of the Polish Succession (1733–5) had underlined the degree to which Continental interventionism was not a necessary policy. That was not the theme in 1745.

John Tucker, a 'New Ally' MP who had unenthusiastically come into office with his patron George Bubb Dodington (another aspect of the layering), reported to his brother back in his constituency of Weymouth: 'Tomorrow we go into the consideration of the army for the year ensuing which it is hoped will pass without any great opposition as the H—ns [Hanoverians] are left out of the estimates.'[4] On 16 January (os) 1745, the ministry won a division over the army by a majority of over 100, a sound victory over the Tories and the Whigs still in opposition, who, together, could only record 113 votes. Tucker noted: 'The army in Flanders was voted yesterday almost unanimously and assurances given of doing what may be judged for the general good on both sides to extricate us out of the present melancholy situation.' On 28 January (os), the Committee of Supply supported the money for the army in Flanders that year, with only one MP speaking against.[5]

However, already prior to the Jacobite rising in late 1745, there was concern that the war would not fulfil the political or strategic hopes of the ministry. John, 2nd Viscount Chetwynd, a former diplomat who was one of the 'New Allies', wrote in December 1744 to John, 1st Earl Gower, another 'New Ally', about a third: 'I did hope to hear that Lord Chesterfield was to go to The Hague where things must be well settled, or you cannot go on with your foreign affairs.'[6] Dutch support was regarded as crucial for Britain to do well in the Low Countries. Once he arrived in The Hague, Philip, 4th Earl of Chesterfield found 'complete anarchy', but also a very large Dutch army and, in large part as a result, a heavily taxed nation.[7]

Concern about the direction and implementation of policy was not restricted to critics, present or former. The ministry was dismayed by French success in the Austrian Netherlands where, on 11 May 1745, Marshal Saxe had won a major battle over Allied forces at Fontenoy, before obtaining the capitulations of Tournai (20 June), Ghent (15 July), Bruges (19 July) and Ostend (23 August). In response to the fall of Ghent, Harrington, then with George in Hanover, pressed Newcastle on the need to prevent an invasion from France.[8] In May 1745,

4   John to Richard Tucker, 15 Jan. (os) 1745, Bod. MS. Don. C. 107 fol. 71.

5   John to Richard Tucker, 24 Jan. (os) 1745, Bod. MS. Don. C. 107, fol. 79; John to Pryse Campbell, 24 Jan. (os) 1745, Carmarthen, CRO., Cawdor Muniments, Box 138.

6   Chetwynd to Gower, 26 Dec. (os) 1744, NA. PRO. 30/29/1/11 fol. 287.

7   Chesterfield to Gower, 9 Feb. 1745, NA. PRO. 30/29/1/11 fol. 288.

8   Harrington to Newcastle, 20 July 1745, NA. SP. 43/36.

Newcastle was careful to locate the source of political criticism that Austria was not doing enough to defend the Austrian Netherlands (Belgium), as: 'begins already to be flung out (and that by persons of consideration and such as are supposed to be the most disposed to carry on the war)'. This situation led Newcastle, who commented that subsidies to foreign powers were too great, to press the need for winning over Prussia.[9] Despite likely hostility from George II, alliance with Prussia had apparent strategic and political benefits for Britain. It would protect Hanover and enable Austria to concentrate on fighting France, thus reducing the burden on Britain and making the British contribution to war in the Low Countries more effective. There would also be benefits in terms of opposition to the Bourbons in Italy, as Austria would also be able to devote more resources there. Moreover, such an alliance was seen as likely to lessen domestic criticism of British foreign policy, notably on the grounds of allegedly favouring Hanover.

The trade-off between foreign affairs and domestic politics was strong, but varied; with some issues particularly crucial. Pelham correctly noted the continued sensitivity of everything bound up in Hanover, or possibly relating to it. He wrote to Chesterfield, a politician, in opposition from 1733 to 1744, as well as a diplomat:

> Whatever assistance we give to you in Holland creates for us here greater difficulties in carrying on the King's business at home. Your friends at The Hague call for ever more Hanoverians into Flanders, and ... your friends here call for the sending away those that are still there.[10]

Thus the location and financing of Hanoverian troops were politically contentious.

Popularity was a key theme, goal and problem for Newcastle; the popularity (in Britain) of foreign allies as well as of the ministry. Noting in August 1745 that Austria's conduct in the Low Countries, where there was repeatedly only a grudging Austrian contribution to Allied operations, made its cause unpopular, he argued that this would be more so when it was known that Austrian policy had blocked the chance of reconciliation between Britain and Prussia. Moreover, there was continued pressure for a trans-oceanic war. The *London Evening Post*, an influential opposition newspaper, claimed, on 19 January (os) 1745, albeit without reason, that corruption had led to the turn from a naval

---

9   Newcastle to Harrington, 21 May (os), 14, 21 June (os), 9 Aug. (os) 1745, NA. SP. 43/37.
10   Pelham to Chesterfield, 15 Feb. (os) 1745, BL. M. 645 (13).

and colonial war to an army one entailing subsidies to allies, an unacceptable policy to the opposition. This focus provided the basis for political attacks. Opposition Whigs who had joined the ministry were mocked by *Old England*, an opposition London newspaper, on 6 April (os) 1745 for the convenience of their changing view: 'What an alteration happened the moment our virtuous Patriots came themselves to fill the seats of ministerial power? The war then from being a damned, villainous, wicked, unjust, Hanoverian War, became a very true, genuine, English war.'

Publications contested foreign policy, with pro-government writers repeatedly linking policy directly to the struggle for liberty within Britain. A preface to the collected edition of the 1745 issues of the *Political Cabinet* claimed:

> It was published chiefly in the view of giving the Public a just idea of the present system of affairs in Europe; to warn them of the destructive views of the House of Bourbon, as well as of the necessity of strongly supporting the House of Austria. Politics are so delicate, so extensive, and abstruse a nature, and understood by so few who are heated by them; that the editor believed it would be a meritorious act, to endeavour to lead his countrymen into the right path in this respect, so far as his slender abilities would permit. He was the more induced to this, as the happy liberty we enjoy in this island (and may it flourish eternally!) is abused by numberless writers, whose only view is to support themselves, at the expense of truth, of their country; and consequently of every thing, in this world, that ought to be most sacred among men ... a just abhorrence of GALLIC tyranny.[11]

The Pelhams had strengthened their control of the British ministry by having Carteret replaced as Secretary of State in 1744 by William, Earl of Harrington. A former diplomat (as William Stanhope) with a high reputation, and an experienced former Secretary of State for the Northern Department (1730–42), he was regarded as amenable by George, in part due to his army background. Crucially, Harrington was not Carteret and had long experience of working with Newcastle, who had been his directing Secretary of State and then counterpart as Southern Secretary. The reluctance of George to accept the exclusion of Carteret, and the 'partiality' he publicly showed him,[12] however, made the political as well as ministerial situation unstable in 1745. The atmosphere of politics at Court was captured as a result of the eagerness with which George's

---

[11] *Political Cabinet* II (London, 1745), pp. iii–v.

[12] John to Pryse Campbell, 9 Dec. (os) 1744, Carmarthen, CRO, Cawdor Muniments, Box 138.

views were recorded. Thus, as an instance of the cascading nature of information, Newcastle's confidant, Andrew Stone, described a conversation with Pelham, who recounted a meeting with George in which foreign affairs played a role irrespective of Pelham's very different ministerial responsibilities as First Lord of the Treasury:

> His Majesty talked warmly of the project of attacking the King of Prussia which Mr Pelham no otherwise argued against than by saying that it would be impracticable to enter into new engagements for conquests to be made, of that kind. But he did not think what he said made any impression.

In turn, George told Harrington that Carteret was 'a man of the greatest abilities this country ever bred'.[13] Praising a predecessor in this fashion was typical of the King's insensitivity.

Carteret was certainly more willing to consider action against Prussia, action that would help Hanover, but that would expose the British ministry to domestic political criticism. George's views therefore threatened ministerial and parliamentary stability. Nevertheless, until the Carteret issue was pushed to a new crisis in February 1746, by George, Granville (Carteret), and the Pelhams, albeit for different reasons, it was possible to handle this threat and to manage the politics both of foreign policy and of strategy.

In its issue of 16 February (os) 1745, *Old England* emphasised the role of popular pressure in leading to the fall of Carteret the previous year: 'The People, by whose voice alone that change was effected'. Concerned that the King could protect a minister who did not enjoy Parliament's confidence, a breach of the general understanding of parliamentary monarchy, the paper pressed for a limitation of the Royal Prerogative in this respect. In the event, in accordance with the characteristic nuances of the constitution and with the successful imprecision of the political system, but also reflecting Carteret's political weakness, the relationship between Crown, ministers and Parliament had resolved itself in 1744 in favour of those ministers able to lead Parliament, and was to do so again in 1746.

As a reminder of the role of rulers, the death of Charles Albert of Bavaria, the Emperor Charles VII, in 1745, greatly altered the international context. The extent of public interest in foreign news was suggested by a verse satire that appeared then in London: *The Dead Emperor: or, Reviving Peace. Being some*

---

[13]   Stone to Newcastle, 16 Feb. (os) 1745, BL. Add. 32704 fols 72–3; Russell (ed.), *Bedford*, I (London, 1843), xxxvii–xxxviii.

deep coffee-house speculations on these important subjects. This satire presented a coffee-house discussion of international relations as touched off by news of Charles's death. As another indicator of interest, share prices rose in London on the death of Charles Albert, as it was hoped that Francis Stephen, the husband of Maria Theresa of Austria, would be elected and that this election would lead to peace. Peace was seen as good for share prices. The linkage of patriotism and foreign policy was registered in Tucker's remark that this election was 'most ardently wished for by all good Englishmen'.[14] Indeed, Francis Stephen became the new Emperor, Francis I. He had had a very successful visit to Britain in 1731 and was regarded with favour there, notably by the 'Old Corps' Whigs, who had entertained him then. Although Francis' election did not lead to peace, it marked the effective end of France's longstanding attempt to use Bavaria in order to overthrow the Habsburgs, and was an important part of the background to the Diplomatic Revolution of 1756, the establishment of a Franco-Austrian alliance.

In the shorter term, in 1745, the German question became that of the relations between Austria and Prussia, an issue that had placed Hanover in a secondary position for several decades. These relations were thrown to the fore with the Prussian attack on Austria and Saxony in 1745. From 1745, France concentrated on war in the Low Countries, which was more of a threat to Britain than operations in southern Germany. This concentration reflected the combination and interaction of political and military factors. France could more readily bring its strength to bear in the Low Countries and could attack Austria directly in its possessions there, hoping to make gains that it could employ thereafter in peace negotiations.

The unexpected Prussian attack on Austria in 1745 undermined British foreign policy and led to an upsurge in criticism of Frederick, both in Britain and in Hanover. George's hostility to Frederick primarily arose from the competing interests and ambitions of Hanover and Prussia, and from a personal ire in which envy and anger each played a considerable and aggravating role. This hostility was regarded by Newcastle as inopportune,[15] as it certainly was from the British perspective. Partly as a result, George's hostility to Prussia was important to the politics of foreign policy in Britain. At the same time, irrespective of George's stance, there was a ministerial hostility to Frederick that drew on his unwillingness to accept British views of the need to make opposition to France the organising principle of international relations. Frederick's unwillingness was to a degree shared by George, as he was concerned about the situation in

---

[14] John to Richard Tucker, 26 Jan. (os) 1745, Bod. MS. Don. C. 107 fol. 81.
[15] Newcastle to Harrington, 12 July (os) 1745, NA. SP. 43/37.

Germany, but George matched the British ministry's hostility to Frederick's international stance. This ministerial attitude came to the fore as a result of the Prussian attack on Austria in 1745. The consequent congruence of King and ministers brought a degree of consistency to foreign policy. As a result, George's attempt to bring Carteret back into office in 1746 was less potentially disruptive in policy terms than might otherwise have been the case. At the same time, there was a marked difference between the strong emphasis that George was eager to place on the challenge from Frederick's views and that which the Pelhams were willing to admit.

The background to this difference became that of rebellion at home and instability abroad. The two were linked. Fearful of a French invasion of England, a fear that began in 1745 before the news of the landing of Charles Edward Stuart on 23 July (os), in support of the Jacobite attempt the ministers in London repeatedly pressed for the recall of troops (and then of more troops) from the army in the Low Countries.[16] However, other figures played down the initial danger of the situation because they did not want Britain to weaken her military commitment to the Continent. This was certainly the position of Carteret and of his ally, John, 4th Marquess of Tweeddale, the Secretary of State for Scotland. They initially cast doubt on reports of Charles Edward's landing, and subsequently on his success. Cumberland did not want to weaken the army in the Austrian Netherlands. George himself was less speedy in deciding to return from Hanover than the Lords Justices, the ministers left in London, would have liked. Cumberland sent Lieutenant-General John Ligonier to meet George on his way to London at Utrecht and to press him on the dangerous situation created by French advances in the Austrian Netherlands. Ligonier succeeded, and George deferred the transfer of the British troops. This was symptomatic of his preference for military advice and of a certain lack of sensitivity to domestic political repercussions.

Pressure to recall troops was a clear sign of British weakness within the alliance, and one that threatened the security of the Low Countries while increasing British dependence on Austrian strategic choices. However, with 'hardly any regular force between Berwick and London', in other words to protect eastern England from a Jacobite advance south from Scotland, there was a need for troops in Britain. Newcastle noted on 5 September (os) 1745: 'I have been for some time under great apprehensions.'[17] He was prone to hysterical

---

[16] Newcastle to Cumberland, 20 Aug. (os), Newcastle to Harrington, 27 Aug. (os) 1745, RA. Cumb. P. 4/203, NA. SP. 43/115.

[17] Newcastle to Henry, 3rd Viscount Lonsdale, Lord Lieutenant of Cumberland and Westmorland, 5 Sept. (os) 1745, Carlisle, Cumbria CRO, D/Pen Acc. 2689. See also

anxiety, but even the level-headed were worried. In an atmosphere of growing concern, rumours spread of French landings, one at Poole,[18] and preparations were made against invasion, including for the borrowing of horses to move infantry more speedily.[19]

The British force in Scotland, meanwhile, was outmanoeuvred and then rapidly fell victim to a Highland charge by Charles Edward's men at Prestonpans outside Edinburgh on 21 September (os), leading to a humiliating and total defeat. Elsewhere in Scotland resistance to the Jacobites was limited. The Secretary of State for Scotland was informed from Dumfries that 'the body of the people' were 'extremely hearty in the common cause, but without arms, without officers, and without any advice of any kind from any of the officers of the Crown as if government for some time had fallen into an apoplectick fit'.[20] The weakness of the Hanoverian cause in south-west Scotland ensured that there was no defensive cover against Jacobite advance for north-west England. There were also concerns about attitudes in England. At the end of September, Robert Trevor noted: 'it is apprehended by some good, sensible Whigs that the indifference and lukewarmness of the many is more dangerous than the activity of the few'.[21] As a result, the government needed to rely on the strength and success of regular forces. This crisis in governmental effectiveness and political stability at the local level was unprecedented and the shock waves reverberated round London for months.

Indeed, the relief felt there when Charles Edward retreated from Derby on 6 December (os), and subsequently in response to victory at Culloden on 16 April (os) 1746, reflected the depth of earlier concerns. This relief helped give the government a valuable political opportunity. However, George squandered some of this opportunity, notably as far as he was concerned, by trying to bring back Carteret. As a reminder of the role of hindsight, that critical evaluation would probably have been, and still be, different had he succeeded. The fortunes of monarchy did not always coincide. The Jacobite challenge led, and notably in 1745–6, to a significant rallying to the Crown but not to political success for George. This rallying was seen as the defence of the Protestant establishment, providing ample compensation for earlier discussion about 'that fatal connexion'

Andrew Stone to Edward Weston, 13 Aug. (os) 1745, Farmington, Weston papers, vol. 16.

[18]   Stephen Poyntz to Weston, 15 Sept. (os) 1745, Farmington, Weston papers, vol. 16.

[19]   Flysheet, 2 Jan. (os) 1746, NA. WO. 34/109 fol. 1.

[20]   Charles Areskine, Lord Tinwall, to John, 4th Marquess of Tweeddale, 18 Sept. (os) 1745, NA. SP. 54/26 fol. 92. See also Lord Glenorchy to Tweeddale, 1 Sept. (os) 1745, Edinburgh, National Library of Scotland, Yester papers, vol. 7071, fol. 3.

[21]   Trevor to Robinson, 30 Sept. 1745, BL. Add. 23821 fol. 107.

with Hanover.[22] This theme did not really recur until 1756–7. Providence, moreover, a potent ally to claim, appeared to be at work in the 1745–6 crisis. The '45 resulted in a serious upsurge in anti-Catholic comment[23] that was given a political resonance when a forty-part edition of John Foxe's sixteenth-century anti-Catholic classic *Book of Martyrs* was published. *Old England* complained on 19 October (os) 1745 that this work was not now in churches to the degree that was formerly the case.

In fact, very few Catholics were involved in the '45, and notably in England. Consequently, very few in authority were, in the event, interested in altering the relevant laws about Catholics. More generally, a different social politics to that of traditional anti-Catholicism was provided by that of social cohesion across religious divides. In the *True Patriot* of 19 November (os) 1749, Fielding, writing from the ministerial perspective, recounted a story:

> A gentleman dined with a friend of his, a Roman Catholic, and after dinner these two were drinking in company with a priest who was chaplain to the family: their bottle being emptied, the master of the house sent his chaplain for a fresh bottle. When he was gone, the other, turning to his friend, said, "Do you really think I can wish well to this rebellion? Why, if Popery was established in England, that fellow would have sent me on the message on which I have now sent him."

In 1745, however, doubts about the future, indeed the present, were more urgent. Concern increased about whether Britain received or deserved divine support, concern that was also to be pronounced in 1757 when the next war went badly. In October 1745, Wesley was worried that 'the senseless wickedness, the ignorant prophaneness' of the poor of the city of Newcastle, and the 'continual cursing and swearing, and the wanton blasphemy' of the British soldiers, would endanger divine support.[24] Such support was seen as significant by many, and not only by those of Wesley's enthusiasms.

It is unclear what would have happened had Charles Edward continued his advance. In the event, the Jacobite council decided on 5 December (os) 1745 on a retreat, and that despite Charles Edward's clear wish to press on to London. Due to the failure of his promises of obtaining English and Scottish support, there was a crucial breakdown of confidence in Charles Edward among

---

[22] *London Evening Post*, 26 Mar. (os) 1745.

[23] John to Richard Tucker, 7 Sept. (os) 1745, Bod. MS. Don. C. 107 fol. 120; C. Haydon, *Anti-Catholicism in Eighteenth-century England* (Manchester, 1993).

[24] Wesley to Matthew Ridley, Mayor of Newcastle, 26 Oct. (os) 1745, Morpeth, Northumberland CRO, ZRI 27/5.

the Scottish chiefs. They considered themselves as having been tricked into a risky adventure. Charles Edward had spent too much time with a small cadre of advisers, many of them Irish. His failure to take the chiefs with him forms an ironic counterpart to George II's difficulties with the 'Old Corps' Whigs in 1744–6. However, the totally contrasting circumstances and results underlined the value of George being in power, and also the resilient and flexible character of British parliamentary monarchy.

By retreating from 6 December (os) 1745, the Jacobites made their defeat almost certain, not least because, in combination with bad weather and the Royal Navy, the retreat led the French to abandon a planned supporting invasion of southern England.[25] However, in a significant prolongation of the rising and therefore of its impact on the war on the Continent and on British foreign policy, Charles Edward retreated to Scotland successfully, beating off the army's pursuit. Once there, he regrouped and beat a poorly-led British army at Falkirk on 17 January (os) 1746. Nevertheless, soon after, short of resources, Charles Edward abandoned the Central Lowlands for the Highlands. The dynamic of Jacobite success, an element crucial to setting the agenda, had been lost. Cumberland pursued Charles Edward, and his total victory at Culloden, near Inverness, on 16 April (os) 1746 swept away doubts about Providence. When they revived in 1750, these doubts focused on the more intangible element of an earthquake in London, albeit a small one.

The strengthened reputation of the Hanoverian dynasty in 1745–6, a reputation celebrated in music by Handel, was not matched by the political success of the monarch. Most significantly, illustrating the consequences of the absence of Walpole's influence, George's relations with his ministers were very poor. In part through the Countess of Yarmouth, George also continued to take advice from Carteret, now Earl Granville, and was believed by Newcastle to do so.[26] Such a policy was similar to that of Continental rulers, who could thus focus all the initiative on their own choice. In Britain, however, the needs of parliamentary accountability and management resulted in policy and political consequences that affected royal choice and the process of choice. Ministerial cohesion was a key requirement, or at least an impression that there was more cohesion than division.

In September 1745, George failed to persuade Harrington to form a new ministry that would have enabled him to dispense with the Pelhams. Once the Jacobites had retreated in December 1745, relations with his ministers

---

deteriorated further. George rejected pressure to take Pitt into office as Secretary at War. This was a course Newcastle urged, both in order to broaden the ministry, and to lessen opposition attacks in the Commons, each matters of great concern to the Duke. George treated the demand, on behalf of a bitter and frequent critic of Hanoverian concerns, as an insult. In his eyes, this insult underlined why he disliked the Pelhams, whom he felt limited his options and failed to show due respect, notably over ministerial choices.

In February 1746, with the Jacobites still undefeated, but an assumption that the rebellion was essentially over,[27] the political crisis was brought to a head. The Pelhams and their supporters resigned their posts in the government on 10 and 11 February (os) in order to demonstrate their value.[28] This policy was also to be tried by officeholders against George III in December 1783, but then with much less success. By withholding his confidence from his ministers and, instead, seeking advice from Granville, George II had challenged their position in Parliament. Foreign policy was part of the equation, with the Pelhams reluctant to accept the degree of commitment to the war on the Continent shown by George and Granville.[29] In turn, the collective resignation raised major questions about the nature of the constitution, and raised them publicly. In practice, the constitutional guidelines that sought to define the relationship of Crown and Parliament, such as the Act of Settlement of 1701, were vague, providing scant guidance for most political eventualities, and were anyway dependent upon mutual goodwill. There was, as yet, no received understanding of such central issues as the collective responsibility of the Cabinet, the particular responsibility of the Departmental Head to both King and Cabinet, the special role of the first minister, and the notion that the King should choose his ministers from those who had the confidence of Parliament.

The resignations troubled foreign powers as they struggled to understand them and to assess their consequences.[30] However, the resignations were of short duration. George turned to Granville and to the Earl of Bath (formerly, as William Pulteney, the leader of the opposition Whigs in the Commons from 1725 to 1742) to form a new ministry. On 10 February (os) 1746 Bath, who had pressed George on the need for royal leadership, kissed the King's hands on accepting the post of First Lord of the Treasury, a post he had earlier sought in

---

[27]   John Maule, secretary to Archibald, 3rd Duke of Argyll, to Andrew Fletcher, 6 Feb. (os) 1746, Edinburgh, National Library of Scotland, MS. 16630 fol. 40.

[28]   P. Yorke (ed.), *The Life and Correspondence of Philip Yorke, Earl of Hardwicke* (3 vols, Cambridge, 1913), I, 499; Goodwood, MS. 104 fol. 297.

[29]   Bod. MS. Don. C 107 fols 226–7.

[30]   Re Prussia, Villiers to Harrington, 5 Mar. 1746, NA. SP. 88/68.

1743, only to be defeated then by Pelham. In 1746, in the face of the resignations, Bath and Granville, both of whom were in the Lords, could not find a manager of Commons' business, or, indeed, sufficient supporters in the Commons. Thomas Winnington's refusal to lead the Commons for them was highly important and, in a key display of strength, 192 MPs attended Pelham's levée. Moreover, the City withdrew a loan that had been offered to the government. Edward Harley noted the pressure:

> the supplies [taxes] not being raised, and the monied contractors in the City, Gore, Vanneck and Gideon the Jew, who had agreed with Pelham, declaring they would be off their bargain if he was out, and Granville not having formed a party in the House of Commons.[31]

'No Pelham no money was the City cry.'[32] The major financial interests had close links with the Pelhams and in wartime, there was a desperate need to keep loans flowing to the government. Indeed, in 1745, Stephen Poyntz, a former diplomat and an experienced courtier, wrote enclosing 'the scheme that is handed about for three million of our supply. If it succeeds, it will be owing to the great opinion which the City and whole nation have of Mr Pelham.'[33] The French government was well aware of the 'exorbitant sums' the British ministry was raising.[34]

Within forty-eight hours, Bath and Granville abandoned their attempt in February 1746, forcing George to turn to the Pelhams. He had to admit what he had tried to deny, that he was led by parliamentary men, and was obliged to give posts to those they wanted to bring into office, particularly Pitt, who became Vice-Treasurer of Ireland and, three months later, Paymaster General. The role and significance of the Commons and the City, as opposed to the Lords and the Court, was clearly demonstrated in this crisis. The two latter were important, but could not determine developments, whereas, at least in this crisis, the Commons and the City had done so. That underlined the assumptions

---

[31] Edward Harley, parliamentary diary, Feb. 1746, Cambridge, University Library, fol. 101.

[32] Henry to Stephen Fox, 13 Feb. (os) 1746, BL. Add. 51417 fols 213–14.

[33] Poyntz to Trevor, 9 Jan. (os) 1745, Aylesbury, Buckinghamshire CRO, Trevor papers, vol. 45.

[34] Instructions for Fournier, Director of the Tobacco 'farm' [farmed tax], sent to London to sound British on possibility of peace, 18 Apr. 1745, AE. CP. Ang. 421 fol. 15; *Old England*, 27 Apr. (os) 1745; Vernon to Sir Francis Dashwood, 29 July (os) 1749, Bod. MS. D.D. Dashwood B11/12/6.

of most commentators, including foreign ones, about the nature of the British political system.

The failure, both of the Jacobite '45 and of the attempt to restore Granville, ensured that the Pelhams had a largely clean slate. Moreover, Harrington's willingness to back Granville eventually provided them with an opportunity to bring in a new Secretary of State; although Harrington's opposition to Newcastle's determination to continue the war appears to have been the key factor.[35] Institutional and personal politics played a role. Harrington objected to Newcastle pursuing a secret correspondence with John, 4th Earl of Sandwich, the envoy sent to represent Britain in the peace talks, who was in Harrington's department, as Northern Secretary. Such divisions between the Northern and Southern Secretaries were common, indeed repeatedly a serious institutional flaw with the organisation and implementation of foreign policy, and a key aspect of its politics at ministerial level. George did not try to keep Harrington in office, but significantly subsequently promoted him in the army.

As a successful former envoy in The Hague (1728–32), Philip, 4th Earl of Chesterfield offered much as Secretary of State for the Northern Department, not least because of the determination to strengthen Dutch adherence to the alliance. Moreover, unlike Harrington, whom he replaced on 19 October (os) 1746, Chesterfield was an active, as well as skilled, debater in the Lords. As a result, he strengthened the ministerial side there, providing valuable support for Newcastle, a somewhat muddled speaker, while weakening the opposition side by his departure.

In addition, the recruitment of Chesterfield broadened the Pelhams' alliance with the former opposition Whigs, at the same time that there was no longer a pact between the latter and Carteret and Pulteney. A sceptical Tucker had suggested in January 1745: 'the Pelhams seem only to have taken in the Opposition to walk over their backs to the Closet again but the path is reckoned so slippery that they will fall by the way'.[36] In fact, the Pelhams had eventually succeeded in winning royal acceptance. The Closet referred to the room where the King saw his ministers for confidential discussions, and thus to royal confidence. The well-accepted significance of the Closet underlined the continued role of the monarch, and also of personal links as opposed to institutional practice, and, linked to this, of conversation rather than correspondence.

---

[35]   Giuseppe Ossorio, Sardinian envoy to London, to Charles Emmanuel III, 28 Oct. 8, 11 Nov. 1746, AST. LM. Ing. 52.

[36]   John to Richard Tucker, 22 Jan. (os) 1745, Bod. Ms. Don. C. 107 fol. 77.

Having consolidated power in Britain in this fashion, the Pelhams used it to try to regain control of the situation in Europe, reviving and directing the alliance against France, and providing a strong British and British-financed military commitment in the Low Countries.[37] This attempt, however, was to be defeated by France and, in a related but separate fashion, to be totally derailed by the weakness and divisions of the alliance, each factor interacting with the other. A caustic Richard Rolt was to argue that the Pelhams adopted the policies they had rejected when advanced by Carteret.[38] Yet there was an important difference, and not only in tone. In terms of British politics, the emphasis by the Pelhams, not on protecting Hanover, but on an alliance designed to defend the Low Countries, proved a winning formula. The former Whig opposition was now totally fragmented. As a clear indication of a support for Continental interventionism, Bedford, Gower and Sandwich had already made clear their opposition to a 'war merely naval' when, on 21 November (os) 1745, Pitt had moved in Parliament for the strengthening of the navy.[39] There was opposition to continuing to pay Hanoverian troops,[40] but the 'New Allies' were prepared to vote for the Hanoverian troops in April and May 1746, a marked reversal on their earlier position.

Indeed, the degree of political support for the government's strategy facilitated a successful response to the onerous burdens of foreign policy, notably the costs of war and foreign subsidies. These costs were seen as a factor in the politics of domestic support. Trevor observed in March 1746: 'What will, I fear, render this land war unpopular in England, and consequently impracticable, is our allies presumption upon our opulence; and expecting to be paid, and prayed for fighting their own quarrels.'[41] Henry Fox, a Lord of the Treasury, explained to his brother in April: 'the first misfortune is the want of money, no more can be raised this year'.[42] Nevertheless, the war was continued, even though the financial situation underlined a fundamental question about the long-term viability of the policy; and did so on a regular basis.

So also with the problems posed by Britain's allies. Fielding wrote, in the *True Patriot* on 27 May (os) 1746:

---

[37]   Newcastle to Cumberland, 7 Apr. (os) 1746, NA. SP. 54/30 fol. 122.

[38]   R. Rolt, *The Conduct of the Several Powers of Europe engaged in the late General War* (4 vols, London, 1749–50), IV, 242.

[39]   Henry Fox to William, Lord Hartington, 28 Nov. (os) 1745, Chatsworth, Devonshire papers, 330.1.

[40]   Edward Harley, parliamentary diary, Cambridge University Library, fol. 92.

[41]   Trevor to Robinson, 26 Mar. 1746, BL. Add. 23822 fol. 245.

[42]   Henry to Stephen Fox, 2 Apr. (os) 1746, BL. Add. 51417 fol. 234.

> Whoever attends to public conversation, which is the only way to know the
> general sense of mankind as to particular points, cannot but be thoroughly
> satisfied that there is nothing more commonly the object of amazement and
> distaste than the present conduct of the Dutch.

The impact of this view was clear from ministerial correspondence. Harrington had already instructed Robert Trevor to get the Dutch to declare war on France: 'which is by all ranks of people most strongly insisted on here'.[43] Fox linked this issue and news from abroad with the parliamentary situation: 'The Dutch, who very much wanted peace, will promise nothing, so that the debate will be opened under all possible disadvantages.'[44] Indeed, it was reported that the problems of relations with the Dutch had played a role in the ministerial crisis,[45] a rumour that reflected the wartime sensitivity of the state of Britain's alliances.

The issues posed by allies were increased because of failures in campaigning, notably defeat at French hands at Roucoux on 11 October 1746, the battle fought that year in the Low Countries. Now returned to the Continent from Scotland, Cumberland lacked manpower comparable to his French opponents, and was part of a coalition that found it difficult in the Low Countries to grasp the initiative, to respond adequately to French advances, or, indeed, to co-operate in strategic terms. In turn, in Britain, the opposition sought to exploit repeated British military failure by implying maladroit or malevolent political intervention, and/or a pattern of poor appointments to military posts because of corruption and party interest.

Britain was not alone in having problems with allies. So also did the competing alliance system.[46] However, the resulting public discussion was more difficult politically in Britain than in the other powers on either side (bar the United Provinces), both because it was public in Britain and due to the nature of the political situation there. Moreover, the Dutch were not the sole problem for Britain among her allies. There were also grave concerns about the bitter and

---

[43]   Harrington to Trevor, 3 Jan. (os) 1746, NA. SP. 84/416 fol. 40.

[44]   Henry to Stephen Fox, 2 Apr. (os) 1746, BL. Add. 51417 fol. 235.

[45]   John to Richard Tucker, 3 Apr. (os) 1746, Bod. Ms. Don. C. 108 fol. 5.

[46]   Bishop of Rennes, French envoy in Spain, to Argenson, French Foreign Minister, 17 Jan. 1746, AE. CP. Espagne 488 fol. 909; Renaud, French envoy in Munich, to Puysieulx, French Foreign Minister, 1 May 1748, AE. CP. Bavière 129 fol. 4; re Prussia and Spain, Champeaux to Rouillé, French Foreign Minister, 16 Apr. 1755, AE. CP. Ang. 438 fols 413–14.

longstanding disputes between Austria and Sardinia, disputes that hampered the war effort in southern Europe.[47]

The deficiencies of alliance politics affected both British foreign policy and domestic opinion. In particular, peace negotiations and the rumour of such negotiation, which became more persistent from early 1746, opened up the possibilities of change within the British alliance system, and led to discussion accordingly, both domestically and abroad. However, in March 1746, the British government rejected a French project for a peace settlement that made no mention of the Hanoverian Succession and that demanded the return of Cape Breton to France. The French were also aware that support for the Jacobites would compromise them with the Dutch and with Frederick II who appeared a possible intermediary. The issue was sensitive with Protestant powers.

A second French peace project, which again demanded this return, but provided for the Hanoverian Succession, was rejected on 31 May (os). This was after the views of George, Newcastle, Bedford and Hardwicke, in opposition to the project, overcame those of Harrington and Pelham, in support of it, and that despite Harrington's warning that the Dutch might otherwise support a separate peace. On the pattern of the negotiations leading to the Peace of Utrecht signed in 1713, Anglo–French–Dutch negotiations finally began at Breda in late 1746 and lasted until the following March. As was generally the case, these negotiations provided an opportunity not only to resolve differences between competing alliances, but also to exploit those within them. In October 1746, Puysieulx, the French plenipotentiary at Breda, wrote to d'Argenson, whom he was soon to replace as Foreign Minister, to discuss the possibility of dividing the hostile alliance.[48]

The negotiations also reflected hopes about the course of the campaigning, notably the consequences of the Austrian invasion of Provence on 30 November 1746, an invasion encouraged by the British and supported by the Royal Navy. The invasion was in part mounted to divert French efforts from the Low Countries. George told Ossorio that the invasion would enable the dictation of peace terms to France.[49] However, both sides encountered supply problems in the winter campaign and the Austrians were distracted by a rising in their rear in Genoa. The French successfully counter-attacked on 21 January 1747, and by 3 February the invaders had recrossed the Var.

---

[47]   Sandwich to Robinson, 23 Feb. 1747, BL. Add. 23824 fols 147–8.
[48]   AE. CP. Hollande 402 fol. 22.
[49]   Ossorio to Charles Emmanuel III, 17 Jan. 1747, AST. LM. Ing. 53

Colonial hostilities with France were restricted largely to the capture of the French fortress on Louisbourg on Cape Breton Island in 1745 by New England militia supported by British warships, and to the loss of the British East India Company's trading station at Madras (Chennai) in 1746. Louisbourg threatened the British position in the western Atlantic and on the North Atlantic seaboard, and acted as an important stopping point from France en route to the French West Indies. Moreover, it was seen as a protection for the entrance to the St Lawrence valley, the centre of French Canada. Well-fortified and at great cost, Louisbourg was designed to resist attack from the sea, and was more vulnerable by land, while the morale of the garrison was low. In April 1745, as Commodore Peter Warren blockaded the harbour, the New England militia landed nearby. The attackers then bombarded the land defences, and Warren's blockade reduced the food available to the defenders. With the walls breached and Warren able to force his way into the harbour, the governor capitulated in June. In celebration, the guns were fired in London.

The capture of Louisbourg complicated the idea of peace with France and spawned ambitious plans for further British campaigns against Canada in 1746 and, to a lesser extent, 1747. These plans anticipated a far greater commitment of British resources to North America than had been seen in 1745. Hopes were high of imperial expansion, with extensive and bold discussion in the press, as well as planning by ministers and the military. Bedford, the First Lord of the Admiralty and a determined supporter of the retention of Cape Breton, was the principal advocate of a campaign against Canada in 1746, and Pitt was a supporter. The acceptance of this project owed much to Newcastle's determination to win over the 'New Allies' against Granville, a determination that was on the pattern of his policy of wooing opponents in 1739 and, even more, 1742 by heeding their foreign policy demands. The campaign, which the Cabinet agreed to on 3 April (os) 1746, was the return for the 'New Allies' support for a continuation of the war on the Continent: it helped the British effort seem 'national'.[50] Unlike in 1739–41, when Britain was only at war with Spain, these hopes now centred on Canada, not the Caribbean. Such schemes showed not only an ability to adapt to circumstances, both diplomatic and strategic, but also the determination of British imperial protagonists to find something with which to justify their hopes. Their urgency was strong because it was argued that imperial expansion

---

[50]   Vincent, French agent, to Puysieulx, 5 Mar. 1747, AE. CP. Ang. 423 fols 86–7; A.H. Buffington, 'The Canada Expedition of 1746: Its Relation to British politics', *American Historical Review*, 45 (1939–40), pp. 552–80, a more generally significant piece; K. Hotblack, *Chatham's Colonial Policy* (London, 1917), pp. 44–6.

was an answer to domestic problems, and because it was thought that the war could not continue for too long.

However, the government was made cautious in 1746 by the continued Jacobite threat, as well as the experience of failure in 1711 (against Quebec) and 1741 (against Cartagena),[51] while Newcastle expressed concern that success against France would make the war last longer as the French would not wish to accept the loss. Moreover, he was rightly worried that the Dutch would be opposed to continuing a war that they would see as fought for British colonial gains. Indeed, tensions between the two powers had been to the fore when the Dutch had refused to co-operate with, let alone support, Britain against Spain in 1739. In late 1745, the Dutch backed a peace plan that included the return of Cape Breton to France. In turn, in January 1747, the British government rejected the Dutch demand for the return, thus helping wreck the peace talks at Breda.[52] Adverse winds were the official explanation for the failure to launch a new attack on Canada. In practice, there was a range of factors. The inability to defeat the French fleet until two battles were won off Cape Finisterre in 1747 was significant, as it led to concerns in 1746 about the security of Scotland, Ireland, Nova Scotia and Newfoundland. In fact, the French attempt to regain Louisbourg failed in 1746, with the fleet sent hit hard by disease and shipwreck. There was also a clear political dimension. Cumberland's opposition to the Canada project, which distracted from the war on the Continent, was important, as was Newcastle's wish to win his support, and Hardwicke's concern about the possibility of a French invasion of Scotland.

As yet, as a result of the failure to attack Canada as Bedford wanted, global expansion was an aspiration rather than a reality; albeit with the important exception of Louisbourg, which, thereby, became politically sensitive. Indeed, Haslang, a perceptive diplomat, saw its return as a major difficulty affecting any peace plan because the 'nation' would be against such a step.[53] This issue prefigured the situation in 1755 when the government's options in negotiations with France were greatly affected both by ministerial differences and by the pressure of public opinion.

---

[51]   Hardwicke to Newcastle, 2 Apr. (os) 1746, BL. Add. 32707 fol. 5.

[52]   Newcastle to Hardwicke, 2 Apr. (os) 1746, BL. Add. 35408 fols 220–1. For more general issues, R. Pares, 'American versus Continental Warfare, 1739–1763', *English Historical Review*, 51 (1936), pp. 429–65, and N.A.M. Rodger, 'The Continental Commitment in the Eighteenth Century', in L. Friedman, P. Hayes and R. O'Neill (eds), *War, Strategy and International Politics* (Oxford, 1992), pp. 39–55.

[53]   Haslang to Preysing, 11 Feb. 1746, Munich, Bayr. Ges., London 217.

Chapter 5

A Failing Alliance System, 1747–8

The high hopes of 1746, the sense of a recovery from acute crisis and a new beginning brimming with attractive possibilities, could not be sustained. The pressure of events was a key and repeated friction, but so also were two more structural factors. First, for both foreign policy and British discussion thereon, there was the inherent assumption–realisation dichotomy that arose as hopes were raised and then dashed. This was very much apparent with the total and unexpected failure to realise the high expectations placed on the results of an Orangist revival in the United Provinces, which, indeed, occurred in 1747.

Second, and on occasion linked to the first factor, there was the more serious problem for all powers of sustaining and managing alliances. This problem was accentuated in wartime because it was then that the requirement for co-operation and action was most pressing. Moreover, strategy ceased to be abstract and became a matter of immediate issues of prioritisation and resource commitment. Partly for this reason, the distinction frequently made in modern discussion of strategy between strategy and policy is not really helpful. The policy of alliances was frequently no more than declarations of intent, and some alliances were devices of convenience and expediency rather than a true unity of purpose. In addition, powers in alliances often made incompatible promises to their various allies. In contrast, the wartime emphasis on strategy made it necessary for allies to address these incompatibilities and to make, and then to implement, policy choices. In this context, the same individuals were responsible for strategy, policy, and the defence of policy, which underlines the mistake, or at least difficulty, of differentiating them. Looked at differently, during wartime, strategy crowded out policy, and notably so when the war went badly. To an extent this was the situation for Britain and the other powers, whether allies, opponents or neutrals, during 1747 and 1748.

Nevertheless, it would be misleading to ignore the extent to which, for all powers, wartime combinations and calculations were increasingly matched by the consideration of the post-war order, consideration which was an aspect of both policy and strategy and, to a degree, a goal of both. This consideration ensured that manoeuvring for advantage and position was significant for all of the powers. The Wars of the Spanish (1701–14) and Polish (1733–5) Succession had each led to dramatic new alignments, between Britain and France, and between Austria and France, respectively. There was no reason to believe that the same would not be the case anew. Indeed, the War of the Austrian Succession was to be followed, although not immediately, by rapprochement between Austria and Spain, and, later, between Austria and France. Moreover, a new alignment between Britain and Spain had appeared a prospect even before the war ended, and was sought by the British ministry.

For Britain, unlike most European states, there was the political difficulty that any major change would need to be explained and defended in Parliament and debated in print. Linked to this need came the reiteration of themes about the nature of politics. These themes were no less potent through being well-ventilated, indeed providing a prime topic for political commentary, one that was more urgent because it was wartime. The interplay of ideas and interests, and of top-down and bottom-up views of politics, was seen in a pamphlet of 1747:

> the People are volatile and unthinking; easily prejudiced against their real friends and genuine interest. The pulpit and press have had infinite sway among them, and have often preached and wrote them out of their wits, and from their duty; and pro tempore [for a while] from their interest. But this [their interest] has, in the main, such hold of their minds, that it will warp them sooner or later, from their errors and prejudices.[1]

Domestic politics were a concern as ministers considered how far, by strengthening the alliance system with Austria and the Dutch, they could both bring the war to a close, and begin the post-war world. Ministers had to evaluate how far these processes required reaching out to other powers as well. Both Spain and Prussia in particular were assessed as potential helps to peace and as possible post-war allies for Britain. Bridging, and complicating, these two options was the idea that other powers could be recruited to strengthen the alliance system. However, although clear in concept, these speculations posed major problems. The views of existing allies, notably Austria and Sardinia, had to be considered, and, linked to this, Britain's hopes from these allies. It was also necessary to assess the likely consequences in terms of the political debate over foreign policy within Britain, and in a variety of milieux from George II's 'Closet' to the public sphere.

---

[1]   Anon., *An Apology for the Conduct of a Late Celebrated Second-rate Minister* (London, 1747).

The possibility that the latter would become more complex, and the ministry less stable, rose markedly in 1747 when the restless Frederick, Prince of Wales went into opposition to his father's ministers and, thus, to his father. This decision was troublesome for the government for both historical and prospective reasons. The historical challenge was clear. George II's opposition while Prince of Wales had greatly exacerbated the political problems created by the Whig Split of 1717–20. Moreover, Frederick's previous opposition from 1737 had not only infuriated George II but also destabilised the Walpole ministry, both within the Whig élite and electorally. This was especially so in Cornwall, the county that, because of its unmatched number of parliamentary boroughs, was most over-represented in Parliament and one where Frederick had influence because he was Duke of Cornwall as well as Prince of Wales. Frederick's opposition had proved highly significant in the 1741 election, and the changing parliamentary arithmetic stemming from these results helped lead to Walpole's fall in 1742, after which Frederick had ended his opposition.

The prospective challenge therefore was clear. Under the Septennial Act, the next election had to be held at the latest in 1748. So far all the Parliaments under the Act, passed in 1716 in order to strengthen the Whig ministry by replacing the need, under the Triennial Act of 1694, to face more frequent elections, had fulfilled their full seven-year term, with the exception of that in 1727, which had to be held then under the Act in order for a new monarch to have a new Parliament. Holding an election in 1748 would give Frederick and his supporters opportunities to win additional backing. The supporters were a motley group of opposition Whigs, among whom George Bubb Dodington, a talented former diplomat and minister, and John, 2nd Earl of Egmont were the most prominent. However, there was the possibility of more backing from among Whigs critical of the Pelhams.

The views of the heir were of particular importance, and were certainly of interest to foreign envoys. Although, like his father in his last years, fit and well, George II had been born in 1683 and was therefore old by the standards of the age. Indeed, even if he lived as long as his long-lived father, George I (1660–1727), he would scarcely complete more than two sessions of a new Parliament. Frederick thus appeared the rising star, which meant that ambitious politicians and foreign diplomats needed to consider how best to secure, or appear to secure, his favour.

Moreover, while the ministry included Newcastle, a master of patronage, as well as Pelham, who directed the Treasury, there was a sense that it might be less adroit electorally than that of Walpole. The very process of the opposition in the 1720s and 1730s building Walpole up as a master of corruption and manipulation had the consequence that his successors did not appear so adroit, which was indeed the case. In addition, if the able and highly experienced Walpole had failed with the 1741 election, the fourth election he had sought to direct, it was questionable whether his inexperienced successors would do any better in 1748, their first.

This situation helps explain why the ministry decided to go early, gain the initiative, and hold the election in 1747. This was an unprecedented and unexpected, but entirely legal, step. Parliament was dissolved on 18 June (os), a day after the end of the session. Despite the opposition having a good case about the intractable and costly nature of the Continental commitment,[2] this move totally wrong-footed them, and notably the group round Frederick. It had not as yet built up the necessary political alliances, nor worked at rifts within the ministry, as the much longer-established opposition had successfully done in 1741.

Partly as a result, the ministry won a convincing verdict in the general election of 1747, as well as a far more successful result than that in 1741. After the 1747 election, there were 338 ministerial supporters, 97 opposition Whigs and 117 Tories; with six seats unfilled due to double returns, where someone is elected to more than one seat. Its supporters could, and did, argue that the ministry was backed not only by both Houses of Parliament, but also by the 'vast majority' of the electorate, at least as measured by the results.[3] Elections provided a clear sign of this which other states lacked. In the *Jacobite's Journal* of 26 December (os) 1747, Fielding contrasted the government favourably with the Carteret ministry of 1742–4:

> We have an Administration not consisting of one absolute Prime Minister, supported only by his tools and dependants, and obnoxious to the Great Men in the Nation; but an Administration composed really of all the Great Men, whose abilities of any kind make them worthy of any place in it; supported by both Houses of Parliament, and, as appears by the last election, by a vast majority of the whole realm.

This concept of the 'Great Men', and of their necessary significance, is instructive for the political and social assumptions of the period. It looks toward the emphasis on the greater Whig lords, notably the Rockinghamite Whigs, in

---

2   Anon., *Cry Aloud and Spare Not; or, Plain useful Facts and Remarks, as a Preparative to the present, sudden and General Election. Addressed to the Worthy Independent Electors of Westminster* (London, 1747).

3   Fielding, *Jacobite's Journal*, 26 Dec. (os) 1747.

the opposition to George III. The election result and the attendant demoralisation of the opposition, both that under Frederick and the Tories, ensured that the ministry enjoyed a strong position in Parliament. As a consequence, the ministry was able to hold off any serious challenge over the peace negotiated in 1748. That is an approach to the timing of the election based on domestic considerations and one that can be readily advanced.

It is, however, also appropriate to consider foreign policy and military developments more directly when assessing this timing. In 1747, the ministry was faced by grave strains within Britain's alliance system, as well as by major and repeated French military successes in the Low Countries, and by the prospect of yet more soon. The two problems were closely linked in a dangerous dynamic. Both the United Provinces and Austria were making formidable efforts and the prospect of fighting on without success was very unwelcome for them as it was for Britain. French successes increased the strain in the alliance system, not least by sapping support for the war in the United Provinces and by encouraging the Austrians to make efforts and seek gains elsewhere. In turn these trends, which magnified the political consequences of French success, weakened military resistance to the French in the Low Countries, and made its continuation an issue. In an attempt to strengthen Dutch commitment, George supported the restoration of Orangist control in the key Dutch provinces of Holland and Zealand, a measure in which the threat of force played a role in overthrowing anti-Orangist provincial governments. This was linked to the formal declaration of war on France by the Dutch, a step sought by Britain since it had declared war in 1744. In 1747, George took an assertive line and was happy to maintain a squadron of warships in Dutch waters, even against the advice of the Admiralty.

Failure against the French made it more likely that any peace would entail politically problematic compromises, for Britain as for its allies. Indeed, one pamphleteer suggested that the ministry wished to guard against the threat of impeachment for negotiating a pusillanimous treaty.[4] There is no evidence to support this claim, but it captures the sense of a close relationship between foreign policy and politics. The likelihood that Britain would have to return Louisbourg (which was interchangeably used in Britain in discussion with Cape Breton) was increasingly sensitive politically as public opinion came to focus on its retention, on the prospects which it apparently offered and on the alleged politics of the issue.[5]

---

[4]   *A Letter from a Travelling Tutor … containing Good Advice to the Independent Electors of Great Britain* (London, 1747), pp. 22–4.

[5]   Ossorio to Charles Emmanuel III, 12 Aug., 11 Nov. 1746, AST. LM. Ing. 52.

John, 4th Earl of Sandwich was then a diplomat, but he was also a borough patron at Huntington, which returned two MPs, as well as a key member of the Bedford group of 'New Allies'. These were former opposition Whigs, among whom John, 4th Duke of Bedford was most prominent, who were now in government. As such, Sandwich's advice to Newcastle, however unwelcome to the more experienced and older figure, was politically relevant. Indeed, Sandwich was a prime instance of the overlap of diplomacy, policy and politics, an overlap that was to be greatly lessened by the institutionalisation of diplomacy in the nineteenth century. This overlap was highly significant as a means of registering political pressures in foreign policy, and vice versa. Sandwich felt able to comment both on public opinion and upon the likely plans of the opposition. Arguing that the retention of Cape Breton by Britain was very important, he wrote:

> I believe the generality of our nation think they see the value of it on their side; and are ready to continue the war for the defence of it, or to express their rage and resentment in the strongest terms if it is given up. All opposition in Parliament seems to be attentive to that point, their writings, as well as the language of their leaders from the first to the last sufficiently show that it is there they intend to form their attack because it is upon that question that they are sure of having the people on their side.

Sandwich thought there would be less fuss if Gibraltar was ceded to Spain.[6] However, George II disapproved of such a step, while Newcastle, referring to the popular view, but also drawing on his long experience of sensitivities over the issue, notably in the 1720s, had already argued that Gibraltar and Minorca should be retained: 'How shall you and I pass our time, who are known to be so much for the trade and commerce, and maritime interests of this country, if we give up, upon any account, our maritime possessions, in the Mediterranean.'[7] Newcastle's reference to the Mediterranean is instructive because this aspect of maritime policy was to be superseded by concern about North America. A willingness to cede Gibraltar was also the case for Bedford, who preferred to retain Cape Breton, and for Chesterfield who very much wanted peace;[8] but, as Ossorio correctly noted, no ministry would dare to do so,[9] because of the likely public response. The idea was to recur in 1756, being raised by Fox in

---

6   Sandwich to Newcastle, 24 Mar. 1747, BL. Add. 32807 fol. 221.
7   Newcastle to Sandwich, 10 Feb. (os) 1747, BL. Add. 32807 fol. 90.
8   Ossorio to Leopoldo Del Carretto di Gorzegno, Sardinian Foreign Minister, 18 Apr. 1747, AST. LM. Ing. 53; Anon., *An Apology for a Late Resignation* (London, 1748).
9   Ossorio to Chavanne, 14 Apr. 1747, AST. LM. Ing. 53.

the aftermath of the loss of Minorca to French attack and when considering how best, in the absence of military success, to regain that island. This issue underlined the extent to which military failure brought up unwelcome questions of prioritisation, as, in a different context, did its diplomatic counterpart. The resolution of such prioritisation could be postponed until decisions had to be reached, as in peace negotiations. However, such postponement made the latter more problematic because, in the meanwhile, issues had been raised in debate.

Sandwich was convinced that the administration must stand on the foundation of 'popularity'.[10] This certainly made sense of the position of the 'New Allies'. If, in contrast, a reliance on popularity did not capture the reality of 'Old Corps' Whig political practice, nor the assumptions raised by Fielding in the *Jacobite's Journal*, Newcastle, nevertheless, wanted to win elections. In 1747, therefore, the diplomatic and military situation, as well as likely political developments, made an early election attractive, rather than one held in the shadow of unwelcome news from abroad.

Each approach to explaining why the election was held early can be argued, and with support from contemporary sources. This serves as a reminder, in discussing political influence and assessing causation, that it is crucial to look across the range of often very different sources, rather than, as in some accounts, adopting a clear interpretative account and looking for sources accordingly. Another conclusion from this point, a conclusion valid for other episodes, is that when the surviving sources clearly point toward one explanation, this may be because contrary sources have not survived. In this light, the extent to which ministers did not keep diaries is important. Moreover, whereas for some ministers, notably Newcastle, there is important and extensive surviving private correspondence, both letters to him and those from him, this is not the case for all, and particularly for Granville and Harrington. In addition, it is necessary to remember that the revelatory nature of private correspondence was of less significance for contemporaries than its use as a tool of persuasion.

For 1747, the key element was that both the domestic and the international dynamic were in accord in making an early election attractive. Thus, the factors encouraging an early election were cumulative, not alternative, a situation that indeed reflected the desired one for government activity. This situation encouraged the looking for supporting arguments.

Having won the election, the ministry found that Britain's international position deteriorated more than had been anticipated. This was true of the campaigning itself, with Britain and her allies defeated in the Austrian

---

[10]   Sandwich to Bedford, 29 Aug. 1747, BL. Add. 32809 fol. 210.

Netherlands at Lawfeldt on 2 July 1747, the major battle of that year. The French capture of Bergen-op-Zoom later in the year, a siege of this major Dutch fortress brought to a close by a surprise storming, led to increased pressure for peace in the Cabinet,[11] as well as affecting Dutch opinion. This deterioration in Britain's position was also apparent with the lack of commitment shown by Austria to Britain's idea of how best to conduct the war. In March 1747, Ossorio had commented that, although the government stood firm against a torrent of criticism, it said it would have to yield if Britain's allies did not do their bit.[12]

As a consequence, success in the 1747 general election did not suffice for the government. Instead, amidst general uncertainty,[13] foreign policy threatened to spin out of control in 1748. It could not deliver the desired outcomes. In addition, alternative goals and policies were offered from within the ministry and the diplomatic corps. This situation left ministers, diplomats and commentators unclear what options could, and would, be followed. Moreover, the uneasiness of ministers about the views of George II increased. This uneasiness had slackened after the total failure of Carteret/Granville's return to office in February 1746, but it revived, albeit in a more diffuse fashion. A new source of political instability had been created by defeat and failure, one very different to that posed in 1747 by Frederick, the opposition, and the prospect of new elections. Instead, in 1748, the multiple, but uncertain, problems of foreign policy and of military developments encouraged interest in peace. Newcastle reflected: 'the months of March, April, and May, are those I most fear. Then, I apprehend, will be the danger of an attempt, either on Breda or Maastricht, or perhaps on both' of those Dutch frontier fortresses.[14]

Interest in peace threw up questions about how Britain's interests were to be advanced. These questions involved prioritisation, and that led both to issues for individual ministers and to the attribution of policies to particular groups. The need for foreign powers to understand how policy would be pursued made this process especially significant for them. The juxtaposition of Crown and nation was a particular theme in understanding British policy. This theme drew on the longstanding critique of Hanoverian interests. Thus, in June 1748, François de Bussy, formerly an envoy in London (as well as being, code-named '101', a longstanding secret agent for Britain), in a memorandum designed to instruct a new French envoy, remarked that the 'North' of Europe was of concern for the particular interests of George and his family, but the 'South' more so for

11　Ossorio to Charles Emmanuel III, 29 Dec. 1747, AST. LM. Ing. 53.
12　Ossorio to Gorzegno, 3 Mar. 1747, AST. LM. Ing. 53.
13　Robinson to Fawkener, 27 Dec. 1747, RA. Cumb. P. 30/241.
14　Newcastle to Sandwich, 29 Dec. (os) 1747, BL. Add. 32810 fol. 425.

the 'nation'.[15] Thus Bussy, who had accompanied George to Hanover in 1741, a time when the prospect of French invasion of the Electorate had greatly affected George's policy, and, allegedly, that of the British government, saw Hanoverian concerns as a key element.

British interests and anxieties were also expressed in terms of relations with other powers. In assessing these interests and their consequences, Britain was greatly affected by rivalries between allies, notably between Austria and Sardinia. These rivalries threatened to cause volatility, making it difficult to continue the wartime alliance into the subsequent peace. In addition, there was concern that the breakdown of the wartime alliance would create possibilities for France, as had happened in 1713. This was not only a view held in London. Aware of Anglo-Austrian tensions, which were considerable on both parts, Frederick II regarded it as likely that Austria would seek to improve relations with France[16] as had been attempted after the Wars of the Spanish and Polish Successions.

Although William Murray, the Solicitor General, a prominent parliamentary speaker for the ministry, in the Commons on 29 January (os) 1748, referred to the 'nature of the peace we want, which must be such as would not break the present alliance, without which no peace could be lasting',[17] there was the sense of new, or newly-revived, possibilities for Britain. These possibilities opened up divisions over policy, as well as debate over how it was being formulated. Key new possibilities were understandings with Spain, France and Prussia; and each was to be explored. Bilateral negotiations with Spain in 1747–8 focused on differences over an establishment for Don Philip in Italy, and over Spanish pressure for the return of Gibraltar and Minorca by Britain. Newcastle refused to yield over the latter.[18]

Relations with Prussia, however, as on earlier occasions, opened up significant differences over the role of George II. Horatio Walpole, a veteran former diplomat and younger brother of Sir Robert, pressed the case for an understanding with Frederick, arguing that fears of him were imaginary and that opportunities for better relations had not been pursued.[19] This was a criticism of the impact of George's views, one in part shared by Chesterfield who unsuccessfully pressed George to send an envoy to Berlin.[20]

---

[15] Bussy, memorandum, June 1748, AE. MD. Ang. 40 fol. 142.

[16] *Polit. Corr.* VI, 130–3.

[17] Dudley Ryder, diary, Sandon, Ryder papers 25 R247.

[18] S. Conn., *Gibraltar in British Diplomacy in the Eighteenth Century* (New Haven, Connecticut, 1942), pp. 145–58.

[19] Walpole to Newcastle, 28 Dec. (os) 1747, BL. Add. 9147, fol. 14.

[20] HMC. *Polwarth*, V, p. 255.

Walpole's intervention, in pursuit of a policy he had already energetically pressed for in the late 1730s and 1740, was instructive as he had no formal responsibility in the field of foreign policy. However, he felt able to discuss an approach to Frederick, both with Cumberland and with those 'in the greatest intimacy and confidence' with Newcastle, in order to advance his proposition that such an approach offered the best means to negotiate peace.[21] Horatio Walpole's role reflected the porous character of the decision-making process, and therefore its overlap with politics within the Whig élite. The small size of the foreign policy bureaucracy increased the influence of outsiders able to suggest policies. That Cumberland revised a memorandum on peace with Spain,[22] was critical of the Dutch failure to act in support of Britain, and read and commented on diplomatic correspondence,[23] indicated his significance. His sensitivities were believed to be a factor in the discussion of the war in the royal speech to Parliament opening the session.[24] Moreover, Cumberland was believed to be influential with Newcastle, who was pleased to note the Duke's 'great approbation' when he proposed Henry Legge as envoy to Berlin.[25] Thus, those discussing policy constituted a group larger than those formally responsible. This was important to the broader politics of policy.

At the same time, Walpole, although regarded as close to Pelham,[26] was outside the core group of ministers. In November 1747, it was Cumberland, Newcastle, Hardwicke, Chesterfield and Pelham who discussed increasing the size of the force to be deployed in the Low Countries. The following February, George wanted a memorandum by William IV of Orange shown to Cumberland, Newcastle, Hardwicke, Bedford and Pelham,[27] the change due to the new Secretary of State. In April 1748, Newcastle communicated the memorandum of a conversation with the Austrian and Saxon envoys to Hardwicke, Bedford, Pelham, Dorset (Lord President of the Council), Gower (Lord Privy Seal), and Grafton (Lord Chamberlain), and, after they approved, orders were accordingly sent to Cumberland and Sandwich. Another letter sent by Newcastle to

---

[21]   Walpole to Newcastle, 28 Dec. (os) 1747, BL. Add. 9147 fol. 15.

[22]   Memorandum submitted to Cumberland, 31 Dec. (os) 1747 and revisions, RA. Cumb. P. 30/346–8.

[23]   Cumberland to Sandwich, 29 Dec. (os) 1747, RA. Cumb. P. 30/335.

[24]   Ossorio to Charles Emmanuel III, 23 Jan. 1748, AST. LM. Ing. 54.

[25]   William Bentinck to Newcastle, 2 Jan. 1748, C. Gerretson and P. Geyl (eds), *Briefwisseling en Aanteekeningen van Willem Bentinck* (Utrecht, 1934), p. 344; Newcastle to Sandwich, 19 Jan. (os) 1748, BL. Add. 32811 fol. 87.

[26]   Gisors, *Journal of Visit to England*, 8 Mar. 1754, AE. MD. Ang. 1 fol. 73.

[27]   Newcastle to Sandwich, 17 Nov. (os) 1747, BL. Add. 32810 fol. 286; Newcastle to Cumberland, 25 Feb. (os) 1748, RA. Cumb. P. 32/113.

Sandwich was endorsed as having been communicated to, and approved by, Hardwicke, Bedford, Pelham and Dorset.[28] These were indeed 'Great Men', to adopt Fielding's formulation. They were socially as well as governmentally prominent. The aristocratic character of Whig government and of this specific ministry was very pronounced.

Long accustomed to George's stubbornness over relations with Prussia, Walpole argued that a mention of the argument would have little impact, and that therefore it was necessary to create a broader pressure for action: '[it] should be represented at large and may be done with equal duty and submission in a way that may afford time and leisure for the serious considerations'. Walpole claimed that Newcastle's clear support for the measure would influence the other ministers. He also emphasised the public impact: 'Your Grace [Newcastle] loved Popularity once, and if you are in earnest why not take the most effectual way to get it.' Walpole also argued that popularity could be won for the Crown by asking Parliament for its support. In offering this view on how Parliament could elicit backing for the Crown, Walpole added the warning that it posed a danger, for he suggested that, 'sooner or later', the matter would be 'stirred there', and, indeed, that the opposition was considering such a course.[29]

The public dimension was not only of interest to Walpole, a member of the Commons from 1710, with only brief interludes where he was not an MP, and a foreign policy expert aware of the varied consequences of Parliament's role. From The Hague, Sandwich also mentioned the danger of criticism:

> unless you clear up that matter, you will leave an opening to those who are not friends of the government to accuse you of having neglected a measure, which it is the universal opinion of people in England would have extricated us out of our difficulties.[30]

Indeed, Sandwich presented that issue, and, thereby, foreign policy as a way to transform politics. Emphasising the need to convince the public that the government had tried everything, Sandwich added:

> judge what a point this will be for an Opposition to work upon. That party is now at a low ebb, but a change of circumstances will change their condition; and with

---

[28] Memorandum, 7 Apr. (os), Newcastle to Sandwich, 19 Apr. (os) 1748, BL. Add. 32812 fols 31, 80.

[29] Walpole to Newcastle, 28 Dec. (os) 1747, BL. Add. 9147 fols 15–17.

[30] Sandwich to Newcastle, 5 Jan. 1748, BL. Add. 32810 fol. 411.

the successor to the throne at their head, and a supposed neglect of this nature to work up the spirit of the people they may soon again become formidable.[31]

Given the political difficulty of the Prussian option, notably with George, as well as distrust of Frederick,[32] it was not surprising that interest was shown, instead, in the possibility of peace with Spain, a goal also attributed to 'the difficulties they are now in more than ever – from the internal state, and management of their domestic concerns, which make them extremely uneasy'.[33] Britain's concern about allies was matched by France's impatience with Spain,[34] an indication of the problems posed by allies.

The reconsideration of Britain's position encouraged by failure in war and the prospect of peace therefore revealed the range of opinions available to the government. The latter underlined the number of stakeholders in policy and the extent to which they were far from equal. Correspondingly, this situation underlines the significance of the survival of documents. Private letters provide a crucial supplement to the official, institutional correspondence. The net effect in 1748 was a policy debate, volatility, and confusion under the pressure of a deteriorating military situation, that was the subject of comment by contemporaries, including foreign diplomats. They could emphasise different points in describing the situation, and that remains the case with scholarship today.

Debate was scarcely unique to Britain, but, in part as a result of it, Britain in 1748 appeared an unreliable ally. Ossorio was concerned that George's particular regard for Hanover, a regard that, he argued, increased its concern about Austria, as well as the government's preference for settling with Spain, would all lead to Sardinia being neglected.[35] Leaving aside such specific anxieties on the part of individual allies, there was a more general sense that British policy and Britain's alliance system were uncertain and adrift. Indeed, this perception captured the situation. There was an echo of the position in 1735 and 1741, in each of which the international context had become very threatening for British policy and hopes.

What is instructive is the weight placed upon George's views. There was a certainty that he sought gains for Hanover, notably neighbouring East Friesland,

---

[31]   Sandwich to Newcastle, 5 Jan. 1748, BL. Add. 32810 fol. 411.

[32]   R. Lodge, 'The mission of Henry Legge to Berlin, 1748', *Transactions of the Royal Historical Society*, series 4, 14 (1931), pp. 1–38.

[33]   Le Man, Spanish agent in London, to Duke of Huescar, 19 Jan. 1748, BL. Add. 32812 fol. 20.

[34]   Puysieulx to Richelieu, 4 Feb. 1748, AN. KK. 1372.

[35]   Ossorio to Charles Emmanuel III, 2 Jan. 1748, AST. LM. Ing. 54.

acquired by Frederick II in 1744, and/or compensation for his claims on it in the shape of the secularisation of neighbouring Wittelsbach prince-bishoprics, especially Hildesheim and Osnabrück, the latter of which alternated between a Hanoverian and a Catholic and, throughout this period, was in Catholic hands. At the same time, this policy could be rationalised by the Hanoverians in terms of trying to stop these bishoprics passing into hostile hands,[36] thus increasing Hanover's vulnerability. The ambiguities of this important issue were exposed by Baron Haslang, the longstanding Bavarian envoy. He noted that whereas George's fear of Prussia led to attempts to build up a restraining alliance system that would include German Catholic rulers, including Bavaria and the other Wittelsbachs, there were also plans to agree with Frederick over a secularisation plan that would benefit both him and George, but take territories from the Catholics.[37]

Concern about Hanoverian interests was regarded as a key element in broader British diplomatic relations, notably with Prussia and Austria.[38] Separately, there was an opinion that George and Newcastle wished to fight on with France, whereas most of the Council sought peace. This was the view of Bedford, and of Haslang, who was in touch with Chesterfield whom he presented as pro-Prussian.[39] Indeed, Chesterfield's resignation as Secretary of State on 6 February (os) 1748 was treated as a sign that the war would continue,[40] against the background of a shift in talk from peace to war.[41] In 1748, the King's backing for Newcastle was presented as crucial in overcoming Council support for peace, and this backing was seen as obtained via Newcastle approaching Cumberland. According to Ossorio, who had longstanding close relations with Newcastle as well as seeing Cumberland, Newcastle had also profited from rivalry between Cumberland and Chesterfield. At the same time, Ossorio reported his certainty that Newcastle would back peace if he could obtain the desired conditions.[42] Obtaining these conditions, and thus peace, was presented as a way to thwart

---

[36] Newcastle to William IV of Orange, 6 Jan. (os) 1748, T. Bussemaker (ed.), *Archives ou Correspondance Inédite de la Maison d'Orange-Nassau*, 4th ser. 1 (Leiden, 1908), pp. 537–9.

[37] Haslang to Preysing, 19 Jan. 1748, Munich, Bayr. Ges., London 220.

[38] Haslang to Preysing, 2, 12 Jan., Preysing to Haslang, 6 Jan. 1748, Munich, Bayr. Ges., London 220.

[39] Newcastle to Sandwich, 19 Jan. (os) 1748, BL. Add. 32811 fols 87–8; Haslang to Preysing, 2, 5, 12, 16, 19 Jan., 20, 23 Feb. 1748, Munich, Bayr. Ges., London 220; Ossorio to Charles Emmanuel III, 19 Jan. 1748, AST. LM. Ing. 54.

[40] Lagau, French agent in Hamburg, to Ministry of Marine, 11, 18 Mar. 1748, AN. AM. B⁷ 365.

[41] Haslang to Preysing, 30 Jan. 1748, Munich, Bayr. Ges., London 220.

[42] Ossorio to Charles Emmanuel III, 2 Feb. 1748, AST. LM. Ing. 54.

'the enemies of the government'.[43] Despite rumours that Pelham, who had criticised Austria in Parliament, would resign if Chesterfield did, there were no further ministerial departures at this point, and the rumours are implausible.[44] Newcastle was presented as overly dominant,[45] but that was not as he saw himself. Indeed, Cumberland was regarded by some as the key player.[46]

Chesterfield's replacement, Bedford, also wanted a speedy peace but was more discreet than the critical Chesterfield who had told Hugh, 3rd Earl of Marchmont that Newcastle backed the war in order to secure royal support.[47] Bedford had wanted Sandwich to succeed Chesterfield, but Pelham considered Sandwich a partisan of war, while George was wary of his critical attitude to Hanover and rejected his expenses as a diplomat. As a result, Sandwich, instead, went to the Admiralty.[48] In accordance with George's orders,[49] Newcastle himself replaced Chesterfield in the Northern Department and, in turn, was replaced by Bedford. However, from the outset, relations between the two were uneasy. Bedford had a notoriously violent temper and hated contradiction.[50] Ministerial departures frequently involved clashes of personalities and style, but policy differences were also significant. The same was also true of divisions among French ministers, divisions that were reported in the British press.[51]

In contrast to the many commentators who reported simply in terms of Court and ministerial divisions, Newcastle brought in the parliamentary dimension. Informing Sandwich that he and Cumberland had wanted the Earl to succeed Chesterfield, Newcastle added:

> But, to tell you the plain truth, the pacific party in the House of Commons (which, by the by, as now constituted, is the whole House of Commons) and, more particularly, some certain part of the Old Corps, and almost all the new corps, were so alarmed at the resignation of the pacific Lord Chesterfield; and had such a dread of another warlike Secretary; that they expressed such

[43]   Sandwich to Cumberland, 6 Feb. 1748, RA. Cumb. P. 31/198.

[44]   Sir Charles Wyndham, Tory MP to Lord Bathurst, 12 Feb. (os) 1748, BL. Loan 57/74 fol. 31; Newcastle to Sandwich, 9 Feb. (os) 1748, BL. Add. 32811 fol. 197.

[45]   Frankland to Robinson, 11 Feb. (os) 1748, Leeds, Vyner Mss., 2833 no. 743.

[46]   Legge to Anson, 11 Feb. (os) 1748, BL. Add. 15956 fol. 201.

[47]   HMC. *Polwarth*, V, p. 272.

[48]   Bedford to Anson, 12 Feb. (os) 1748, BL. Add. 15955 fol. 161; Russell (ed.), *Correspondence of John, Fourth Duke of Bedford, II* (London, 1843), pp. x, xii.

[49]   Newcastle to Sandwich, 9 Feb. (os) 1748, BL. Add. 32811 fol. 197.

[50]   Sandwich to Anson, 30 Jan. 1748, BL. Add. 15957 fol. 41; Ossorio to Charles Emmanuel III, 23 Feb. 1748, AST. LM. Ing. 54.

[51]   *Daily Advertiser*, 29 Jan. (os) 1748.

apprehensions, and uneasiness, at the supposed design in your favour, that very ugly consequences were flung out; and I really think it was not certain but some parliamentary attempt might have been stirred up to embarrass affairs. I am very sensible that many who were forward in expressing their fears ... were much more angry with me than with you ... means were found to create some doubts in the King at this time ... You cannot imagine how pacific this House of Commons is; to a degree that, except the Solicitor General [Murray], there is hardly a man that does not almost insinuate, more or less, the necessity of making any peace.[52]

Granville also referred to parliamentary pressure for peace and suggested that it might lead to the formation of 'a party ... to force the King to peace'.[53] As soon as the ministry was reconstituted, Newcastle pressed for a speedy end to the war,[54] a process decisively encouraged by the Dutch admitting that their situation was much worse than they had suggested.[55] This admission made it unclear whether the war could be continued in the Low Countries and suggested that France would make rapid gains in the campaigning season that was about to begin.

Another dimension of domestic pressure was provided by merchants seeking the resumption of trade to Spain. They discussed this with the Spanish agent and the interception of his dispatches made Newcastle aware that representations to Parliament from London and Bristol were being encouraged. The publication of Spain's peace proposals was seen as another basis for encouraging opposition.[56]

While the ministry focused on the diplomatic strategy and military operations that were to be adopted to ensure an acceptable post-war situation, public debate had different priorities. In the peace discussions at the close of the War of the Spanish Succession (1702–13 for Britain), there had been more concern in this debate about the European situation, in large part because the fate of the Spanish monarchy and its extensive European dominions had been so contentious during the war. Instead, in 1748 the focus was on the maritime and imperial dimensions of any settlement with France. The two naval victories off Cape Finisterre on 3 May (os) and 14 October (os) 1747, notably the second, on 14 October (os), had been severe blows for the French. Their fleet could no longer escort large convoys bound for their colonies, and this vulnerability destroyed the logic of the French imperial system, and encouraged Newcastle to focus on

52   Newcastle to Sandwich, 12 Feb. (os) 1748, BL. Add. 32811 fols 213, 216.
53   Le Man to Huescar, 13 Feb. 1748, BL. Add. 32811 fol. 155.
54   Newcastle to Sandwich, 12 Feb. (os) 1748, BL. Add. 32811 fols 148–53.
55   Newcastle to Cumberland, 25 Feb. (os) 1748, RA. Cumb. P. 32/113.
56   Le Man to Huescar, 16 Feb. 1748, BL. Add. 32811 fols 169, 171.

naval activity if the war unavoidably continued.[57] The Royal Navy ended the war in a rich glow of success that helped to sustain the maritime patriotism that had become increasingly important in the definition of national interests.

The weakness and demoralisation of the opposition in Parliament after the 1747 election, which indeed led to a very easy session in 1748[58] despite the deteriorating military situation, ensured that the press was the focus of discussion of this definition and of related criticism of the ministry. Indeed, in its issue of 21 January (os) 1748, the *Westminster Journal* declared: 'no peace can be sold to us which is not founded on the reduction, at least, of the French commerce, and the ruin of the naval power of France'. On behalf of the ministry, a critical Fielding pointed out that, while the opposition wanted peace, they also expected France to yield,[59] a contradiction more generally true of the opposition stance, at once critical and expectant. The *Westminster Journal* was of more particular interest because copies were being sent to the French government. In the issue of 6 February (os) it referred to 'the British Americans', a new identity:

> Whatever the creed of some persons may be, mine, that of the British Americans and all Englishmen who judge with knowledge and impartiality, is, that to people and secure New Scotland [Nova Scotia], to reduce Canada, and open a communication betwixt our settlements in Hudson's Bay and those on the Ocean, should be one of the principal objects in view in a war against France. Let us turn out these bad neighbours while we have power and lawful authority, lest they in time cause us to remove. It is of much more concern to us than who has the possession of Italy. I had almost said, of the Netherlands.

In April, Newcastle complained about 'being pelted with pamphlets and papers every day'.[60] Press criticism of the government, however, did not affect parliamentary developments. The situation there in part was a result of the 1747 election. In addition, changing attitudes toward the war played a role. Frederick Frankland, an observant ministerial MP, observed:

> As common danger generally unites parties, so I never saw a sessions of Parliament wherein there has hitherto been so much harmony and confidence. Our ministers have more than once seemed to bespeak peace and called upon the House [of

---

57   Newcastle to Sandwich, 19 Jan. (os) 1748, BL. Add. 32811 fol. 88.
58   Charles Wyndham to Charles, 6th Duke of Somerset, 28 Mar. (os) 1748, Exeter, Devon CRO. 1392 M/L18 48/1.
59   *Jacobite's Journal*, 8 Oct. (os) 1748.
60   Newcastle to Sandwich, 1 Apr. (os) 1748, BL. Add. 32812 fol. 12.

Commons] to declare their sentiments, but they have not been answered, but cautioned to take care what peace they *refused* as well as what they accepted?[61]

Frankland's correspondence with the husband of his niece, Thomas Robinson, who had preceded him in representing Thirsk in Parliament on the Frankland interest, provided the envoy in Vienna with a useful guide to British politics. Like an increasing number of ministerial supporters, Frankland was fearful of the consequences of another campaign.[62]

Parliamentary support meant money. On 13 May (os) 1748, George II thanked MPs: 'for the ample provision you have made for the service of the current year. Nothing could have contributed so much to the putting an end to the calamities of war, and reducing our future expenses, as these well-judged supplies.' In the aftermath of electoral success, the ministers had found that the domestic constraint that was most pressing was the financial, not the political. Newcastle, who in January accepted that it would not be possible to raise comparable sums for 1749, changed his tone about raising funds for 1748. He complained in March, significantly making Cumberland aware of the factor: 'money is so scarce, that it cannot easily be got at any rate, or for any service'.[63] There was a lack of credit in the market and the value of government stock fell. Raising money for the war hit stock values as assets were liquidated.[64]

Finance was linked to strategy, with interventionism and alliance politics a cause of heavy expenditure. In contrast, Velters Cornewall, a Tory MP for Herefordshire who had been recruited by the Prince of Wales, pressed the case in the Commons on 8 February (os) 1748 for a naval war.[65] Bad military news from the Low Countries compounded the difficulties created for a divided and mistrustful ministry[66] by the fact that the country had been continually at war since 1739, a situation contrasting with the far shorter War of the Quadruple Alliance but, instead, reminiscent of the politically divisive War of the Spanish Succession. This news also sapped Dutch support for the war.

---

[61]   Frankland to Robinson, 15 Jan. (os) 1748, Leeds AO, Newby Hall Mss 2833, no. 71.

[62]   Frankland to Robinson, 2 Feb. (os) 1748, no. 72.

[63]   Newcastle to Sandwich, 22 Jan. (os), 16 Feb. (os) 1748, BL. Add. 32811 fol. 103, 220; Newcastle to Cumberland, 11 Mar. (os) 1748, RA. Cumb. P. 32/245.

[64]   Frankland to Robinson, 23 Feb. (os) 1748, Leeds Archive Office, Newby Hall Mss 2833 no. 75.

[65]   Cobbett, *Parliamentary History*, XIV, 158–9.

[66]   R. Harding, *The Emergence of Britain's Global Naval Supremacy. The War of 1739–1748* (Woodbridge, 2010), pp. 330–1.

Following the decisive defeat of the Jacobites in 1746, and the election results in 1747, the peace treaty negotiated at Aix-la-Chapelle (Aachen) in 1748 therefore lowered the political temperature in Britain and greatly eased the situation for the ministry. Although the preliminaries were agreed months earlier and signed by Britain and France in April, the definitive treaty was not signed until 18 October 1748. Neither Austria nor Sardinia were happy about the terms and they did not sign until 23 October and 20 November. Despite Austrian reluctance, Charles Emmanuel III received part of Austrian Italy, as agreed in 1743, while Don Philip, the half-brother of Ferdinand VI of Spain and son-in-law of Louis XV, gained Parma and Piacenza from Austria. However, for Britain, the peace was based on the principle of the status quo antebellum, the return to the pre-war situation. France returned its gains in the Low Countries, as well as Madras, which had been captured from the British East India Company. Britain returned Cape Breton, while the disputed Canadian border was referred to commissioners. France also agreed to recognise the Protestant succession in Britain and to expel Charles Edward Stuart, which underlined his failure in Scotland and reiterated the expulsion of 'James III and VIII' after the War of the Spanish Succession.[67]

Peace was much wanted in Britain,[68] which had been at war since 1739. Peace, indeed, led to a sustained rise in share prices, a key indication of the overlap of politics with government, and of the dependence of both on news. Such financial confidence made it easier to handle government borrowing. A sense of fortuitous timing was captured by John Barker, a Presbyterian cleric prominent in London, who observed: 'How happy was it for this country that a Parliament was chosen when the people were in humour. And a peace made while we had any money to carry on the war.'[69] In the *Jacobite's Journal* on 14 May (os) 1748, Fielding also noted the importance of conjuncture, a point that is relevant when considering evidence:

> Whoever will be pleased to cast his eyes backward for one month only, and recollect the gloomy prospect which the situation of public affairs then presented; the dreadful apprehension which prevailed in every mind, and discovered itself in every countenance; arising from the daily decline of national credit, from the apparent strength of our enemies, and from the manifest weakness or perfidy of

---

[67] R. Lodge, *Studies in Eighteenth-Century Diplomacy, 1740–1748* (London, 1930); C. Baudi Di Vesme, *La Pace di Aquisgrana* (Turin, 1969).

[68] Alt to William VIII of Hesse-Cassel, 30 Apr., 3 May 1748, Marburg, 4f Eng. 249.

[69] Barker to Philip Doddridge, 5 May (os) 1748, G.F. Nutall (ed.), *Calendar of the Correspondence of Philip Doddridge DD* (London, 1979), p. 274.

our allies, must be obliged to own, when he compares it with the pleasing scene now shifted on the stage, that no nation hath ever had a quicker transaction from evil to good ... we ought, with one accord to cry, BLESSED ARE THE PEACE-MAKERS ... surely no people were ever more sick, more weary of a war, than we were of this.

Peace greatly helped Pelham, the First Lord of the Treasury, 'this pupil of the late corrupter',[70] in other words a protégé of Walpole, who himself had died in 1745. The political and governmental situations were transformed and Pelham was now in a position to pursue Walpolean policies: fiscal restraint, preserving a Whig monopoly of power and the status quo in the church, and trying to preserve peace. Indeed, in 1748, Pelham wrote to a ministerial colleague, John, 1st Earl Gower, the Lord Privy Seal: 'Peace you know is my mistress; and war a rival I fear, as well as watch.'[71]

Significantly, Pelham also based this view on the opinion of his constituents, writing after 'a full meeting of Gentlemen ... almost all in good humour, our peace is popular with all parties'.[72] This claim is instructive for it raises the question of what constituted popular opinion. In the Commons, Pelham represented the eastern division of Sussex, a grain exporting region very much under the influence of Newcastle and his family, who had considerable property and significant electoral influence there. The leading magnate in the western division, Charles, 2nd Duke of Richmond, was an ally whom Newcastle kept informed of foreign policy.[73] In 1748, grain exports bridged from an issue in local to one in national politics. Aware also of the international implications, not least in terms of the Dutch response, a concerned Newcastle wrote to assure Sandwich, then envoy in the United Provinces:

There has been an unlucky accident happened in the House of Commons, relating to the exportation of the corn. Some officious, designing fools had given out that, in order to prevent carrying corn to France, there must be a total prohibition of all exportation. The country gentlemen and some *others* were so alarmed at this, that without considering the consequences, or knowing what had passed in Holland, they came to a resolution against prohibiting the exportation of corn; but this is only general, and cannot authorise the carrying it to France; which, as all commerce is, is prohibited by the Declaration of War. This has given me a good

[70]   *Universal Spectator*, 12 Feb. (os) 1743.
[71]   Pelham to Gower, 9 Aug. (os) 1748, NA. PRO. 30/29/1/11 fol. 311.
[72]   Pelham to Gower, 18 Aug. (os) 1748, NA. PRO. 30/29/1/11 fol. 313.
[73]   Newcastle to Richmond, 1 Jan. (os) 1747, Goodwood, Richmond papers, Mss 104.

deal of concern; but we will try, if we cannot find out some method, to set it right, by strengthening the prohibition to France.[74]

Pressure from the agricultural interest was seen as a factor.[75] The return of peace, and the resulting ability to export grain free of controversy, brought the prospect of particular benefit to both divisions of Sussex and also to East Anglia, just as British grain exported had benefited from neutrality during the War of the Polish Succession. In the event, grain exports to France, where bread had been very scarce and expensive in 1748,[76] increased markedly in 1749.

There was also a longer-term trend that began in the mid-1740s. Sustained population growth led to greater demands on the rural economy, with food prices rising rapidly despite good harvests. High yields could be combined with high prices, unlike earlier when more limited population growth had helped keep prices down causing serious problems in the agrarian economy in the 1720s and 1730s. As agricultural wages in the 1740s or, indeed, more generally, did not rise greatly, demand for food increased the prosperity of farmers and rental income, providing more money for agricultural improvement and encouraging investment in it. This prosperity helped to counter the serious wartime problems for landowners caused by the rise in the Land Tax arising from wartime expenditure. Thanks to rural prosperity, downward pressure on rents ceased, assisting landowners. The reduction in political tensions from the late 1740s, a reduction noticeable in the 1747 and 1754 elections, by comparison with those of 1734 and 1741 (seen for example in the marked decline in the number of seats contested), owed much to political factors, but the greater ease of landowners and tenants was also significant.

The perception of public opinion is clearly different if the focus is on the press, rather than on the opinion cited by Pelham. This, indeed, is the focus of much modern work. Newspapers captured a tranche of opinion, in particular urban opinion, that was critical of government and the peace terms. Written and published in towns, notably London, and distributed from them, most newspapers proved less successful in capturing rural opinion or less interested in presenting its perspectives. There was a European dimension in newspaper criticism of government, with Puysieulx, the French Foreign Minister, also

---

[74]   Newcastle to Sandwich, 29 Jan. (os) 1748, BL. Add. 32811 fol. 125. cf 16 Feb. (os) fol. 220.

[75]   Zamboni to Landgrave Ludwig VIII of Hesse-Darmstadt, 9 Feb. 1748, Darmstadt E1 M10/6.

[76]   *Westminster Journal,* 6 Feb. (os) 1748; spy report, Lyons, 24 Feb. 1748, NA. SP. 84/445 fol. 73.

noting 'libelles' against the peace in the cafés of Paris.[77] However, the scale of such discussion was far greater in Britain, while a key element was whether, as a result of its constitution and politics, Britain would show a different response to this criticism. In Continental terms, this meant the government being weak enough to let it be intimidated by popular criticism.[78] In terms of foreign policy, specifically the ethos of ministers and diplomats, this was an unacceptable response. Outside this context, however, it was possible to see this political response to criticism in a different and more positive light. In practice, the parliamentary strength of the British ministry ensured that the peace did not cause it significant political difficulties. In November 1748, Newcastle was convinced that Parliament would support the treaty: 'I think we can have no opposition. There are few, very few, who do not seem pleased, and own how well, and how soon, our great affair has been brought to a conclusion.'[79]

Given this parliamentary position, there was a strong sense that existing policies and governmental personnel would last until the ministerial revolution that was expected to follow the eventual accession of Prince Frederick once the elderly George died. Frederick was the hope of Newcastle's Whig opponents as well as, less consistently, of many Tories. The disappointment of the latter about being let down by opposition Whigs in 1742 and 1744 was countered by a fear of redundancy if acting alone combined with the total failure of the Jacobite option in 1745–6. Thus, Tories were willing to look to Frederick. Whatever the domestic politics, Newcastle was certain that the course of foreign policy was clear. He wrote to Pelham: 'Do but concur in the necessity of supporting the Old System and Alliance, and all will do well, this you know was, and always must be, my point.' Cumberland agreed: 'Whatever slips our allies make, they may be overlooked, provided there is hopes of pursuing the old system, and maintaining the old alliance.'[80] Pelham, meanwhile, was confident that the experience of the recent war had left the population reluctant to be drawn hastily into another struggle. He thus saw a major change from the situation in 1739. This view was ironic as developments in 1754–5 were to reveal a much more complex situation as far as public attitudes were concerned.

[77] Puysieulx to Belle Isle, 17 June 1748, Duc de Broglie, *La Paix d'Aix-la-Chapelle* (Paris, 1895), p. 260.

[78] Puysieulx to Richelieu, 29 June 1748, AN. KK. 1372.

[79] Newcastle to Cumberland, 25 Nov. (os) 1748, RA. Cumb. P. 41/238; Newcastle to Walter Titley, envoy in Copenhagen, 7 Mar. (os) 1749, BL. Add. 32816 fol. 207.

[80] Newcastle to Pelham, 21 July (os) 1748, NeC 642; Cumberland to Newcastle, 20 Oct. 1748, BL. Add. 35464 fol. 133.

Chapter 6

Responding to the Peace, 1749–51

International crisis and internal governmental division threatened British foreign policy in 1749. They made the opportunities, for new policies and new alignments, created by the end of the war appear troubling and uncertain. This was not new, as the ends of the Wars of the Spanish Succession and Quadruple Alliance, in 1713 and 1720 respectively, indicated, and as that of the Seven Years' War in 1763 was also to show. However, Britain had done less well in 1739–48 than in either of the two previous wars or than in that which was to follow. In particular, the situation challenged Newcastle who, as he repeatedly showed, was temperamentally unable to cope with uncertainty, a characteristic fully noted by others. Uncertainties related to the international contest as well as to domestic responses. Newcastle rationalised his attitude with reference to what he saw as a dangerous international situation; although considered from a different perspective, the uncertainties of this situation did, indeed, create dangers, some of them potentially very serious.

At the same time, there were reasons for optimism. In particular, Spain was far more favourably inclined to Britain than in the late 1730s. Indeed, in a marked reaction against the policies followed under Philip V, who had died in 1746, his successor, Ferdinand VI (r. 1746–59), sought a settled Europe, while he wished also to ease commercial and colonial differences with Britain. Complaints about Spanish restrictions on British trade in the New World continued,[1] but they did not gain significant traction. In contrast, France seemed a far more dangerous power to British commentators than it had done in the late 1730s. Then, there had been concern about French policy and strength, but much of this concern rested on Austria's alignment with France and the opportunities this apparently irrational breach with the 'Old System' presented to France. Now, the situation was different and far more troubling. In 1745–8, France had repeatedly demonstrated that the revived alliance that had earlier fought France in the War of the Spanish Succession in 1702–13 was now both weak and unsuccessful. Winning the support of Austria apparently could not solve Britain's strategic problems, notably the defence of the Low Countries.

---

[1]   *Protestor*, 28 July 1753.

Moreover, France after 1748 appeared far stronger and more menacing than after the War of the Spanish Succession. Whereas the accession in 1715 of the infant Louis XV, the great-grandson of Louis XIV, was an obvious sign of dynastic vulnerability, and was accompanied by the establishment of a regency that proved highly divisive as well as willing to ally with Britain; by 1748 Louis had a clear succession and seemed fully in control of the political situation. In addition, France profited greatly from its recent military successes. Its military reputation was high, notably that of Marshal Saxe, and France offered much as a potent ally. The French government claimed in 1749 to be in a position to put 150,000 troops into the field. There were also reports that the French navy would be greatly increased.[2] That France had been heavily defeated at sea by Britain in 1747 was far less significant for potential allies than its repeated victories on land in 1745–8, victories over British, Dutch and Austrian forces. This contrast between sea and land led to a major difference in perception about respective power, between British public opinion and the views of other powers. This difference played a significant role when the contrast between land and sea power reached a crisis situation in 1755–6.

It was unclear in 1748 what Britain could do if France did not hand back its conquests in the Low Countries as it had promised to do.[3] In the event, the French proved accommodating.[4] However, French approaches for good relations with Britain,[5] which would have been a real diplomatic revolution, did not receive a particularly positive response in London. Although the British government was very happy to see both powers act to restrain their allies in the Baltic,[6] echoes of the highly contentious alliance between the two powers in 1716–31 were not wanted for political and diplomatic reasons. Such echoes would have been unacceptable both to 'Old Corps' Whigs, notably Newcastle, seeking to differentiate themselves from the highly contentious Walpole legacy, and to their 'New Allies' acquired in 1742, 1744 and 1746, most of whom had always conspicuously rejected that legacy. This political tension would have played out against the background of a highly unsympathetic press and a critical public opinion. If the domestic context was scarcely conducive for a realignment with

---

[2]   Anon. report from Paris, 13 Jan. 1749, sent to London by British espionage network, NA. SP. 84/451 fol. 13.

[3]   Ossorio to Charles Emmanuel III, 10 Jan. 1749, AST. LM. Ing. 55.

[4]   Newcastle to Dayrolle, 20 Jan. (os) 1749, NA. SP. 84/450 fol. 27.

[5]   Yorke to Bedford, 19 Feb., Yorke to Hardwicke, 5 Apr. 1749, BL. Add. 32816 fol. 90, 35355 fol. 34; Puysieulx to Durand, 14 Mar. 1749, AE. CP. Ang. 425 fol. 406.

[6]   Bedford to Yorke, 27 Feb. (os), 13, 20 Mar. (os) 1749, Lord John Russell (ed.), *Correspondence of John, Fourth Duke of Bedford*, II (London, 1843), pp. 10–13, 15, 18–19, 22.

France, there was also the issue, as when the possibility recurred in 1772, 1786–7, and 1792, that the international consequences would have been undesirable: Britain would have jeopardised relations with other powers, notably Austria, Russia and Sardinia, and would have taken on undesirable commitments.

If better relations with France were scarcely unproblematic, the apparent challenge to the British alliance system posed in any event by French strength was accentuated by the extent to which France's might-be allies represented disruptive possibilities to the international system and to Britain's allies and would-be allies. Among France's might-be allies, this was notably so of Prussia, which still had very bad relations with Austria, but was also the case with Sweden and Denmark, both of which challenged Russia's ambitions and interests in the Baltic. However, the French government repeatedly emphasised its wish for peace and its intention to restrain those who might trouble it.[7] This stance raises the question whether more could have been done in Britain, by co-operating with France, to settle international tensions. A managerial analysis to international relations suggests a positive answer, but there was a host of domestic and international challenges to such an approach. This situation prefigured that for the period from 1762 when suggesting a more active policy of caution to international commitments.

In domestic terms, in contrast with the firework celebrations in Green Park, London on 27 April 1749, there was in 1749 and the early 1750s a strong sense of disappointment, across the British political spectrum, notably that the 1748 peace was humiliating and, at best, incomplete. This was particularly so on the part of the opposition, not only in the press, but also with what was presented as the 'Party of the Prince of Wales'.[8] The return of Cape Breton was widely and repeatedly castigated, and became a lasting issue.[9] In addition, there were less incessant complaints that Britain provided hostages for its observance of the peace, and not vice versa,[10] and also that the Bourbons had made gains in Italy at the expense of Austria, thus threatening the balance of power.[11] As an

---

[7]   Argenson to Valory, 3 Mar. 1746, NA. SP. 78/331 fol. 439; Puysieulx to Hautefort, 8 Nov. 1750, AE. CP. Aut. 248 fol. 26.

[8]   *Westminster Journal*, 7 Jan. (os) 1749; *Remembrancer*, 7 Jan. (os) 1749; Alt to William VIII of Hesse-Cassel, 7 Jan. 1749, Marburg, London, 250.

[9]   Admiral Vernon to Sir Francis Dashwood, 29 July (os) 1749, Bod. Ms. D.D. Dashwood B11/12/6; J.M. Sosin, 'Louisbourg and the Peace of Aix-la-Chapelle, 1748', *William and Mary Quarterly*, 14 (1957), pp. 516–35; H. Mimler, *Der Einfluss kolonialer Interessen in Nordamerika auf die Strategie und Diplomatie Grossbritanniens... 1744–1748* (Hildesheim, 1983).

[10]   Anon, *The Two Most Famous Ostriches* (London, 1749); *Remembrancer*, 21 Jan. (os) 1749.

[11]   *Remembrancer*, 15, 22 Oct. (os), *Old England*, 17 Dec. (os) 1748.

acknowledgement that interventionism could bring benefits, it was claimed by critics that the ministry could have made more from the advance of the Russian army into Germany, an advance Britain had subsidised.[12] Reports that Gibraltar would be restored to Spain[13] were groundless, but spread doubt about the determination of the government. The debate over the peace also brought up the issue of constitutional authority and power. The *Remembrancer* claimed on 14 January (os) 1749:

> The advice of the Parliament was reasonable to be taken, because it was a Parliamentary War: And if so, the wisdom and authority which had been consulted on the war, ought to have been consulted also on the peace, that they might judge for themselves, whether it was for their honour or interest to accept of the terms proposed or not.

Ironically, there were also bitter complaints in France about national honour being compromised in the peace terms, notably with the expulsion of Charles Edward Stuart, to which end the British applied repeated pressure. These complaints were driven home on the Crown with the inaccurate rumour that Madame de Pompadour, the mistress of Louis XV, had betrayed French national interests in return for a British bribe.[14] Whereas in Britain, the nature of parliamentary monarchy put the ministers in the firing line, in France criticism focused more closely on the Crown. It would have done so even more had contemporaries been aware of the *Secret du Roi*, the secret foreign policy of Louis XV to support the candidature of the Prince of Conti for the Polish throne and, linked to this, to limit Russian power in Eastern Europe.[15] Hostility to Britain played an increasingly significant role in French patriotic sentiment.[16] Nevertheless, as a reminder that cross-currents were not only seen there, that view co-existed with popular hostility in France toward Austria,[17] hostility indeed that was to sap the alliance with Austria negotiated in 1756.

---

   [12]   *Remembrancer*, 21 Jan. (os) 1749.

   [13]   *Craftsman*, 4 Feb. (os) 1749.

   [14]   T.E. Kaiser, 'The Drama of Charles Edward Stuart, Jacobite Propaganda, and French Political Protest, 1745–1750', *Eighteenth-Century Studies*, 30 (1997), p. 375.

   [15]   E. Boutaric (ed.), *Correspondance secrète inédite de Louis XV sur la politique étrangère* (2 vols, Paris, 1886).

   [16]   E. Dziembowski, *Un nouveau patriotisme française, 1750–1770: La France face à la puissance anglaise à l'époque de la Guerre de Sept Ans* (Oxford, 1998).

   [17]   T.E. Kaiser, 'The Austrian alliance, the Seven Years' War and the Emergence of a French "National" Foreign Policy', in J. Swann and J. Félix (eds), *The Crisis of the Absolute Monarchy. France from Old Regime to Revolution* (Oxford, 2013), pp. 167–79.

With a motivation based on a reading of the international situation, and not of domestic politics, which, to him, tended to mean Parliament rather than public opinion, Newcastle thought it urgent, as well as necessary, both to protect and revive the alliance with Austria and the Dutch, and to strengthen it against likely challenges. Newcastle claimed to base his judgement on 'how the facts really stand',[18] but he tended to see these facts in the light of his strong suppositions, and to plan his resulting strategy with an often frenetic zeal to overcome these challenges. The two challenges that appeared most apparent, the security of the Low Countries and the future of the Empire, were each highlighted by recent events.

The strengthening of the Barrier Forts in the Austrian Netherlands was apparently crucial to their defence against another French attack, as well as that of the United Provinces, and that of British strategic interests in the Low Countries. These interests were varied. They included financial and economic concerns, as well as the security of the route to Hanover, and the risk of another attempted invasion of Britain. The last had been highlighted by the French invasion plans and preparations of 1744–6. Dunkirk, already a French port, was bad enough, but, in the event of another war, Ostend and the Scheldt in French hands was more threatening as a prospect. As a result, there was a short-lived British interest in gaining Ostend as part of the peace, or, at least, providing troops for its garrison, an interest on the part of Newcastle and Sandwich, that picked up earlier discussion of such an option.[19]

The speed with which the Barrier Forts had fallen to French attack in the recent war suggested a need for their rapid and radical repair and improvement. Moreover, these forts became a convenient explanation of failure in the recent war, an explanation, in practice, that exaggerated their significance in the campaigning, and, notably, at the expense of battles. The defence and siege of fortifications were to play an important role in the Seven Years' War in Europe, but less so than in the conflicts of 1688–1748. In part, this situation reflected the absence of campaigning in the Low Countries during the Seven Years' War, but there had also been a shift toward greater significance for battle. Yet, fortifications represented an important force multiplier and a tangible demonstration of alliance co-operation, and it is easy to understand why Newcastle placed such a weight on the issue.

---

[18] Newcastle to Sandwich, 25 Dec. (os) 1747, BL. Add. 32810 fol. 391.

[19] J. Black, 'Territorial Gain on the Continent: An Overlooked Aspect of Mid-eighteenth Century British Foreign Policy', *Durham University Journal*, 86 (1994), pp. 43–50.

Newcastle repeatedly found neither Austria nor the Dutch willing to pay what it took to restore and strengthen the Barrier Forts, or even to pay a reasonable share. As a result, there was no strengthening of the defences of the Austrian Netherlands. Part of a broader failure of economic and strategic hopes,[20] this issue was corrosive. It rarely featured at the forefront of British foreign policy, but it was a key topic in diplomatic negotiation and complaint. Moreover, the failure of Britain's allies to do what was deemed necessary played a role in public discussion in the press. The discussion, both public and governmental, repeatedly failed to devote due weight to the views of these allies. These views included different conceptions of their interests to those held in Britain, as well as a degree of bitterness and suspicion, of Britain and other allies, stemming from the recent war. Pragmatic issues were to the fore, rather than the sentiment and emotion that Newcastle was apt to deploy. Bitter about Britain, Maria Theresa saw her need for its alliance as arising from her fear of Prussia.[21] This raised the issue of whether that fear could be better addressed by another alignment for Austria and, more particularly, what would happen if Britain's relations with Prussia changed, as was indeed advocated by Horatio Walpole, Legge and others in 1748. In the British press, there was more coverage of the problems facing the United Provinces, notably financial difficulties,[22] than those confronting Austria. The latter proved difficult to explain in a sympathetic fashion.

In addition, the Imperial Election Scheme was to become an issue in the press. This Scheme was, and is, a much discussed aspect of Newcastle's foreign policy.[23] To an extent the attention is disproportionate because it leads to a serious underplaying of British policy toward Spain and, to a lesser extent, the

---

[20]   P.G.M. Dickson, 'English Commercial Negotiations with Austria, 1737–1752', in A. Whiteman, J.S. Bromley and P.G.M. Dickson (eds), *Statesmen, Scholars and Merchants* (Oxford, 1973), pp. 81–112.

[21]   Maria Theresa to Zöhrern, envoy in London, 31 Jan. 1749, HHStA. Englische Korrespondez 97.

[22]   *Daily Advertiser*, 13 Feb. (os) 1749.

[23]   D.B. Horn, 'The Origins of the Proposed Election of a King of the Romans, 1748–1750', *English Historical Review*, 42 (1927), pp. 361–70; R. Browning, 'The Duke of Newcastle and the Imperial Election Plan, 1749–1754', *Journal of British Studies*, 7 (1967–8), pp. 28–47 and 'The British Orientation of Austrian Foreign Policy, 1749–1754', *Central European History*, 4 (1968), pp. 299–323; H.M. Scott, '"The True Principles of the Revolution": The Duke of Newcastle and the Idea of the Old System', in J. Black (ed.), *Knights Errant and True Englishmen: British Foreign Policy, 1660–1800* (Edinburgh, 1989), pp. 55–91; Black, 'The British Attempt to Preserve the peace In Europe, 1748–1755', in H. Duchhardt (ed.), *Zwischenstaatliche Friedenswährung in Mittelalter und Früher Neuzeit* (Cologne, 1991), pp. 227–44.

Italian states. Nevertheless, the Scheme did come foremost. It also led to the eventual swallowing of diplomatic strategy by tactics, in terms of how best to win the support of individual German rulers for the Scheme. The Scheme reflected Newcastle's determination to have 'a system'[24] as well as his repeated concern about developments that might arise. This anticipation of the future was an aspect of his continual concern, but also a product of his tendency to plan, and, in doing so, locate the present as a stage to a future he sought to control. The past also held up warnings for Newcastle:

> I can see the follies and the vanity of the court of Vienna, but I see the danger and ruin of being dependent upon France. I was once catched in the year 1725 [a reference to the anti-Austrian Treaty of Hanover] ... no consideration shall ever catch me again.[25]

The extent to which the imperial succession had helped cause conflict in 1740–1 after the Emperor Charles VI died, providing an opportunity for Frederick to attack in 1740, and for others to follow, left Newcastle determined to pre-empt the prospect of another such episode by ensuring that the succession was settled. With a Habsburg again in place, Austria would be stronger and, he hoped, better able to meet British expectations. As a result, Newcastle focused on the election of a King of the Romans, the title of the designated successor to the Emperor. The Emperor was then Francis I (r. 1745–65), the husband of Maria Theresa of Austria. Newcastle's candidate was their son, Joseph, who would later be the Emperor Joseph II (r. 1765–90).

This project reflected a concern with dynastic factors as a key element in international relations, both as goal and means. Such a concern might appear redundant in light of the trans-oceanic issues and comparative fiscal strength that were to come to the fore from 1754, but Newcastle was scarcely alone in his focus. The results of the election of a non-Habsburg as Emperor in 1742, the pro-French Bavarian Charles VII, appeared salutary,[26] but that issue scarcely exhausted concerns about royal successions and dynastic enhancement. The '45 demonstrated the continued relevance of Jacobitism, and this relevance was very much seen in Europe in terms of dynastic challenge rather than the other issues also involved in Jacobitism. In addition, in the early 1750s, the Swedish and Polish successions were matters of great concern. Moreover, in the late 1740s, a

---

24 Newcastle to Hardwicke, 17 Nov. 1748, BL. Add. 35410 fol. 91.
25 Newcastle to Cumberland, 22 Oct. (os) 1748, RA. Cumb. P. 40/166.
26 Bedford to Rochford, 8 Dec. (os) 1750, NA. SP. 92/58 fol. 396.

range of British ministers and diplomats had emphasised links between dynastic possibilities and the balance of power. In 1747, the plan for the marriage of a Saxon prince to a daughter of Louis XV, with the former succeeding eventually to the Polish throne, was regarded as a threat.[27] Linked to the house of Orange, Dutch politics were also presented in a dynastic light.

The Imperial Election Scheme, which George also vigorously espoused,[28] entailed the need to win the backing of the German princes who could vote, namely the nine Electors of the Holy Roman Empire, and that need meant providing them with financial support and diplomatic backing. France (and Prussia) in turn sought to encourage opposition to this election, which was inherently a demonstration of diplomatic predominance, and which, due to Newcastle's commitment, very much became such a demonstration. The British did not respond positively to the French suggestion that the two powers co-operate to try to settle differences over the Scheme.[29] As a result, there was a market in support, and one in which success appeared uncertain and the reliability of the Electors highly problematic. Subsidies, hitherto, for Britain, a key element in the diplomacy and politics of wartime policy, thus became so for peacetime as money was used in an attempt to cement international support, and in a very public fashion with the subsidies debated in Parliament.[30]

More generally, in Britain the Scheme opened up a new politics in the debate over foreign policy, as well as a new debate in its politics. In particular, peacetime subsidies, and the commitments they entailed, were widely unwelcome. This was so in the press and in parliamentary debates. Indeed, this unpopularity became an argument used by the government in pressing allies to be compliant with British negotiating positions.[31] In addition, a lack of support, let alone enthusiasm, for such subsidies was also the case for key figures within the government, notably Pelham and Hardwicke, but not only them. Newcastle complained: 'I see a great inclination to lie by, and engage as little as possible.' Foreign diplomats reported that all the Council, bar Newcastle, were opposed to the subsidies.[32] This disagreement reprised an earlier one of money allegedly owed to Austria

[27]   Hanbury Williams to Chesterfield, 28 Oct., Chesterfield to Burrish, 10 Nov. (os) 1747, NA. SP. 88/69, 81/96.

[28]   Zamboni to Kaunitz, 6 Mar. 1752, HHStA. England, Varia 10 fol. 104.

[29]   Albemarle to Bedford, 20 Jan. 1751, Russell (ed.), *Bedford*, II, 66–8.

[30]   J. Black, *Parliament and Foreign Policy in the Eighteenth Century* (Cambridge, 2004), pp. 89–92.

[31]   Newcastle to Holdernesse, 4 Jan. (os), Holdernesse to Newcastle, 22 Jan. 1751, NA. SP. 84/457.

[32]   Newcastle to Cumberland, 25 Nov. (os) 1748, RA. Cumb. P. 41/238; Perrone to Charles Emmanuel III, 5 June 1749, AST. LM. Ing. 55.

as part of wartime backing.[33] These diplomats also captured another tension, that between support by the Hanoverian ministers for the policy of winning allegiance via subsidies, and opposition by their British counterparts bar Newcastle,[34] who argued that it was necessary to provide subsidies in order to win allies.

The ministerial controversy has attracted scholarly attention,[35] although often without the scrutiny of foreign diplomatic archives that offers interesting amplification of ministerial views in the shape of comments made to diplomats. The closeness between Newcastle and the Sardinian envoy ensures that his reports are of particular interest. Distinguishing between the constitutional acceptability of peacetime subsidies and the current more critical views of the 'nation',[36] Perrone reported that Newcastle thought that the nation might accept such subsidies in a year or two.[37] For Newcastle, in contrast, the international competitive context was crucial: the Duke argued to his colleagues that Britain needed to respond to the French use of subsidies to win allies.[38] However, Chesterfield told the French envoy that experience and fiscal problems ensured that a part of the ministry, supported by the opinion of the entire nation, was resolved not to pay peacetime subsidies.[39]

As often in a clash that could be described in terms of Continental versus Oceanic policies, a key element in practice was that of implementation. For many, this issue took precedence over the more general question described in policy terms. Opposition to such subsidies was, correctly, seen by observers to rest not only in their goal, but also in their being perceived as useless.[40] This view reflected not just experience, but also a perception of international relations that contested the instrumentalist confidence in mechanistic theories and assumptions. In particular, there was criticism of the approach repeatedly displayed by Newcastle, that of the ready manipulation of the balance of power in order to serve British interests. Instead, on the part of the critics of subsidies, there was a lack of confidence in an ability to construct a system, a lack of confidence that reflected critical views on human motivation and behaviour.

---

33 Ossorio to Charles Emmanuel III, 28 Jan. 1749, AST. LM. Ing. 55.
34 Perrone to Charles Emmanuel III, 26 June 1749, AST. LM. Ing. 55.
35 D.B. Horn, 'The Cabinet Controversy on Subsidy Treaties in Time of Peace 1749–50', *English Historical Review*, 45 (1930), pp. 463–6.
36 Perrone to Charles Emmanuel III, 28 Aug. 1749, AST. LM. Ing. 55.
37 Perrone to Charles Emmanuel III, 25 Dec. 1749, AST. LM. Ing. 55.
38 Newcastle to Hardwicke, 25 Aug. (os) 1749, BL. Add. 32719 fol. 69.
39 Mirepoix to Puysieulx, 2 Sept. 1749, AE. CP. Ang. 427 fols 8–9.
40 Mirepoix to Puysieulx, 2 Sept. 1749, AE. CP. Ang. 427 fol. 9.

In the case of Count Kaunitz, the Austrian Chancellor from 1753, the British ministry was to come to share such views in 1756, but there was already criticism of the demands arising from the Imperial Election Scheme.

As another element in the controversy over the Scheme and subsidies, the uncertain relationship between the British 'constitution' and political realities was indicated by the different views outlined by ministers, diplomats and commentators. Thus, responding to Dutch pressure for a subsidy to Clemens August, Archbishop-Elector of Cologne, a ruler who was only significant because of his Electoral vote, Holdernesse: 'laid great strain upon the difficulty I supposed His Majesty would be under, from the nature of our constitution, in granting subsidies to foreign princes in time of peace'.[41] By 1750, however, under pressure from George and Newcastle, the ministerial situation had changed, with Bedford and Pelham being willing to spend money to win allies, and being in favour of the Imperial Election Scheme. Significantly, Cumberland was also mentioned.[42] For George and his Hanoverian ministers, there were cross-currents. In particular, George was both highly suspicious of Frederick II[43] and determined to try to block pro-French moves in the Wittelsbach-filled prince-bishoprics of north-west Germany that were close to Hanover: Osnabrück and Paderborn. He sought Dutch and British assistance to help block these moves.[44] A major pluralist, the Archbishop-Elector of Cologne from 1723 to 1761, held these bishoprics. The sense of a rivalry between Austrian and French parties extended to other prince-bishoprics, notably Liège,[45] and, more generally, across Europe.

Subsidies to the Archbishop-Elector of Cologne had also been highly contentious in 1729–30, helping to divide Sir Robert Walpole from the key Secretary of State, Charles, 2nd Viscount Townshend. This legacy was not to the fore in the early 1750s, although it was instructive because, in 1729–30, the subsidies had been sought while Britain was allied to France and against Austria. Moreover, the prospect of war then ensured that the Electorate, its Westphalian prince-bishoprics, and its Rhine crossings, were strategically important as means of supporting Hanover and the Dutch against Austrian and Austrian-allied, notably Prussian, attack. The very different rationale for such subsidies in the

---

[41] Holdernesse to Newcastle, 8 July (os) 1749, NA. SP. 84/449 fol. 68.

[42] Perrone to Charles Emmanuel III, 26 Mar. 1750, and to Gorzegno, 11 May 1750, AST. LM. Ing. 56. For Cumberland's influence, Ossorio to Charles Emmanuel III, 24, 28 Jan., 11 Feb. 1749, AST. LM. Ing. 55.

[43] Bedford to Albemarle, 4 Mar. (os) 1751, Russell (ed.), *Bedford*, II, 73–4.

[44] Holdernesse to Prince of Orange, 6 Jan. (os) 1749, NA. SP. 84/447 fol. 116.

[45] Cressener to Keith, 2 Feb. 1749, BL. Add. 35465 fols 82–3.

early 1750s can be seen as a sign of flexibility or, as Newcastle presented it, as a return to Britain's 'true' interest in opposing France. However, aside from the issues of limited value and inconsistency, there was also that of the cost of subsidies. Concern about the size and management of the National Debt made this cost particularly unwelcome.

In 1751, Granville (formerly Carteret) returned to office, as Lord President of the Council. This post denied him specific ministerial responsibility for foreign policy, but ensured that he was available to support interventionism in the Cabinet. Although foreign diplomats were to see him as challenging Newcastle in 1755, he certainly proved ready earlier to accept his new, subordinate position. This was an indication both of the Pelhams' strength and of George's willingness to accept the exigencies of parliamentary monarchy, as had not proved the case in 1744 and 1746. That Granville was now part of a ministerial system dominated by the Pelhams was a sign to foreign envoys and domestic commentators, but he was also seen as a protégé of the King and had indeed received the prestigious Order of the Garter in 1749. Granville's appointment both demonstrated George's significance and was a clarification of the King's close relationship with the Pelhams. As such, this was an important step. There were also policy aspects. Granville was regarded as the prime developer of the Imperial Election Scheme in Britain.[46] He knew and cared more about Imperial politics than Newcastle did.

Whatever the views of individual ministers, much of the press did not change opinion in the early 1750s, but remained hostile to the Imperial Election Scheme and the related policies, notably peacetime subsidies. The wide range of opposition was kept active by the frequency with which the issue of subsidies was discussed, and especially in Parliament. As a result, opposition over policy interacted with, and drew on, the more specific issue of opposition over its cost.

The net consequence of the Imperial Election Scheme and the emphasis on subsidies was to sap the support that did exist for interventionist politics and policies, and to affect their legacy. Indeed, well before the crisis of Britain's Continental policy in 1756, a crisis that was part of the wider-ranging European Diplomatic Revolution, this policy had become politically toxic. This toxicity, however, was greatly underplayed due to the parliamentary strength of the government. This strength did not prevent parliamentary attacks, but they could not prevail in either House. The Abbé de la Ville, an experienced French diplomat, pointed out in 1749 that, for several years, there had been

---

[46] Mirepoix to Puysieulx, 18 Aug. 1751, AE. CP. Ang. 432 fol. 129; Mirepoix, Portrait de la Cour d'Angleterre, Nov. 1751, AE. MD. Ang. 51 fols 158–61.

unprecedented fierceness in the attacks by opposition parliamentarians, but that, despite this, the resolutions of Parliament had very much conformed to ministerial wishes.[47]

More than one reading of this situation is possible, for the pattern was similar with the attacks on British foreign policy, notably the Anglo-French alliance, in the late 1720s. These attacks also were unsuccessful, being defeated in successive sessions, but they contributed to a position of political vulnerability, one in which the association of the government with the alliance was made a matter of contention and one in which results were contested. Ultimately, the issue of the reliability of the alliance in terms of the securing of national interests had become the crisis of the 1730 parliamentary session, with French repairs to the privateering base of Dunkirk, in defiance of the Peace of Utrecht in 1713, the cause of contention as Walpole struggled to control the Commons. This crisis helped lead to the government pursuing a new diplomacy, in the shape of the alliance with Austria negotiated in 1731.

The subsidy issue can be regarded as different in that the Imperial Election Scheme had already run out of steam by 1753 due to what were, in the eyes of the British ministry, the excessive demands, unhelpful policies, and unreliability of the German states. Thus, unlike with the French alliance in 1730–1, domestic political criticism was not the key element. It did not, for example, explain the persistent difficulties the British encountered in dealing with the Elector Palatine. However, the fundamentals of the Scheme finally collapsed in 1756 with the end of the Anglo-Austrian alliance as part of the Diplomatic Revolution. In another light, the new alliance with Prussia that was an aspect of this Revolution, in turn, involved fresh, but different, interventionism and a subsidy, as did the hiring of foreign troops, notably from Hesse-Cassel. These were 'sold' politically by Pitt, but, eventually, these subsidies became an item of rising political and governmental concern in Britain, which helped to lead to the end of the subsidy system and the Prussian alliance in 1762. Thus, in a parallel with the earlier French alliance, the theme of the parliamentary opposition in the early 1750s[48] did eventually have an effect. In part, this was because opposition arguments influenced government policy, or, rather, in a crucial difference, the policy, first, of a ministry facing a new international situation (1756), and, then, of a new government (1762–3).

---

[47]   La Ville, 'Angleterre-sur l'etat politique de a Royaume', 1749, AE. CP. Ang. 427 fol. 411.

[48]   *Westminster Journal*, 18 July 1752.

There was no such degree of influence, however, in the short term, although that is not the same as there being no influence. The easing of the political situation, both domestic and international, in the late 1740s led to a slackening in parliamentary attendance as there appeared scant prospect of the opposition achieving any successes. Diplomats reported that there was nothing interesting in Parliament.[49] On 18 January (os) 1749, the ministry carried a division on the size of the army by 295 to 114, a majority seen as likely 'to make things go on easily' for the ministry.[50] The ministry was to go on to block, by 221 to 120 votes, an opposition demand for the disclosure of parliamentary papers designed to further criticism of the peace. Alt argued that this division reflected the 'nation's' pleasure with the coming of peace. On 16 November (os) 1749, in the debate on the Address, the opposition failed to gain traction, and the ministry easily won a Commons division on the contentious issue of Dunkirk on 5 February (os) 1750.[51]

Moreover, as an aspect of a more general decline of party affiliation and rivalry,[52] a number of Tories went over to the ministry, including Sir Miles Stapylton, MP for Yorkshire, who was rewarded in April 1750 by being made a Commissioner of Customs, and Henry, 3rd Viscount Downe who, having been adopted by a meeting of Yorkshire Whigs, won Stapylton's seat in an unopposed by-election later in April. Re-elected in 1754, Downe died in 1760 of wounds incurred fighting with the army as a brevet lieutenant-colonel in Germany, a reminder of the varied overlap of peace and war at the individual level. Another instance of lessened partisanship came from Pitt. In government from 1746, Pitt in 1750 told the Commons why he had tempered his earlier criticisms of Walpolean foreign policy and become, instead, an advocate of caution, an about-turn he reiterated in 1751.[53]

In the meanwhile, in the early 1750s, repeated opposition failure in Parliament, and the strong sense that this would not change,[54] did not preclude

---

[49]   Ossorio to Charles Emmanuel III, 6 Jan. 1749, AST. LM. Ing. 55.

[50]   Frederick Frankland to Thomas Robinson, 19 Jan. (os) 1749, Leeds Archive Office, Newby Hall Mss 2834; Ossorio to Charles Emmanuel III, 4 Feb. 1749, AST. LM. Ing. 55; Alt to William VIII of Hesse-Cassel, 31 Jan. 1749, Marburg, 4f England, 250.

[51]   Alt to William VIII, 21 Feb. 1749, Marburg, 4f England, 250; H.R. Wyndham (ed.), *The Diary of the Late George Bubb Dodington* (3rd edn, London, 1785), pp. 16–17.

[52]   J.C.D. Clark, 'The Decline of Party, 1740–1760', *English Historical Review*, 93 (1978), pp. 499–527.

[53]   Cobbett, *Parliamentary History*, XIV, cols 694, 801.

[54]   A.N. Newman, 'Leicester House Politics, 1749–51', *English Historical Review*, 76 (1961), pp. 577–89; H.R. Wyndham (ed.), *The Diary of the Late George Bubb Dodington* (3rd edn, London, 1785), pp. 33–7.

a wider debate about policy in the press. This debate, which focused as much on what was held to be the underlying culture of government as on specific policies, drew on a strong sense of cultural alienation from France, a sense that was linked to political divisions, although frequently only in a general fashion. In 1749, a pamphleteer suggested that the vigour of opposition to the presence of French actors in London had passed: 'Parading with the Independent Flag, the Cry of French Strollers, and other emblems of confusion, which used to animate and ring-in our unthinking friends, is now no more.'[55] However, the issue played a role in the bitterly-contested Westminster election of 1750, being directly linked to the choice of candidates: 'Ye Electors! Who hate all the frenchified clan, If you love your selves, choose not the Minister's Man.'[56] Culture wars were presented as both serious and as readily spanning the English Channel, as with the *Queries Submitted to the Serious Consideration of the Worthy Electors for the City and Liberty of Westminster* (1749). These included: 'Whether a man can be sincere, in his professions, to serve the interests of Great Britain, who appears publicly in defence of our natural enemies, and treats all such of his constituents, who are not frenchified, as a mob?' and

> Whether the French Ministry could contrive a speedier, or more effectual method to subdue a people, and reconcile them to their despotic government, than by forcing their language, manners, and follies upon them, in the comedies now represented in the Haymarket [theatre].

In the event, in a campaign that started in late 1749 and continued into 1750, Granville, Viscount Trentham, who had supported the players, was elected for Westminster, in part due to significant expenditure by his father, John, 1st Earl Gower, and his brother-in-law, John, 4th Duke of Bedford, a prominent urban landowner. Both men were key 'New Allies' of the ministry. However, the controversy over the election continued. Jacobites were involved in the unsuccessful petition against the Westminster result in 1751. Contention over the issue drew on, and sustained, unease about the intentions of the social élite and the ministry, unease that, in part, focused on the 'New Allies'. They exemplified the fear of betrayal. This unease could also be seen, although less urgently than in the mid-1740s, in attacks on the role of Hanoverian interests. Thus, a 1749 caricature, *The Conduct of the Two B[rother]s*, presented the Hanoverian horse as

---

[55]   [P. Leigh], *The Dying Groans and Last Farewell to the World of the H.B. of the City of Westminster* (London, 1749), p. 3.

[56]   *Peg Trantum in the Suds, or No French Strollers. A New Ballad* (London, 1749), verse 10.

licking up Britannia's blood, Britannia having been dismembered by the Pelhams. This was a brutally vivid account of Britain's alleged fate, one directly linked to government policy.

Cultural unease and the debate about Continental policy both contributed to a sense that the government did not understand national interests; and, indeed, could not understand them. Alongside subsidies, and other signs of a mishandled and misconceived Continental policy, notably alleged favour for Hanover, came popular anger at the failure to fulfil expectations over North America, specifically those raised from 1745. Concern over these two elements, Continental and North American, supported each other and ensured that the public debate over interests and policy included a coherent opposition critique. This critique was to be deployed to successful political effect in the mid-1750s.

The unpopularity of the Continental policy was in part a matter of its apparent redundancy, a redundancy that challenges a key theme in this book, that of crisis. On the one hand, it is easy to support this theme of crisis for 1749–51 by reference to ministerial correspondence and press comment, notably about French intentions and British vulnerability. However, at the same time, there was a marked slackening in tension, and certainly in contrast to the recent war. This slackening was encouraged by the extent to which the Baltic crisis of 1749 did not, as was feared, lead to war between Russia and a French- and Prussian-backed Sweden, a conflict that might have strengthened France at the expense of Britain's potential partners, and, indeed, involved Britain. As a consequence of the reduction in tension, there was apparently less of a need for Britain to affirm its international system by supporting the Imperial Election Scheme, or, indeed, the alliance with Austria, other than as a deterrent, and the former very much as a long-term deterrent. Deterrence, however, did not provide a reason that commanded popular backing, or even consistent ministerial support, let alone enthusiasm.

Had the sceptical Pelham been as powerful or (somehow) charismatic a ministerial and political figure as Walpole had been, then it is likely that Newcastle would have had less success in pushing his policies of commitment and cost, and certainly in the absence of an international crisis. Paradoxically, such a situation might well have ensured that, when war with France recurred, it would have been easier, politically, to press for a Continental alignment not compromised by recent quarrels and costs. Such counterfactuals may appear problematic, but they capture the way in which contemporaries considered issues. Plans, such as the Imperial Election Scheme, but also alliances in general, were discussed by contemporaries, both ministers and commentators, in terms of counterfactuals, which, indeed, were crucial to the forward-looking dimension of mechanistic accounts of international relations. It would be unhelpful today not to discuss the viability of plans and speculations unless with reference to counterfactuals, both those advanced at the time and others advanced with the benefit of hindsight. Furthermore, these counterfactuals underline real and possible relationships across time that indicate the uncertain and varied character of such links alongside their significance. Pelham, himself, was able to rationalise the government's policy, and his response to it, by arguing that the Scheme would help stabilise Germany, not least by separating the German rulers from France. As a result, he came to justify the Scheme as a means to ensure 'quiet' and thus control expenditure,[57] an approach that eased his relations with his brother.

Foreign policy in the early 1750s was affected, but not necessarily moulded or determined, by public criticism. Indeed, there was no certain relationship between the two. Ministerial strength in Parliament certainly did not prevent a practice of heeding public opinion that was commented on by diplomats and that did not match their social assumptions or political views. In 1750, Perrone presented the government's decisions to send away a troupe of French actors and to abolish the Act to cut the interest on the National Debt, as leading the well-intentioned to fear that the 'nation' would become accustomed simply to follow its whims, and, therefore, to the ministry acting accordingly.[58] The 'nation', indeed, was the key term, not only with the frequent juxtaposition of nation and King,[59] but also with Newcastle seeing the 'nation' as a unity and force that the government would have to be aware of.[60] For Mirepoix, the relevant phrase, alongside the nation, was public opinion, with the government presented as not daring to try anything contrary.[61] The nation and public opinion acted as theme, analysis, and rhetoric for domestic politics, in a similar fashion to the liberties of Europe and the balance of power for foreign policy.

The pressure from public opinion, in so far as it was (variously) discerned, shaped and expressed, operated in two contrary directions in 1749–51: in discouraging expensive commitments on the Continent and in encouraging trans-oceanic expansionism and opposition to France. It is all too easy to focus on the return of Louisbourg after the Treaty of Aix-la-Chapelle and to argue, therefore, that the ministry was not willing to respond to popular views, and, in this case, on a clearly crucial issue. This was not in fact the case. Both ministers

---

[57] Pelham to Hugh, Earl of Marchmont, 1 Sept. 1750, G.H. Rose (ed.), *A Selection from the Papers of the Earls of Marchmont* (3 vols, London, 1831), II, 388–9.
[58] Perrone to Charles Emmanuel III, 22 Jan. 1750, AST. LM. Ing. 56.
[59] Perrone to Charles Emmanuel III, 22 Jan. 1750, AST. LM. Ing. 56.
[60] Newcastle to Hardwicke, 25 Aug. (os) 1749, BL. Add. 35410 fol. 130.
[61] Mirepoix to Puysieulx, 3 Jan. 1750, AE. CP. Ang. 428 fol. 9.

and diplomats were aware of a context of scrutiny, and could respond accordingly. Thus, Pelham wrote to his brother about Nova Scotia in June 1750: 'Had we done nothing, we might have been blamed, in time to come: And had we done that, publicly, and no more, all the coffee houses in town would have been full of their wise animadversions.' Coffee houses were indeed a prime forum in which events were commented on, and thus recorded, and policy was debated. John Tucker commented on 'coffee house statesmen'. The close relationship between coffee houses and the press made the former, which subscribed to newspapers, more significant. Newspapers were read and discussed in coffee houses, while several papers used coffee houses as bylines. In 1756, a pamphleteer referred to having 'studied many years at the fireside of that illustrious school of politics, usually called the Smyrna Coffee-House, under those consummate adepts in that science who read daily lectures at that place'.[62] Opposition leaders had used a map when considering whether to raise Nova Scotia in Parliament.[63]

Nova Scotia was not the sole issue in which non-ministerial views had to be considered. With regard to control over the Caribbean sugar island of St Lucia, which was contested with France, Yorke, from the Paris embassy, put the focus on Parliament. As the recipient was his father, Hardwicke, the letter carries further credence:

> I am very cautious of saying too much on this subject to the Commissaries, as I would not willingly be brought to the Bar of the House, for any advice given, in a point which, as a national one, will certainly cause a greater clamour, whatever is the event.[64]

There was also tension over control of the island of Tobago.[65] In contrast, the ministry's decision, in response to Spanish concerns, not to send two frigates in order to explore the Pacific[66] did not become a public issue. In Europe, there were attacks on the ministry for failing to prevent France from repairing Dunkirk,

[62]　Pelham to Newcastle, 26 June (os) 1750, BL. Add. 35410 fol. 258; John to Richard Tucker, 3 Apr. (os) 1746, Bod. Ms. Don. C. 108 fol. 5; *Gray's Inn Journal*, 17 Aug. 1754; Anon., *A Serious Defence of some late Measures of the Administration* (London, 1756), p. 4.

[63]　H.R. Wyndham (ed.), *The Diary of the late George Bubb Dodington* (3rd edn, London, 1785), p. 28.

[64]　Yorke to Hardwicke, 9 Sept. 1750, BL. Add. 35355 fol. 292.

[65]　Henry Grenville, Governor of Barbados, to brother George, 5 Jan. (os) 1749, HL STG 24 (16).

[66]　Bedford to Keene, 24 Apr. (os) 1750, Russell (ed.), *Bedford*, II, 48–9.

a dangerous privateering base, the condition of which was regulated by treaty. This issue resonated due to a long sensitivity about it.[67]

As Secretary of State, Bedford made it clear to foreign envoys that the nation did not want new European commitments or war.[68] His tone was scarcely that of a seeker after deterrence through alliance building, which was the position repeatedly taken by Newcastle. Goal and process were both involved in Bedford's views on policy. With reason, he was seen as an opponent of subsidies.[69] Whereas Newcastle and Granville were able to overcome their past differences, Newcastle found this more difficult with Bedford, one of the 'New Allies'. Socially and politically, Bedford did not prove eager to defer to Newcastle, who blamed Sandwich for what he saw as inappropriate diplomatic instructions sent by Bedford.[70] As an instance of the importance attributed to George, Newcastle's willingness to support the Imperial Election Scheme was attributed to his need for the King's support against Bedford.[71] In practice, Newcastle actively sponsored the Scheme because of his views on the European situation and not as a result of domestic political calculations.

In June 1751, as the parliamentary session came to a close, Bedford was replaced as Secretary of State by a more pliant figure, Robert, 4th Earl of Holdernesse, who, as a diplomat, had worked with Newcastle, and who, unlike Bedford, had no significant independent political position. Nor did Holdernesse seek one. With reason, George thought Bedford indolent, proud and obstinate. He also suffered from violent rheumatism and gout.[72] George's unwillingness, however, to remove Bedford at Newcastle's behest, ensured that the Pelhams got Sandwich out of the Admiralty, which led Bedford to complain to George on 13 June and to resign the following day.[73]

Politics and policy are both in part a matter of tone. By late 1751, there was a general sense that the tone of British foreign policy was very different to the situation at the beginning of 1750. This was certainly the view of foreign diplomats, whose perception was a key way in which British policy was fixed as far

---

[67]   *Protestor*, 14 July 1753.

[68]   Mirepoix to Puysieulx, 30 Jan. 1750, AE. CP. Ang. 428 fol. 77; Perrone to Charles Emmanuel III, 26 Feb. 1750, AST. LM. Ing. 56.

[69]   Alt to Landgrave, 16 July 1751, Marburg, 4f England, 248.

[70]   Bedford to Yorke, 23 Mar. (os), Newcastle to Hardwicke, 26 Mar. (os) 1749, BL. Add. 32816 fols 276–8, 35410 fols 116–17.

[71]   Mirepoix to Puysieulx, 18 Aug. 1751, AE. CP. Ang. 432 fol. 129; Mirepoix, Portrait de la Cour d'Angleterre, Nov. 1751, AE. MD. Ang. 51 fol. 162.

[72]   Anon. to Edward Trelawny, Governor of Jamaica, 14 June (os) 1751, Washington, Library of Congress, microfilm reels, Vernon-Wager papers, reel 93.

[73]   Russell (ed.), *Bedford*, II, 82–3, 86, 89.

as contemporaries were concerned. These diplomats saw a more assertive British stance, both in Europe and overseas, and argued that the ministry was driving the process. This was an important point as far as the situation overseas was concerned, because the assumption hitherto on the part of most diplomats had been that governmental policy was driven by, and in response to, public opinion. Instead, in November 1751, Saint-Contest, the French Foreign Minister from 11 September, and a minister who lacked the interest in reconciliation with Britain shown by his predecessor, Puysieulx, claimed that it was the government that excited the British nation. He wrote that the government made the nation believe that Britain alone had the right to make settlements on the Guinea coast in West Africa, that half of Canada belonged to them, and that France usurped their Caribbean possessions, a reference to St Lucia and Tobago. Saint-Contest also claimed that there was no equivalence between the conduct of the British and French governments.[74]

The West Indies had been a cause of tension in 1749, notably a dispute over Tobago.[75] These disputes slackened, although concern continued to be expressed, both in the press[76] and in political circles. In late 1750, Rear-Admiral Charles Knowles MP pressed Bedford, Pelham, Halifax and Thomas, Viscount Dupplin, a MP and member of the Board of Trade, on the vulnerable state of Jamaica and the strength, in contrast, of France's Caribbean islands.[77] Attention, instead, focused on North America, where the potential for serious dispute had existed since the peace. Nova Scotia was a keen issue, with the British ministry convinced that the French did not wish to end disputes over it, and angered at reports that France proposed to publish favourable pamphlets in Britain. The press provided a steady stream of news about Nova Scotia, with an impression of French aggression there.[78] Nova Scotia appeared far more immediate as an issue than the affairs of the more distant, remote, and obscure North American interior. It was certainly easier for the press to report on Nova Scotia. Moreover, unlike the interior, Nova Scotia raised the issues of naval power, oceanic geopolitics and maritime trade. Each of these played a sensitive role in British public debate over foreign policy. Collectively, they were of great weight.

Nova Scotia thus represented a continuation of the sensitivity shown over the return of Louisbourg, a sensitivity to be seen again in 1758 when the issue

---

[74] Saint-Contest to Mirepoix, 4 Nov. 1751, AE. CP. Ang. 432 fol. 225.

[75] R. Rolt, *The Conduct of the Several Powers of Europe* (4 vols, London, 1749–50), IV, 635.

[76] For continued concern, *Old England*, 18 May (os) 1751; *Newcastle Journal*, 18 Jan. 1752.

[77] Knowles to Trelawny, 27 Nov. (os) 1750, Vernon-Wager papers, reel 93.

[78] *Old England*, 14 Sept. (os) 1751, 8 Aug. (os) 1752.

of its return anew was raised in the Commons.[79] They were linked issues as Cape Breton Island was very close to Nova Scotia. Failure over Louisbourg could be linked to the future of Nova Scotia in an indictment of the ministry, while concern over Louisbourg was a spur to finding an acceptable solution over Nova Scotia. Granville told Perrone that the situation risked becoming similar to that with Spain at the end of the 1730s, with a disputed trans-oceanic issue leading to war. Governmental anxieties about the views of the nation[80] were frequently referred to in diplomatic correspondence.

In practice, Saint-Contest was exaggerating in November 1751 when he claimed that the government was exciting the nation. Newcastle certainly played the key role in ensuring the parliamentary implementation of the provisions necessary for the Imperial Election Scheme. At the same time, he made clear the need to handle matters with care, and to take advantage of circumstances, in order to ensure popular backing. Newcastle told Perrone that Frederick II's choice of a Jacobite as his envoy to Paris would anger the nation and make it easier to win support for a subsidy to Russia,[81] a step seen as necessary in order to restrain Prussia. In the case of trans-oceanic issues, there was not in practice the active governmental hostility of France discerned by Saint-Contest, but the possibility that fear of domestic criticism was preventing a sincere attempt to settle matters with France.[82] Domestic political implications were to the fore in trans-oceanic issues because there were none of the international alliance or military exigencies that arose in wartime.

With no Hanoverian dimension, the politics, domestic and international, of trans-oceanic issues were less complex than those of Britain's policies on the European Continent. There was an anti-French dimension to the interventionist diplomacy on the Continent, and notably in terms of preventing an unwelcome future. Moreover, this dimension could be deployed in order to seek domestic and international support. However, as with the case of Carteret's diplomacy in the early 1740s, there was also the belief that British policy was primarily directed against Prussia, which led to a cross-current in policy. This direction was presented by Newcastle as made necessary by Frederick II's support for France. Thus, deterring Prussia was seen as an aspect of deterring France. This was the case at a variety of levels. Thus, Knowles, who was very concerned about the naval balance with the Bourbon powers, linked this oceanic theme with that of rivalry

---

[79] Rigby to Bedford, 7 Dec. 1758, Russell (ed.), *Bedford*, II, 371–2.
[80] Mirepoix, Portrait de la Cour d'Angleterre, Nov. 1751, AE. MD. Ang. 51 fols 164–6.
[81] Perrone to Charles Emmanuel III, 9 Sept., 4 Nov. 1751, AST. LM. Ing. 56.
[82] Yorke to Hardwicke, 24 Aug. 1751, BL. Add. 35355 fols 366–7.

with Prussia in the shape of the latter planning to supply the Bourbons with Baltic naval stores.[83] This link provided an economic dimension to geopolitics.

Nevertheless, contrary to Newcastle's view, there was a widespread assumption that the key element in the drive to deter Prussia was that of supporting the Hanoverian interests of George II. Newcastle did not appreciate the unpopularity of his policy. For a politician who had considerable experience in political management, there was a degree of naivety and wish-fulfilment in his response. Thus, Newcastle referred to the subsidy to Russia to keep troops on its frontier with Prussia:

> That, alone, will make the Russian subsidy as popular here as I, in my conscience, think it makes it necessary. I think, I can find, that those, who are the most adverse to subsidies, begin to see the necessity of this measure; or, at least, that it will not be withstood.[84]

This attitude was designed to confront ministerial critics as much as parliamentary opponents. Yet subsidies were unpopular. The failure to appreciate the serious political consequences of this unpopularity if the ministry lost control over the dynamics of the international and/or domestic political situation were to help put it on the defensive in the mid-1750s.

Newcastle's lack of realism may have been a consequence of his clear strength in the government. For, far from the elderly, but robust,[85] George II, born in 1683, dying, it was his elder son, Frederick, Prince of Wales, born in 1707, who died, on 20 March (os) 1751. A burst abscess in one of Frederick's lungs, possibly the result of an old sporting injury, was held responsible. This put an end to the attempts by Newcastle and Granville to recruit his support against Bedford and Cumberland,[86] and to the varied negotiations Frederick's advisors had been conducting in order to build up his strength. Frederick, indeed, had a capacity to challenge established links because he was able to attract support, or the prospect of support, across the political spectrum.[87] Frederick's death led also to an end of speculation on his stance on foreign policy, a stance generally

---

[83]   Knowles to Trelawny, 27 Nov. 1750, Vernon-Wager papers, reel 93.

[84]   Newcastle to Hardwicke, 13 Mar. (os) 1750, 6 Sept. (os) 1751, NA. SP. 84/454 fol. 261, BL. Add. 35412 fol. 15.

[85]   Lady Anson to Marchioness Green, 12 Oct. 1751, Bedford, CRO. L30/9/3/31.

[86]   A.N. Newman (ed.), 'Leicester House Politics, 1750–60', *Royal Historical Society, Camden Miscellany*, 23 (1969), pp. 193–5.

[87]   G. Glickman, 'Parliament, the Tories and Frederick Prince of Wales', *Parliamentary History*, 30 (2011), pp. 120–41.

reported as pro-Austrian. In contrast, his brother, Cumberland, was seen as more favourable to Prussia.[88] Newcastle benefited politically from Frederick's death. That it was followed three months later by the removal of Bedford was no coincidence. Newcastle saw himself as strong enough to part with the Duke, and also believed it was necessary to act. One commentator observed: 'The two Dukes were like wrestlers waiting on opportunity of giving each other the trip and Mr. Pitt moderating till the death of the Prince of Wales, which throw the power on the side of the Duke of Newcastle.'[89]

Whatever the dynastic situation, parliamentary support for the ministry carried weight abroad and, moreover, was believed to do so. In January 1753, Yorke reported from The Hague: 'The Lords' Address is much admired, and the assurances of strengthening His Majesty's hands, and the extraordinary zeal about the security of the succession, are thought to carry a more extensive meaning than the bare words seem to imply.'[90] Parliament's stance was seen as affecting Britain's appeal as an ally. Providing Yorke, two months later, with details of the ministry's parliamentary strength, Newcastle added:

> I know great industry has been used to represent in foreign courts that these affairs had created such difference and uneasiness here, as would entirely engage the King's whole attention; and prevent His Majesty from concerning himself at all with affairs abroad.[91]

In practice, the ministry appeared in firm command of the situation.

---

[88]   Klinggraeffen, envoy in London, to Frederick II, 24 Jan., and reply, 11 Feb. 1749, *Polit. Corr.* VI, 368; Ossorio to Charles Emmanuel III, 31 Mar. 1749; Mirepoix to Puysieulx, 3 Jan. 1750, AE. CP. Ang. 428 fol. 7; Ignace Koch, Secretary to Maria Theresa, to Count Kaunitz, Austrian envoy in Paris, 17 Apr. 1751, H. Schlitter (ed.), *Correspondance secrete entre ... Kaunitz ... et ... Koch* (Paris, 1899), p. 97; Re Frederick's support for negotiations with Bavaria, Haslang to Preysing, 2 Jan., 25 Feb., 22 May 1750, Munich, Bayr. Ges.; Perrone to Charles Emmanuel III, 12 Mar. 1750, AST. LM. Ing. 56.

[89]   Anon. to Trelawny, 14 July 1751, Vernon-Wager papers, reel 93.

[90]   Yorke to Hardwicke, 19 Jan. 1753, BL. Add. 35356 fol. 115.

[91]   Newcastle to Yorke, 23 Mar. 1753, NA. SP. 84/462.

Chapter 7

The New Order Under Strain, 1752–3

His Majesty's fleet (though at a very great expense) is in a better condition than it ever was known to be in time of peace: – and the great effect which the superiority of the King's navy the last war had towards obtaining the peace shows how necessary and effectual the keeping up that fleet may be for the preservation of it.

Newcastle, 1753[1]

The years 1752 and 1753 saw the development of the themes of the previous three years discussed in the previous chapter. The political context, however, had changed with the unexpected death of Frederick, Prince of Wales in March 1751 and the consequent collapse of his political interest. As for much of his adult life, Frederick's intentions had been very unclear, but his death removed the cause of speculation, and, in minimising political risk, greatly helped the government. However, domestic politics thereafter were not static. Newcastle's ability to fall foul of whichever of his colleagues was the other Secretary of State had led to the fall of Bedford in June 1751. On the one hand, ministerial stability thereafter continued until 1754. Speculations about changes were part of the staple of diplomatic reports, but, in practice, the ministry had rarely been so stable, even when Sir Robert Walpole's power was at its height.

Indeed, Britain was presented by many commentators, and with reason, as stronger and more stable than France in the early 1750s. Seeking to persuade Francis I, the Emperor, of the wisdom of co-operating with Britain to push through the Imperial Election Scheme, the British envoy John, 3rd Earl of Hyndford, countered the idea that French opposition was a prohibition:

examine France, on the side of its interest, whether it be so, or not, at present to begin a war when neither its trade, marine, nor finances have recovered their strength, when Louis XV's expenses exceed by a third the expenses of Louis XIV.[2]

---

[1] Newcastle to Keith, 22 Oct. 1753, NA. SP. 80/192. For the Austrian response, Keith to Newcastle, 3 Nov. 1753.

[2] Hyndford to Newcastle, 11 Apr. 1752, NA. SP. 80/190.

On 11 November 1752, the *Newcastle Journal* carried a London report that claimed: 'We see that all-grasping power, which would assume universal influence, perplexed by internal disputes.' Indeed, the introduction of the *vingtième* tax in 1749 led to protests. Calling for reduced government spending and lower taxes, the *Parlement* of Paris sought to give responsibility for overseeing financial policy to the *parlements*. In 1753, George commented to Perrone on the bad state of France and the weakness of its ministry.[3] This view is instructive because it qualifies the usual comparison of Britain and France.

So also with ministerial disputes. Foreign diplomats highlighted those within Britain, but those elsewhere could be drawn to the attention of British diplomats by foreign ministers who employed the British technique of referring to them in order to excuse policy. Thus, in 1749, Puysieulx told Yorke that he was under pressure from colleagues who wished France to hold onto some of its conquests in the Austrian Netherlands until the Allies had fulfilled their obligations under the peace treaty.[4]

Perspectives, however, varied. *Old England*, on 25 November 1752, noted 'the reviving spirit of that people giving more vigour to the proceedings of their Parliament', the latter the habitual misinterpretation of the *Parlement* of Paris.[5] In turn, the paper warned about the danger of Britain becoming 'a military power', a reference to persistent opposition distrust of the Captain General, Cumberland. In an instance of the variety and malleability of historical references, he was repeatedly depicted as a would-be Richard III, a usurping uncle of the future George III.[6] More mundanely, Newcastle was also troubled by Cumberland, seeing him as a supporter of rival members of the Whig élite, notably Bedford. Cumberland's links were closest with a group of Whig grandees whose relations with Newcastle were cool at best. Newcastle made it clear that he was confident both that Bedford and Sandwich would lose royal favour if they launched a formal opposition, and also that the forthcoming general election, which had to be held in 1754 at the latest, would produce the result he desired.[7] Cumberland's reputation reflected the paradox that the legacy of 1689 made France a natural enemy, but that the same legacy and bias against a large army limited the British capacity to fight France.

Unexpectedly, in 1753, the government's eclectic reform policy led to a serious political storm over Jewish naturalisation. There was a strong strand of

---

3   Perrone to Charles Emmanuel III, 25 Jan. 1753, AST. LM. Ing. 57.
4   Yorke to Bedford, 19 Feb. 1749, BL. Add. 32816 fol. 90.
5   For example, *Whitehall Evening Post*, 14 June, *Protestor*, 3 Nov. 1753.
6   *Commons Debate on Regency Bill*, 16 May (os) 1751, p. 1036.
7   Perrone to Charles Emmanuel III, 9 Sept. 1752, 8 Mar. 1753, AST. LM. Ing. 57.

disquiet over immigration. Opposition to any naturalisation Bill for foreign Protestants had been predicted in 1748.[8] The new Act was essentially designed in order to attract Jewish merchants to London and to help financial figures linked to Pelham.[9] More generally, however, the Act, passed on 7 June 1753, was an important part of the foreign policy of the government, for this policy had a significant financial component, one moreover linked to domestic as well as international politics. Britain was in competition to act as the key state in a global financial system, one centred on the Atlantic but spreading more widely, and notably to South and East Asia. Diaspora financial networks were important to this system, especially, in Europe, the Huguenots (Protestants who had had to leave France, in 1685) and the Sephardi Jews. The former had benefited from a naturalisation law only requiring that they took communion in the Church of England. The latter were of particular significance for facilitating Britain's position in the trade with Portuguese Brazil and with Spanish America, the major sources of bullion in the Western world, and that in a period where the metallic basis of fiscal strength was more significant than over the last seventy years.

With this bullion, Britain was readily able to manage trades on which it had a negative balance, which was true of a number of important trades, notably with Russia, Turkey, India and China. These trades gave Britain key advantages in satisfying Western markets, both domestic and colonial. These advantages enabled Britain to be the most significant entrepôt state in the world, a state whose commerce focused on London, the centre of government. Thanks to the bullion, it was also possible to provide money for subsidies to European allies: policy could be implemented. Britain's political significance was further enhanced by its major importance as a source of loans. This significance helps explain Britain's role in the Imperial Election Scheme. In 1749, for example, Saxony sought permission to raise a loan in London as a means to re-establish its finances and take the international role it ought to do.[10] Moreover, the diaspora networks helped Britain to draw on Dutch wealth and financial connections, a major source of finance and credit for Britain and a significant aspect of its strength in the international financial system.

---

[8] D. Statt, *Foreigners and Englishmen: The Controversy about Immigration and Population, 1660–1760* (Newark, Delaware, 1995); Zamboni to Landgrave Ludwig VIII of Hesse-Darmstadt, 9 Feb. 1748, Darmstadt E1 M10/6.

[9] Alt to Landgrave William VIII of Hesse-Cassel, 25 May 1753, Marburg, 4f England 254; Haslang to Preysing, 6 June 1753, Munich, Bayr. Ges., London 227.

[10] Hanbury Williams to Newcastle, 16 Jan. 1749, NA. SP. 88/70.

Thus, British policy and Britain's ability to act as a major power were again linked to domestic politics. The Jewish Naturalisation Act was also part of a reform pulse after the War of the Austrian Succession ended in 1748. This reform pulse was designed to prepare Britain for a further international conflict and, more generally, to strengthen the state. In part, reform policies arose in response to specific problems and issues, notably the post-war concern over a crime wave that was linked to the demobilisation of about 80,000 men into a crowded labour market. There were highway robberies by disbanded soldiers and sailors across the country.[11] The contrast between the costly fireworks that celebrated peace and the state of poor veterans was captured by commentators.[12] The problems of large-scale gin-drinking exacerbated social worries and moral panic.[13] In his speech to Parliament on 15 November 1753, George expressed concern at the crime rate. In contrast to the emphasis on mechanistic themes in the thought of the period, there was a significant understanding of society as organic.

The reform pulse was also designed to be proactive, and that in a number of contexts. Domestic ones were significant. Some changes reflected developments that preceded these years, such as those associated with Methodism. Moreover, there were contrasts and cross-purposes between some of the reform policies. At the same time, there was an essential commonality in the reform pulse, that of anxiety and of preparation for struggle in a troubling international context.

This drive for preparation linked foreign and domestic policies, and both to key themes in political discussion. As in the war years, there was a perception that Britain and France were competing in terms of fiscal strength and stability, and that this was a key element in international relations. Upset by the poor state of the finances of his ally France,[14] on which he sought information,[15] Frederick wanted to know whether Britain could afford to pay subsidies to its allies.[16] The ability to afford was linked to the willingness to pay. Although concerned to limit subsidies,[17] Newcastle observed in 1753 that expenditure was crucial: 'I know, the King of Prussia's dependence is that the court of Petersburg [Russia] will do

[11]   Sir James Kinloch to Lord Braco, 5 Jan. (os) 1749, Aberdeen UL, Duff of Braco papers, 2727/1/214.

[12]   Joseph Spence to William Burrell Massingberd, 15 Feb. 1749, Beinecke, Osborn Shelves, C455 12/66.

[13]   N. Rogers, *Mayhem: Postwar Crime and Violence in Britain, 1748–53* (Oxford, 2013).

[14]   Frederick to Lord Marshal, 1 Sept. 1753, *Polit. Corr.* X, 63–4.

[15]   Frederick to Knyphausen, *Polit. Corr.* X, 475.

[16]   Frederick to Michell, 23 Oct. 1753, 12 Mar. 1754, *Polit. Corr.* X.

[17]   Newcastle to Hanbury Williams, 9, 28 July 1752, HW.

nothing in this respect without money; and that there will be no inclination here, in the present circumstances, to give it them.'[18] Indeed, Frederick saw British money as the great 'cloche' of the international system, a mechanistic image of the operation of the latter.[19] Such images were very important to the way in which people thought and expressed themselves about international relations, and thereby helped sustain patterns of thought. Thus, the Jewish Naturalisation Act was located not only in domestic political controversy,[20] but also in a broader context. Similarly, Hardwicke's Marriage Act, that had also caused controversy in 1753 (it came into force in March 1754), was located in a broader social context focused on views about social mobility.

Ministerial changes and the prospect of more and of changes in rulers encouraged a considerable degree of volatility, not least because many rulers and ministers, particularly new ones, were not pledged to specific policies. This was an issue affecting views of Britain, as the likely policies of the future George III were unclear. In the shorter term, however, the key change in question occurred abroad, although not at once. In 1753, the alteration in the Austrian government when Kaunitz became Chancellor led to mistaken speculation that he would back Britain, and that this could prove the basis for a new security system, bringing new life to the exhausted Anglo-Austrian alliance.[21] There was also speculation that Kaunitz would lead Austria towards France, as former Chancellor Sinzendorf had sought to do in 1728 and as Bartenstein had done in 1735. However, the difficulty of relying on professions of friendship was also a theme.[22] Indeed, Count Starhemberg, the Austrian envoy, reached Paris in January 1754 without instructions to change Austrian policy.

Rumour played a major role in encouraging preparation for struggle because, especially in 1753, there was much speculation about imminent attacks. Most diplomats and commentators simply reported such speculation, which helped encourage and spread alarm. Others presented it as an aspect of an interacting system in which deterrence played a role. Thus, in March 1753, Joseph Yorke observed:

---

[18]   Newcastle to Keith, 21 Sept. 1753, NA. SP. 80/192.

[19]   Frederick to Michell, 14 May 1754, *Polit. Corr.* X, 475.

[20]   T.W. Perry, *Public Opinion, Propaganda, and Politics in Eighteenth-Century England: a Study of the Jew Bill of 1753* (Cambridge, Massachusetts, 1962).

[21]   Newcastle to Yorke, 18 May, Newcastle to Keith, 6 July, Keith to Newcastle, 21 Dec. 1753, NA. SP. 84/463, 80/192; Frederick II to Klinggraeffen, 18 May, Frederick to Lord Marshal, 29 May 1753, *Polit. Corr.* IX, 427, 437–8.

[22]   Saint-Contest to Aubeterre, 7 Nov. 1753, AE. CP. Aut. 252 fol. 269.

The preparations, rumours of encampments, magazines, augmentations, and many other such articles, I attribute to the persuasion they are in at the Court of Versailles that because we are attentive to our navy, that therefore we mediate some great design by sea. I have many proofs of their suspicion, and if that is so, does not good policy require that they should keep us in check by demonstrations towards the Empire, and Flanders, which last is our weak side and therefore the most likely to draw our attention, and prevent us from going to great lengths.[23]

British concern about Flanders, and the Austrian Netherlands more generally, made not only the state of the Barrier an acute issue, but also French works at neighbouring Dunkirk. These issues attracted press concern[24] and also diplomatic and political comment.[25]

This troubling context offers a way to consider the attempt to advance British interests in Europe and overseas. The Imperial Election Scheme and the development of Nova Scotia, the Continental and the Oceanic, both take on additional meaning, not as opposites in policy, but as aspects of the same drive to improve relations, one that was very different to the 'salutary neglect' detected by some contemporary commentators in the 1720s and 1730s. In turn, there was a perception that French policy had a similar unity. Holdernesse was to claim in 1756:

The conduct of the Court of France, ever since the Peace of Aix-la-Chapelle [1748], has evidently shown, that their immediate aim was at the power and influence of Great Britain, which had stood in the gap, and prevented the ruin of the Liberties of Europe, and their ambitious aim at universal dominion: – For there is not a part in the world in which the commercial interests of these kingdoms are concerned, from whence complaints of the most grievous nature, of French encroachments, have not come to the King's ears.[26]

Aspects of the same drive, however, did not mean agreement over implementation and priorities. Indeed, the lack of such agreement was highly significant in the politics of the period, although the focus was on priorities not implementation. This led not only to the disagreements seen in the press and in Parliament, but also to important tensions within the Whig ministry. Thus, there was a major

---

[23]   Joseph to Philip Yorke, 23 Mar. 1753, BL. Add. 35363 fol. 324.
[24]   *Whitehall Evening Post*, 14 June 1753; *Protestor*, 14 July 1753.
[25]   Yorke to Newcastle, 26 June 1753, NA. SP. 84/463; Council meeting, 21 Aug. 1753, BL. Add. 32995 fol. 26.
[26]   Holdernesse to Keith, 21 June 1756, NA. SP. 80/197 fols 170–1.

disjuncture between the strategic and operational dimensions of policy, and, more particularly, the strategic and the political. This was to be a disjuncture that was exacerbated by anxiety and one that was triggered by specific crises. As a result, although the logic of British policy was forward-looking and based on a secure understanding of international interactions, it was vulnerable to the problems of the short-term. Newcastle exemplified this tension.

The year 1752 began with significant political endorsement for Newcastle's Continental interventionism, and, more especially, for the Imperial Election Scheme. The Saxon treaty was strongly approved in the Commons on 22 January (os). Newcastle was self-serving in thinking that this approval would lead to 'universal approbation throughout the whole kingdom'.[27] Bedford's attack in the Lords failed. The attack met with a weak response by Newcastle, but an effective one by Granville.

Newcastle was more acute in observing that a failure for Britain to benefit from the 'extraordinary expense' of subsidy treaties would create political difficulties for the government.[28] This was a warning to diplomats, British and foreign, that foreign governments did not wish to heed, nor, indeed, Newcastle to pursue the logic of. So also with the growing disquiet about the situation in the Low Countries. Concern about Austrian attitudes toward the Barrier were matched by worries about Dutch isolationism, worries that offered a counterpoint to the possibility that Britain might do the same. Noting that his views were also those of the King, Newcastle feared that 'the whole system of Europe would be overturned'.[29] From The Hague, Yorke picked up a sense of flux, one based on the strains in existing alliances:

> I see that the King of Prussia is upon the watch to pick us up. He is smoother than he has been a great while, and from no other motive, but because he is wise enough to see, that if the Imperial Court [Austria] drives us much further, we must change our system whether we will or no.[30]

There was also concern about Austrian unhelpfulness over the Imperial Election Scheme, a concern driven home on Newcastle because he accompanied George to Hanover.[31] Travelling back via Brussels, Newcastle held discussions with the ministers about the tariff for the Austrian Netherlands and ended up highly

---

27 Newcastle to Hanbury Williams, 24 Jan. (os) 1752, HW.
28 Newcastle to Hanbury Williams, 24 Jan. (os) 1752, HW .
29 Newcastle to Yorke, 21 Jan. 1752, NA. SP. 84/458.
30 Joseph to Philip Yorke, 7 Apr. 1752, BL. Add. 35362 fol. 299.
31 Newcastle to Holdernesse, 4 June 1752, NA. SP. 36/118 fols 330–1.

dissatisfied.[32] The extent to which his views were being shaken by experience was significant. He expressed his anger with Austria freely on his return to London.[33] Although continuing to try to breathe some life into the Imperial Election Scheme,[34] he argued that peacetime subsidies were impossible.[35] Meanwhile, the French government claimed that Parliament would be mindful of the state of the Scheme. Saint-Contest, the Foreign Minister, felt certain that the British ministry would seek unanimity among the Electors, rather than a plurality, as it would not wish to present Parliament with a division in place of the unanimity it had predicted.[36] Parliament was certainly a factor cited by British diplomats, who were anxious about what the ministry could say, as well as by others who thought the issue would affect the date on which the session opened.[37] In the event, it did so with great success for the ministry.[38]

The British government sought to ease relations with France over the Imperial Election Scheme, but without success. This led to a more general reluctance to seek 'any system' with France although Newcastle returned to the idea.[39] Despite warnings that failure would discredit British policy,[40] the Scheme failed as a result of the difficulties of winning over the Electors, notably the Elector Palatine, who was backed by France. That would have been bad enough, but doubts about Britain's alliance system were more serious. Indeed, Newcastle argued that Austria's stance encouraged France to act 'the double part which they now do'.[41] There was criticism from Gerlach Adolf von Münchhausen, the head of the Hanoverian ministry, on the grounds that Austria's conduct arose from the British decision to discuss the Scheme with France, but Newcastle and the Hanoverian representative in London responded that 'rejecting those overtures from France to make all easy, would never have been born in England'. They also pointed out that Austria had already shown an obdurate approach. Newcastle

---

[32] Newcastle to Yorke, 1 Dec. 1752, NA. SP. 84/461.

[33] Perrone to Charles Emmanuel III, 14 Dec. 1752, AST. LM. Ing. 57.

[34] Newcastle to Wrede, 19 Dec. 1752, Munich, Bayr. Ges., London 226.

[35] Perrone to Charles Emmanuel III, 28 Dec. 1752, AST. LM. Ing. 57.

[36] Saint-Contest to Grevenbrock, 9 Jan. 1753, AE. CP. Palatinat 78 fol. 9.

[37] Joseph to Philip Yorke, 9 Jan. 1753, BL. Add. 35363 fol. 318; reporting Dutch opinion, Bonnac to Saint-Contest, 10 Jan. 1753, AN. KK. 1400 fols 40–1.

[38] Newcastle to Yorke, 12 Jan. 1753, NA. SP. 84/462; Alt to Landgrave William VIII of Hesse-Cassel, 6, 20 Feb. 1753, Marburg, 4f England, 254.

[39] Newcastle to Holdernesse, 26 July 1752, NA. SP. 36/119 fol. 139; Newcastle to Keith, 23 Jan. 1753, NA. SP. 80/191.

[40] William Bentinck to Holdernesse, 11 July 1752, BL. Eg. 3481 fol. 51.

[41] Newcastle to Hardwicke, 12 July 1752, BL. Add. 35412 fol. 173.

was backed by George,[42] and, blamed for being led by the Austrians, Hyndford, the envoy in Vienna, was recalled. He had been a protégé of Münchhausen.[43] Even Hyndford, however, warned Maria Theresa of Austria that there was a danger of Austria losing 'the English Nation',[44] an instructive approach and phrase. Seeking to represent the latter, *Old England* deployed 'common sense' in order to argue that the Scheme was of no benefit for Britain.[45] Governmental sensitivities were apparent, Yorke writing to his father Hardwicke:

> I shall be very sorry to see the English ministers reduced to the hard necessity of producing anything to justify a measure they have failed in, such a situation would be productive of much mischief, would perhaps revive a drooping opposition and throw us back into our ancient spirit of squabbling.[46]

The general sense of disquiet was given particular starts when rumours spread of possible conflict. In 1752, George thought Prussia might intervene militarily in the Jülich-Berg succession dispute, and was also worried about Prussian threats to Saxony. Such concerns led to flurries of speculation and diplomatic activity.[47] None resulted in conflict, but there was a parallel with the uncertainty in British trans-oceanic relations with the Bourbons. As in the latter case, although Newcastle could refer to 'the general Law of Nations',[48] there was no agreed or easy basis for peaceful international settlement of disputes. Instead, there was a reliance on deterrence, although, in the case of the threat to Saxony in early 1753, the British ministry was at pains to emphasise that it had no general defensive engagements against aggression in Europe:

> The King will always be ready to employ his good offices for the service of the King of Poland, and for preventing any steps which may endanger the peace of the Empire; But His Majesty cannot make himself a party where he is none, or act in consequence of engagements which he did not think proper to take.[49]

---

[42]   Newcastle to Pelham, 26 July 1752, BL. Add. 35412 fol. 209.

[43]   Newcastle to Pelham, 26 July, Hanbury Williams to Henry Fox, 27 July 1752, BL. Add. 35412 fol. 208, 51393 fol. 109.

[44]   Hyndford to Newcastle, 5 Aug. 1752, NA. SP. 80/190.

[45]   *Old England*, 1 Aug. (os) 1752.

[46]   Yorke to Hardwicke, 26 Aug. 1752, BL. Add. 35356 fol. 71.

[47]   Yorke to Newcastle, 16 Sept. 1752, NA. SP. 84/460; Newcastle to Albemarle, 18 Oct. 1752, NA. SP. 78/245 fol. 160.

[48]   Newcastle to Yorke, 19 Jan. 1753, NA. SP. 84/462.

[49]   Newcastle to Hanbury Williams, 12 Jan. 1753, HW; Newcastle to Yorke, 12 Jan. 1753, NA. SP. 84/462.

The concerns of 1752 led to anxiety in early 1753 that Frederick was planning an attack on Hanover, an opinion communicated by Austria.[50] In turn, Frederick sought information on Hanoverian military preparations[51] and also saw a wide-ranging international conspiracy being created against him, one envisaged by Count Brühl, the Saxon minister, and involving Britain, Austria and Russia.[52] Newcastle saw the crisis as demonstrating the need for the Imperial Election Scheme.[53] Austrian and Russian support was sought in the event of a Prussian attack.[54] Again, rumours circulated, for example of an Anglo-Russian negotiation to transport Russian troops to Holstein, which might lead to a Hanoverian attack on Prussia.[55] In London, the Cabinet discussed the issue on 6 February and agreed that Britain had to defend Hanover. Granville saw this as a crucial deterrent to Prussia, while Newcastle thought Prussia would not attack.[56] As later in 1755, there were doubts about French intentions in 1753[57] and very conflicting reports about French military preparations,[58] as well as those of Prussia, Austria and other powers.

The British readiness to seek the support of Austria and, in particular, Russia matched the requirements of the Hanoverian government.[59] This closeness could have led to political problems in Britain, but the crisis proved short lived and, despite Newcastle's sensitivity on the point,[60] was not generally seen in terms of Britain protecting Hanover. Frederick declared by his envoy in Hanover that he had no invasion plans.[61] However, the crisis was instructive for what it showed about international relations and also concerning both the apparent propensity

[50] Keith to Newcastle, 17 Jan. 1753, NA. SP. 80/191; Perrone to Charles Emmanuel III, 25 Jan. 1753, AST. LM. Ing. 57.

[51] Frederick II to Michell, 20 Jan. 1753, *Polit. Corr.* IX, 318.

[52] Frederick to Lord Marshal, 20 Jan. 1753, *Polit. Corr.* IX, 315.

[53] Newcastle to Keith, 23 Jan., 30 Mar. 1753, NA. SP. 80/191.

[54] Newcastle to Keith, 2 Feb., 9 Mar. 1753, NA. SP. 80/191.

[55] Vergennes to Saint-Contest, 5 Feb. 1753, AE. CP. Palatinat 78 fol. 104.

[56] Ryder diary, 6 Feb. 1753, Sandon.

[57] Newcastle to Yorke, 13 Feb. 1753, NA. SP. 84/462.

[58] Yorke to Newcastle, 3, 10, 13, 17, 20 Apr. 1753, NA. SP. 84/463; Joseph to Philip Yorke, 10 Apr. 1753, BL. Add. 35363 fol. 326.

[59] Newcastle to Hanbury Williams, 20 Feb. 1753, HW; W. Mediger, *Moskaus Weg nach Europa: der Aufstieg Russlands zum europäischen Machstaat im Zeitalter Friedrichs des Grossen* (Brunswick, 1952), pp. 452–5, and 'Great Britain, Hanover and the Rise of Prussia', in R. Hatton and M.S. Anderson (eds), *Studies in Diplomatic History* (London, 1970), pp. 209–10; J.P. LeDonne, *The Grand Strategy of the Russian Empire, 1650–1831* (Oxford, 2004), pp. 87–9.

[60] Perrone to Charles Emmanuel III, 5 Apr. 1753, AST. LM. Ing. 57.

[61] Newcastle to Yorke, 16 Mar. 1753, NA. SP. 84/462.

of conflict and the possibility of avoiding it, as conspicuously did not happen in 1756. In March 1753, Maria Theresa assured Keith that Austria would fulfil its engagements if Frederick attacked Hanover, and the warning she offered, that Britain approaching France to use its influence on Prussia risked making France too powerful, scarcely suggested that Austria might approach France.[62] The Russian willingness to provide military assistance pleased George and the ministry and subsequently made it easier to take a firm line over North America while also leading to a failure to appreciate that this technique for managing European developments might not work on another occasion. The British emphasis was on Russia being willing to act against any further aggrandisement by Prussia, rather than against Prussia as currently constituted, and this was clearly seen as designed to prevent any war to regain Silesia and weaken Prussia.[63] This, however, did not match Austrian priorities. The sense of linkage led to suggestions that 'the addition of Russia to our system' would lead France to yield to British pressure to demolish harbour works at Dunkirk.[64]

Less apparent over Europe since the departure of Bedford, ministerial differences were more readily apparent in trans-oceanic policy. There was a new version of the tension that had been to the fore in 1739, as disagreement then over how best to confront Spain was linked to tension within the ministry, notably increased assertion on the part of Newcastle against Walpole. In 1752–3 an older Newcastle, who in the House of Lords debate on the Saxon treaty, had attacked the reliance only on 'our wooden walls',[65] a criticism of the 'blue water' reliance on naval strength, faced other ministers with different priorities. Notable was the group termed recently the 'authoritarian Whigs', among whom George, 2nd Earl of Halifax, Bedford and Sandwich were important,[66] a group that, to a degree, looked to Cumberland. This group was concerned with North America. In part, this was a case of concern with the trans-oceanic interest as a whole, but the priorities with North America were somewhat different to those in the West Indies. The emphasis was on long-range power projection, the geopolitics of forts, winning over local Native tribes, laying claim to vast tracts of land, and the availability of force. This was an emphasis different to that of building up

---

[62]   Keith to Newcastle, 9 Mar. 1753, NA. SP. 80/191.

[63]   Newcastle to Keith, 6 July 1753, NA. SP. 80/192.

[64]   Yorke to Hugh Jones, Under-Secretary in Northern Department, 6 July 1753, BL. Add. 35432 fol. 108.

[65]   Notes on Debate, Warwick, Warwickshire CRO, Newdigate papers, CR136 B 3012/44.

[66]   S. Kinkel, 'The King's Pirates? Naval Enforcement of Imperial Authority, 1740–76', *William and Mary Quarterly*, 3rd ser., 71 (2014), p. 8.

the navy and its trans-oceanic capability. These ministers were particularly keen on developing the British position in Nova Scotia, whereas Pelham was seen as opposed, because of the cost and the potentially damaging impact on relations with France. Newcastle was presented as influenced by Pelham.[67] As a security for the British position there, Halifax pressed in 1751 for the stationing of two warships off Nova Scotia, a measure opposed by the Board of Admiralty.[68] Cost again was an element. The press voiced concern over Nova Scotia.[69]

The definition of the North American border with France had been left to negotiation by commissioners in the Peace of Aix-la-Chapelle. However, the difficulty of settling the matters in dispute were accentuated by expansionism on the part of both Britain and France.[70] Moreover, this expansionism was linked to marked volatility among the Native American tribes and in their relations with Britain and France. The end of the war meant that trade between France and French North America resumed. This resumption provided France with opportunities to win over Native Americans by providing goods and purchasing furs, and thus reversing a loss of French influence during the recent war.[71] Moreover, the French stepped up their defences in North America. The loss of Louisbourg in 1745 and subsequent anxieties about possible British attack led to a post-war determination to strengthen France's position. The colony cost more than the revenues it produced, but its retention was increasingly seen as a geopolitical necessity.[72]

Interest in containment and concern about British expansion[73] had led the French, in 1749, to send a small force into the Ohio Valley, which offered a shorter route from New France, French-held Canada, to the French settlements

---

[67]   Mirepoix to Saint-Contest, 12 Nov. 1751, AE. CP. Ang. 432 fol. 235.

[68]   Halifax to Newcastle, 6 Mar. 1751, BL. Add. 32724 fol. 165; Perrone to Charles Emmanuel III, 22 Apr. 1751, AST. LM. Ing. 56.

[69]   *Old England*, 8 Aug. (os) 1752.

[70]   T.C. Pease (ed.), *Anglo-French Boundary Disputes in the West 1749–1763* (Springfield, Illinois, 1936); M. Savelle, *The Diplomatic History of the Canadian Boundary, 1749–63* (New Haven, Connecticut, 1940); M. Pedley, 'Map Wars: The Role of Maps in the Nova Scotia/Acadia Boundary Disputes of 1750', *Imago Mundi*, 50 (1998), pp. 96–104.

[71]   W.R. Jacobs, *Diplomacy and Indian Gifts: Anglo-French Rivalry along the Ohio and Northwest Frontiers, 1748–1783* (Stanford, California, 1950).

[72]   C.M. Desbarats, 'France in North America: the Net Burden of Empire during the First Half of the Eighteenth Century', *French History*, 11 (1997), and 'The Cost of Early Canada's Native Alliances: Reality and Scarcity's Rhetoric', *William and Mary Quarterly*, 3rd ser. 52 (1995).

[73]   President of the Council of Marine to M. de la Galissonière, 2 Jan. 1749, BN. AN. Colonies, B89.

in the Illinois Country, and then on to distant Louisiana in the south. The Ohio Valley was also attractive to Virginians seeking land to the west across the Appalachians, as well as to imperial strategists thinking of how best to disrupt French plans. In 1747–8, the Virginia House of Assembly and the British government had given the Ohio Company, a newly-chartered group of Virginia landowners and London merchants, title to a third of a million acres. This was a vast stake that represented a bold land grab, one likely to engender confrontation with France. Essentially, expansionism, which in wartime appeared normal and necessary, became bellicose in peacetime. It represented a disturbing blending of the two states, and one that the British colonial authorities lacked the power and will to differentiate and the British government the determination to seek to do.

In turn, the resulting policies were regarded as a threat to British North America. The disputes between the two powers were made more serious by the British belief that there was a French plan to weaken fatally their position there, and that it was necessary to act vigorously to show the French that they should abandon this plan. This was an understandable stance on the part of British commentators, although there was also a degree of British paranoia and French hyperbole about French intentions. This perception had different force and connotations for colonial interests, the British public debate, and the ministry.

By the summer of 1753, concern about French moves was widespread at the centre of the ministry, with the Board of Trade reporting news from New York that the French had sent 6,000 troops to build forts on the River Ohio, a serious exaggeration of the numbers involved. The Halifax/Bedford/Sandwich/Cumberland connection were not the sole players. The Council decision on 21 August 1753

> that, with regard to the settlement said to be intended to be made by the French on the River Ohio, general orders should be sent to the several governors in North America, to do their utmost, to prevent, by force, those, and any such attempts, that may be made, by the French, or by the Indians, in the French interest,

was taken not by these men, but by Newcastle, Hardwicke, Pelham, Granville, Anson, and Ligonier, the Lieutenant-General of the Ordnance.[74] The representatives of the military, Anson and Ligonier, played a role. However, the key element was the Pelhams, a group that included not only their confidante Hardwicke but also Newcastle's ally Granville. Moreover, Anson was closely linked to the Pelhams. North America was not the sole issue. The Council

---

[74] Council memorandum, 21 Aug. 1753, BL. Add. 32995 fol. 27.

ordered Albemarle in Paris to protest about French policy in the West Indies and over Dunkirk. Holdernesse argued that it was now necessary to act firmly.[75] Kaunitz warned Keith that France was thinking of attacking British North America.[76] At this stage, Newcastle and Pelham were directing much of their attention to the forthcoming elections.[77]

Meanwhile, an interesting indication of a relative lack of public interest in high politics was provided by the press. Appearing on 10 November 1753, the last issue of the *Protester* offered instructive reflections on the relationship between politics and the public mood:

> In a Paper War the same precautions should be taken as in a war of execution ... Plausible grounds for a rupture may be found at any time: But all times are not alike favourable for coming to action ... no opposition can be carried on with any efficacy, but in the name of the People, and for popular considerations: And if they cannot be pressed into the service, the whole proceeding grows ridiculous, and would soon deserve the name of Quixotism rather than Patriotism ... Almost all the popular topics which used to have the swiftest and surest operation, I have, at times, laid before them: And have found them as cold with regard to every one of them ... all that they seem to desire, at present, is a noise and a bustle for the sake of adding to the amusements and diversifying the chat of the day ... of the various points, which have been agitated for some years passed, only the French players [actors] and the Jews Act, have made any manifest impression on the minds of the People ... They may satisfy themselves with what they see, and reconcile themselves to what they feel, under a persuasion that, being in general free and unmolested, they need not ruffle the current, by nice disquisitions, and fruitless cavillings.

This account throws critical light on the thesis of this book that there was a mid-century crisis and the perception of crisis. However, as the 1930s, the decade of the National Government and economic modernisation in southern England as well as of Appeasement, shows, there is nothing incompatible between a sense of crisis and an engagement, at the same time, with a very different agenda of present concerns. Certainly in 1753, the focus was on the Jewish naturalisation agitation and not on the situation in North America. The government was presented

---

75   Minutes 21 Aug. 1753, BL. Add. 32995 fol. 26; Perrone to Charles Emmanuel III, 30 Aug. 1753, AST. LM. Ing. 57.
76   Keith to Newcastle, 19 Sept. 1753, NA. SP. 80/192.
77   Lady Anson to Marchioness Grey, [1753], Bedford, CRO, Lucas papers, 30/913/43.

as yielding to popular opinion to Jewish naturalisation[78] with the Repeal Act receiving the Royal Assent on 20 December. This repeal ensured an easier time in the parliamentary session that began in November 1753, and also helped confirm the trend of assuming that decisions were made through such yielding to pressure. As a result, the issue helped affect the wider international perception of British policy and politics, that of popular volatility[79] and government responses. The latter perception also owed much to a general election being due in 1754. As Newcastle knew, Frederick did not believe that the British ministry would place the burden of a Russian subsidy on the 'nation'.[80] He was informed from London of a tension between George and the Hanoverian ministry, both willing to meet all Russian demands, and a less willing British ministry.[81]

At the same time, the government was more clearly in control politically than when it had been threatened by Prince Frederick. The latter's death had brought his eldest son, George, the future George III, born in 1738, back into the orbit of his grandfather, for George II did not extend to his daughter-in-law, Augusta, nor to his numerous grandchildren, the loathing he had shown for his troublesome eldest son. That Augusta came from the ruling house of Saxe-Gotha helped as she had no links with the Whig aristocratic families. The education of the future King caused controversy in late 1752 when his sub-Governor, Andrew Stone, Newcastle's political factotum, was implausibly seen as pushing unwelcome Tory views. In early 1753, Stone successfully defended himself before the Council from the charge of being a Jacobite, still a potent accusation; and an attack on the issue in the House of Lords was defeated by the ministry. The crisis indicated the continued traction of Jacobitism as an issue, the sensitivity of the topic of the future ruler's opinions,[82] and also the ability of George II and the Pelhams to overcome attacks. Simon, 1st Earl Harcourt, the Governor, or head of the Prince's household, a critic of Stone, resigned in December 1752. He was succeeded in 1753 by James, 2nd Earl Waldegrave, a socially adroit courtier who enjoyed considerable favour with George II and was

---

[78] Alt to William VIII of Hesse-Cassel, 10 Aug. 1753, Marburg, 4f England 254; Joseph Yorke to Hugh Jones, 23 Nov. 1753, BL. Add. 35432 fol. 184.

[79] Frederick II to Klinggraeffen, 6 July 1754, *Polit. Corr.* X, 370.

[80] Frederick to Klinggraeffen, 24 July, Frederick to Count Podewils, 25 July, Frederick to Lord Marshal, 16 Aug. 1753, *Polit. Corr.* X, 27, 51–2; Newcastle to Keith, 21 Sept. 1753, NA. SP. 80/192.

[81] Michell to Frederick, 3 Aug. 1753, *Polit. Corr.* X, 48.

[82] Perrone to Charles Emmanuel III, 22 Feb., 1 Mar. 1753, AST. LM. Ing. 57.

then close to the Pelhams. Perrone presented the Pelhams as triumphant in all respects, while Newcastle emphasised the government's strength in the Lords.[83]

The real threat from Jacobitism proved marginal in these years. Alexander Murray of Elibank played a central role in the so-called Elibank Plot of 1751–3, a series of projects that included the murder or seizure of George II as a prelude to an invasion by Charles Edward. However, these projects were betrayed by Alistair MacDonell, the British agent Pickle. Significantly, Jacobitism played little role in the reports of foreign envoys, let alone the speculations and plans of foreign powers. After Culloden, Jacobitism appeared totally dependent on foreign help. Aside from Jacobite schemes for an attack on George himself, their plans were reliant on international help. This dependence underlined the value to Britain of being at peace. The potential significance of Jacobitism in the 1750s is generally underrated by modern scholars due to its failure to materialise during the Seven Years' War and due to the linked failure of French invasion plans. That, however, was not a knowledge enjoyed by contemporaries. Instead, it was the very opposite that appeared the case. The outbreak of conflict with France in the 1740s had given new force to Jacobitism and there appeared every possibility that the same might recur. It was only with hindsight that the fundamental change in the Scottish Highlands following the '45 toward a more stable and loyal Scotland became apparent. At any rate, the situation in England appeared more significant. Concern about Jacobitism helped engage interest in the state of public opinion.

France was not the sole issue when considering the international dimension of Jacobitism. Ever anxious, Newcastle was concerned in 1753, when it was rumoured that Charles Edward Stuart was in Prussia, about Frederick providing help to the Jacobites:

> As it is possible that some encouragement may be given to the Jacobites from thence; care is taken to have all the coast of Scotland watched, and well guarded, against anything that may come, either to the West Coast of Scotland or to the North East.[84]

The Prussian port of Emden was seen as a threat. In reality, there was scant danger, and concern soon ebbed. Without a navy, Prussia posed far more of

---

[83]   Perrone to Ossorio, 11 Jan. 1753, AST. LM. Ing. 57; Newcastle to Yorke, 23 Mar. 1753, NA. SP. 84/462; Newcastle to Hanbury Williams, 23 Mar. 1753, HW.

[84]   Newcastle to Joseph Yorke, 19 Jan., 9 Mar. (quote), Newcastle to Robert Keith, 22 Oct. 1753, NA. SP. 84/462, 80/192; Perrone to Charles Emmanuel III, 11 Jan. 1753, AST. LM. Ing. 57.

a threat to neighbouring Hanover. For geopolitical and naval reasons, it was France that was the threat. The Lord Marshal, a Jacobite exile who was Prussian envoy in France, suggested that Frederick look at the Jacobite option,[85] but, while keen to establish the nature and severity of opposition in Britain,[86] and willing to provide secret encouragement, Frederick thought the current international situation inappropriate, although he thought Jacobite action might succeed if George died soon, leaving a regency. Newcastle sought information from Austria on Jacobite intrigues in France.[87]

Baron Rosencrantz, the experienced Danish envoy, argued that political stability was due to the absence of an effective opposition leader; while Haslang, his Bavarian counterpart, claimed that this factor would lead to ministerial victory in the elections. As a result of the lack of such a leader, Rosencrantz claimed that there was a failure to appreciate the depth of popular anger with the system of ministerial manipulation. He also commented on the size of the National Debt.[88] Alongside the perception that he was in control,[89] George's age was seen as a serious problem.[90] The suggestion that major issues had not been overcome was both prescient and one that alerted foreign governments to continued instability in Britain. Yet history is experienced and perceived in the conjunctures of the moment. These condition the understanding of the longer term, of the results of the past and the prospects for the future. This provides a context within which to assess the perceptive suggestions of foreign diplomats.

The political, diplomatic, and military problems of 1754–7, problems that became acute from 1756, revealed that there were indeed weaknesses in the apparently stable order of 1751–4 that followed the death of Frederick, Prince of Wales. Nevertheless, problems have to be placed in perspective, a situation that does not tend to occur when there is a sense of crisis. However weak the foundations of stability, notably in the international system, the situation both abroad and in the British Isles was far less difficult and troubling than during 1739–48. Britain was not at war, Jacobitism had been defeated, and it was easy to suggest that Russia could be used to deal with threats in Europe.[91] Yet there

---

[85] Lord Marshal to Frederick, 16 Feb., 7 May, Frederick to Lord Marshal, 29 May, 26 June 1753, *Polit. Corr.* IX, 356, 437–8, 457.

[86] Frederick to Lord Marshal, 21 July 1753, *Polit. Corr.* X, 21.

[87] Newcastle to Keith, 22 Oct. 1753, NA. SP. 80/192.

[88] Rosencrantz to Frederick V of Denmark, 27 Feb. 1753, Manchester, John Ryland Library, Eng. Mss. 669 no. 3; Haslang to Preysing, 6 June 1753, Munich, Bayr. Ges., London 227.

[89] Frederick to Michell, 10 Nov. 1753, *Polit. Corr.* X, 149–50.

[90] Anon. memorandum, 31 Jan. 1754, AE. MD. Ang. 51 fol. 200.

[91] Anon. memo on Anglo-Russian links, Sept. 1753, AE. MD. Ang. 40 fol. 244.

was still the fear that war might recur, Jacobitism might revive and the alliance system prove weak and ineffective.

The ministry was divided in its anxiety over North America and its responses. However, as with Britain's Continental alliance system, there was already growing concern by 1753, in the case of North America, over the viability of existing policy and over the related position of the ministry. The demand for resolve in North America was soon to transform the policy and political environment as a whole. This transformation reflected recent changes in the political environment in Britain, notably in assumptions about Britain's identity and interests.[92] The political usage of empire helps to explain why the tension between Britain as a European state and Britain as an imperial power was increasingly settled in favour of the latter as far as contemporary commentators were concerned. This change, which became a tipping point, was linked to the reconceptualisation of empire so that it became less a matter of the British Isles with some trans-oceanic outliers, and, instead, more an understanding of Britain's destiny and position across the Atlantic, spanning the ocean and, later, oceans. The former understanding of empire had proved readily compatible with the idea and strategic practice of Britain as a European state; but the latter was far less so.

At the same time, links were drawn between the European and trans-oceanic spheres, and not least because Continental ministers and diplomats saw French expansionism and trans-oceanic rivalry with Britain as of significance and as worth mentioning to British counterparts.[93] Newcastle, who presented himself as faced by colleagues more fearful of war with Prussia and Spain, saw a strong alliance system in Europe as a crucial aid to Britain in the colonies. Rejecting the argument that a Russian subsidy would only benefit Hanover, he informed his friend Hardwicke:

> The situation in Europe requires it, except we give up all pretence to holding the balance and, upon all occasions, yield to the encroachments of France upon our trade and possessions in the West Indies, perhaps both Indies, in America, and everywhere else.[94]

---

[92]   B. Harris, *Politics and the Nation: Britain in the Mid-eighteenth Century* (Oxford, 2002).

[93]   Keith to Newcastle, 19 Sept. 1753, NA. SP. 80/192.

[94]   Perrone to Charles Emmanuel III, 23 Aug. 1753, AST. LM. Ing. 57; Newcastle to Hardwicke, 21 Sept. 1753, BL. Add. 32732 fol. 699.

Mirepoix had pointed out in 1751 that the government realised that it was impossible to restrict a war with France to the oceanic sphere.[95]

The configuration of politics did not inevitably lead toward crisis. Aside from the ability to put to one side issues with Spain,[96] where Britain sought Austrian diplomatic assistance,[97] British and French differences over India led to conflict there, but this conflict was handled without the two powers coming to war more generally. In part, this outcome reflected the nature of each state and their empires: the states were composite structures with a varied amount of delegation. In the case of India, both Britain and France assigned governmental authority to monopoly trading companies. Moreover, these companies retained authority. There was no equivalent to the loss of authority seen with the British Royal African Company, the position of which finally collapsed in the early 1750s, in the face of continued opposition from independent traders combined with an unviable cost structure. The retention of authority by the East India Companies, however, was not the sole factor as the companies required military support from the state, notably in the case of warships. As a separate issue, there was a functional element, that of a distance from Europe in India far greater than in the case of the New World. As a result, there was a need to permit a delegation of responsibility to the companies comparable to that of the authority they wielded.

In the New World, the links to Europe were closer than in the case of India. In part, this was due to relative proximity. However, it was also the case that royal authority was greater. For Britain, this authority was conditional, due to the role of provincial assemblies and also of the Hudson Bay Company, but, even so, it was greater than in India. Yet that itself was not the only issue in explaining the contrast between developments in India and in North America where differences led to full-scale war. In particular, it is necessary to note differing circumstances within North America: it proved easier for Britain and France to finesse differences in Nova Scotia short of conflict than in the case of the Ohio River valley. In theory, the scale of the latter, as well as the role of Native Americans, provided opportunities for compromise and buffer zones. However, in the context of rising anxiety and of a post-war determination, by both Britain and France, to reverse perceived losses and disadvantages, this very flexibility created not only opportunities for making gains, but also greater room for fear. Thus the flexibility led toward conflict, just as trans-Atlantic proximity

---

[95] Mirepoix, Portrait de la Cour d'Angre, Nov. 1751, AE. MD. Ang. 51 fol. 166.

[96] L.H. Gipson, 'British Diplomacy in the Light of Anglo-Spanish New World Issues, 1750–1757', *American Historical Review*, 51 (1945–6), pp. 627–48.

[97] Newcastle to Keith, 22 Oct. 1753, NA. SP. 80/192.

had already caused concern on the imperial periphery to become politically dangerous in the metropole.

North America had greater bite as an issue because there was widespread concern in the early 1750s that France was successfully using the peace in order to improve its navy and challenge Britain's position in every area. Thus, rivalry in India, West Africa and the West Indies was fitted into a common pattern that made North America more challenging.[98] Anxiety in the London press was reprinted in provincial newspapers.[99] These issues linked economic and strategic concerns, creating a sense that all was related in a more general crisis.[100] The focus of anxiety was France; but there were also issues with Spain, notably over American trade and over British logging on the Caribbean coast of Central America.[101] Opposition newspapers directed attention to Spanish depredations, and to an allegedly corrupt ministerial neglect in response.[102] There was a call for merchants to petition Parliament to consider the issue and, in particular, the failure of the peace treaty to address it.[103] The ministry was able to prevent the issue from coming to Parliament by promising to press Spain hard.[104]

These concerns, like accounts of exploration,[105] looked ahead to the major theme of British foreign policy in the 1760s, trans-oceanic interests. However, the pursuit of these interests also echoed the opposition to Spain's New World position prominently seen in 1738–41. Given the emphasis in the early 1750s on Continental interventionism, and not only in the shape of the Imperial Election Scheme, it is instructive that there were also anticipations of elements of the 1760s in aspects of this very interventionism, as well as echoes of the caution shown by Walpole in the 1730s. Thus, Newcastle was cautious about taking on commitments, notably in Eastern Europe, and particularly with reference to Saxony-Poland. With reference to the accession of Augustus III, as Elector of Saxony, to the 1746 Treaty of St Petersburg, Newcastle wrote to Keith:

---

98   Zamboni to Kaunitz, 7 Aug., 11 Sept. 1752, HHStA. England, Varia 10 fols 121–4, 140.

99   *Newcastle Journal*, 15, 22, 29 Aug. (os) 1752.

100   M.J. Schumann, 'Mercantilism, Communications and the Early Prehistory of the Seven Years' War, 1749–1754', *Nuova Rivista Storica*, 89 (2005), pp. 83–104.

101   Zamboni to Kaunitz, 18 Sept. 1752, HHStA. England, Varia 10; Newcastle to Keene, 15 Jan. 1753, BL. Add. 32842 fol. 153; Mirepoix to Saint-Contest, 14 Feb. 1754, AE. CP. Ang. 437 fol. 54.

102   *Old England*, 23 Sept. 1752.

103   *Old England*, 30 Sept. 1752.

104   Alt to William VIII of Hesse-Cassel, 15 Jan. 1754, Marburg 4f England 255.

105   *Newcastle Journal*, 19 Jan. 1754, re the North-West Passage to the north of North America.

Both the Empresses have general defensive alliances, and, consequently, mutual guarantees with the King of Poland, as Elector of Saxony; but His Majesty has none; and, therefore, it cannot be expected, unless some great and public utility should arise from it, which does not at present appear, that the King should take any new burden upon himself upon this accession, or enter into any new engagements with the King of Poland upon it.[106]

Newcastle could sense long-term threats to Britain's position from developments in Eastern Europe, but did not know how best to respond. He was concerned that Frederick might stir up the Turks to attack Austria or Russia or both (a report corroborated by the Emperor[107]), while Prussia attacked Saxony-Poland, whereas, in his view, France preferred a to create a league to act after the death of Augustus III in order to have a candidate elected King of Poland. The latter represented a revival of the anxieties centred on the last vacancy in the crown, which, occurring in 1733, when Newcastle was a Secretary of State, had led to a major international conflict, but there were also more specific new concerns. Newcastle reported that Frederick was after Polish Prussia which: 'if it could be obtained would add great strength, and weight, even by sea, and, particularly, with regard to the trade of the Baltic, to His Prussian Majesty's power, which we feel, but too much, at present'. He went on to note that 'the remedy' was 'more doubtful'. While seeing the views of Saxony, Austria and Russia on the Polish succession, and urging the taking of steps to secure the election of Augustus' son, 'the Prince of Saxony', Newcastle emphasised that Britain was not a principal: if Poland was attacked 'the King will act that part which the circumstances of his own kingdoms, and the general interest of Europe, may require of him'.[108] George and Newcastle were both concerned about the issue.[109] Moreover, the Imperial Election Scheme was let drop.[110]

Nevertheless, despite its flaws, Newcastle's system was still in place, and, indeed, had been greatly strengthened by the Treaty of Aranjeuz of 14 June 1752, under which Austria, Sardinia and Spain guaranteed other's Italian possessions. The sense that between them Britain, Austria and Russia dominated Europe was a striking feature of the diplomatic correspondence of the period and in his speech to Parliament on 15 November 1753, George did not need to bring

---

[106] Newcastle to Keith, 30 Mar. 1753, NA. SP. 80/191.
[107] Keith to Newcastle, 25 May 1753, NA. SP. 80/191.
[108] Newcastle to Hanbury Williams and Keith, 20 Apr. 1753, HW.
[109] Perrone to Charles Emmanuel III, 3, 10 May 1753, AST. LM. Ing. 57.
[110] Reporting Holdernesse, Perrone to Charles Emmanuel III, 20 Dec. 1753, AST. LM. Ing. 57.

anything particular to attention over foreign affairs. At this stage, Newcastle felt that Kaunitz had brought an improvement to Austrian policy.[111] Newcastle's system was to collapse in 1756, in part because in 1755 he sought to use and extend it without adequately considering the views of his allies, but this clash of interests should not detract from the earlier strength of the system.

The crisis of 1753 looked forward to those in 1755–6 in a variety of ways. These included Newcastle's uncertainty over the situation and how best to respond[112] as well, allegedly, as divisions within the ministry. Thus, Pelham was reported as seeking to avoid bellicose steps, such as the dispatch of a fleet to the Baltic, on the grounds of cost, while Halifax argued that it was very clear that France did not wish to settle differences over North America. Indeed, Frederick wondered whether it was best to approach Pelham for a secret negotiation to settle commercial disputes with Britain.[113] Newcastle was also concerned about changes within the French ministry.[114] The issues in Europe at dispute in 1752–3 did not press hard on anxieties and divisions within the British ministry, but the concerns and tensions that were to ensure a different response in 1754 were already clear. In particular, there was the issue of whether the Elector of Hanover could and would be made to pay for the King of Britain,[115] and, if so, with what consequences in terms of foreign policy and domestic, notably ministerial, politics. Newspaper criticism in Britain about Hanoverian influences, inappropriate peacetime subsidies and the failure to secure trans-oceanic issues in dispute with France and Spain,[116] looked toward the political problems that were to arise in 1755.

---

[111] Newcastle to Keith, 30 Nov. 1753, NA. SP. 80/192.

[112] Perrone to Charles Emmanuel III, 12 Apr. 1753, AST. LM. Ing. 57.

[113] Perrone to Charles Emmanuel III, 5 Apr. 1753, AST. LM. Ing. 57; Frederick to Michell, 20 Nov. 1753, *Polit. Corr.* X, 159.

[114] Perrone to Charles Emmanuel III, 24 May 1753, AST. LM. Ing. 57.

[115] La Touche to Saint-Contest, 5 May 1753, AE. CP. Prusse 171 fol. 240.

[116] *Protester*, 23 June 1753.

Chapter 8

Towards War with France, 1754–5

The growing crisis over North America was to interact with tensions in British politics following the unexpected death of Henry Pelham on 6 March 1754. The resulting unstable political situation lasted until 1757 and, in large part, 1758, and greatly tested the suppositions and practices of the British constitution and British politics. This test exposed the problems of operating parliamentary monarchy and the ambiguities of constitutional practice, as well as the impact of death, which was a theme of the period, with the deaths of Frederick, Prince of Wales (1751) and Pelham, as well as the expected death of George II. At the same time, the political situation only became so serious due to the very difficult international situation. Furthermore, this difficulty did not come to the fore at once. As a result, the ministry was able to overcome the initial problems caused by Pelham's death, and their aftermath, although this recovery left a weaker ministerial position that affected the response to developments abroad.

The death occurred against a threatening background. Britain had unresolved differences with France in North America and was worried about the dispatch of French warships to India, there was concern about the security of Hanover, and a general election was imminent. In political terms, the principal issue in foreign policy was not, as it was to become later in 1754, that over North America, but instead over whether the ministry would yield to George's wish for a subsidy for Russia, a subsidy also backed by Austria. Pelham was opposed to such a peacetime subsidy and the Council had judged the terms unacceptable in August 1753, but an anxious Newcastle wished to please the King. The British counter-project, which the Austrian envoy in London thought as generous as Britain could afford, was, however, not regarded as sufficient by the Russians.[1] This was the continuing agenda of Continental interventionism and subsidy treaties, albeit one directed to Hanover's security rather than the Imperial Election Scheme. The European situation appeared more threatening because, in January 1754,

---

[1]   Mirepoix to Saint-Contest, 10 Jan. 1754, AE. CP. Ang. 437 fols 17–21; Frederick to Michell, 4 Feb. 1754, *Polit. Corr.* X, 232; Haslang to Preysing, Munich, Bayr. Ges., London 229; Alt to Landgrave William VIII of Hesse-Cassel, 3 May 1754, Marburg, 4f London, 255; Council memorandum, 21 Aug. 1753, BL. Add. 32995 fols 27–8; Colloredo to Chernuishev, Russian envoy in London, 12 Nov. 1753, NA. SP. 100/53.

France negotiated separate alliances with Denmark and Sweden, while there was concern that France was trying to win Sardinia.[2]

Although Mirepoix predicted that Pelham's death would change the scene at court entirely, as much for general affairs as for domestic ones,[3] Newcastle was able to reconstitute the ministry after Pelham died without reference to foreign policy and without having to take into office those whom he disliked. In that respect, Pelham's death was similar to that of Wilmington in 1743, but with the difference that Pelham's replacement of Wilmington had brought him into a ministry in which the 'Old Corps' Whigs shared power with former opponents, notably Carteret, who were still serious rivals. In 1754, in contrast, Newcastle himself replaced Pelham, which was an indication of the significance he attached to the Treasury and of the difficulty of trusting another politician in that role. Holdernesse, a pliant Secretary of State, was continued in office and was joined, as the other Secretary, replacing Newcastle, by Sir Thomas Robinson, a courtier and former ambassador to Vienna (1730–48). He was also given management of the Commons, replacing Pelham. Newcastle had initially sought to entrust the management of the Commons to Fox. Fox, however, refused to accept the task when he ascertained that Newcastle intended to retain full control of all government patronage, including the secret service money, and to manage the forthcoming general election. Such an allocation of roles would have left Fox without the power to give substance to his management. In contrast, with no independent power base, and far less political (particularly parliamentary) ambition than Fox, Robinson was dependent on Newcastle.[4] To that extent, there was an integrated ministry comparable to that under Pelham. In addition, as a courtier who, moreover, appreciated the nuances of German politics, Robinson was highly acceptable to George.

While Robinson, who was regarded as pro-Austrian, led the Commons for the remainder of the session, which ended on 6 April, Newcastle successfully took over Pelham's role as the manager of the imminent general election. In the event, as anticipated, there were few contests, and the ministry was left in a dominant position. Indeed, as Newcastle had predicted in 1753,[5] the 1754 election was a major triumph for the ministry, the easiest of the elections under George since that which had followed his accession in 1727. Moreover, the election was seen as a triumph. The hopes of opponents were shattered. Having

---

2   Perrone to Charles Emmanuel III, 3 Jan. 1754, AST. LM. Ing. 58.

3   Mirepoix to Saint-Contest, 7 Mar. 1754, AE. CP. Ang. 437 fol. 76.

4   Joseph to Philip Yorke, 22 Mar. 1754, BL. Add. 35364 fol. 7; Perrone to Charles Emmanuel III, 17 July 1754, AST. LM. Ing. 58.

5   Perrone to Charles Emmanuel III, 8 Mar. 1753, AST. LM. Ing. 57.

reported that a sweeping victory was likely, diplomats, British and foreign, were able to comment on the triumph.[6] That another election would not need to be held until 1761 underlined the triumph.

The Oxfordshire election proved particularly hard-fought and, although atypical as a contest, throws instructive light on developments in politics and notably outside the major urban constituencies. The government committed money on the Whig side, while, in a determined effort to contest the ambition of the Whig aristocrats, the Tories spent more than £20,000. Both sides sought to mobilise public support: the Tories raised more than £8,000 by public subscription, while the Whigs proved eager to use the press. George, 2nd Earl of Macclesfield wrote of his eldest son, Thomas, Viscount Parker, one of the Whig candidates:

> Lord Parker received your letter this day; and I entirely agree with Lady Susan, that the printing, by way of a handbill, the Letter Concerning the Papists and the State of the Popish Religion in Oxfordshire, published in Jackson's last Journal [*Jackson's Oxford Journal*] will be of considerable advantage to our Cause. But as Jackson has already incurred so much displeasure for having given that letter a place in the paper, he may possibly be unwilling to reprint it … we think to print a good number of them in this town, and send them by the first opportunity, to yourself, and our other friends in Oxfordshire to be properly dispersed by you and them.

Accordingly, Macclesfield had 1,500 copies printed in London: 'in a large character that such may be more easily read, as it may be thought proper to tie upon posts, or in other convenient places.'[7] In the event, there was a double return for Oxfordshire, with both sides claiming victory. After a lengthy dispute, the House of Commons settled the matter the following year, as usual, on the basis of party strength in the Commons; and the Whig candidates were declared elected in April 1755.

Despite the electoral triumph, Robinson was not strong enough, personally or politically, to deal with the political uncertainties and divisions of the Whig élite, let alone with those that were to arise from the move towards war with France. In November 1754, Joseph Yorke, the envoy in The Hague, an MP and a son of Lord Chancellor Hardwicke, wrote to his brother Philip, Viscount

---

6　Haslang to Preysing, 19 July 1753, Munich, Bayr. Ges, London 227; Michell to Frederick, 20 Nov. 1753, *Polit. Corr.* X, 169.

7　Macclesfield to Thomas Bray, 26, 29 Jan. 1754, Exeter College, Oxford, Bray papers.

Royston, also an MP, that: 'the situation of America gives me less uneasiness than that of our home system, for if we break to pieces there, the New World will be a prey to the usurpers,'[8] the latter a reference to the French. The Yorke family provided an instance of the way in which, among the Whig élite, personal ability was hardening into well-connected power and position. A similar process had occurred with Freemasonry which had initially been more potentially radical and less aristocratic.

Robinson's background as a diplomat and courtier was particularly reflected in his view of himself as defending the King's interests. He wrote to a longstanding diplomat in December 1754: 'Our affairs in Parliament have been a little disturbed, by the private affairs of some ambitious gentlemen, who have been desirous of more power than the King intended to give them.' Pitt 'said that the King might as well have sent his jack-boot to govern the House of Commons as Sir Thomas Robinson.'[9] Initially, the attacks on Robinson and the ministry could be held off. In the Commons, as so often, Pitt was stronger in oratory than in the political arithmetic of creating a significant impact in terms of support. Bayntun Rolt told George's mistress, Lady Yarmouth, that these attacks would not signify unless 'Mr Pitt and Mr Fox were of accord,'[10] which appeared highly unlikely. Won over to back the ministry, Fox was allowed to join the Cabinet that December.

The persistence and adaptability of the ministry, however, was to be tested as had not been the case under Pelham. This was due to a development that was at once long-term and immediate. Competition between Britain and France over the interior of North America came to a crisis. In 1752–4, the French drove out British traders from the Ohio Valley, intimidated Britain's Native American allies, and constructed forts between Lake Erie and the junction of the Allegheny and Monongahela rivers. The renewal of French aggression threatened to exclude the British from the interior. Although the British government had no wish for war with France, and was more concerned about the position in Nova Scotia, it could not accept French claims in the Ohio Valley, and the Virginia authorities had been instructed to defend British claims. In August 1753, the decision was taken in London to order the dispatch of thirty cannon for use in the forts to be built on the Ohio.

On 17 April 1754, a 500-strong French force obliged the small colonial garrison of 40 men in Fort Prince George (near modern Pittsburgh) to surrender.

---

8   Joseph to Philip Yorke, 1 Nov. 1754, BL. Add. 65364 fol. 15.
9   Robinson to Benjamin Keene, 12 Dec. 1754, Leeds, Archive Office, Vyner papers, no. 11863; Ilchester (ed.), *Letters to Henry Fox*, p. 100.
10   Bayntun Rolt diary, 25 Nov. 1754, Bristol, University Library.

George Washington, a land speculator keenly committed to westward expansion, advanced, as colonel, at the head of a small advance force of 40 Virginia militia supported by 12 Native Americans, into the contested area. He surprised and defeated a smaller French advance detachment on 28 May. The French, in response, advanced south in greater numbers, at least 1,000 French and Native Americans. Rapidly constructing Fort Necessity in response, Washington had more than 400 men: mostly 'provincials' of the Virginia Regiment, and some South Carolinians. However, the French and Native Americans penned Washington's force in, killing most of the horses, and driving off or killing all the cattle. Washington's choice for a fort was poor, but he thought he would be reinforced, and that there would be no true siege. He also worried about any sort of retreat where his men could be caught in the open. Outfought in an exposed position, Washington was obliged to surrender at Fort Necessity on 3 July. The humiliating capitulation terms included the evacuation of the Ohio region for a year and a day.

These border hostilities led to fear of French attacks on the British colonies, including Nova Scotia.[11] That this fear was rapidly and strongly expressed in Britain as well as in British North America reflected the extent to which news and opinion circulated within the British Atlantic. Due in part to the substantial settler presence, the British Atlantic operated as a world in which initiatives stemmed from both sides of the Atlantic. At the same time, the sensitivity of the issue of North American security reflected the extent of recent developments in British North America, for this was the first occasion in which events there in the interior resonated so widely. At that point, the British had fewer than 900 regular troops in North America. Meeting on 26 June, the Cabinet resolved on measures to maintain the frontiers. An over-excited Newcastle warned: 'All North America will be lost, if these practices are tolerated.' He presented France as untrustworthy and as ignoring clear warnings.[12] Formerly frenetic over German politics, Horatio Walpole now focused on the French threat in North America.[13]

The economic argument was also voiced. William Murray, the Attorney General, wrote to Newcastle that, at this rate, the French would become the

---

[11]   William Shirley, Governor of Massachusetts, to George, 2nd Earl of Halifax, 20 Aug. 1754, S. Pargellis (ed.), *Military Affairs in North America 1748–1765* (New York, 1936), p. 25.

[12]   Cabinet minute, 26 June, Newcastle to Horatio Walpole, 29 June, Newcastle to George, 3rd Earl of Albemarle, envoy in Paris, Newcastle to Granville, both 5 Sept. 1754, BL. Add. 33029 fol. 124, 32735 fol. 597, 32850 fol. 218–19, 32736 fol. 432.

[13]   Walpole to Robert Dinwiddie, 15 July 1754, HL. HM. 9406.

'masters of the tobacco trade'.[14] There was, in fact, no French threat to the tobacco-producing areas near Chesapeake Bay. Nevertheless, Murray powerfully captured the widespread sense that developments in the hinterland would have an impact closer to the coast, and the economic sensitivity of imperial arguments, as well as the extent to which Scottish interests were centrally involved: Glasgow was the main importing port for tobacco. Profit from its import and processes brought liquidity into the Scottish economy. There was no sense of Scotland's interests as separate to those general to Britain.

Mutual distrust was a key element in the developing crisis. The French repeatedly argued that Britain was stirring up hostile moves by Native Americans.[15] Emphasising French moderation, Rouillé, the French Foreign Minister, added that the chance of successful negotiations was lost as a result of British military steps and that, once clashes had begun, their consequences would be difficult to contain.[16] With good reason, Rouillé also claimed that the British presentation of North American geography was deeply flawed, in that the French presence in the distant Ohio River valley did not represent a threat to the British colonies as there were intervening mountains.[17] However, that, indeed, was the British view. Thus, Holdernesse feared that in the Ohio Country, France was seeking to get a position to 'open a way for an attack upon Pennsylvania or Virginia',[18] while Robinson was concerned about France wanting 'to have an opening into the Bay of Fundy' on the west side of Nova Scotia.[19] In turn, Rouillé inaccurately argued that if in the Ohio Valley, the British would be in the centre of the French colonies and able to invade Canada and Louisiana.[20]

The limited frontier conflict over the Ohio River valley blew up, in Britain, but not France, as a major governmental and political issue, with all the resulting pressure for action. In these circumstances, with a strong war group and argument coming to the fore both within the government and more generally,[21] whatever the ministry did appeared insufficient and slow, and could be made to appear so by critics. Moreover, the ministry fractured, with those pressing for a firm commitment in North America gaining traction, in part as a result

---

[14]   Murray to Newcastle, 7 Sept. 1754, BL. Add. 32736 fol. 438.

[15]   President of the Council of Marine to Antoine-Louis Rouillé, French Foreign Minister, 18 Aug. 1754, AN. AM. Colonies B[100].

[16]   AE. CP. Ang. 437 fols 296–7.

[17]   Rouillé to Mirepoix, 3 Feb. 1755, AE. CP. Ang. 438 fol. 79.

[18]   Holdernesse to Yorke, 11 Mar. 1755, NA. SP. 84/468.

[19]   Robinson to Keene, 11 Mar. 1755, Leeds AO., Vyner papers, no. 11835.

[20]   Rouillé to Mirepoix, 3 Feb. 1755, AE. CP. Ang. 438 fol. 80.

[21]   Haslang to Wreden, 16 May 1755, Munich, Bayr. Ges., London 230.

of Newcastle's characteristic concern about the domestic political situation. In this, Newcastle repeated the stance he had taken during the 1739 political crisis over relations with Spain. The significant contrast in 1754–5, not least with an election not as close as it had been in 1739, was that the opposition was much weaker and more of the bellicosity came from within the government. Despite French assurances, the government decided, in late September 1754, to send two regiments to North America to conduct operations there to enforce British claims and, thereby, to protect the British position. Cumberland, the Captain General, Fox, the Secretary-at-War, and Halifax, the expansionist President of the Board of Trade, all politicians supportive of a firm stance and critical of Newcastle, pressed the government to be firm.[22] These rivalries were understood abroad and played a key role in the analysis of British politics. Frederick, who sought to follow British politics with great attention, saw them in terms of a rivalry between Fox and Newcastle, with the former having the crucial direction of the Commons.[23] The French envoy sought to encourage Newcastle to dispense with Fox, whom he thought wished to replace the Duke. In a parallel, British ministers regarded the French ministry as divided and as including bellicose ministers, a view shared by the Austrian envoy in Paris.[24]

In an attempt to ease matters, Mirepoix, the well-connected French envoy, was sent back to London, returning on 8 January 1755. On 10 January he had an audience with George, who underlined his wish for peace, but said that he was obliged to provide British colonists with protection.[25] Newcastle told Mirepoix, who, however, doubted his grasp of detail about North America, that the government had made naval preparations only to satisfy popular opinion.[26] This approach to ministerial politics was well-founded, but incomplete. It presented Britain in terms of a parliamentary ministry and not, as was more appropriate, as a parliamentary monarchy. Indeed, the position and views of George were significant, both in so far as North America was concerned and also more generally. Like Newcastle and the Secretaries of State in 1754–5, George's policy horizon was not focused on the trans-oceanic sphere. Instead, he was

---

[22] T.R. Clayton, 'The Duke of Newcastle, the Earl of Halifax, and the American Origins of the Seven Years' War', *Historical Journal*, 24 (1981), pp. 571–603.

[23] Frederick to Klinggraeffen, 7 Jan. 1755, *Polit. Corr.* XI, 5; Mirepoix to Rouillé, 23, 30 Jan. 1755, AE. CP. Ang. 438 fols 43, 57–8.

[24] Robinson to Keene, 11 Mar. 1755, Leeds AO, Vyner papers, no. 11835; Starhemberg to Kaunitz, 27 Mar., 8 Mar. 1755, J.C. Batzel, 'Austria and the First Three Treaties of Versailles, 1755–1758', (PhD., Brown, 1974), p. 47.

[25] Mirepoix to Rouillé, 16 Jan. 1755, AE. CP. Ang. 438 fol. 15.

[26] Mirepoix to Rouillé, 16, 23 Jan. 1755, AE. CP. Ang. 438 fol. 5, 16, 18, 45.

concerned about the situation in Europe, and that at a time in which Britain's alliance system was clearly under strain. In addition, this strain was readily apparent to George on his lengthy visits to Hanover in 1753 and 1755 and through his discussions with diplomats. Divisions within the ministry, whether explicit or implicit, made the King's views of considerable importance. The lack of collective ministerial responsibility and Cabinet cohesion meant that there was no alternative to seeking to maintain royal support. That ministers were appointed by, and answerable to, the King had become more significant because the ministry was divided and vulnerable.[27] The absence of an effective manager of the Commons after Pelham's death was an additional major problem, and one that became more serious, or at least was perceived as more serious, as a public political crisis apparently became imminent.

At the same time, alongside the role of George, there were the views of the royal family over policy, although without there being the acute division seen in the earlier case of Prince Frederick. Precisely because there was not this division, the opinions of Cumberland were more relevant as he was a player in the debate within the ministry, as well as attending Parliament.[28] Although without the constitutional basis of the King's governmental and political role, Cumberland's stance was also of great political importance. In part, this situation reflected Cumberland's closeness to the monarch, but his position in the military and his links with specific ministers, notably Fox, were also significant. Cumberland was able to talk to ministers, and they regarded his views as a matter of comment. For example, Robinson informed Newcastle that he had been told by Cumberland that the government should fix France's imperial boundaries in North America, and that, once this was achieved, clear instructions should be issued to the British commander: 'that he may not be liable to future reproaches from one or the other colony, or be sacrificed one day or other, to the clamours of merchants at home or their interested correspondents abroad'.[29] Thus Cumberland appreciated the problems created by domestic political pressures, but in response was inclined to denigrate these pressures, an approach very different to that of Newcastle. Cumberland's attitude was at one with his view that problems could, and should, be overcome, and through firmness. Cumberland offered a harsh view of the trans-Atlantic linkage in news and opinion.

In part, the changes in British policy, notably the more aggressive stance in North America, reflected not only domestic and American developments, but

[27] Mirepoix to Saint-Contest, 14 Mar. 1754, AE. CP. Ang. 437 fol. 85.

[28] Richard Blacow to Thomas Bray, 26 Mar. 1755, Exeter College, Oxford, Bray papers.

[29] Perrone to Charles Emmanuel III, 11 July 1754, AST. LM. Ing. 58; Robinson to Newcastle, 22 Sept. 1754, BL. Add. 32736 fol. 563.

also Britain's position in the changing power relationships and vulnerabilities on the Continent in response to the possibility that conflict would spread to, and in, Europe. In this context, there was a desire to show firmness, which Newcastle and Holdernesse claimed would lead France to back down,[30] and a concern that the trans-Atlantic situation might spin out of control and endanger Britain's position elsewhere. French naval preparations led a meeting of ministers on 16 January 1755 not only to determine that Mirepoix's proposals were inadmissible but also to decide on British preparations.[31] At the same time, the ministry sought to keep the issue out of Parliament in order to make a settlement with France more likely.[32]

Mid-January saw a heightening of preparations, with Britain ordering the readying of 17 ships of the line. Diplomatic speculation was directed to the month at which squadrons would be ready to sail,[33] the size of the fleets being readied,[34] and the need to match the moves of the other power.[35] Contrasts between assurances and actions sowed distrust,[36] while the pace was set by repeated reports of preparations. Robinson captured the combination of freneticism and resolve: 'We shall not, we must not, be behind with them [the French]. If they will treat; we will treat. If they will decide by the sword, we must be ready for them.'[37]

Military preparations made the possibility of peace appear transient.[38] There was also the anxiety that, once prepared, the French fleet might attack, including possibly the British Isles. Meanwhile, the British ministry was interested in a joint evacuation of the contested territory in North America and a resumption of negotiations.[39] The designation of the Ohio country as to be left to the Native Americans with the British and French able to pass 'in a peaceable manner, for the sole purposes of travelling and trading' represented an attempt to provide a long-term settlement, but one that scarcely matched the aspirations of the colonists.[40] This prefigured the unsuccessful suggestion in 1814 that a buffer

---

[30] Perrone to Charles Emmanuel III, 23 Jan. 1755, AST. LM. Ing. 59.
[31] Ministerial meeting, 16 Jan. 1755, BL. Add. 32996 fols 5–6.
[32] Mirepoix to Rouillé, 16 Jan. 1755, AE. CP. Ang. 4387 fols 22–3.
[33] Yorke to Holdernesse, 21 Jan. 1755, NA. SP. 84/468.
[34] Mirepoix to Rouillé, 23 Jan. 1755, AE. CP. Ang. 438 fols 42–3.
[35] Mirepoix to Rouillé, 30 Jan. 1755, AE. CP. Ang. 438 fol. 54.
[36] Rouillé to Mirepoix, 3 Feb. 1755, AE. CP. Ang. 438 fol. 81.
[37] Robinson to Keene, 27 Jan. 1755, Leeds, Archive Office, Vyner papers, no. 11834.
[38] Mirepoix to Rouillé, 10 Feb. 1755, AE. CP. Ang. 438 fol. 122.
[39] Perrone to Charles Emmanuel III, 30 Jan. 1755, AST. LM. Ing. 59.
[40] Ministerial meetings, 7, 10 Feb. 1755, BL. Add. 32996 fol. 25, 29–30; Mirepoix to Rouillé, 10 Feb. 1755, AE. CP. Ang. 438 fols 118–19.

zone occupied by independent Native Americans be established between British-ruled Canada and the United States. Meetings between Mirepoix and Robinson went reasonably well in early 1755, but the former voiced the threat that any conflict might become general and that France could seize the Low Countries and hold it until the dispute was settled.[41] Fear of this encouraged a renewed British approach to Austria 'for establishing some defensive system' in Europe.[42]

Meanwhile, preparations for war continued, with 35 ships of the line commissioned on 14 February and the pressing (forcible enrolment by press gangs) of sailors. In addition, differences over maps hindered the negotiations, and the French repeatedly argued that Britain misrepresented the position in the American interior.[43] The British stance was unacceptable to France. Newcastle and Robinson proved unwilling to accept the Appalachians as a boundary for Britain beyond which France could occupy the Ohio country. Robinson told Mirepoix that British ministers lacked the room for manoeuvre of their French counterparts, only for the envoy to say that the resulting irresolution might lead to war.[44] Failing to appreciate Britain's approach, and notably to understand a willingness there to seek a solution, the French government judged the British position over the Ohio country unacceptable and referred to refusing to buy peace.[45] The detailed British provisions certainly involved France abandoning positions and the British being able to trade on Lakes Ontario and Erie, the latter of which greatly challenged the French position in Canada, as well as in the Ohio country.[46] By mid-March 1755, the negotiations appeared unlikely to be able to lead to any agreement.[47]

In meetings with Mirepoix on 20 and 21 March 1755 respectively, Robinson and Newcastle sought to rescue the negotiations, claiming that the counter-project Robinson had delivered on 7 March, which Rouillé had rejected, was a basis for negotiation and not an ultimatum. Newcastle added that the Ohio issue was less important to Britain than Nova Scotia, although, as far as the Ohio issue was concerned, he stated that it would not be possible to accept a threat to the British colonies or a block on trade with Native Americans. Mirepoix told Newcastle

---

41   Holdernesse to Yorke, 11 Feb. 1755, BL. Eg. 3446 fols 32–3.
42   Holdernesse to Yorke, 14 Feb. 1755, NA. SP. 84/468.
43   Mirepoix to Rouillé, 21 Feb., Rouillé to Mirepoix, 24 May 1755, AE. CP. Ang. 438 fols 195–6, 439 fols 97, 101–61; Bonnac to Rouillé, 21 Feb. 1755, AE. CP. Hollande 488 fol. 106.
44   Mirepoix to Rouillé, 28 Feb. 1755, AE. CP. Ang. 438 fols 232–40.
45   Rouillé to Mirepoix, 5 Mar. 1755, AE. CP. Ang. 438 fols 247–50.
46   Ministerial meeting, 20 Feb. 1755, BL. Add. 32996 fols 34–6.
47   Holdernesse to Keith, 11 Mar. 1755, BL. Add. 9147 fol. 59; Rouillé to Mirepoix, 17 Mar. 1755, AE. CP. Ang. 438 fols 285–6

that the latter needed to show more firmness in pursuing peace and also that the instructions given to the fleets should be concerted in order to avoid the risk of a clash. He was very jaundiced about British foreign policy, presenting it as lacking a plan and being led by the 'fermentation accidentelle de leur interieur'.[48] The report sent to Paris on the parliamentary debates on 25 March for raising money dwelt on pressure in the Commons over the American issue.[49]

Rouillé correctly saw the instructions given to British provincial governors and naval commanders as key elements,[50] and also argued that there was a fundamental contrast between a British government driven by mercantile demands and a French counterpart that did not take this approach.[51] Concerned that French moderation would be interpreted as timidity, and convinced that no British ministry could persuade the nation to accept a fair settlement, the French government instructed Mirepoix to cease to make approaches.[52] Frederick saw the British ministry as boxed in by the unrealistic hopes they had raised with the nation.[53] This was a reasonable view, but also one that exaggerated the degree of agency possessed by the ministry. Mirepoix was more hopeful,[54] but presented the ministry as swayed by a hostile political environment and unable to settle matters before the fleets put to sea when matters would become more dangerous.[55]

The context within which the French ministry received these reports was set by its very critical response to the parliamentary debates on 25 March and, more specifically, to what it saw as the failure of the British ministry to provide a lead capable of disabusing parliamentarians of their flawed ideas. Press criticism of France contributed to the same end. This theme of a public let down by inadequate leadership and swayed by misleading information was one that Rouillé had already offered.[56] In turn, British ministers meeting at Newcastle House on 3 April, thought the way forward blocked by the French stance.[57] In a note presented by Robinson on 5 April, the British government declared that, until peace terms were settled, it would not be possible to concert instructions to governors and commanders. Five days later, a ministerial meeting recommended

[48]   Mirepoix to Rouillé, 22 Mar. 1755, AE. CP. Ang. 438 fols 297–30.
[49]   Anon. report, AE. CP. Ang. 438 fols 312–16, at fols 315–16.
[50]   Rouillé to Mirepoix, 27 Mar. 1755, AE. CP. Ang. 438 fol. 333–5.
[51]   Rouillé to Mirepoix, 27 Mar. 1755, AE. CP. Ang. 438 fol. 336.
[52]   Rouillé to Mirepoix, 17 Mar. 1755, AE. CP. Ang. 438 fols 280–3.
[53]   Frederick to Klinggraeffen, 29 Mar., *Polit. Corr.* XI, 97; Haslang to Preysing, 1 Apr. 1755, Munich, Bayr. Ges, London 230.
[54]   Mirepoix to Rouillé, 28 Mar. 1755, AE. CP. Ang. 438 fols 339–42.
[55]   Mirepoix to Rouillé, 1 Apr. 1755, AE. CP. Ang. 438 fols 344–5.
[56]   Rouillé to Mirepoix, 3 Apr., 19 Feb., 1755, AE. CP. Ang. 438 fols 348–51, 171–2.
[57]   Ministerial meeting, 3 Apr. 1755, BL. Add. 32996 fol. 69.

intercepting French reinforcements at sea and Admiral Boscawen hoisted his flag at Portsmouth on 9 April, sailing from Spithead on 21 April.[58] In response, Mirepoix recommended that he be recalled to France.[59]

The key element was the political atmosphere in Britain. Crucially, it was not only opposition commentators who called for firmness toward France. To the French, there was a capitulation by the British government to a hostile public mood,[60] a capitulation that the government should avoid.[61] This capitulation was not only seen by French commentators.[62] This reading of British politics proved significant in the French response to the crisis,[63] and, in turn, this response supported this reading. Observers, British and foreign, joined in the opinion that the nation wanted war.[64] This mood developed very rapidly, in part because it drew on strong currents of suspicion. Moreover, there were signs of commitment across the country; and the reporting of them helped make them normative, which was, indeed, the intention. For example, the *Bristol Journal* of 19 April 1755 declared:

> The corporation of this city, being duly sensible that the having His Majesty's fleet speedily manned is of the utmost importance upon the present critical conjuncture; has promised a reward of two guineas to every able seaman, and of one guinea and a half, to every ordinary seaman (additional to His Majesty's royal bounty) who, within Bristol, volunteer for the navy.

Within the extensive circulation area of this paper, it also noted that the Fraternity of Free and Accepted Masons at Carmarthen had done the same, offering £1 to every volunteer. From Tunbridge Wells, a popular spa destination, Lord George Sackville wrote that 'the shopkeepers' were very 'stout' for war.[65]

---

[58]   Boscawen to John Clevland, Secretary to the Admiralty, 9, 21 Apr. 1755, NA. Admiralty Papers 1/481 fols 5, 51.

[59]   Mirepoix to Rouillé, 25 Apr. 1755, AE. CP. Ang. 438 fol. 448.

[60]   Mirepoix to Rouillé, 23, 30 Jan., 8, 10 Feb. 1755, AE. CP. Ang. 438 fols 46–7, 59, 111, 122; Starhemberg, Austrian envoy in Paris, to Kaunitz, 16 Jan. 1755, Batzel, p. 44.

[61]   Rouillé to Mirepoix, 5 Mar. AE. CP. Ang. 438 fol. 250.

[62]   Perrone to Charles Emmanuel III, 20 Mar. 1755, AST. LM. Ing. 59; Bonnac to Rouillé, 14 Mar. 1755, AE. CP. Hollande 488 fol. 136.

[63]   Mirepoix to Rouillé, 13 Mar., Rouillé to Mirepoix, 17 Mar. 1755, AE. CP. Ang. 438 fols 227, 280.

[64]   Perrone to Charles Emmanuel III, 6 Mar. 1755, AST. LM. Ing. 59; Holdernesse to Keith, 11 Mar. 1755, BL. Add. 9147 fol. 59.

[65]   Sackville to Sir Robert Wilmot, Derbyshire RO., Catton Collection, WH 3448.

Although there were concerns about the tax implications[66] the public was more united than might have been anticipated given the serious divisions at the end of the previous war and over the peace terms. Indeed, Holdernesse felt able to claim that, with regard to supporting the British position, 'there is but one voice in the whole nation upon this subject'.[67] There are no reliable sources for the public mood in this crisis, or, at least, reliable as understood in twentieth-century terms. However, that is a retrospective assessment, and contemporaries were able to make do with the judgements they advanced, and were used to doing so. In that light, there is no doubt that public opinion was regarded as supportive of a firm stance towards France; indeed as pressing for firmness. In terms of the political culture, as well as constitutional practice, that view was not seen by all commentators as necessarily requiring an equivalent governmental policy, but it was regarded as important to the debate over policy within government. Wide public interest familiarised large numbers with imperial issues and colonial interests and shaped an 'active public consciousness of empire'.[68]

The pressure for an outcome judged satisfactory was less politically acute as the parliamentary session moved towards its close. Newcastle had had, as he had predicted,[69] a satisfactory session, which ended on 25 April 1755. However, there was the strong prospect of a marshalling of opposition during the summer aimed at causing trouble when Parliament resumed if there was not a satisfactory settlement.[70] Alongside tension within the ministry, there were rumours that Newcastle was seeking Tory support, which was certainly the case with disputed election petitions.[71] His attempt to win Pitt round to act as Commons' spokesman for the ministry failed, however, and Newcastle remained reliant on Fox despite the tensions between them.

Separate to disagreements over claims were those over process. The British regarded it as unacceptable that France should continue in possession during the negotiation of what had been, in their view, unreasonably seized. In turn, the French regarded the British refusal to send orders to the colonial governors in

---

[66]   Francis, 1st Earl of Guilford to Sanderson Miller, 18 Mar. 1755, L. Dickins and M. Stanton (eds), *An Eighteenth-century Correspondence: Being the Letters ... to Sanderson Miller* (London, 1910), p. 230.

[67]   Holdernesse to Robert Keith, 11 Mar. 1755, BL. Add. 9147 fol. 59; Bonnac to Rouillé, 21 Mar. 1755, AE. CP. Hollande 488 fol. 147.

[68]   M. Peters, 'Early Hanoverian Consciousness: Empire or Europe?', *English Historical Review*, 122 (2007), pp. 663, 667.

[69]   Perrone to Charles Emmanuel III, 5 Dec. 1754, AST. LM. Ing. 58.

[70]   Perrone to Charles Emmanuel III, 6 Mar. 1755, AST. LM. Ing. 59.

[71]   Richard Blacow to Thomas Bray, 13, 18 Mar., John Clark to Bray, 13 Mar. 1755, Exeter College Oxford, Bray papers.

North America not to act as a threat. Linked to this difference came the issue of the reinforcements that could be brought across the Atlantic.[72] In response to British troop moves, France decided to send 3,000 troops to Canada.[73] On 24 March, however, the British Council agreed that a squadron should be deployed off Louisburg to stop the French landing troops. The French wished to settle the immediate crisis over these troops, postponing the matters in dispute to subsequent negotiations, but the British wanted a settlement of the entire dispute and were unwilling to offer the suspension of hostilities deemed necessary by the French.[74]

Mirepoix presented Newcastle, in the face of Cumberland's support for Granville, as no longer in control of government policy, and of the ministry as unwilling to defy the public mood. He also suggested a shift in British goals; away from pursuing interests in North America and towards destroying the French navy, a measure that allegedly led to orders to Boscawen to attack the French fleet.[75] Rouillé was hopeful that something could be salvaged through talks with Robinson and also suggested approaching Granville.[76] Assuring Mirepoix that George wanted peace, and urging him to ignore the newspapers, Robinson told the envoy on 5 May that he was ready to negotiate, but Mirepoix correctly underlined the danger of a clash at sea between the fleets.[77] Alongside the narrative of a British ministry driven by public opinion[78] came that of a ministry divided between Newcastle and Granville.[79]

Concern over the potential domestic consequences led British ministers to be reluctant to commit themselves on paper,[80] but discussions with Mirepoix continued during May with the British showing firmness over Nova Scotia, but Rouillé nevertheless confident of British ministerial sincerity.[81] On 14 May, Mirepoix delivered a memorandum sent from Paris on 9 May, to which Robinson delivered a response on 7 June. The latter indicated major differences

---

[72]   Yorke to Holdernesse, 25 Feb. 1755, NA. SP. 84/468; Rouillé to Duke de Duras, French envoy in Spain, 11 Mar. 1755, AE. CP. Espagne 517 fol. 193.

[73]   President of Council of Marine to Marquis de Duquesne, 17 Feb. 1755, AN. Colonies, B 101.

[74]   Memorandum on meeting with Mirepoix, 7 Mar. 1755, BL. Add. 32996 fols 44–5; Rouillé to Mirepoix, 2 May 1755, AE. CP. Ang. 439 fols 15–8.

[75]   Mirepoix to Rouillé, 5 May 1755, AE. CP. Ang. 439 fols 24–6.

[76]   Rouillé to Mirepoix, 9 May 1755, AE. CP. Ang. 439 fols 47–51.

[77]   Mirepoix to Rouillé, 6 May 1755, AE. CP. Ang. 439 fols 6–10.

[78]   Mirepoix to Rouillé, 10 May 1755, AE. CP. Ang. 439 fol. 66.

[79]   Rouillé to Mirepoix, 9 May 1755, AE. CP. Ang. 439 fol. 51.

[80]   Mirepoix to Rouillé, 15 May 1755, AE. CP. Ang. 439 fol. 77.

[81]   Rouillé to Mirepoix, 24 May 1755, AE. CP. Ang. 439 fol. 96.

in negotiating position, while, meanwhile, trouble was expected from action in the Atlantic.[82] Boscawen had been sent reinforcements when the size of the French squadron that had sailed from Brest on 3 May was known. To Mirepoix, neither George II nor Newcastle were displaying sufficient grip in maintaining peace.[83] It was also suggested that the British ministry needed to be able to show something for the major costs incurred in supporting the British position.[84] To Newcastle, in contrast, the French memorandum was unreasonable, but it ought to be possible by vigorous defensive measures to ensure a reasonable peace. From Hanover, Holdernesse emphasised George's concern for peace but, at the same time, his refusal to lessen 'the necessary means of defence'. This position was presented as requiring action by Britain and her allies, the former 'to recover such of His Majesty's possessions as have been unjustly invaded'.[85]

Aware of the general report that the British would attack the French fleet, and of British assurances of a sincere desire for peace, Rouillé was reduced to waiting on events and hoping that Britain would not attack.[86] He thought Robinson's response unsatisfactory, and no real advance on the British stance earlier in the year.[87] The British government argued that any action in, or off, North America did not provide an excuse for war in Europe, but, at the same time, suspected that France would strike there.[88] On 18 June, Newcastle suggested that it would be impossible to avoid war as there was insufficient willingness to compromise over American disputes.[89] Indeed, on 16 June, Robinson, while contemptuous of the French negotiating position, also noted that the British government had not allowed the pursuit of negotiations to prevent its preparations for action:

> Everything is in motion, to recover self-evident encroachments in America. Our colonists, with the few regular troops there, will be beginning to beat up the French quarters, in five or six places, at a time, where they have been silently creeping in upon us. What may happen at sea, God knows. We look upon our American colonies in the North as blocked, if not besieged... If France is willing

---

[82] Mirepoix to Rouillé, 7 June 1755, AE. CP. Ang. 439 fols 166–8.

[83] Mirepoix to Rouillé, 7, 18 June 1755, AE. CP. Ang. 439 fols 169, 192.

[84] Haslang to Wreden, 16 May 1755, Munich, Bayr. Ges., London 230.

[85] Newcastle to Hartington, 17 May 1755, HP. Chatsworth papers; Holdernesse to Keith, 20 May 1755, NA. SP. 80/196 fols 3–5.

[86] Rouillé to Bonnac, 18 May 1755, Rouillé to Aubeterre, 17 June 1755, AE. CP. Hollande 488 fol. 263, Aut. 254 fol. 176.

[87] Rouillé to Mirepoix, 15 June 1755, AE. CP. Ang. 439 fol. 183.

[88] Holdernesse to Keith, 31 May 1755, NA. SP. 80/196 fols 36–9.

[89] Peronne to Charles Emmanuel III, 19 June 1755, AST. LM. Ing. 59.

to do us justice, – she may do it with honour, by doing it at once, before she knows that we have done it for ourselves in North America.[90]

On 1 July, the Council considered the negotiation with France as in effect broken off.[91] Mirepoix soon after followed up with a memorandum complaining of the conduct of the colonial authorities of Virginia.[92]

Meanwhile, on 10 June, a naval attack by Admiral Boscawen, on the French force that had left Brest for Canada on 3 May, greatly ratcheted up the dispute. Partly due to fog, most of the French reinforcements of 3,650 men reached Canada, however, this peacetime attack, which captured two ships and 800 troops, did not achieve its purposes. To the concern of British ministers,[93] there was no equivalent to the successful attack on a Spanish fleet off Sicily in 1718, an attack, intended to support the Austrian position in Sicily, that led to war between Britain and Spain. However, Boscawen's attack similarly proved crucial to the deterioration in relations between the British and French governments. Bussy was at once recalled from Hanover and Mirepoix from London. The envoys had first sought assurances that Boscawen had not received instructions to attack, but the ministers had refused to provide them. Holdernesse told Bussy 'that his court could not be surprised that His Majesty should endeavour in the present circumstances to prevent any considerable reinforcement being sent into America'.[94]

Moreover, a British expedition advancing on the French base of Fort Duquesne (Pittsburgh) was successfully ambushed on 9 July by a French and Native American force. The British suffered heavy casualties (977 killed or wounded out of 1,459) including the commander, Major-General Edward Braddock. Fresh from Britain, Braddock's regulars lacked experience of North American operations, and this battle, a 'terrible drawback' in Robinson's phrase, reaffirmed France's dominance of the Ohio Country and underlined the issues involved in operations in the interior.[95] British attacks on the border between

90   Robinson to Keene, 16 June 1755, Leeds, Archive Office, Vyner papers, no. 11840.
91   Council meeting, 1 July 1755, BL. Add. 32996 fols 160–1.
92   Mirepoix to Rouillé, 3 July 1755, AE. CP. Ang. 439 fols 221–3.
93   Hardwicke to Anson, 14 July 1755, BL. Add. 15956 fol. 23.
94   Rouillé to Bussy, 18 July 1755, AE. CP. Br-Han. 52 fol. 16; Holdernesse to Keith, 26 July, 28 Aug. 1755, NA. SP. 80/196 fol. 139, BL. Add. 35480 fols 59–60; Ruvigny de Cosne, Secretary of Embassy in Paris, to Holdernesse, 20, 21, 24 July 1755, BL. Add. 35480 fols 64–70.
95   Robinson to Keene, 28 Aug. 1755, Leeds AO. Vyner Mss, no. 11843; M.C. Ward, '"The European Method of Warring is not Practical here": The Failure of British Military Policy in the Ohio Valley, 1755–1759', *War in History*, 4 (1997), pp. 247–63.

Nova Scotia and Cape Breton were more successful,[96] but attracted less attention. Due both to developments in North America, and to a more general sense of competition and crisis, pro-government writers presented Britain as driven to war. One pamphleteer claimed: 'It is the over-grown power of that nation, and the rapid progress the French are continually making in their commerce, that forces us into a war.'[97] Public interest was seen in announcements of new maps of America and in the publication in London of the 1662 discussions over Nova Scotia as recounted in the correspondence of the French envoy.[98]

As the dynamic of military developments and domestic pressures in 1755 made war with France far more likely, this threw the security of the Low Countries and Hanover to the fore, as it was assumed that the conflict would spread there. The strategic vulnerability of Hanover ensured that the issues of politics and force in the Empire (Germany), and more generally on the Continent, were reconceptualised away from the Imperial Election Scheme and the question of the future stability of the Habsburg state (Austria) and, instead, to more immediate concerns of defence. The earlier agenda had still been the main theme in 1754. Thus, in August 1754, Newcastle had told Perrone that the maintenance of Britain's subsidy policy was vulnerable to the Austrian failure to re-establish the Barrier, as the lack of an effective Barrier meant that France would be able to break all connections between Britain and the Continent, so that all other arrangements would signify nothing. The projected treaty with Russia was regarded as dependent on Austria.[99] Problems in the alliance with Austria, nevertheless, ensured that there was speculation about existing and possible alignments. In December 1754, Joseph Yorke first reported Prussian insinuations of better relations with Britain and the Dutch, and then added his fear that Austria's unhelpful policy over the Barrier threatened the collapse of Britain's system. At the same time, alongside his dated view of the danger of 'France's acquiring a real universal monarchy, which the conduct of the House

---

[96]   D.S. Graham, 'The Planning of the Beauséjour Operation and the Approaches to War in 1755', *New England Quarterly*, 41 (1968), pp. 551–66; C.M. Hand, *The Siege of Fort Beauséjour, 1755* (Fredericton, 2004).

[97]   Anon, *An Answer to a Pamphlet, called, A Second Letter to the People* (London, 1755), p. 16.

[98]   *Daily Advertiser*, 3 Aug., 5, 10 Sept. 1755; *Letters and Negotiations of Count d'Estrades in England* (London, 1755); M. Day, 'The Roots of Empire: Early Modern Travel Collections and International Politics in the Long Eighteenth Century', in M. Farr and X. Guégan (eds), *The British Abroad Since the Eighteenth Century, II. Experiencing Imperialism* (Basingstoke, 2013), pp. 22–8.

[99]   Perrone to Charles Emmanuel III, 15 Aug. 1754, AST. LM. Ing. 58.

of Austria is bringing about in a hurry', Yorke presciently noted that, 'to alarm the Austrians with a Prussian negotiation is dangerous too'.[100]

Indeed, Austrian policy in 1755 increasingly focused on the prospect of war between Austria and Prussia, and other elements in the international system were seen as subsidiary. Both Britain and France were potential distractions to such a war, as much as sources of help. In order to be able to focus on Russia, Austria did not wish to help Hanover if it was attacked by France, and nor did it want a French attack on the Austrian Netherlands. The French envoy was told in May 1755 that Austria had no engagement with Britain over North America and did not wish to join in the struggle between Britain and France if it was extended to Europe.[101] Kaunitz, instead, pressed Keith on the need for Britain and Austria to co-operate against Prussia, a 'new power [that] had quite changed the old system of Europe', and, to that end, wanted Britain to be sure of Russia.[102] In turn, the Austrians were unwilling to provoke France by sending troops to the Austrian Netherlands as the British pressed, not least in order to influence the Dutch.[103] The Austrian Council refused on 17 June. This was troubling as the French were making major military preparations, and notably at Givet from which it would be possible to advance into the Low Countries.[104] Austria sending troops to the Austrian Netherlands might please Britain, but would not help Austria against Prussia. While George was angry at Austria's stance, British ministerial suspicions of Austro-French negotiations were strong by the summer.[105] These suspicions encouraged the idea of Britain turning to Prussia to prevent a French attack on Hanover, or, indeed, a supporting Prussian attack. The Hanoverian ministers suggested that Prussia might guarantee Hanoverian neutrality. Frederick rejected a French approach in June to be ready to attack Hanover.

However, in Britain, the very popular anger directed at France was also aimed at the traditional remedies for vulnerability on the Continent: subsidy treaties, which, despite the government's serious financial situation,[106] it pursued in 1755. These treaties were seen by critics as at one with what was (misleadingly) presented as a pliant trans-oceanic approach to France. Thus, a demand for

[100]   Joseph to Philip Yorke, 10, 24 Dec. 1754, BL. Add. 35364 fols 24–5.

[101]   Aubeterre to Rouillé, 26 Feb., 7 May 1756, AE. CP. Aut. 254 fols 85–8, 146; Kaunitz to Colloredo, 27 Aug. 1755, HHStA. Englische Korrespondenz 107.

[102]   Keith to Holdernesse, 22 May 1755, NA. SP. 80/196 fols 29–32, quote fol. 32.

[103]   Holdernesse to Keith, 20 May 1755, NA. SP. 80/196.

[104]   Holdernesse to Keith, 17 June 1755, NA. SP. 80/196 fols 71–2.

[105]   Holdernesse to Keith, 31 May, 17 June 1755, NA. SP. 80/196 fols 57, 77; Perrone to Charles Emmanuel III, 3 July 1755, AST. LM. Ing. 59.

[106]   Newcastle to Holdernesse, 11 July 1755, BL. Add. 32857 fols 2–3, 43.

changes in policy affected attitudes toward the recent attempt to build up a deterrent system on the Continent. While concerned to demonstrate to George 'the regard we have had to His German dominions,'[107] Newcastle warned Gerlach Adolf von Münchhausen, the senior Hanoverian minister, about the impossibility of Britain entering into a general plan for war on the Continent, essentially because of a hostility to subsidy treaties.[108]

Tension within the ministry included Holdernesse's willingness to go to greater lengths than his colleagues.[109] He accompanied George to Hanover. A key division was over subsidy treaties, with Holdernesse in Hanover seeking to develop an alliance network that matched George's ambitions. This included an attempt to win the support of Bavaria and Saxony by renewing subsidy agreements,[110] as well as a Russian alliance designed to influence Austria and Prussia. In an echo of established approaches, the British pressed Austria to help in winning over Bavaria, only to meet with an unhelpful response.[111] Holdernesse was concerned to help ensure that government 'measures go down in Parliament,'[112] but drew different conclusions to those arrived at by Newcastle who sought to avoid an overly ambitious subsidy system.[113] George meanwhile spent many hours on military reviews.[114]

On 9 August 1755, Pitt told Hardwicke that he would require prior consultation about the policies he was to defend in the Commons. It was unclear what it would take to defend Hanover and how it would be possible to reconcile this need with other goals, and within the parameters of what was politically acceptable. This proved a serious problem for both Pitt and newspapers that adopted a similar stance until 1758, although far more so when in, or supporting, government than from the comfortable shelter of opposition.

The prospect of war with France in North America posed an immediate problem: it was unclear how far this conflict could be limited to North America and the high seas. There were examples of a geographical limitation in conflict. Thus, in 1733–5 and 1741–4, while at war with Austria, France had supported and maintained a neutrality for the Austrian Netherlands, in large part in order

---

[107]   Newcastle to Holdernesse, 11 July 1755, BL. Add. 32857 fol. 54.

[108]   Newcastle to Münchhausen, 25 July 1755, BL. Eg. 3481 fol. 133; Newcastle to Holdernesse, 25 July 1755, BL. Add. 32857 fol. 357.

[109]   Holdernesse to Yorke, 25 May 1755, BL. Eg. 3446 fol. 116.

[110]   Holdernesse to Burrish, 20 May, 14 July 1755, NA. SP. 81/105.

[111]   Holdernesse to Keith, 17 June, Keith to Holdernesse, 27 June 1755, NA. SP. 80/196.

[112]   Yorke to Holdernesse, 6 June, Holdernesse to Yorke, 22 June 1755, BL. Eg. 3446 fols 152, 164.

[113]   Newcastle to Holdernesse, 29 Aug. 1755, BL. Add. 32858 fols 332–3.

[114]   Richard Potenger, Under-Secretary to Hanbury Williams, 17 June 1755, HW.

to influence British and Dutch attitudes. As another instance of restraint, the French, in 1755, unlike in 1744, were not interested in the idea of supporting Jacobite schemes, although rumours to the contrary circulated and Newcastle was concerned.[115] Rouillé observed in April that the Jacobites were not capable of overthrowing the British government and that any plan seeking that end was chimerical. A memorandum in the French archives argued that it would be foolish for France to invade Britain unless she had control of the sea and that such control would require the destruction of the Royal Navy.[116] In August, 'James III and VIII', from his exile in Italy, approached the French government, claiming that while Anglo-French relations had been good he had kept his distance, but that now war appeared likely and the only way to obtain a solid peace would be to restore the Stuarts. Arguing that he enjoyed considerable support in England and Scotland, James stated that the arrival of a French force would lead the Jacobites to rally, and that, if they could not invade from France, an invasion from Sweden should be attempted. James regarded an attack on Hanover as complementary, rather than an alternative, as he claimed that such an attack would indirectly increase the chance of a revolution in England. The French reply was limited to compliments. In October 1755, the Jacobites added details of their alleged support in Wales.[117] The British government instructed the Customs Service in Scotland to keep its eyes open for secret correspondence.[118]

A Jacobite proposal in January 1756 that the French invade between Rye and Winchelsea with 6,000 men, carried from Dieppe and Boulogne in small ships while the British fleet was held back from the defence of the coast by adverse winds, was regarded as underestimating the strength of the British army.[119] This was a realistic assessment, although the ability of Charles Edward to reach Scotland in 1745 had cast an unflattering light on the effectiveness of the Royal Navy. Two months later, Rouillé, denying any French concert with the Stuarts, argued that experience revealed that the overthrow of the British government could come only from domestic action.[120]

---

[115]   Keene to Robinson, 28 Apr. 1755, Leeds, Archive Office, Vyner papers, no. 11838; Newcastle to Holdernesse, 11 July 1755, BL. Add. 32857 fol. 43.

[116]   Rouillé to Mirepoix, 3 Apr., Mirepoix to Rouillé, 10 Apr. 1755, AE. CP. Ang. 438 fol. 349, 389, 439 fol. 272.

[117]   Count of Lismore to Monsieur, 12 Aug., 21 Oct., reply, 9 Sept. 1754, AE. CP. Ang. 439 fols 278, 371–2, 287.

[118]   Anon. minute, 20 May 1755, BL. Add. 32996 fol. 109.

[119]   AE. CP. Ang. 440 fols 26–7.

[120]   AN. KK. 1402, p. 257.

Although willing to use Jacobites to provide information,[121] the Jacobite option was a high-risk one for France. The *Monitor* on 16 August 1755 referred to the 'obsolete name of Jacobitism'. Instead, in 1755, it was fully appreciated in London that the French had a ready response to their vulnerability in North America, namely the prospect of attacking Hanover. In 1741, an advance towards Hanover had led George, as Elector, to yield and to back French interests in the Empire. In 1755, there was the prospect of a reprise of such an advance, by France and, in this case, its ally Prussia.[122] Indeed, such an advance might well secure the alliance. This possibility linked the strategic weakness of Hanover to the political vulnerability of the British ministry, for pressure on Hanover risked counteracting any British gains in North America. This vulnerability preceded that which was to be shown when Minorca fell to French attack in 1756, and underlined the dependence of the ministry's political situation on the state of international relations. As such, the situation in 1755 appeared similar to that in 1741 when Hanover was threatened with attack and, in addition, there were no significant successes for Britain in the war with Spain. By the fall of Minorca in 1756, the situation was to have deteriorated and to be similar to that which had confronted the Walpole ministry later in 1741 after the failure of the much-anticipated attack on Cartagena.

In 1755, as in 1739 towards Spain and 1741 towards France, the international dynamic toward action was to be matched in Britain by a domestic one. The ministry was divided, and this was a cause of weakness in resisting the pressure for action. These historical echoes from 1741 are significant, because the key political figures in 1755, George, Newcastle, Fox, Robinson and Pitt, were all players in 1741; only Cumberland, a younger figure, had lacked a public role, although he supported his father against his elder brother, Frederick. In 1755, Cumberland was presented as a key political figure, with deteriorating relations with France linked to Newcastle's weakness in the face of the Duke.[123]

As North America came to the fore from 1754, Britain's Continental options were increasingly discussed in terms of an apparently imminent war with France. Although war was not declared until 1756, both Britain and France continued hostile acts in North America and at sea, attacking each others' warships and trade. The deteriorating international situation made parliamentary support increasingly important for the ministry, not least in order to ensure the passage of subsidy treaties. In April 1755, Newcastle drew attention to the need to

---

[121] Bonnac to Rouillé, 31 July 1755, AN. KK. 1401, p. 589.

[122] Reporting Perrone, Perrone to Charles Emmanuel III, 14 Aug. 1755, AST. LM. Ing. 59.

[123] Mirepoix to Rouillé 25 Apr. 1755, AE. CP. Ang. 438 fol. 444.

strengthen the ministry's position in the Commons.[124] George was ready to help. From Hanover, Holdernesse reported to Newcastle in June that:

> The King entered much into conversation upon parliamentary and party matters and said you had promised to write me word at a proper time how *some people* stood affected to his measures, in short the King seems in that kind of temper at present that I am persuaded he would willingly give ear to any proposal you might now think proper to make.[125]

Newcastle was clear about the link between politics in the Commons and the state of foreign affairs, and saw the voting of support to Hanover as the key issue. He argued that George had to allow the ministers to seek 'the assistance of those who are necessary for us'.[126]

In July 1755, Newcastle had observed, 'sea war, no continent, no subsidy is almost the universal language'. He also reflected that fighting would serve to cover the ministry from criticism on the grounds of incurring the costs of military preparations but not then acting, a criticism aimed at Walpole, for example in 1729.[127] In practice, subsidy treaties could be passed, as the session in the winter of 1755–6 was to show.[128] Indeed, the *Monitor* on 16 August 1755 offered an account of subsidies that captured nuances. Its maxims included not only placing 'our chief dependence' on the navy, but also:

> To engage in no foreign alliances where the interest of Britain is not immediately and essentially concerned; and, when alliances may be judged necessary, and any foreign subsidies are to be granted; to prefer alliances with Russia, the Empress Queen [Maria Theresa], the King of Prussia, the King of Sardinia, and other great powers, to those with petty German princes, who have always failed us; and to proportion the subsidies to the abilities of our own nation, and not to the wants of those who apply for them.

---

[124] Newcastle, memorandum, 18 Apr. 1755, BL. Add. 32996 fols 81–02.

[125] Holdernesse to Newcastle, 29 June 1755, BL. Add. 32856 fol 380.

[126] Newcastle to Holdernesse, 11 July 1755, BL. Add. 32857 fols 43–4, 53–4.

[127] Newcastle to Holdernesse, 25 July 1755, BL. Add. 32857 fols 357, 363 (quote); Perrone to Charles Emmanuel III, 17 July 1755, AST. LM. Ing. 59.

[128] Henry Digby to Hanbury Williams, 23 Dec. 1755, BL. Stowe 263 fol. 3.

Nevertheless, as the session neared, trouble was increasingly anticipated, including with the encouragement of the Court of the young Prince George.[129] In late 1755, a major press and parliamentary attack was mounted on subsidy treaties with Hesse-Cassel and Russia which, it was claimed with reason, were essentially for the defence of Hanover, albeit if attacked in the growing crisis in Anglo-French relations, and which, it was alleged, would make it harder to devote resources to the struggle in North America.[130] Signed on 30 September 1755, the Anglo-Russian treaty promised mutual assistance in case of attack, provided for British subsidies to Russia, and stipulated that for four years Russia was to maintain an army near the Livonian frontier from which it could threaten East Prussia. The political acceptability of subsidies was lessened by the strains in Britain's relations with Austria and the Dutch, which ensured that a wider rationale for the subsidies appeared less credible and that, in the event of both peace and war, alliance burdens would not be shared.[131] Moreover, the cost of the treaties led to criticism, as when Newcastle tried to justify the Russian treaty to Dodington on 10 October.[132]

As a result of Robinson's limitations as a manager, and in light of expected attacks by Pitt, Fox saw George on 26 September and subsequently replaced Robinson as Secretary of State and Commons' leader.[133] Newcastle pronounced himself satisfied with this change, although there were doubts on that head, not least from foreign envoys. Robinson reassured Keene that the change was only in order to obtain parliamentary support for the existing policies. He added that

> the stuff which an English House of Commons is composed of ... is not a field for a man who has consumed the most part of his life abroad, and especially when he is too old to begin a science the merit of which is perhaps mostly owing to *habit*.[134]

---

[129] George Sackville to Sir Robert Wilmot, 20 Sept. 1755, Matlock, CRO. Catton Collection, WH 3449; Richard Rigby to 2nd Earl Gower, 1 Oct. 1755, NA. PRO. 30/29/1/14.

[130] *Monitor*, 6 Sept. 1755.

[131] Holdernesse to Yorke, 30 July, 3 Aug. 1755, BL. Eg. 3446 fols 182, 187.

[132] H.R. Wyndham (ed.), *The Diary of the Late George Bubb Dodington* (3rd edn, London, 1785), p. 494.

[133] Newcastle to Lady Catherine Pelham, 26 Sept. 1755, BL. Add. 32859 fols 219–20; Alt to William VIII of Hesse-Cassel, 10 Oct. 1755, Marburg, 4f England 258. The key work is J. Clark, *The Dynamics of Change: The Crisis of the 1750s and English Party Systems* (Cambridge, 1982). See also P.A. Luff, 'Henry Fox and the "Lead" in the House of Commons 1754–1755', *Parliamentary History*, 6 (1987), pp. 33–46.

[134] Robinson to Keene, 9 Oct. 1755, Leeds AO, Vyner papers, no. 11844.

Opening Parliament on 13 November, George referred to the active measures taken on land and at sea, mentioned the need for 'large supplies' (taxes), and ended: 'There never was a situation in which my honour, and the essential interests of Great Britain, called more strongly for your zeal, unanimity, and dispatch.' The second, however, was to be very much lacking over the following two years.

That day, in the debate on the Address, Pitt, in a declaration of open opposition to the government, spoke for over ninety minutes. He condemned what he presented as the Hanoverian focus of foreign policy and the past failure to take sufficient note of the defence of North America, stressed the importance of the navy, and offered a very Whiggish account of the royal position: 'the King owes a supreme service to his people'; whereas the people had no such obligation to Hanover. Attacking the subsidy treaties, 'he said that measure would hang like a millstone about the neck of the minister who supported it and sink him into disrepute amongst the people'.[135] And yet the government won a clear majority: 311 to 105. Henry Legge's refusal to countersign a warrant for payment, and his parliamentary attack on the subsidy treaties, led to his dismissal as Chancellor of Exchequer. He had already made it clear that he could not approve of the treaties.[136]

On 10 December 1755, Thomas Potter, MP for Aylesbury and an ally of Pitt, albeit a politician with a reputation for dissipation, told the Commons that the subsidy treaties were: 'illegally concluded, as being made for the defence of Hanover without consent of Parliament, in violation and defiance of the Act of Settlement'. The ready response of parliamentarians to the raising of constitutional points, the extent to which they were graspable, and the flexibility they offered as points for debate, affected the significance of these points in the discussion of foreign policy. Issues of foreign policy could serve, apparently, to show whether ministers could be relied upon to protect the constitution, which was another aspect of the protection of national interests. In the same debate in response, Fox attacked Pitt and the attempt to create 'the fatal distinction ... of Englishman and Hanoverian'.[137] The government's majorities were substantial, with divisions of 318 to 126, 289 to 121, 263 to 69, and 259 to 72 in the

---

[135] Gilbert Elliot to his father, Lord Minto, 15 Nov. 1755, NLS. Ms. 11001 fol. 15; Walpole, *Memoirs of George II*, II, 69–72; Farmington, HW papers, vol. 63 fol. 22.

[136] Legge to Fox, 17 Oct. 1755, BL. Add. 51388 fol. 132.

[137] Fox to William, 4th Duke of Devonshire, 19 Dec. 1755, Chatsworth House, Devonshire Mss 330/87; Pryse Campbell to Mr White, 18 Dec. 1755, Carmarthen, Cawdor, Box 138; Walpole, *Memoirs of George II*, II, 95–102.

Commons, and of 85 to 12 in the Lords. Moreover, on 26 November, land tax at four shillings in the pound had been agreed to without a division.[138]

These majorities suggested that the ministry would have no problem in persisting with its policy, and, thereby, raises the question whether it could have been maintained, but for the loss of Minorca in 1756 and the subsequent political storm over incompetence, if not worse. The examples of the recent past, notably the Walpole ministry's ability to survive a serious parliamentary storm over Dunkirk (1730) and to secure approval for a settlement with Spain (1739), were not encouraging as, aside from the serious problems in Parliament, each issue had exacerbated serious divisions within the ministry. The danger in 1755–6 that a parliamentary storm would become a central plank in a crisis within the ministry, and thus lead to a change in policy, was readily apparent. The government no longer had confidence in its ability to secure parliamentary support for its policies, and was wary about the political vulnerability and costs of its policy. A pamphleteer who anticipated Edmund Burke's later thesis admitted in 1755 that his own view was:

> diametrically contrary to all printed politics of these times. And though I do not think myself accountable not even to my constituents, for my conduct in Parliament, yet it would be a kind of insolence should I refuse to arm my friends ... I am well aware what vast advantage the Antisubsidizers have in sounds. *Hanover, Hanoverian Interests, the Naval Power of Great Britain, her Situation as an Island, her Commerce, and her Detachment from the Continent*, are popular, plausible, and, when not carried into extravagance, proper topics of argument. But they ought to have their bounds. When our Crown was settled on the present Royal Family, the Nation well knew the connexion between it and Hanover.[139]

This, however, was not a view that had strong traction in the public debate in 1755, at least in so far as subsidies to powers on the Continent were concerned.

---

[138]   Rigby to Bedford, 26 Nov. 1755, Russell (ed.), *Bedford*, II, 171–2.

[139]   Anon., *Reflections upon the Present State of Affairs, at Home and Abroad ... In a Letter from a Member of Parliament to a Constituent* (London, 1755), pp. 4, 40.

Chapter 9

The Diplomatic Revolution and the Crisis of 1756

At a time when the honor of Great Britain seemed daily perishing, when our most valuable possessions were abandoned to the enemy; when the sword of France, as yet unsated with American blood, carried slaughter and conquest through all our richest colonies, when we were the jest of all the tittering courts in Europe; the exigence was certainly alarming and called aloud for an alteration of men and measures.

Test, 20 November 1756

The outbreak of large-scale hostilities in North America in 1755 did not lead immediately to a declaration of war, but attempts to maintain peace proved feeble. This situation directed much of British public attention to the cause, course, and possible consequences of British operations in North America. Indeed, in terms of the long-term development of British power and the politics of empire, these operations were to be of great significance. In 1756, however, the British failure to achieve any striking success in North America, or indeed anywhere, was striking. There was nothing to compare with the capture of Louisbourg in 1745. Instead, 1756 saw defeats in North America. Forts Ontario, George and Oswego were lost. These defeats reflected not only British military inadequacies, but also the military capability of the French–Native American alliance there and its ability to seize the initiative. This failure also thwarted Newcastle's hope that success in North America would counteract failure elsewhere, a hope directed to domestic as much as international needs.[1] In addition, war came to Europe where Britain's diplomatic position and ambitions collapsed; which greatly exacerbated the diplomatic consequences for Britain of the outbreak of conflict in North America. A reminder of the role of both spheres serves to correct claims that the Diplomatic Revolution, and international relations more generally, were dominated by the German question, and that other issues were thereby peripheral.[2]

---

[1] Viry to Charles Emmanuel III, 20 July 1756, AST. LM. Ing. 60.
[2] B. Simms, *Europe. The Struggle for Supremacy, from 1453 to the Present* (New York, 2013).

In response to the apparent threat from Prussia as well as France, the British government had followed a policy since the early 1730s of seeking to strengthen relations with Austria and Russia, each of which was in a position to put military pressure on Prussia and to resist France's alliance system. However, in 1755–6, the likelihood of war with France accentuated British concern about Hanover sufficiently to cause a search for additional security. This policy vindicated earlier views and criticisms that the Hanoverian commitment would indeed affect British policy, and to a limiting, if not detrimental, effect. In 1755, money allotted to the Civil List, over which Parliament had no control, was used to negotiate subsidy treaties for Hanover,[3] while George turned to Prussia. This approach reflected George's significance to foreign policy as well as his views: not only George's quest for security for Hanover, but also his perception of the state of Britain's alliances. That the crucial negotiations with Frederick occurred as a result of George's lengthy visit to Hanover in 1755 underlined his significance. At the same time, Mirepoix correctly assessed George's position when he reported that the king did not care much about the North American colonies and did not want war with France, but that he had no intention of trying to improve the situation for Hanover by making concessions over North America, and, indeed, had no power to make such a suggestion.[4] Despite the suggestions of critics, there was no equivalent in the case of George to the French *Secret du Roi*, a large-scale and sustained secret diplomacy.

Particular British concern focused on Austria, not least because there was an awareness of the vulnerability of the Austrian Netherlands to French attack. At the same time, there was the danger that France might gain control of all or part of the Austrian Netherlands, possibly by accepting an exchange for the Austrian gain of Bourbon territories in Italy, notably Parma.[5] This possibility raised a serious challenge to British interests, but also the question as to how best to defend them in these particular circumstances. Britain's ability to affect both developments in Italy and the equations of power in northern and southern Europe was very limited.

Fear of Russia helped lead Frederick in 1755 to pay heed to suggestions made through the Duke of Brunswick that he agree to remain neutral in any Anglo-French conflict, which was a goal advanced by Newcastle and the Hanoverian

---

   [3]   C.W. Eldon, 'The Hanoverian Subsidy Treaty with Ansbach (1755): A Typical German Subsidy Treaty of the Eighteenth Century', *Journal of Modern History*, 12 (1940), pp. 59–68.

   [4]   AE. CP. Ang. 438 fol. 305, 439 fol. 169.

   [5]   Mitchell to Holdernesse, 14 May 1756, NA. SP. 90/65; Yorke to Keith, 13 June 1756, BL. Add. 35480 fol. 195.

ministers.[6] Alliance with Britain would apparently free Frederick from the threat of Russian attack, whereas, if he provided France with assistance, he would face Russia and possibly Austria as well. As a result, Frederick, unimpressed anyway by French policy, accepted British proposals. By the Convention of Westminster of 16 January 1756, the two powers agreed to guarantee their respective possessions and to maintain peace in the Empire by jointly opposing the entry of foreign forces.

Better relations with Prussia might seem to solve the strategic problems for Hanover and Britain, but it soon became clear that there was no ready answer to these problems. The British government had hoped that Frederick would be able not only to guarantee Hanover and provide assistance if it was attacked, but also to help settle, or at least contain, Anglo-French differences. Newcastle told Francesco, Count of Viry, the Sardinian envoy, that he wanted to reconcile Austria and Prussia and to establish a system to restrain France.[7] Similarly, it was anticipated that Prussia and Russia could be reconciled.[8] There were also hopes that Spanish offers to be a channel for Anglo-French negotiations could be fruitful.[9] Thus, in what was an accumulation if not confusion of hopes, there appeared to be many opportunities to change the situation for the better.

Instead, these hopes proved fruitless. The Convention of Westminster was presented by the British to the Austrians as freeing Austria from the apprehension of Prussian attack and therefore allowing her to concentrate on resisting France. Instead, as Hardwicke had suggested,[10] the Convention destroyed the system Britain had been seeking to create and thus ensured that, in trying to prevent this very outcome, the war would extend to the continent where Britain was vulnerable. This was because the Convention led Britain to lose the alliance of Russia and the possibilities that this offered. Tsarina Elizabeth and her Chancellor, Bestuzhev, had seen the British alliance as a step that would further their plans for war with Frederick and, to that end, had been prepared to heed British pressure not to pursue a border dispute with Turkey.[11] Regarding him

---

[6]   Newcastle to Münchhausen, 25 July 1755, Hanover, Hannover, 91, I, 22 fol. 16; Münchhausen and Steinberg to Newcastle, 26 July 1755, BL. Eg. 3481 fols 136–7.

[7]   Newcastle to Devonshire, 7 Mar. 1756, BL. Add. 32863 fols 215–16; Bonnac to Rouillé, 1 Mar. 1756, AN. KK. 1402, p. 226; Viry to Charles Emmanuel III, 8 Mar. 1756, AST. LM. Ing. 60; Holdernesse to Keith, 23 Mar. 1756, NA. SP. 80/197 fols 41–4.

[8]   Holdernesse to Mitchell, 11 May 1756, NA. SP. 90/65.

[9]   Fox to Devonshire, 9 Mar. 1756, History of Parliament Transcripts, Chatsworth papers.

[10]   Hardwicke to Newcastle, 28 July 1755, BL. Add. 32857 fols 397–8.

[11]   Hanbury Williams to Keith, 8 July, Hanbury Williams to James Porter, envoy in Constantinople, 8 July 1755, BL. Add. 35480 fols 22–5.

as a challenge to their influence in Eastern Europe, they sought to revive the schemes that had existed during the War of the Austrian Succession for a joint attack by Austria, Hanover, Russia and Saxony. The prohibition in the Anglo-Russian treaty of 1755 of separate negotiations with the 'common enemy' was regarded as referring to Frederick, and Russian anger with the Convention of Westminster led them to refuse to ratify the treaty. The Russians were taken by their animosity to Frederick towards better relations with France. Moreover, Frederick does not appear to have appreciated the reaction in France where the Council decided on 4 February 1756 not to renew the alliance with Prussia.

In what was to be described as the Diplomatic Revolution, Austria and France negotiated an alliance, Kaunitz approaching Louis XV through Madame de Pompadour.[12] Austria also sought to harm Anglo-Russian relations, and successfully so. This dramatic change tested British assumptions about the proper order and operation of the international system. The commonplaces of diplomatic correspondence illustrated this. Thus, in March 1756, Walter Titley wrote from Copenhagen asking his counterpart at Vienna to give his regards to whoever was appointed Austrian envoy: 'making him the hearty tender of my services, that we may justly and confidentially pursue the main object of our respective courts; which I take to be always the same with regard to Denmark'. Titley also referred to 'the opposite interest', and, in contrast, to Britain's alliances with Prussia and Russia as completing 'that ancient system whereby the Liberties of Europe were formerly supported'.[13] Such an analysis and prospectus, one apparently valid since the Anglo-Austrian Treaty of Vienna of 1731 (Titley had been at Copenhagen since 1729), now, however, crumbled into dust. The First Treaty of Versailles signed by Austria and France on 1 May 1756 was a defensive alliance which specifically excluded the Anglo-French war. Maria Theresa promised her neutrality in that conflict.

The situation was more testing for Britain because the new alliance between Austria and France was to be a wartime alliance, whereas the Austro-French alignment of 1735–41 had been a peacetime one that posed only a latent threat, to Britain and others. In contrast, in 1755–6, it appeared that, because of the weaknesses of British foreign policy and the successes of its British counterpart, France would be able to concentrate its energies on fighting Britain. Britain's alliance system certainly collapsed. Irrespective of their view of Prussia, neither Austria, Russia nor the Dutch displayed any interest in 1755–6 in supporting

---

12   L. Schilling, *Kaunitz und das Renversement des Alliances* (Berlin, 1994); M. Schumann and K.W. Schweizer, *The Seven Years War: A Transatlantic History* (Abingdon, 2008).

13   Titley to Robert Keith, 10 Mar. 1756, BL. Add. 35480 fols 139–40.

Britain or in protecting Hanover from an anticipated attack. Sardinia, Spain and Portugal were not to back Britain, which instead was threatened, as in 1739–41, by the prospect of a conflict without allies. Moreover, this was more serious than in 1739–41 because the enemy now was France, not (less powerful) Spain.

The British position was challenged in European waters as well as North America. Between 1745 and 1755, France and Spain had launched warships with a total displacement tonnage of nearly three times that launched by Britain, ensuring that the British superiority in warship numbers, already seriously eroded in the 1730s, was further hit. Such shipbuilding meant that reports of improvements to French ports, notably Dunkirk, were a matter of concern in Britain.[14] Due to the problems posed by the organic nature of ships' parts, new boats were more seaworthy. The altered naval strength led to a degree of caution on the part of the British government and Admiralty that did not match public expectations about British achievements.

In 1756, France rapidly won a major success. The British government hoped that the arrival in the Mediterranean of a fleet under Byng would render French naval preparations at Toulon ineffective.[15] However, instead, the French moved quickly, landing troops on the nearby British Mediterranean island base of Minorca on 18 April. This expedition was a dramatic step which demonstrated the French ability to set the agenda. As a result of such a clearly hostile move, which lacked the ambivalence of developments in North America, war on France was declared on 17 May.

The French invasion was made more significant, in terms both of international relations and of British politics, by the abject failure of Byng to compensate for it by relieving the Minorca garrison besieged in Fort St Philip. On 20 May, thirty miles off Minorca, Byng was unable to defeat a French fleet of comparable size. The British manoeuvred to take full advantage of the wind, while the French remained on the defensive. Contrary to the well-established rules of eighteenth-century naval warfare, the fleets were not parallel as they approached one another on the same tack. Instead, Byng was converging on Galissonière's fleet at an angle, so that the two vans were closer together than the two rears. This track allowed the French to concentrate their broadsides on Byng's van before the entire British line could come into action. One of these broadsides shot away the topmast of the sixth British ship in the line, causing it to stop, thereby threatening to entangle Byng's remaining ships. Instead of breaking his line and passing around the damaged ship to continue his attack, Byng chose

---

[14]   *Whitehall Evening Post*, 14 June 1753.
[15]   Fox to Bristol, 19 Mar. 1756, NA. SP. 92/64.

to stop to dress the line of his fleet. As the rear of his force therefore attempted to sort itself out, it was beyond effective cannon range and unable to influence the battle. There was a failure to concert operations between the parts of Byng's force. The van, commanded by Rear Admiral Temple West, engaged the French at close quarters and was badly pummelled by heavy, raking French broadsides. By the time Byng had the rear of his fleet ready, West's force was mangled and the British fleet was in no condition to renew its attack. That night, the fleets further separated. After refitting his ships, Byng conducted a council of war with his captains. In light of the now-weakened state of the fleet, the council was 'unanimously of the opinion that the fleet should immediately proceed to Gibraltar', the nearest British position. This was a decision that sealed the fate of the now deserted garrison on Minorca.

The net effect was to generate not only a public storm in Britain, but also a collapse of confidence in, and on the part of, the ministry. What had been reasonable, and certainly defensible, strategic and operational decisions by the ministry and its agents, based on the assessment of resources and threats, had unravelled due to the pressure of events. When news of Byng's defeat was finally confirmed in Britain, he was abused at length in print, while his effigy was burned in many cities. A series of public displays of a lack of confidence drove this agitation home and provided new material for it. On 20 August, the Lord Mayor, aldermen and councillors of London waited on the King, presenting an Address blaming the government for the loss of Minorca, as well as for failures in defending North America, the former apparently serving to locate the latter. James Wallace, one of the two Under Secretaries in the Northern Department, presented this Address in a positive light, as, indeed, he needed to do if popular pressure was not to be seen as damaging. His letter to Mitchell was an instance of the way in which diplomats had to be kept informed of domestic politics, not least in order to counter critical comments about British stability and policy:

> This day, the City of London has begun the dance of Addresses for an Enquiry etc, by waiting upon the King with theirs. It is very dutiful towards His Majesty, and no less hearty as to granting of subsidies; and the whole drawn with decency; so that it may possibly do more good than hurt; as the rest of the corporations are all gaping after the effect of it at court.[16]

There were also more specific concerns about the recent failure, concerns arising from the real and alleged importance of Minorca to Britain's commercial and

---

[16]   Wallace to Mitchell, 20 Aug. 1756, BL. Add. 6823 fol. 13.

political interests in the Mediterranean. Ministerial anxiety did not only relate to the political consequences, although they were important.[17]

Court-martialled, Byng was found guilty of failing to do his utmost to relieve Fort St Philip or to destroy the French warships, and was sentenced to death. The court added a recommendation for a royal pardon because they did not believe that his failure had arisen from cowardice or disaffection. This recommendation led to a renewed outburst of public anger. The navy was not supposed to fail, and a strong belief in naval invincibility was the bedrock of public faith in the government. If the British could not rule the waves, Britain itself might be conquered. If the navy would not do its duty, who would? This point was driven home because Byng's father had won the striking victory over a Spanish fleet off Sicily in 1718, the battle of Cape Passaro.

In practice, the failure to press home the attack on the French was a command decision that had more to do with the navy's rigid adherence to the Permanent Fighting Instructions than with the inability of the commanders. Moreover, as a key strategic element, the wish to preserve forces in home waters against a threatened French invasion affected the number of ships that could be spared for Byng. If the government had acted in accordance with French plans, keeping more warships in home waters than was, in the event, necessary, that did not mean that its response was inherently wrong; only poorly implemented, or, at least, unsuccessful. The latter was an important distinction, but one that left (and leaves) room for contention.

The public's rage over the loss of Minorca, combined with the political vulnerability of the Newcastle government, ensured that there was little possibility of a fair allocation of responsibility. Byng's supporters claimed that the ministry was making the admiral a scapegoat for its own negligence.[18] Leaving aside the alleged negligence, the accusation of scapegoating was reasonable.

British agents had reported the danger of a large-scale invasion of Britain,[19] and the French government certainly began to receive a new tranche of Jacobite memoranda advocating such action.[20] The risk of invasion had kept most of the navy in home waters, blockading the French fleet, and thus unable to support Byng. This posed a relationship between European and trans-oceanic tasks very

---

[17] Newcastle to Hardwicke, 19 July 1756, BL. Add. 32866 fols 211–12; Hardwicke to Horatio Walpole, 22 Aug. 1756, papers of Thomas Walpole in the possession of Matthew Holland. These papers have been purchased by the Lewis Walpole Library.

[18] Anon., *Observations on the Conduct of the Late Administration; Particularly in Regard to our Loss of Minorca* (London, 1757), pp. 2–12.

[19] Dayrolle (Brussels) to Fawkener, 20 Apr. 1756, RA. Cumb. P. 47/12.

[20] For example 12 June 1756, AE. CP. Ang. 440 fols 231–7.

different to that offered by Continental interventionism, but, again, with a trade-off between these tasks. Moreover, until the prospect of French invasion was addressed, there would only be so much strength that it was possible to commit to either Continental or trans-oceanic enterprises. This point, however, was politically problematic given the widespread unwillingness in public discussion to appreciate the consequences of British vulnerability. In addition, the British task was complicated by Dutch neutrality, unlike in 1689–97, 1702–13, and 1744–8, for this neutrality deprived Britain of the assistance of the Dutch navy.

Thus, in diplomatic, strategic and domestic terms, a crisis was faced in 1756. There was a collapse of confidence both within and concerning the Newcastle ministry. Not only its policies, but its ability to execute them, were a source of great uncertainty, and both within Britain and on the part of foreign observers. This sense encouraged debate over both goals and the remedies that should be sought in adopting particular strategies, notably a trans-oceanic one. However, underlying much of the debate, there was a collapse of confidence, due to an absence of success, alongside the misplaced belief on the part of some that all could be readily achieved provided the will was there.

Meanwhile, the loss of Minorca meant that Britain would need somehow to achieve sufficient success to obtain its return. Newcastle argued that this return was necessary for trade and to help Italian allies, by which he essentially meant Sardinia.[21] There were obviously more pressing domestic political reasons. The recovery of the island itself by attack was rendered difficult because, as Newcastle pointed out, French invasion preparations obliged Britain to conserve forces at home,[22] an argument also made by government supporters in response to bitter press criticism, notably, but not only, over Minorca,[23] and a course pressed by Frederick II.[24]

In response to the threat of invasion, Hanoverian troops were sent to England, landing at Chatham on 20 May 1756. There was also pressure for a strong militia. The possibility of a run on the Bank of England was rumoured in the case of invasion. This would create a liquidity crisis, and led to the suggestion that money be taken out of the Bank and stored in a safe place so that there should be ready money for the military.[25] Moreover, there were concerns about

---

[21] Viry to Charles Emmanuel III, 12 May 1756, AST. LM. Ing. 60.
[22] Viry to Ossorio, 12 May 1756, AST. LM. Ing. 60.
[23] Viry to Charles Emmanuel III, 25 May 1756, AST. LM. Ing. 60.
[24] Mitchell to Holdernesse, 27 May 1756, NA. SP. 90/65.
[25] Anon., 'Measures proposed...', [1756], RA. Cumb. P. 46/128.

the vulnerable nature of poorly-fortified Ireland.[26] Any French invasion would be on behalf of the Jacobites, which underlines the degree to which the Jacobite threat still had meaning, both militarily and in people's minds. Frederick urged the British government to be mindful of the threat of action on behalf of the Jacobites, and Berlin was the source of reports about links between France and the Jacobites.[27] Frederick, furthermore, claimed that Kaunitz had warned that the British royal family might suffer from Austrian anger, although that remark was as much a reference to Hanover,[28] and one designed to benefit from British distrust of Austria.

The crisis over British military strategy interacted with that over diplomacy, each giving point to the other. The two crises produced challenges for politicians while playing a role in their struggles over policy and power. However, the complexity and nuances of the situation were such that political alignments within the ministry could be differently explained. For example, alongside questions about how best to act against France, it was possible to present divisions in terms of the rise of the 'party' committed to alliance with Frederick, a party, allegedly led by Cumberland, Bedford, and Fox, which was very angry with Austria.[29] This view was soon supplemented by one of a government divided over whether Britain should seek to counterbalance the Franco-Austrian alliance, the approach attributed to George, Newcastle and the Secretaries of State, or should follow a more cautious approach, one that entailed a withdrawal from interventionism.[30] The two issues were linked with the observation that ministerial critics of Austria were now advocating an abandonment of Continental interventionism.[31] Alliance with Prussia was an alternative if it entailed the commitment of troops to the Continent, but that was not the automatic corollary of the alliance.

In a fast-moving situation, views were not fixed and instead, overlapped. Nevertheless, the overwhelming theme was of an abandonment of the alignment of the early 1750s, at least to an extent. Newcastle was torn; angry with Austria, but unwilling to take steps that might make a return to the old system of alliance

---

[26]   Henry Conway to Devonshire, 7 Oct. 1756, Derby, Library, Catton Collection, WH 3450.

[27]   Mitchell to Holdernesse, 4 Sept. 1756, NA. SP. 90/66.

[28]   Mitchell to Holdernesse, 12 Aug. 1756, NA. SP. 90/66.

[29]   Viry to Charles Emmanuel III, 13, 17 May 1756, AST. LM. Ing. 60.

[30]   Viry to Charles Emmanuel III, 11, 18 June 1756, AST. LM. Ing. 60.

[31]   Viry to Charles Emmanuel III, 2 July 1756, AST. LM. Ing. 60.

with Austria impossible. George was also angry with Austria, and prepared to say so.[32]

At the same time, there were immediate strategic issues, namely the threat of a large-scale French attack on Britain or Hanover. Alliance with Prussia was seen by Britain to focus on protection against the risk of French attack, notably on Hanover.[33] The constraints facing the ministry were not simply international and military. Indeed, Newcastle told Viry that it was difficult to conduct matters in Britain as he wanted.[34] Within this context, the government, nevertheless, emphasised parliamentary backing, and presented support for Hanover as 'a national quarrel', as the national honour was engaged in supporting Hanover if attacked as a result of measures taken in North America.[35] In relations with Prussia, the stress was placed on the domestic perception, Holdernesse writing:

> there is no other means of inducing this country to contribute efficaciously towards these His Majesty's views, but by a determination on the part of the King of Prussia to throw off all reserve, and act openly against France for the defence of His Majesty's territories if unjustly attacked in consequence of a British quarrel.[36]

For Frederick, however, the key issue was not the protection of Hanover, but relations with Austria, which continued to wish for the return of Silesia. Despite British wishes,[37] he withdrew troops from the Rhineland, where they could cover Hanover from French attack, and, instead, attacked Austria. Well aware of Austro-Russian military preparations to begin war, Frederick launched a pre-emptive strike. In order to deny a base to the gathering coalition against him, Frederick first, en route for Austria, invaded Saxony on 28 August. Aside from applying on land a breach of the law of nations that the French claimed the British had pioneered with Boscawen's attack at sea in 1755,[38] this was a dangerous move. Louis XV felt obliged to succour Augustus III of Saxony, his heir's brother-in-law, and this obligation added a powerful motive to French antipathy to Frederick. Indeed, Frederick helped to precipitate both a hostile Franco-Russian *rapprochement* and a strengthening of the Austro-French

32 Viry to Charles Emmanuel III, 24 Sept. 1756, AST. LM. Ing. 60.
33 Holdernesse to Mitchell, 9 July 1756, NA. SP. 90/65.
34 Viry to Charles Emmanuel III, 9 July 1756, AST. LM. Ing. 60.
35 Holdernesse to Mitchell, 9 July 1756, NA. SP. 90/65.
36 Holdernesse to Mitchell, 6 Aug. 1756, NA. SP. 90/65.
37 Holdernesse to Mitchell, 10 Aug. 1756, NA. SP. 90/66.
38 Mitchell to Holdernesse, 25 Sept. 1756, NA. 90/66.

alliance. News of Prussia's attack was communicated by Michell, its envoy in London, on 4 September.[39]

The outbreak of conflict on the Continent, following the formal declaration of war between Britain and France in May as a result of the invasion of Minorca, affected a British government facing a difficult situation. On the one hand, there was, despite the claims of Jacobites, a considerable degree of national cohesion in Britain. The anonymous author of a pro-government pamphlet *A Letter to the King of xxx [France]* discerned a fundamental unity in opposition to France:

> Our Ministry (as you well know) have done much against you, the Opposition are angry that they have not done more. The race of your old friends, whom you used to know by the name of Tories is extinct and lost. If a love of Liberty, zeal for the commerce and glory of Britain, and for the basis of it, the Protestant succession, in the illustrious House of Hanover, are criterions [sic] of Whiggism; we are a nation of Whigs.

The author then asked the question why there were complaints about the ministry, attributing them to the national 'humour [character] and climate, as well as our constitution'. Ascribing opposition in this fashion to 'barometrical' factors was commonplace and going too far. Instead, a degree of essential unity, in the sense of opposition to France, was present.[40] Understandably, however, that scarcely appeared to be the case from the perspective of Newcastle, who was 'vastly low-spirited and dejected'.[41] His already distrustful relationship with Fox collapsed, in part under the strain of the humiliating loss of Minorca. Fox did not wish to face the pressure of blame without the reality of power. The situation was exacerbated by Pitt's use of public outrage in his encouragement of Instructions and Addresses. These were deployed from constituencies to their MPs and to the Crown. Josiah Tucker, a Bristol cleric who wrote on economic issues and was a protégé of Robert Nugent, a member of the Treasury Board, and of Hardwicke, referred to 'the epidemical madness of addressing, instructing etc'.[42] Caricatures were also used, as in *The English Lion Dismember'd*.

---

[39]　Holdernesse to George, 4 Sept. 1756, BL. Eg. 3425 fol. 29.

[40]　Anon., *A Letter to the King of xxx* (London, 1756), pp. 5–8.

[41]　Alexander Hume Campbell to Hugh, Earl of Marchmont, 15 July 1756, HMC, *Polwarth* V (London, 1961), p. 322.

[42]　P. Langford, 'William Pitt and Public Opinion', *English Historical Review*, 88 (1973), pp. 54–79; M. Peters, *Pitt and Popularity: The Patriot Minister and London Opinion During the Seven Years War* (Oxford, 1980).

Moreover, there was no good war news. The navy was constrained by a set of tasks, focused on invasion deterrence and commerce protection, that forced it into a reactive operational stance. In September, Anson, the First Lord of the Admiralty, drew the attention of his ministerial colleagues to the dire consequences of the problems posed by maintaining the blockade of France's leading Atlantic naval base:

> My Lord Anson ... represented the condition of the squadron under the command of Vice Admiral Boscawen, that the crews of the ships are very sickly, that the ships must necessarily return in order to be refitted, and that, upon the whole, the fleet would run the utmost hazard, were it to continue cruising off Brest, beyond the middle of the next month.[43]

The following month, Bedford, then Lord-Lieutenant of Ireland, complained about ineffectiveness as well:

> What we have been doing with our fleet this summer, but endeavouring to hedge in the cuckow, which, as must always be the case, we have been utterly unable to effect? For many ships and forces have been stole away from the different ports of France to America, and with this additional disadvantage, that whilst we are wearing out our ships and sailors by keeping the French fleet within their harbours, they are, without any waste of men or ships, getting themselves into a condition of being able to drive us off their coasts in a very short time.[44]

Convoying trade provided another arduous task that did not bring political benefits, but, instead, was accompanied by complaints.

Described as 'the Primum Mobile of the whole Administration',[45] Newcastle sought to deal with the crisis by winning over opposition. To him, this meant neutering hostility by accommodating it in terms of posts in the government. This was a policy he had seen work in 1720 when Walpole had been brought back into government and one he had repeatedly used with success from 1742. Posts, however, were not the sole issue. Personal drive and political ambition proved key issues. Indeed, drawing out the constitutional implications, *A Letter to the King of xxx* commented on:

---

[43]   Cabinet Minute, 29 Sept. 1756, BL. Add. 51376 fols 85–6.

[44]   Bedford to Henry Fox, 14 Oct. 1756, Earl of Ilchester (ed.), *Letters to Henry Fox* (London, 1915), p. 93.

[45]   Anon., *An Answer to a Pamphlet, called A Second Letter to the People* (London, 1755), p. 3.

those ingredients which compose the power a British statesman may aim at. It is not any peculiar office, rank, or station, but a secret energy and confidence annexed to it, without which that office or station may not give the possessor that full sufficiency and content that may be the object of his ambition. Therefore be not surprised that a man with us may be Secretary of State, Chancellor of the Exchequer, Paymaster of our Forces, or in any other post to which you are used to annex the idea of our Premier, and yet not, possesses that plenitude of power which constitutes a minister, and which ambition may think its due. Indeed the terms minister and ministry are so vague and ill-understood in our language, as well as constitution, that I find it difficult to form, much more to give a true idea of it.[46]

After a dispirited Fox, who lacked not only Newcastle's confidence but also Pitt's political energy and drive, resigned in October 1756, Newcastle persuaded George to allow him to offer Pitt a Secretaryship of State in return for his support. Approached by Hardwicke on 19 October, Pitt, however, did not seek Newcastle's solution, a reconstitution of the ministry to bring him in and thus strengthen the Duke, but instead a total change of it and its policies. This was the complete Whig renewal that critics (correctly) argued had not taken place with the fall of Walpole in 1742. Pitt demanded the resignation of Newcastle, as well as an inquiry into recent setbacks, a step designed to expose Newcastle's role in Byng's failure. He also pressed for the dismissal of foreign troops in British pay, troops largely intended for the defence of Hanover. Determined that he should not simply defend government policy in the Commons, which was what Newcastle sought, and what Fox had rebelled against, Pitt insisted that a scheme of measures be adopted that he could approve and defend, a theme of his political career.

The King rejected Pitt's terms which, indeed, were in part aimed against the royal position. Newcastle, unsuccessful in his attempt to find a Commons' leader other than Fox or Pitt, told George that he could not engage to conduct business in the Commons and resigned on 27 October. This was pressure on the King that was different from that in 1746 when he had been forced to abandon the attempt to form a ministry without the Pelhams; but, nevertheless, pressure again. George was obliged to accept Fox or Pitt, both of whom were unpalatable. Lady Betty Waldegrave reported a discussion between her father, Granville, 2nd Earl Gower, the Lord Privy Seal, and the King about Fox. The King's concern with his own independence and with status emerged clearly. He complained about Fox:

---

[46] Anon., *A Letter to the King of xxx* (London, 1756), pp. 11–12.

the ambition of that man is not to be gratified. I have done more for him than any
one person. He has power enough. I will give him no more. If he quits me now
and throws everything into confusion, the whole world will blame him. I have
made his brother an Earl, over all the Barons' heads.

Indeed, the brother in question, Stephen Fox, was made Earl of Ilchester in June
1756. This was an instance of social mobility as Stephen and his younger brother
Henry were the sons of Sir Stephen Fox, who had begun life as a footman, before,
as Paymaster of the Forces, making a fortune which he invested in property. In
reply, Gower showed how the King had to listen to uncomfortable truths about
his need, as a result of the political system, for people he disliked. Gower said of
Fox: 'He was ready to undertake His Majesty's affairs, provided a proper power
was vested in him, but, without it, he would not pretend to carry on the business
of the House of Commons.'[47] On 27 October, George gave Fox the authority to
form a Fox–Pitt ministry, but Pitt rejected the idea next day.

The Prussian envoy complained that no attention was paid to foreign
affairs,[48] and Frederick was angry about the ministerial instability. In turn,
British diplomats noted a failure from London to respond to dispatches and,
indeed, circumstances,[49] a failure to which the illness of the two Secretaries of
State contributed.[50] The government sought to provide reassurance that the
divisions were about men not measures,[51] but, irrespective of this, there was
the question of the ability of Britain to implement policy. Mitchell reported
of Frederick: 'I cannot bring him to particular explanations till I am able to tell
him an administration is settled in England.'[52] Mitchell argued that the British
ministers were united in their positive views about Frederick, but the latter
proved unwilling to disclose his plan of operations for 1757. He argued that good
intentions would not suffice if the opportunity to plan for the next campaign
was lost, and pressed Britain to act with vigour, including threatening the French
coast and winning the support of Denmark, Sardinia, Turkey and the United
Provinces.[53] Frederick was assured that the changes in the government would

[47]   Betty Waldegrave to her brother, Viscount Trentham, 16 Oct. 1756,
NA. PRO. 30/29/1/17 fol. 962.
[48]   Michell to Frederick, 29 Oct., Frederick to Michell, 9 Nov., Frederick to Mitchell,
10, 14 Nov., 1756, *Polit. Corr.* XIV, 30–2, 38, BL. Add. 6843 fol. 39.
[49]   Mitchell to Hanbury Williams, 18 Dec. 1756, HW.
[50]   Haslang to Wachtendonck, 24 Dec. 1756, Munich, Bayr. Ges., London 231.
[51]   Holdernesse to Mitchell, 3 Nov. 1756, BL. Add. 6832 fol. 98.
[52]   Mitchell to Holdernesse, 17 Nov. 1756, NA. SP. 90/67.
[53]   Mitchell to Holdernesse, 24 Nov., 5, 8, 9 Dec. 1756, NA. SP. 90/67; Frederick to
Michell, 28, 30 Nov. 1756, *Polit. Corr.* XIV, 81, 94.

not lead to any alteration in British policy,[54] and Prussian assistance was sought in arranging a subsidy treaty with Brunswick, which was crucial to the defence of Hanover.[55] At the same time, Hanoverian ministers fed George's uneasiness about alliance with Prussia, a nexus of opinion-generation, if not policy-making, that challenged British politics and policy. There was a danger that British policy would be affected and that Hanover might follow a different path.

Pitt's apparent indispensability in the Commons allowed him to defy Newcastle and Fox and then forced the King to yield. However, George's unwillingness to have Pitt responsible for relations with northern Europe, meant that he had to accept the Southern Secretaryship. In place of Newcastle, an unenthusiastic William, 4th Duke of Devonshire became First Lord of the Treasury on 6 November 1756. A young 'Old Corps' Whig, he had been an MP (1741–9), a member of the Cabinet from 1749, Master of the Horse (1749–5) and Lord Lieutenant of Ireland (1755–6), where he had sought to govern without party. This ministry, however, lacked a parliamentary majority and the auspices for one were not good. There was also the question of how best to define and pursue a foreign policy, both in the context of domestic division and with reference to a rapidly-changing and unprecedented international situation. The public debate was also challenging, with the threat of criticism over both specifics and the general thrust of policy. *Con-Test* outlined the problem in its first issue, that of 23 November 1756:

> There is in all kingdoms a real or permanent, and an accidental or immediate interest. If a potent state should be so ill advised as to pursue an accident or immediate, to the neglect of its real or permanent interest, such an unnatural conduct in them, must influence other powers, to submit to a temporary deviation from those established rules of government, which past experience may have prescribed as most generally essential to public good.

That year, the wider British public were offered a bleaker and readily accessible prospect of the threat from France and its relationship with national weakness in Arthur Murphy's successful play *The Englishman from Paris* (1756), which was very much a comedy with a twist. Jack Broughton, the Frenchified returned traveller, presents the lack of freedom in France as a defence of social privilege:

---

54   Mitchell to Holdernesse, 13 Dec., Potenger to Mitchell, 21 Dec. 1756, NA. SP. 90/67, BL. Add. 6823 fol. 23.

55   Holdernesse to Mitchell, 31 Dec. 1756, NA. SP. 90/67.

> At Paris one of the Canaille [mob] dare not come within the atmosphere of a man
> of condition – there, for sending forty livres to the Lieutenant of the Police, a man
> of quality may run a scoundrel through the body.

His servant, Roger, in contrast, linked British freedom to an active public culture: 'they have such laws there – why a poor servant dare not give his opinion there of the government ... if he does ... he is sent to the Bastille'. This reference to the fortress-prison in Paris was an ironic comment given that, in January 1757, Robert Francois Damiens, a servant, had no trouble in gaining access to the palace of Versailles and stabbing Louis XV. Roger continued, 'Why now here we can talk of folks at the helm and of taxes.' To drive the point home and relate the subject to the international crisis, Jack described the French as naturally ready to break treaties, and linked their ability to give fashions to Europe to their future success in running it.

The reiteration of these themes reflected not only humorous stereotypes, but also a sense of disquiet and a belief that national character could be sapped by élite betrayal. In addition to the sociocultural challenge, religious difference was associated with political rivalry. Richard Rolt, an industrious hack author, wrote in 1753 about 'our liberties ... our religion; both of which are repugnant to the constitution of France'.[56] He was subsequently to write much in praise of Frederick, treating this ally as a Protestant hero. France apparently was not the sole threat. In a cause célèbre, the release, by means of Holdernesse acting in accordance with George's wishes, of a Hanoverian soldier arrested in Maidstone over the theft of handkerchiefs led to concern about the rule of law as well as discussion of masculinity.[57]

There was a fear in 1756 about the functional capability of the British system. Commentators raised the question whether the form of government gave France an advantage in moving more rapidly in a crisis and to implement policy.[58] In part, there were simply the problems of divided authority in Britain, as also, although to a far greater extent, in the United Provinces. These problems were seen when Prussia sought a declaration of the consequences for its trade of the outbreak of war between Britain and France. The Prussian envoy was told

---

[56]   R. Rolt, *Memoirs of the Life of the Right Honourable John Lindesey, Earl of Crawfurd* (London, 1753), p. 13.

[57]   M. McCormack, 'Citizenship, Nationhood and Masculinity in the Affair of the Hanoverian Soldier, 1756', *Historical Journal*, 49 (2006), pp. 971–93.

[58]   Haslang to Preysing and Wachtendonck, 30 July 1756, Munich, Bayr. Ges., London 231.

that no declaration of that kind could be valid, as the King's authority did not reach to cases provided for by law, and that the only method by which the ends which His Prussian Majesty has in view could be obtained would be by a Treaty of Commerce.

Accepting this, Frederick sent proposals, leading Holdernesse to reply that it was necessary first to refer them to the Board of Trade. Although George II was keen on speed, his Secretary of State sent instructions noting that 'from the forms of this government, the business is delayed'.[59] Such delay indicated the subordination of the ministry to the law, as well as the extent to which the administration was not readily responsive to ministerial, still more royal, wishes. However, such delay was not helpful in the fast-changing circumstances of that year. Indeed, Britain's ability to affect, still more direct, the international situation was, at least in part, lessened as a consequence of such processes.

Disquiet, moreover, was voiced by British commentators, although they tended to focus on the supposed weaknesses of the political system, rather than its governmental counterpart. This focus overlapped with anxieties about political and public culture, not least the élite weakness, if not betrayal, highlighted in Murphy's play. The fall of the Newcastle ministry encouraged the sense of unease,[60] if not betrayal. In some respects, Minorca provided an opportunity and symbol for the discussion of existential threats already seen with the Jacobite invasion of 1745. In each case, thanks to the severity of the crisis, the focus was no longer on the alleged impact of Hanover on British policy and politics; although Hanover was not without political consequence, both in specifics and with reference to the general tone of policy discussion. Indeed, in practice, in the 1740s and 1750s, Hanover proved an aspect of contention when matters as a whole were not quite so serious. However, the very nature of Britain as a political system itself became an issue anew in 1756, and thus contributed centrally to the description of the period as a mid-century crisis. Crucially, failure in war coincided with political division and weakness in government, leading William Bentinck to remark 'What will become of this inconsistency and confusion nobody can foresee, much less foretell.'[61]

---

[59] Holdernesse to Mitchell, 11 May 1756, NA. SP. 90/65.

[60] Henry Legge to Earl of Guildford, 9 Nov. 1756, Bod. Ms. North d 7 fol. 67.

[61] Bentinck to Keith, 17 Dec. 1756, BL. Add. 35481 fol. 160.

Chapter 10

A Struggle for Survival, 1757

I am the Chairman of a club of reputable persons, consisting of some gentlemen of fortune, and some not inconsiderable tradesmen, who talk freely enough, at times, of the public affairs; but always under a restriction that I am afraid is seldom observed elsewhere; namely, to propose remedies rather than inflame complaints; and even this, with all the diffidence becoming public individuals.

Letter in *Public Advertiser*, 12 January 1757

If 1756 was difficult, 1757 threatened to be more so. The events of that year were certainly seen by many in that light, both in terms of domestic politics and with regard to the international system. Again, there were international and domestic crises, with these crises arising from serious diplomatic, strategic and political problems, and made more complex by their interactions. As well as Britain, Hanover was confronted by a grave situation, and in each case, there was a fear of dire and speedy consequences. These, indeed, proved to be the case for Hanover. Concern was felt at the most senior level and from the outset of the year. On 5 January 1757, George, in an audience with Haslang in which only the two men were present, expressed his concern about the future of the Empire if Frederick was defeated and what he presented as the balance of power thereby lost. This fear led George to propose that the Electors of Bavaria and the Palatinate should try to mediate between Austria and Prussia.[1]

George's emphasis on secrecy, in this and other matters,[2] was in part directed against his British ministers. Keeping them in the dark led to tension and uncertainty and, in part, represented a failure of British foreign policy. More generally, the Pitt–Devonshire ministry established in November 1756 on the ruins of Newcastle's system proved weak, divided, indifferently led, and unable to cope with the many difficulties it faced. These difficulties included opposition from Newcastle's numerous supporters. The *London Evening Post* complained on 8 March 1757 that, despite the need for unanimity, 'some discarded managers' sought to "keep up" divisions and animosities'. The newspaper

---

[1]   Haslang to Preysing, 7 Jan., Haslang to Wachtendonck, 11 Jan. 1757, Munich, Bayr. Ges. London 233.
[2]   George to Frederick, 7 Jan. 1757, *Polit. Corr.* XIV, p. 251.

offered an instructive approach to politics, one in which party was no longer valid. However, this approach did not capture the consistent reality of factional activity, nor the complicating role of the King.

Aware of division and weakness in London, British diplomats complained of a lack of instructions and information, a lack that focused their concerns.[3] In turn, foreign rulers and envoys discerned division and weakness.[4] Parliamentary support was seen, in Britain and abroad, as a way to affirm Britain's policy, notably its determination to stick to Frederick.[5] However, a persistently sickly Pitt found it difficult to control the dynamic of events in Parliament or in foreign policy, the latter notably because of the unexpected Diplomatic Revolution. This alliance between Austria and France, to which Russia acceded on 11 January 1757, denied Britain the international system that had helped it in its previous three wars with France. On 29 January, with the support of some Protestant princes, the Imperial Diet declared war on Prussia, which put Hanover in a more difficult position. Indeed, the ministers in Hanover appeared receptive to Austrian approaches for a neutrality, and had their own channels to George, not least through his influential mistress, the Countess of Yarmouth.[6] In contrast, Mitchell found the Hanoverian ministry unenthusiastic about his negotiations to bring Brunswick into the Prussian alliance.[7] As a result of concerns about Hanover and George, the Cabinet took an opportunity to bring the subject of the Prussian alliance to an issue with George, in order to show that the government could not take steps to support the defence of Hanover unless upon the basis of the Prussian alliance.[8] On 17 February, Pitt asked the Commons for £200,000 to pay for an Army of Observation to protect Hanover and help Prussia but, in a key political step, this sum did not cover the Hanoverian troops themselves. Instead, they were to be funded out of Hanoverian revenues.[9]

Aside from angering George, the Pitt–Devonshire ministry could not impose itself on events, abroad or at home, and soon lacked the political strength to keep going. Alongside serious political weakness and disunity, there was a related division over strategy, notably between Pitt and Cumberland.[10]

3   Mitchell to Holdernesse, 2 Jan. 1757, NA. SP. 90/68.
4   Viry to Charles Emmanuel III, 14, 18, 20 Jan., 4 Feb. 1757, AST. LM. Ing. 61.
5   Holdernesse to Mitchell, 25 Jan. 1757, BL. Add. 6832 fol. 110.
6   Frederick to Mitchell, 7 Feb. 1757, BL. Add. 6843 fols 67–8.
7   Mitchell to Holdernesse, 8 Feb. 1757, NA. SP. 90/68.
8   Holdernesse to Mitchell, 8 Feb. 1757, BL. Add. 6832 fol. 112.
9   B. Simms, 'Pitt and Hanover', in B. Simms and T. Riotte (eds), *The Hanoverian Dimension in British History, 1714–1837* (Cambridge, 2007), p. 41.
10   R. Whitworth, *Field Marshal Lord Ligonier* (Oxford, 1958), p. 201.

The central position and very different assumptions and policies of both created issues for their colleagues. The two men, however, were not the sole political players. Devonshire discussed foreign relations with foreign envoys, although taking care to keep this secret so as not to offend the Secretaries of State, which really meant Pitt.[11] Moreover, public disquiet over foreign policy remained a factor. Pamphleteers readily linked past policies, present crises, and political factors. Thus, the anonymous *A Letter to His Grace the D—of N----E, on the Duty he owes Himself, his King, his Country and his God, At This Important Moment* (1757) bitterly attacked the support for Hanover that the writer argued had characterised Newcastle's policy and, instead, presented government as the means to pursue 'the Nation's Welfare'.[12] The *London Evening Post* of 13 January 1757 claimed that the last government (the Newcastle ministry) had been ready to give up everything gained by the Peace of Utrecht in 1713. This was, at once, a reference to talk of propriating Spain, notably by returning Gibraltar (and possibly an allusion to the failure to retain Minorca), but also a suggestion that the 'Old Corps' Whigs were worse than the Tories had been in 1713. This approach offered a way to rehabilitate the Tories and to join them to Whigs critical of the 'Old Corps'. The new ministry indeed required new sources of political support, which was the theme of Pitt's politics, although the search for them created tensions within the Whig establishment.

More urgently, there were grain riots. Indeed, 'C.W.', writing in the *London Evening Post* of 5 February, thought that the price of grain, as well as the absence of military success, indicated a lack of divine support. This fear encouraged Edward Weston, a former Under Secretary, to launch, on 8 February, the *Fast*, which contained a call for personal and national religious revival.[13] It is easy to neglect this aspect of politics, but it was highly significant, not least contributing to a mood of crisis; crisis, moreover, that appeared more serious and searching than that simply of political calculation. More prosaically, riots had grave military implications in terms of requiring the deployment of troops at home in order to control the situation. This need represented another aspect of the strategic pressure for home defence. Grain supplies also became an international issue, as with the threat to British grain imports from Poland posed by Russian warships, an issue that led to diplomatic representations.[14]

While they sought to devise and implement policy, politicians and ministers were affected by wider political and social currents. At the same time, the need to

---

[11]   Viry to Charles Emmanuel III, 4, 8 Feb. 1757, AST. LM. Ing. 61.
[12]   Anon., *A Letter to His Grace the D- of N-E* (London, 1757), p. 42.
[13]   Manuscript in Weston's hand, Weston Underwood papers.
[14]   Hanbury Williams to Holdernesse, 17 June 1757, NA. SP. 91/65.

respond to immediate problems, military, diplomatic and political, crowded out attempts to implement coherent systems. For example, there was an interaction between differences over strategy and developing political tensions. Thus Pitt's need to align with the 'Leicester House' supporters of Prince George, the future George III (who lived at Leicester House), encouraged the minister to support expeditions against the French coast because this group wished to differentiate itself clearly from Cumberland's backing for a British-financed army in Germany. These expeditions complicated the oft-proclaimed choice between 'Europe' and 'America', as, in terms of both duration and geography, they became the apparent alternative to a longstanding commitment of troops to the Continent and, more specifically, Germany. As a result, the expeditions could serve as a strategy designed to win over Tories and opposition Whigs. However, the nature of any trade-off between the coastal expeditions and the wider war was unclear and contentious.[15] Meanwhile, the fall of Minorca continued to resonate as an issue. The front page of the *Citizen* declared on 30 March:

> The desire of many of our readers, whom we are always ready to oblige, occasions the Instructions of the City of London, to their representatives, to be this day again inserted, as not yet unseasonable in the present national situation.

Aside from debate within Britain, there was also that with Britain's leading ally, Frederick II, an ally who was made more significant by the lack of any comparable supporter. As a result, for Britain, Frederick was in a very different position to those occupied by Austria, the Dutch, or Sardinia in the War of the Austrian Succession. Frederick had initially hoped that Britain would be able to woo the Dutch,[16] but, under the pressures of campaigning, his aspirations became more narrowly military. In the absence of the dispatch of British troops to Germany,[17] Frederick supported the sending of a British fleet to the Baltic in order to discourage Russian and Swedish attacks,[18] as well as British attacks on the French coast or Ostend as a means to reduce pressure on Prussia[19] or

---

[15]   Anon., *A Letter to the People of England, upon the Militia, Continental Connections, Neutralities, and Secret Expeditions* (London, 1757), pp. 20–1.

[16]   Mitchell to Holdernesse, 25 Jan. 1757, NA. SP. 90/68.

[17]   Frederick to Mitchell, 1758, BL. Add. 6843 fol. 140.

[18]   Mitchell to Holdernesse, 4, 7 Apr., 12 June 1757, NA. SP. 90/68–9; Frederick to Michell, 14 Apr. 1757, *Polit. Corr.* XIV, 501–3; Frederick to Mitchell, 11 June 1757, BL. Add. 6843 fol. 99.

[19]   Frederick to Michell, 14 May, Frederick to Podewils, 11 June 1757, *Polit. Corr.* XV, 36, 161; Mitchell to Holdernesse, 4 Nov. 1756, NA. SP. 90/67.

Hanover.[20] There was uncertainty as to how 'considerable'[21] a diversion might be achieved, but, nevertheless, it came to play a key role in political, strategic and diplomatic discussion.

Political difficulties escalated at the time of onset of the 1757 campaign season, which acted as a pressure for decisions. The fall of the Devonshire–Pitt ministry, with Pitt's dismissal on 6 April, was not followed by the swift creation of a replacement. Instead, there was a protracted period in which various ministerial solutions were attempted.[22] As a result, although Holdernesse had told Michell that, if the government changed, it would still be pro-Prussian,[23] Frederick complained: 'of the little attention that England seemed to have to the affairs of the Continent', added that for nine months, 'ever since our unhappy divisions triumphed at Home', he had 'been amused with fair words', and later sardonically referred to being glad to hear that 'at last, we were likely to have an administration in England' and to his hope that 'the time that has been lost in inaction' would be made up.[24] At the same time, Frederick was also highly critical of the 'slowness' and lack of resolution of the Hanoverian ministry[25] which did not face comparable political problems. However, the *London Chronicle* of 5 April noted past Dutch complaints about the problems created by British political instability. Indeed, the impact abroad of this stability was not solely a subject for Frederick's sarcasm. On 9 April, the *Con-Test* asked: 'How would our foreign enemies, for the distinction is become necessary – How would they triumph, to find our councils so miserably fluctuating, that our ministers are but the servants of a day.' A week later, the paper reported that the fall of Pitt had been greeted with bonfires in Paris.[26] Haslang commented that the spirit of faction reigned more than ever.[27]

Despite Pitt's well-known unpopularity with George, neither Newcastle nor Fox appeared to have a good chance of forming a ministry that could survive in the Commons without Pitt. In large measure, this was because any such ministry would be vulnerable to his devastating oratory if anything went wrong with the handling of the war. Moreover, as key elements, Fox did not have the stomach for

[20] Mitchell to Holdernesse, 2 July 1757, NA. SP. 90/69.
[21] Holdernesse to Cumberland, 7 Sept. 1757, BL. Eg. 3442 fol. 236.
[22] J.C.D. Clark, *The Dynamics of Change: The Crisis of the 1750s and English Party Systems* (Cambridge, 1982).
[23] Michell to Frederick, *Polit. Corr.* XIV, 502.
[24] Mitchell to Holdernesse, 31 Mar., 29 June, 2 July 1757, NA. SP. 90/68-9; Frederick to Michell, 3, 8 June 1757, *Polit. Corr.* XV, 123, 142.
[25] Mitchell to Holdernesse, 4, 7 Apr. 1757, NA. SP. 90/68.
[26] Cf. 11 June 1757.
[27] Haslang to Preysing, 20 May 1757, Munich, Bayr. Ges., London 233.

the fight, and Newcastle had no one of sufficient stature or courage to take Pitt on. There was no equivalent to Walpole or Pelham, both of whom had proved experienced and effective Commons' leaders even if Pelham was no great orator.

While British politicians struggled to form a strong and durable ministry, there was a parallel attempt to produce resolve in Hanover in the shape of the dispatch thither of Cumberland. He disembarked at Stade on 14 April, reaching Hanover two days later. This was a counterpart to the replacement of Pitt in that it represented George's attempt to provide direction to the Hanoverian government and, more particularly, to ensure a common line for Britain and Hanover. As such, there was a parallel with the removal of Townshend in 1716, a key step in bringing on and clarifying the Whig Split of 1717–20. Holdernesse commented: 'His Royal Highness's presence at Hanover will alter the face of affairs, and vigorously carry into execution His Majesty's commands.'[28] Austrian and French approaches for Hanoverian neutrality, approaches that threatened British foreign policy, were rejected. This tension was captured in the person of George: 'The Court of Vienna has an affectation of treating with the King in his Electoral capacity only, and at the same time propose conditions to him directly repugnant to some of his engagements as King.' The Austrian envoy reported that the hands of the Hanoverian ministry were tied, and that the British ministers were more concerned with Prussian than Hanoverian interests.[29] The atmosphere of rumour was indicated by press reports that a neutrality had been agreed.[30]

In the meanwhile, French military moves toward the Lower Rhine increased tension, although Cumberland was given assurances of Prussian assistance if required.[31] Cumberland was assured that the maintenance of these Prussian troops would be paid as any opposition in the Commons could be 'over-ruled'.[32] However, the crisis in Prussia's military situation that June led to Frederick saying that he could no longer send help to Cumberland and Hanover. Instead, referring to the efforts made by Britain in the 1700s 'to preserve the Balance of Power', he called for the dispatch of British troops.[33]

The eventual solution to the domestic political situation, the Newcastle–Pitt ministry, formed, with Devonshire's support, on 29 June 1757, was to last until

---

[28]   Holdernesse to Mitchell, 12 Apr. 1757, NA. SP. 90/68.
[29]   Holdernesse to Mitchell, 29 Apr.. 1757, NA. SP. 90/68; Colloredo to Stahremberg, 29 Apr. 1757, AE. CP. Br. Han. 52 fols 97–106.
[30]   *London Chronicle*, 5 May 1757.
[31]   Cumberland to Holdernesse, 19 Apr. 1757, BL. Eg. 3442 fol. 19.
[32]   Holdernesse to Cumberland, 29 Apr. 1757, BL. Eg. 3442 fol. 33.
[33]   Mitchell to Holdernesse, 29 June, 9 July 1757, NA. SP. 90/69.

October 1761. However, although seen as 'solid',[34] it was not initially clear that the ministry would be successful or lasting. Instead, to many commentators, it appeared likely that the differences between the two protagonists, and their drive to dominate, would soon split the ministry. Pitt's position might have looked weak in terms of the arithmetic of parliamentary management, as he did not command an interest or have any experience in managing the Commons. Nevertheless, thanks to his ability, magnetism, vigour and public resonance, Pitt's position was stronger than anyone else's, although not strong enough for him to direct a ministry by itself. He was especially weak at the royal court, in the House of Lords, and with the leading financial interests.

The different positions in which Newcastle found himself during the serious wartime political crises of 1744–6 and 1756–7 throw much light on the workings of the political system. In the former, it was the Pelhams who could offer the management of the Commons, while Carteret, weakened by his inability to do so, fell in 1744, despite George's support. Moreover, neither George nor Carteret could sustain the latter's return to office in 1746. In 1756–7, in contrast, Newcastle not only faced a very different international situation, but also could not promise a pliant Commons. Without Pelham, he was in a far weaker position. This weakness also owed much to Pitt's ability to strike a popular political resonance, accessible to Whigs and Tories, both within and outside Parliament,[35] a resonance that was disturbing to Newcastle who did not know how to deal with the issue. Moreover, others were aware that he did not know. Pitt's ability to strike this resonance was a skill Carteret had lacked, for personal reasons, thanks to his political baggage, and because of the policies he actively advanced. Parliament, rather than the electorate, was the key issue, because elections were episodic and, due to their necessary timing, did not need to be held in response to great political developments: to changes in the ministry in 1744, 1756 and 1757, or the declaration of war with France in 1756.

There was a broader challenge to the Anglo-Hanoverian polity as a result of the campaigning of that year. Cumberland had been sent to command a Hanoverian and allied force, one that did not include British units, a force that would protect Hanover, which, after the end of the 1756 invasion panic over Britain, was seen as the most vulnerable part of Britain's system. Whatever the attitude of the British public, and there was continuing criticism of Hanoverian influence,[36] the loss of Hanover would become a factor in peace negotiations. Cumberland's force

---

[34] Newcastle to Mitchell, 16 July 1757, BL. Add. 6832 fol. 26.

[35] *London Chronicle*, 30 Apr., 3 May 1757.

[36] *Citizen*, 18, 22, 24 June 1757.

was attacked by a larger French army under the Duke of Richelieu and retreated from 14 June. Although fighting well, Cumberland was defeated at Hastenbeck on 26 July, and Hanover was then rapidly overrun. Acting on his own initiative, and unsurprisingly so given the state of communications between London and Hanover in this period, Cumberland negotiated the Convention of Klosterseven, signed on 10 September. This agreement with Richelieu took the remnants of Cumberland's force out of the conflict and left Hanover neutral.

This outcome was not tangential to the direction of Hanoverian policy because, in an understandable response to the Electorate's vulnerability, there had been earlier interest in neutrality,[37] interest that made Frederick distrust the Hanoverian government.[38] Indeed, the French ambassador in Vienna had pressed Kaunitz to demand Hanoverian neutrality as a way to annoy both Frederick and the opposition in Britain.[39] Hastenbeck and Klosterseven suggested that George had been unwise to reject the Austrian suggestion earlier in the year that Hanover be allowed neutrality in return for granting the French army passage so as to be able to attack Prussia. Hanoverian neutrality posed a major challenge for the British ministry, in both international and domestic terms, indicating, as it did, that there was a lack of clear support for the war in Hanover and implying that the same was true of Britain.

Moreover, the challenge for the ministry extended to the very nature of the state, both constitutionally in Britain, as a parliamentary monarchy, and diplomatically as the dual entity of Britain-Hanover. This nature created multiple political pressures and issues of perception, both for George II and for those who served him. Critical demands were readily apparent. For example, the *Con-Test* of 16 July 1757 argued, with both irony and threat, that if Britain had to commit itself to the Continent, it was clear that George's

> attention to Continental connections, holds but the third place in his royal thoughts: the security of his kingdoms, and the succour and preservation of his dominions in America, happily appear to be the first and second objects of his parental concern.

Hanoverian neutrality threatened the British alliance with Prussia, and indeed the viability, as well as the contents, of British foreign policy. Allegedly in part because it was felt that he was 'so liable to be insulted by the populace',

---

[37] Project of a treaty for neutrality, Apr. 1757, AE. CP. Br- Han. 52 fols 86–96.
[38] Mitchell to Holdernesse, 11 Nov. 1757, NA. SP. 90/70.
[39] Estrées to Rouillé, 6 Jan. 1757, AE. CP. Aut. 256 fol. 37.

the Austrian envoy had been recalled from London in June, which had led to the recall of Keith from Vienna. The structure of British foreign policy was collapsing, with links broken with powers with which Britain was not at war.[40] Attacked by Austria, Russia, France and Sweden, Prussia itself was under great pressure, with the Austrian victory at Kolin (18 June) causing particular anxiety. It led Frederick to press anew for the dispatch of the British fleet to the Baltic.

The Prussian crisis resulted in a sense of the 'Liberties of Europe' as under threat[41] and ensured that there was much pressure for a solution of political difficulties in Britain. The serious danger that Frederick might abandon the struggle,[42] as he indeed considered, made British subsidies to him a matter of significance. Mitchell underlined the need for parliamentary management in a dispatch reporting his assurance to Frederick that the ministry would wish to provide money 'but that, by the constitution, no money could be given, but by Parliament'.[43] Frederick added 'the liberties of Europe, religion and the balance of powers' together in a list when explaining to Cumberland why Britain had to send troops to the Duke's assistance.[44]

As a result of this sense of crisis, reports of Prussian successes, notably at Rossbach over the French on 5 November 1757, were received in Britain with great relief and joy.[45] This made a major contrast with attitudes there toward Continental interventionism in 1755; a contrast that indicated the volatility of opinions, which, in turn, influenced politicians: knowing that public opinion was so changeable is likely to have influenced policy-making. To critics, this was a case of national opinion being easily swayed,[46] but there was also a more specific adjustment, indeed transformation, of attitudes in response both to Britain's international circumstances and to the perception of developments on the Continent. As a consequence, Newcastle was now eager to announce his backing for Frederick,[47] while there was extensive support in Britain for a subsidy to support Prussia.[48] The adjustment was comparable to the rallying

---

[40]   Reporting Kaunitz at second hand, Bristol to Pitt, 29 June 1757, Holdernesse to Keith, 28 June 1757, NA. SP. 92/65, 80/198.

[41]   Hanbury Williams to Holdernesse, 1 July 1757, NA. SP. 91/65.

[42]   Frederick to Margravine of Bayreuth, 16 July 1757, *Polit. Corr.* XV, 251.

[43]   Mitchell to Holdernesse, 29 June 1757, NA. SP. 90/69.

[44]   Frederick to Cumberland, 8 July 1757, *Polit. Corr.* XV, 223.

[45]   Holdernesse to Mitchell, 6 May 1757, NA. SP. 90/68; M. Schlenke, *England und das friderizianische Preussen, 1740–1763* (Freiburg, 1963).

[46]   *Test*, 28 May, *Con Test*, 6 Aug. 1757.

[47]   Newcastle to Mitchell, 16 July 1757, BL. Add. 6832 fol. 26.

[48]   Holdernesse to Mitchell, 16 Aug. 1757, NA. SP. 90/69.

of most opinion in the winter of 1744–5 in favour of the defence of the Low Countries, particularly the support then of the 'New Whigs'.

The Hanoverian neutrality led to much criticism of Hanover[49] and discredited Cumberland who had been widely blamed for the fall of Pitt the previous spring.[50] As a result of his military failure, Cumberland was now marginalised politically. Moreover, Pitt, who had opposed sending British troops to Germany, was able to come to the fore in directing strategy. Had events at home and abroad been otherwise, the political arithmetic of faction might well have created pressure for a very different strategic vision.

Urgent in his demands, Pitt insisted on the disavowal of the Convention, refusing to support payment for the Hanoverian troops while they remained inactive as a consequence of the neutrality. This was an approach that was designed to have an impact on George and on British public opinion. Crucially, Pitt had a solution. At the Cabinet on 7 October 1757, his suggestion that Britain agree to pay the entire cost of the Army of Observation, provided the Convention was disavowed, was adopted. George complied. Moreover, a subsidy for Prussia was agreed. The difficult task of selling this to the public was taken on by Pitt and his allies, the *Monitor* on 3 December presenting the subsidy as a way to save on the cost of sending British troops to the Continent.[51] Hanover, however, was to bear a heavy burden as a result of the resumption of hostilities, one that created problems in the relationship with Britain,[52] and that George felt very strongly.

Prussia's eventual success in 1757 appeared even more significant due to the humiliating failure in late September of a British expedition against the French Atlantic naval base of Rochefort, an expedition intended to challenge the articulation of France's trans-oceanic system. This failure, which owed much to poor intelligence, inadequate co-operation between naval and army commanders, and indifferent and hesitant generalship, led to much criticism of the ministry. The failure also indicated the problems facing the policy of coastal expeditions, problems that were of conception as well as implementation. The political controversy after Rochefort, which included a Commission of Enquiry

---

[49]   Anon., *A Letter to the People of England, Upon The Militia* (London, 1757), p. 18.

[50]   *Citizen*, 16 June 1757.

[51]   C. Eldon, *England's Subsidy Policy Towards the Continent During the Seven Years' War* (Philadelphia, Pennsylvania, 1938); P.F. Doran, *Andrew Mitchell and Anglo-Prussian Diplomatic Relations During the Seven Years' War* (New York, 1986); K.W. Schweizer, *Frederick the Great, William Pitt, and Lord Bute. The Anglo-Prussian Alliance, 1756–1763* (New York, 1991).

[52]   N. Harding, 'Hanoverian Rulership and Dynastic Union with Britain, 1700–1760', in R. Rexheuser (ed.), *Die Personalunionen von Sachsen-Polen 1697–1763 und Hannover-England 1714–1837. Ein Vergleich* (Wiesbaden, 2005), pp. 402–4.

into the conduct of the generals, did not gain the traction of that after Minorca the previous year, in part because there was no comparable humiliation and in part because Pitt was in the ministry. Nevertheless, there was a significant political cost.[53] The popular response was certainly an element when, in August 1757, Pitt proposed, and the Cabinet agreed, to approach Spain offering to return Gibraltar in order to win Spain's support in the war, and thus regain Minorca. Pitt presented regaining this mark of shame as a crucial precondition for peace.[54] Unwilling to enter the war, Spain refused.

Alongside the crisis in Europe, which, to critics, represented the overthrow of a long-failed system,[55] there were others in Britain's maritime and trans-Atlantic strategies. The former confronted the pressure of a range of commitments in the face of a strong French navy, as Holdernesse noted when explaining why it was not possible to send a fleet to the Baltic:

> the strength of the English marine is not equal perhaps to what is thought abroad, owing to the great want of sailors; and yet His Majesty must have a squadron in the Mediterranean, equal at least to the [French] Toulon fleet; one in the Channel, to keep the squadrons of Brest and Rochefort in respect; one in North America; a considerable one in the West Indies, which from the nature of the trade winds is necessarily divided, and one in the East Indies ... It will give you but a melancholy prospect to see the French Marine so very near equal to that of England.[56]

While public calls for colonial security and gains increased, creating more pressure for success, there were few victories to show. Indeed, in the North American interior, the French capture of Fort William Henry at the head of Lake George on 9 August served as another reminder that the initiative there was still held by French forces, and that they could deliver impressive results, while also leaving unclear what this initiative would lead to. The ability of their British counterparts to protect themselves appeared limited and, with it, the prospect of protecting the British colonies.

---

[53] George Quarme to Rockingham, 18 Oct. 1757, Sheffield, Archives, Wentworth Woodhouse papers, R1-111; Viry to Charles Emmanuel III, 18 Oct. 1757, AST. LM. Ing. 62; *Monitor*, 10 Dec. 1757.

[54] Newcastle to Hardwicke, 9 Aug., Hardwicke to Newcastle, 11 Aug. 1757, BL. Add. 32872 fol. 493, 32873 fols 24–5; Pitt to Keene, 23 Aug. 1757, NA. SP. 94/155.

[55] *Monitor*, 9 July 1757.

[56] Holdernesse to Mitchell, 5 July 1757, NA. SP. 90/69; M. Schumann, 'Anglo-Prussian Diplomacy and the Baltic Squadron, 1756–1758', *Forum Navale*, 59 (2003), pp. 66–80.

In 1757, moreover, British efforts focused on a major amphibious operation, directed against Louisbourg, and then Québec,[57] one that could take advantage of naval strength. However, despite sending more forces, there was to be no repetition of the success in 1745. Instead, a combination of a large concentration of French warships and bad weather frustrated British plans. Political factors also played a role. John, 4th Earl of Loudoun, the commander in North America, who was, like many military figures, a protégé of Cumberland, was unwilling to use this theoretical authority with political care and to search for a compromise on the reimbursement and control of colonial troops. As a result, there was scant co-operation between Loudoun and the colonies. This had serious operational consequences. Loudoun was recalled in December 1757.

After three years of operations, British forces had secured Nova Scotia, but as a result of what was derided as the 'Cabbage Planting Expedition', had made no impact on Louisbourg. In the interior, the Ohio River Valley remained in French hands, and the British had been driven from Lake Ontario and towards the Hudson Valley. The resourceful French commander, Louis Joseph, Marquis de Montcalm, had successfully taken, and repeatedly retained, the initiative. There was much disappointment and criticism in Britain, and, again, a sense of failure.[58] This sense related not only to developments in America, but also to what they were believed to betoken for Britain's very existence. Trade as essential to national position and prosperity, a general theme, was given particular force by the current case of North America,[59] which was presented as the new existential battlefield in place of the Jacobite threat. France was depicted as convinced that 'the great project of universal monarchy can never be compassed by the French until they have destroyed our commerce and navigation, which they cannot more effectually do than by worrying us out of the Continent of North America'.[60] As a consequence of these concerns, as well as of more specific worries, there were calls for Britain to gain Nova Scotia and the North American interior.[61] Anxiety led to pressure for expansion and action. The economic significance of North America to Britain's Baltic position, or, at least, the apparent significance, was captured by the *London Evening Post* on 14 July 1757 when claiming that Britain would not send warships to help Frederick:

[57]   Pitt to John, 4th Earl of Loudoun, 4 Feb. 1757, HL. Loudoun papers, no. 2765A.

[58]   Anon., *A Letter from a Merchant of the City of London to the Right Honourable William Pitt Esq* (2nd edn, London, 1757), p. 25; *Citizen*, 29 Mar. 1757.

[59]   Anon., *A Serious Call to the Corporation of London, to address His Majesty* (London, 1756).

[60]   Anon., *A Letter from a Merchant*, p. 26.

[61]   Anon., *A Letter from a Merchant*, pp. 22, 26; *Citizen*, 29 Mar. 1757.

for fear of affronting Russia, which might, in such a case, seize the effects of our merchants there. Thus we feel the ill effects of our neglect of the Northern Colonies, who might long ago have been brought to supply the Mother Country with all kinds of naval stores, and thereby saved the vast sums that have been carried out of this nation, to raise and cherish a cockatrice in the Baltic.

As with other crises, the sense of failure led to alarmist talk, not only about Britain's prospects, but also about national decline and degeneracy. *Con-Test* claimed that 'England must submit to wink at indignity and injustice, till by prudent councils at home, and active valour abroad, she is restored to a capacity of asserting her rights, and avenging past insults and oppressions'.[62] Frederick echoed the theme, linking 'the unhappy state of our internal affairs' to 'the English' no longer being 'the same people, your want of union and steadiness has dissipated the natural strength of your nation', and referring to 'England in her decadence'.[63] Prospects and decline were apparently linked. They also reflected the long-held assumption that the Revolution Settlement that had followed the Glorious Revolution was contingent, much threatened, and dependent on a combination of national resolve, ministerial probity, and the support of Providence. There was no lasting dispensation granting success. An awareness of this existential situation guided responses to the particular circumstances of the moment and to likely developments. An alleged threat to Protestantism was an aspect of the apparently fundamental nature of the crisis, although doubts were expressed on this head.[64]

The crisis was also presented as one that threatened the whole of society, with subsidies to foreign powers meaning that there would be no bread for children or enough money for sailors.[65] The argument of a threat to society was made frequently, most notably in a pamphlet of February 1757 which printed 'The St Giles's Address to Andrew Stone', a Lord of Trade and a significant ally and support of Newcastle. This Address depicted despair among the London poor as their livelihood was threatened, and showed how the war, in the shape of the loss of Minorca, had wide-ranging consequences:

We the lamp lighters, link-boys, dustmen, chimneysweepers, cinder-sifters, carmen, porters, shoe-cleaners, hackney-coachmen, and (late) bruisers of ... St Giles's ... By means of this capture to the enemy, many Turkey merchants, who

---

[62] *Monitor*, 30 Apr., *London Chronicle*, 7 May, *Con-Test*, 9 July 1757.
[63] Mitchell to Holdernesse, 12 June, 11 July 1757, NA. SP. 90/69.
[64] *Crab-Tree*, 12 July 1757.
[65] [Shebbeare], *A Third Letter to the People of England, on Liberty, Taxes, and the Application of Public Money* (3rd edn, London, 1756), pp. 55–6; *Con-Test*, 11 June 1757.

had used to have twenty fires blazing at once, and of course, so many chimnies to sweep, now are forced to do their business at coffee-houses, for want of money to buy coals at home. Their wives call aloud for no coaches, though their own are laid down, their maid servants, which they never did before, sift their own cinders. Their very apprentices, when they cross the way, never pay the link-boy, but cry, like courtiers, another time. And, their porters carry the letters and messages, who used to stay in the warehouse; and, to our utter ruin, pocket the money themselves.[66]

This critique of the conduct of the war was amplified in other writings that developed a criticism of the wealthy for their conspicuous consumption. An anonymous pamphlet of 1757 that offered the programmatic title *Proposals for Carrying on the War with Vigour ... Intended to Demonstrate, That it is not the Dearness of the Labour of the Poor ... which are the real Clog on the Foreign Trade of England* attacked the import of luxury goods such as lace, adding:

> I sincerely wish that our merchants might live like princes, and our traders as if they were the rulers of the Earth, but at this time, when every nation in Europe is setting up, or endeavouring to set up, manufactures in opposition to ours ... there seems to be an ... absolute necessity ... to lay aside the articles of foreign luxury, and return to the old plain English way of living, which will bring with it peace of mind, health of body, an augmentation of people, an increase of shipping and navigation, and a revival of our manufactures and commerce.[67]

The *London Chronicle* complained on 4 June that women were keen to buy imported silks that were clearly French. An argument of the significance of economic warfare was offered with the call in the *London Evening Post* of 12 February for stopping exports of raw wool, adding:

> The encouragement of manufactures in general, together with an utter prohibition to the importing of French wines, laces, silks, brocades, and cambrics etc will distress our great enemy as sorely as our fleets themselves; but both together may bring them to reason.

This rebuttal of luxury was also employed as an argument to place and praise Pitt. Thus, the *London Evening Post* of 27 January, stated that

---

[66] Anon., *Two Very Singular Addresses* (London, 1757), pp. 3–6.
[67] Anon., *Proposals*, p. 54. See also, *London Evening Post*, 1 Jan. 1757.

no acquisitions of wealth or titles can be to him an equivalent for the high regard and esteem he stands in with the Public: Hence we assure ourselves, that no considerations whatever will induce him to swerve from a generous and vigorous prosecution of the most proper measures.

An argument for a revived nation was linked to calls for a militia to protect Britain against invasion. The alternatives presented were of a militia 'all interested in the general weal, rather than ... a rabble of mercenaries, either natives or foreigners'.[68] This was an organic account of the British, rather than a mechanistic view of Britain as a constitutional system. Although contested by critics, notably in the House of Lords,[69] the establishment of a strong militia was presented not only as a national defence policy, but, also, as one for maritime strength and imperial security:

> either we must establish an internal constitutional force for the defence of our own country, and send forth our fleets for the protection of our colonies, or keep our navy at home for the preservation of the former, and leave the latter an easy prey to the first enemy that shall seize upon them.[70]

Meanwhile, the competitive edge war gave to the perception of social problems was indicated by a letter from 'Atticus Police' published in the *Public Advertiser* on 12 January 1757. Referring to famine, the letter attacked the use of grain in alcohol, adding 'what hopes may not the French flatter themselves with, when they are to fight against Englishmen who are scorched in the womb by spirituous liquors and who suck gin from their mothers instead of milk'.

Although the critique focused on society and related issues of morality and policy, there was also a political dimension. This was notably so with the attack on political connections for corrupting the governmental process by allegedly ensuring that inappropriate people were appointed and that the proper functions of Crown, Council and institutions, such as the Board of Admiralty, were thwarted, thus undermining the potential of maritime warfare.[71] This argument was directed both against the 'money interest' and against the use of

---

[68]   Anon., *A Letter to the People of England, Upon The Militia* (London, 1757), p. 10.

[69]   Edward Owen to Weston, 28 Apr. 1757, Weston Underwood.

[70]   C. Jenkinson, *A Discourse on the Establishment of a National and Constitutional Force in England* (London, 1757), p. 46.

[71]   Anon., *The Fatal Consequences of the Want of System in the Conduct of Public Affairs* (London, 1757); *Monitor*, 30 Apr., *Citizen*, 16 June 1757.

party to advance private schemes and to prevent the unity that was required.[72] There was also a broader political critique of the nature and assumptions of the political system. In its issue of 5 April 1757, the *Citizen* criticised the standard assumption:

> that a minister hath nothing else to do than to form a Party, just strong enough to support him at Court, and to carry on his business in national assemblies ... But this is only the quackery of government, which every little state mountebank understands ... The true art of government consists in a general knowledge of mankind, and the particular disposition of the people to be governed ... They are called the vulgar, the mob, the rabble ... and treated as if they were of some inferior species, who are designed only for labour ... They are not, perhaps, very intimately acquainted with the different interests and views of the several Courts of Europe, or the tedious detail of intricate and contradictory treaties, which are sufficient to puzzle the wisest head in Christendom, and even the negotiators themselves would be at a loss to explain; but it is ridiculous to suppose them altogether ignorant of domestic affairs, and the general interest of their country. They judge of public measures both in peace and war, by the effects which they produce on their trade and dealings.

The following day, the paper attacked the additional tax placed on newspapers, a tax that linked élite direction, social politics, fiscal policy, and the standard of living.[73]

Social, moral and political anxieties provided a troubling context. The strategic crisis was different to that in 1744–5: there was no French fleet in the Channel and no Jacobite force in Britain. Yet those had not been in evidence in 1739–43 as the earlier conflict gathered pace. The possibility that failures in 1754–7 would be followed by more dire prospects and outcomes, as had happened in 1744–8, seemed reasonable. Indeed, these fears were to be vindicated by the French invasion attempt of 1759, an attempt designed to assist the Jacobite cause. With a large British fleet near Louisbourg in 1757, and France the conqueror of only a fraction of the British empire, Britain was scarcely a failed power. Nevertheless, a similar comment was also to be valid for 1781–2 in the latter stages of the War of American Independence. In 1757, as in 1781–2, the prospect was bleak. Britain's mid-eighteenth century crisis was scarcely over.

---

[72] Anon, *The Protest* (London, 1757), pp. 25–9.

[73] See also *Citizen*, 7 June 1757. For a critique based on considerations of tax yield, *London Evening Post*, 7 Apr. 1757.

Chapter 11

Conclusions

A fleet is our best security: but then it is not to lie by our walls; nor be confined to the navigation of our own coasts. The way to deliver Rome from the rival ships and hostilities of the Carthaginians was to carry fire and sword upon the African coast. Employ the enemy at home, and he will never project hazardous invasions. Our fleets are able to bid defiance to all the maritime forces of Europe. And as the surest and most rational means to humble the ambition of France is to destroy her power by sea, and her trade from America; no service, but what is directed towards this salutary object of British politics, can be worthy of the attention of a British ministry.

Monitor, 24 December 1757

The gravity of the mid-eighteenth century crisis scarcely appears to prefigure what was to follow. Britain was to emerge victorious from the Seven Years' War (1756–63) and very conspicuously so, such that the terms of triumph became the principal issue in debate within British politics in 1762–3.[1] Commentators in the 1760s were to compare Britain to Imperial Rome at the height of its power repeatedly. If foreign, commentators were to claim that the balance of power had been destroyed, and notably in the naval sphere and the trans-oceanic world. This success ensured that the Seven Years' War was viewed retrospectively in Britain in a positive way, and there was no stress on crisis, although moralists in Britain were to warn of the moral, cultural and political dangers arising from unprecedented wealth.

None of this, however, seemed likely in 1756–7. Indeed, notably from the perspective of those years, the period from 1744 appeared a protracted crisis, with the inter-war years after 1748 apparently given direction by the need to prepare for a new struggle, and to make both nation and state fit for that purpose. Throughout, there was an awareness of threat. In part, this was a dynastic crisis for the Hanoverian regime and its associated values and interests. This was a crisis that appeared feeble in hindsight; but not when French invasion threatened in 1756, when it was considered thereafter,[2] and was attempted in 1759. It

---

[1]   R. Middleton, *The Bells of Victory: The Pitt-Newcastle Ministry and the Conduct of the Seven Years' War, 1757–1762* (Cambridge, 1985).

[2]   Memorandum, 25 Feb. 1757, AE. CP. Ang. 441 fols 17–33; Frederick II to Mitchell, 27 Feb. 1757, BL. Add. 6843 fol. 84.

would be mistaken to see politics as simply a case of the Whig order opposed to Jacobitism, but, at the same time, the continued existence of the latter affected the wider discussion of politics within Britain, notably because Jacobitism had an international dimension. As a related issue, the Whig argument that 'the ignorant and illiterate Vulgar' were manipulated into supporting those with 'execrable designs in favour of Popery and Slavery',[3] a reference to Jacobites, while self-serving, also made public criticism appear dangerous and thus, at least potentially, affected the parameters of debate.

Public criticism, however, was the direction, style and content of British politics; although that situation and the problems posed by such criticism left unclear how political discussion should best be conducted and handled. In part, in the 1740s and 1750s, there was a reiteration and also reformulation of political assumptions. Indeed, the setting of norms, and thus prior to that, the contesting of norms, were major themes as the Revolution Settlement of 1688–9 was worked through a context of weakening party division; which was the situation in the 1740s, even more, 1750s, and, finally decisively, the 1760s. Public debate played a key role in this contestation. For example, belief in the innate value of publication was expressed in the *London Evening Post* of 29 March 1757:

> The freedom of speech, and the freedom of writing, that at present prevails, and, which in some measure, proceeds from the need that all parties have of the press, will bring lasting advantages to this kingdom. Many things have been already so clearly explained, and so fully exposed, that we cannot hereafter be deceived though we may be driven into distress. The nation never fully understood the value of government better, or were ever more cheerfully disposed to support the government.

In its issue of 12 March, the paper had rebutted claims that the press was responsible for the war. Such a debate over the means of discussion played a significant part in the press.

Debate, at the time, in part located Britain's position not only with reference to immediate partisan issues, but also in terms of a long context of developments and events in British history and in Britain's international position. This was a context that, for contemporaries, necessarily looked back, most prominently to the Revolution Settlement, but also with reference to earlier episodes in British history, such as the Hundred Years' War with France. However, the present-day significance of the years 1744–57 for the broader social and ideological picture of

---

[3]   *Jacobite's Journal*, 19 Mar. (os) 1748, cf. 8 Oct. (os) 1748.

British development is unclear. They suggest a false turn, a period of failure, that had to be overcome were Britain to reach sunlit pastures, a pattern subsequently seen when the Napoleonic Wars and World War Two were discussed. The theme of failure overcome in the mid-eighteenth century was to be a major strand in the contemporary and later literature, a history that was created, and that focused in particular on Pitt and on the many achievements of the glorious Year of Victories, 1759. This history was in part designed for polemical and celebratory purposes, not least for the wartime political alliances, those of the political groupings in Britain, of Pitt, Newcastle and George II, and those of Britain and Prussia.[4] These alliances were presented as the causes of victory, as the reasons for success were contested as an aspect of the partisanship of the 1760s, and notably with the emphasis on Pitt. In turn, this approach became the national account, and notably in the nineteenth and early twentieth centuries.

This account is not without weight. The leaders, political and military, of 1758–62, and the policies and contingencies of those years, indeed played key roles in British victory. At the same time, it is instructive to adopt a wider perspective. In particular, it is necessary to look at how and how much the structural factors giving Britain strength and enabling it to use this strength, notably its naval power and its public finances, were affected by the agency and contingencies of the years covered by this book. There were, for example, concerns about the constitutional threat posed by a stronger professional military, concerns that focused on the position and alleged ambitions of Cumberland and that helped ensure there was a shortage of troops.[5] There were suggestions by foreign diplomats that rising opposition in Ireland would affect the British ability to respond to the mid-century crisis as there would be a need to have more troops there.[6]

Nevertheless, there was significant strengthening of the British military state in the period, which was particularly apparent with the navy. In 1749, as a result of long war service, including damaging operations in the Caribbean, the battle fleet in good condition had been greatly reduced, and the dockyards could not cope with requirements for repair and replacement. This problem was overcome in the early 1750s, not least through using the private sector to build new ships. The 1749 visitation of the royal dockyards revealed corruption and inefficiency. There was resistance in the Navy Board to proposals for radical reform, but there was considerable success in making the existing machinery work more smoothly.

---

[4]   F. De Bruyn and S. Regan (eds), *The Culture of the Seven Years' War. Empire, Identity, and the Arts in the Eighteenth-century Atlantic World* (Toronto, 2014).

[5]   D. Baugh, *The Global Seven Years War, 1754–1763* (Harlow, 2011), pp. 203–5.

[6]   Perrone to Charles Emmanuel III, 10 July 1755, AST. LM. Ing. 59.

As a result, the naval mobilisation of 1755 proceeded relatively smoothly. The public–private partnership heavily involved in the contracting out of army supply had also improved.[7] More generally, the Seven Years' War was to demonstrate many deficiencies and problems in the British military state, for example in the supply of gunpowder, but there had been a qualitative improvement in British government and military organisation and activity since the early 1740s. This improvement proved crucial to Britain's ability to act successfully in the New World as well as to fulfil military tasks in Europe and in European waters such as maintaining a blockade of France's major Atlantic naval base of Brest, which was no easy task.

The relationship between domestic politics and foreign policy, however, remained more troubled. There were notable divisions in British opinion over policy and its implementation. Offering a perspective very different to that of Jane Austen during the Napoleonic Wars, William Hotham wrote to his brother from Bath about Admiral Byng in March 1757: 'People's violence in general, and the ladies in particular, is to me something very shocking.'[8]

At the same time, it is mistaken to imagine that this situation was uniquely British, or simply a consequence of parliamentary government. Frederick observed of Russia in 1756: 'there had been lately great diversions and dissensions at that Court'.[9] Moreover, there was a strong sense in Britain and elsewhere that public opinion could play a role in a number of states, and also institutions, notably the *Parlement* of Paris, a body often reported in the British press as the Parliament of Paris,[10] and thus both accommodated to the language of British politics and also misrepresented. The following January, the Austrian envoy in Paris commented on the hostility of French public opinion, seeing it as habitually opposed both to Austria and to the French government.[11] This was an echo of French views about British popular assumptions.

British politics did not simply involve political management and opinion within Britain. The problems of managing a 'multiple polity' were also significant.

---

[7]   R. Middleton, 'Naval Administration in the Age of Pitt and Anson, 1755–1763', in J. Black and P. Woodfine (eds), *The British Navy and the Use of Naval Power in the Eighteenth Century* (Leicester, 1988), pp. 109–112; G.E. Bannerman, *Merchants and the Military in Eighteenth-century Britain: British Army Contracts and Domestic Supply, 1737–1763* (London, 2008).

[8]   William to Charles Hotham, 14 Mar. 1757, Hull, University Library, Hotham papers, DD Ho 4/6.

[9]   Mitchell to Holdernesse, 27 May, NA. SP. 90/65.

[10]   Bristol to Pitt, 13 Apr. 1757, NA. SP. 92/65.

[11]   Starhemberg to Kaunitz, 31 Jan. 1757, quoted in J.C. Batzel, 'Austria and the First Three Treaties of Versailles, 1755–1758' (PhD., Brown University, 1974), p. 271.

In terms of the politics of foreign policy, the issue was not Ireland. Instead, in Britain, the tie to Hanover created serious problems for both politics and foreign policy, the last notably in early 1757 as the alliance with Prussia was gravely threatened by discussions about foreign policy. This situation contributed to the major difficulties that faced the British and Hanoverian ministries in late 1757. However, despite contentious politics arising in Britain from the link with Hanover, British foreign policy and the related politics were not essentially a response to the need to protect Hanover. Instead, throughout the period covered by this book, there was the longstanding concern to create a coalition to resist France, a concern that reflected views across the Whig spectrum, as, even more, did that to ensure a dynamic purpose and energy to such resistance. France, and not Hanover, dominated the public debates.

The ministerial rationale for the wish to establish an anti-French coalition, and (separately) the reasons publicly given for it, were different by 1755–6 to the situation in the 1740s. The emphasis was increasingly on the political and strategic implications of British imperial commitments and, as a contentious add-on, the consequences for Britain's position in Europe. It was not solely in order to justify their own strategic choices that British ministers felt able to claim, as in 1757, that 'the result of the great struggle, between England and France, ... will determine the conditions of the future peace'.[12] The greater stress on Britain's oceanic and imperial position[13] did not mean that ministers sought to remove Britain from Continental power politics, but it did influence the governmental approach as well as greatly affect the public perception of Britain, in Britain and abroad. Instead of Britain being seen abroad as part of a European system seeking to counter any hegemonic power, notably France, the British were increasingly presented across Europe as an empire determined to monopolise the trade of the world. This view was advanced at a time of greater public interest in trade as an aspect of national identity, and of governmental concern to use commercial expansion to strengthen the nation as well as the state.[14] This argument looked toward an approach that was to be strongly taken toward, indeed against, Britain after the Seven Years' War.

At the same time, alongside this 'modern' theme, notably of the significance of commercial competition, the criticism of Britain's mercantile dominance was

---

[12] Holdernesse to Mitchell, 17 July 1757, NA. SP. 90/69.

[13] For a qualification, D. Ahn and B. Simms, 'European Great Power Politics in British Public Discourse', in W. Mulligan and B. Simms (eds), *The Primacy of Foreign Policy in British History, 1660–2000* (Basingstoke, 2010), pp. 79–101.

[14] Describing Russian attitudes, Douglas to Rouillé, 23 May 1756, Paris, BN. Naf. 22009 fol. 119.

an aspect of a conservative theme, namely a longstanding disdain for mercantile people and concerns. A similar approach, ironically, was to be taken by British commentators when explaining why the Dutch did not act in what they considered an appropriate international role. Holdernesse warned in 1756 that:

> The support of the Freedom of Navigation, as artfully insinuated and coloured by France, is an argument by which that power means to lead all neutral states to carry on her commerce, and enable her to increase her military marine force, or to engage them, if that should be prevented, in an open opposition to the English fleet ... Holland ... the clamours of the merchants, who think of their own private emoluments more than the public good.[15]

For some British commentators, the imperial emphasis was expansionist, and for others defensive. Despite the claims of protecting British interests and treaty rights, the defensive had not been a theme and attitude that was pronounced when British commentators, angered by Spanish depredations on British trade, hopefully considered action against Spanish America in the late 1730s and early 1740s. However, the situation was very different as far as France was concerned, for there were strong fears that French expansion in the North American interior threatened the British colonies.

Wherever the emphasis, there was also a widespread realisation, following the return of Louisbourg, that the European situation was not only important, but could be determinant as far as imperial goals were concerned, or, at least, with respect to their implementation. This realisation encouraged the idea that success in Europe for Britain and its allies, or, at least, the avoidance of failure, would free up trans-oceanic opportunities. This idea had a powerful peacetime component in terms of the establishment of a strong alliance able to act as a deterrent against France and failure, and to prevent an impression of vulnerability. Thus, policy and strategy were linked. The deterrent, moreover, was multi-purpose. It could serve to protect specific interests, in the shape of Hanover and the Low Countries, as well as the more general sense of the proper nature and operation of the European system. The latter appeared the best way to guide against unwanted contingencies, such as, notably in 1753, a conflict over the Polish succession.

Under the crunch of crisis, however, this situation broke down in 1755. The unity of British foreign policy was shattered. An expansionist, aggressive,

---

15   Holdernesse to Keith, 21 June 1756, NA. SP. 80/197 fol. 186. See also Holdernesse to Hanbury Williams, 25 June 1756, NA. SP. 91/63.

opportunistic and optimistic North American policy, in essence adopted for domestic political reasons (domestic including colonies), and in response to urgent anxiety about North America, was pushed to the fore; but at the same time that the weaknesses, if not failings, of Britain's Continental alliance system became more apparent. Whereas in North America, British ministers had only to consider their own politics and policies in framing their response to French policy, as well as their own assumptions about French intentions, on the Continent there was the diplomatic, strategic and political problem of the agenda being set by allies, and, indeed, being obviously set. Defending the new alliance with Frederick II in 1756, Holdernesse argued that Austria had no reason to complain as Britain had never intended to support an aggressive war against Prussia and, specifically, that the alliance with Russia was seen as preventive.[16] However, while an accurate statement of British policy, that was not the view of Britain's allies; while, subsequently, from his attack on Saxony, Frederick was repeatedly to show that he did not intend to let Britain set his agenda, and thus the agenda for the alliance in Europe.

Paradoxically, an aspect of this failure was to leave Britain, in at least one major respect, in a less difficult position in 1756–7, indeed until 1793, than had been the case hitherto. Due to alliance between Austria and France from 1756, there was no longer the need for Austria and, therefore, Britain to defend the Low Countries, or, indeed, the possibility for Britain to do so. This meant that British forces could not be deployed there. This ended the hopes, as in 1709 and 1744, of invading France across its land frontiers, but also ensured that the Low Countries would not need to be protected from French invasion. However, the absence of an Austrian alliance was serious for a range of reasons, not least that the Austro-French alignment helped ensure that the now far more vulnerable Dutch would not oppose France. In addition, there were more specific factors that did not relate to the military situation on the Continent. These included the value, however declining, of the Dutch navy, not least in balancing the French and Spanish navies, and the use of Dutch troops against Jacobite action and the threat of such action. There was also the danger that ports in the Austrian Netherlands, notably Ostend, would enhance French invasion prospects, and the risk that Austria would cede part of the territory to France, as, indeed, was considered. The French occupation of Ostend and Nieuport for the duration of the war, a clause in the Second Treaty of Versailles signed on 1 May 1757, was

---

[16]   Holdernesse to Keith, 23 Mar. 1756, NA. SP. 80/197 fols 44–5.

soon known.[17] Thus, an issue that had played a role in English/British policy for centuries, and most recently in 1744–8, that of resisting French expansion in the Low Countries, was again to the fore, but in a different shape.

With neither Austria nor the Dutch any longer part of the British alliance system, there was no prospect of defending the Low Countries. Moreover, Dutch neutrality and Austria's alliance with France apparently lessened the need to undertake a task that repeatedly proved very difficult.[18] This situation further pushed the emphasis onto the maritime and trans-oceanic dimensions of British policy, neither of which had alliance implications, other than in terms of organising support from the colonists. Moreover, the lack of this need to defend the Low Countries helped make Hanover appear more of a strategic and political appendage to Britain. Hanover could no longer be so readily presented, either practically or rhetorically, as it had been in the 1740s, as part of a broad alliance system focused on opposition to France, and thus in line with traditional British interests. In addition, Hanover was no longer protected by French priorities in the shape of France being more concerned to expand into the Low Countries, as had been the case in 1744–8. Instead, Hanover was successfully invaded in 1757.

Similar problems of practicality in execution and, indeed, compatibility with wider British strategy affected the new alliance with Prussia. Pitt's rhetorical skills, combined with Frederick's military ability, were to postpone this problem until the early 1760s and to make the ending of the alliance politically toxic for George III and the Bute ministry. Moreover, in the meanwhile, these skills and this ability were to prove crucial to British politics and strategy during the years of victory. This outcome, however, appeared implausible in 1756–7 as Frederick confronted a formidable range of challengers. Indeed, in June 1756, Holdernesse suggested that, if Russia allied with France, as it was to do in 1757:

> the decided superiority of France, in conjunction with such an ally may force the King, however unwilling His Majesty may be, to give up *all* thoughts of intermeddling in the affairs of the Continent. I can by no means admit the King of Prussia, when not in alliance with France, to be, in any degree, formidable to the Empress of Russia.[19]

---

[17]   Newcastle to Holdernesse, 11 July 1755, BL. Add. 32857 fol. 45; Mitchell to Holdernesse, 18 May 1757, NA. SP. 90/69.

[18]   A.R. Limm, '"Fairly Out-generalled and Disgracefully Beaten": The British Army in the Low Countries, 1793 to 1814' (PhD, Birmingham, 2015).

[19]   Holdernesse to Keith, 21 June 1756, NA. SP. 80/197 fol. 178.

This suggestion highlighted a fundamental development in Continental power politics, one that affected British strategic and diplomatic capability. British success on the Continent from 1759 was to disguise this shift, notably the consequences of the unprecedented wartime alignment of France, Austria and Russia, but it was to prove a major factor in the 1760s, one, indeed, that the crisis of 1756–7 had demonstrated. The depth of this crisis led to great relief when news of a Prussian victory over an Austrian army was received in May 1757, Holdernesse noting 'my Office was crowded with messengers from the City, to enquire if the report was well founded'.[20] The news resonated around the country, James Gollop writing from distant Berwick about the 'glorious event'.[21] Prussian victory provided an aura of success that offered an apparently stable basis in international relations and foreign policy for the establishment of a new ministry in London. Capturing the extent of changes in opinion and anticipating the later transformation in opinion, the *Test* commented on 28 May 1757 on:

> the precarious vicissitude of human affairs ... do we not all remember the time when the King of Prussia, to use the blackguard expression of a certain eminent personage, 'Stunk in the nostrils of every Englishman?'. When the English language was exhausted in odious appellations? ... And now how reversed are the opinions of the people? Imagination has not in all her stores of lavish ornament colours sufficiently gaudy to adorn his favourite home ... his alliance is now allowed to be natural; a great orator [Pitt] loves to touch his little finger ... I shall not be surprised if I should find this heroic, philosophic, warlike, enterprising monarch [Frederick], in some future political conjuncture, the d-mndest, vilest, most detestable etc and the Queen of Hungary [Maria Theresa], now a bitch, set upon two legs again, and adored in every print-shop.

the last a reference to caricatures. Relief was even more the case when Frederick unexpectedly and conclusively defeated the invading French at Rossbach on 5 November 1757. Holdernesse assured Mitchell that the victory 'has filled the world with surprise and admiration. It is impossible to describe to you the universal joy that this great event has spread throughout the whole nation.'[22] This result, however, threw up both a problem and a solution for the ministry. The possibility that France might approach Prussia, resuming the former alliance between the two powers, led to the question of whether the British 'Nation'

---

[20] Holdernesse to Mitchell, 6 May 1757, NA. SP. 90/68.
[21] Gollop to John Tucker, 31 May 1757, Bod. MS. Don. B. 19 fol. 158.
[22] Holdernesse to Mitchell, 22 Nov. 1757, NA. SP. 90/70.

would heartily enter into a Continental war[23] in order to satisfy Frederick. Simultaneously, the popular enthusiasm aided 'the intentions of those in power in the exertion of the strength and assistance of this nation.'[24] The enthusiasm certainly addressed the political consequences of the policy.

At the same time, in addition to concern about the constraints posed by popular attitudes, a degree of flexibility, alongside wishful thinking, in the British discussion about international relations was indicated in the diplomatic correspondence. Holdernesse conveniently argued in 1756 that Russia's interest was internal improvement, not external expansion, and that that interest should lead to alliance with Britain, with which there was a positive balance of trade, and thus support for the British commercial system, including its security from French attack in North America.[25] Instructions were sent to Hanbury Williams accordingly.[26] However, despite the significance of British trade for Russia,[27] they proved fruitless. This was a major blow for British foreign policy.

The viability not only of Britain's alliances and foreign policy, but also of the Revolution Settlement within Britain was also at issue in 1756–7, and appeared to be at issue. Political division and governmental instability did not help Britain as it struggled with extremely difficult diplomatic and military circumstances. In the *Jacobite's Journal* of 29 October (os) 1748, Fielding had pointed out (as others had done) a contrast between Britain and most other European states, as well as the misleading consequences that might thereby arise:

> it is one of the unhappy consequences which too often attends the liberty of writing in free countries, to have their weakness exposed, and their secrets divulged to the whole world. And this, perhaps, may be one reason of the disadvantageous light in which the politics of such countries may have sometimes appeared, when compared to those of more absolute governments.

Alongside administrative flaws, political weakness, and policy drawbacks, it is appropriate, however, to draw attentions to strengths in the British system. There were important elements of dynamism not seen elsewhere, other than in certain respects in the United Provinces. These included the role of international trade, in economic, social, fiscal and political terms, Britain's relative freedom from state and corporatist control, the size and political importance of the capital,

---

23   Mitchell to Holdernesse, 25 Dec. 1757, NA. SP. 90/70.
24   Edmond Thomas to Mitchell, 10 Dec. 1757, BL. Add. 6861 fol. 298.
25   Holdernesse to Keith, 21 June 1756, NA. SP. 80/197 fol. 179.
26   Holdernesse to Hanbury Williams, 25 June 1756, NA. SP. 91/63.
27   Hanbury Williams to Holdernesse, 26 Mar. 1757, NA. SP. 91/65.

and the place of urban life as an aspect of the activity and autonomy of the middling orders. There was also significant economic development and a degree of cultural confidence. In *The Progress of Poesy* (1757), Thomas Gray followed poetry's development from Classical Greece and Rome to modern England.

At the political level, and in comparative terms, the relative weakness of the Court was palpable and notably in 1744, 1746 and 1756–7, as far as the choice of ministers was concerned.[28] At the same time, George was no cipher. This was true for Britain, but also for Hanover. Indeed, like Frederick, as he sought to make the alliance work to Prussia's benefit, George could be cross about 'dilatory proceedings at Hanover', where there were few formal restrictions to his power.[29] In Britain, the importance of Parliament was readily apparent, alongside the positive consequences that arose, notably its ability to raise funds, and the significance of national legislation and consciousness. Thus, in May 1757, Holdernesse emphasised the willingness of the peers in the House of Lords to support the defence of Hanover if attacked in consequence 'of measures taken for the defence of the rights and possessions of the Crown of Great Britain; for assisting the King of Prussia, and for supporting the Protestant cause in the Empire'.[30]

Whether or not expressed in terms of dynamism, development or change are not inherently incompatible with the idea of Britain as an *ancien régime* society.[31] Instead, taking on board this idea, the situation referred to can be seen as one of the most significant features of a British *ancien régime* that, however, was different in character to those on the Continent, varied as the latter indeed were. There were stately homes as grand as the chateaux and schlosses on the Continent, but there was no comparison on the latter to parliamentary leadership of the type exercised by Pelham or Pitt, nor to the dynamism of London. Even when the British ministry was strong and felt secure, there was still an awareness of the role of public pressure. Britain, therefore, was not an inflexible Church–State society, nor a stagnant and corrupt Whig oligarchy. Instead, the essentials of the political system were a difficult, but working, compromise. Parliamentary monarchy, the method and ideology that was put in place as the result of the Glorious Revolution and the Revolution Settlement required compromise and an understanding of nuance. Parliamentary monarchy involved policy in the midst of debate, as well as debate focused on policy; and neither of these

---

[28]   *Con-Test*, 14 May 1757.
[29]   Holdernesse to Cumberland, 6 May 1757, BL. Eg. 3442 fol. 56.
[30]   Holdernesse to Cumberland, 17 May 1757, BL. Eg. 3442 fols 78–9.
[31]   For this idea, J.C.D. Clark, *English Society, 1660–1832* (2nd edn, Cambridge, 2000). See more recently, his *From Restoration to Reform, 1660–1832* (New York, 2014).

processes, especially the former, was easy. To some commentators, British and foreign, this situation suggested that Britain was inherently unstable. Indeed, from the perspective of government, both then and if adopted by modern commentators, it is easy to see that the fall of ministries and ministers, notably in 1742, 1744 and 1756, the more frequent sense that ministries might fall, and the regular business of having to defend policy against sometimes ill-informed and generally partisan opposition, can appear causes of weakness, and notably in terms of competition with other powers.

Yet, however inconvenient, or prone to 'the reports of shallow coffee-house graduates in politics and the idle declamations of overheated pamphleteers,'[32] debate and contention revealed a political structure that was adaptable, and certainly not rigid. Any concentration on politics as contention, and on the clash of groups and ideas, risks distracting attention from the degree of co-operation and toleration that did exist, and from the extent of consensus that this suggested. Indeed, the very possibility of recruiting support from those hitherto in opposition, as repeatedly happened from 1742 to 1757, helps explain this clash of groups and ideas, but also its general limitation. Criticism might be labelled factious, but it was not generally seen as seditious, and nor was it seditious if the logic of opposition politics is accepted, namely that of persuading the monarch to change the ministry. Thus Jacobitism, and the response to it, did not define the political system, nor explain its tensions. The '45, the Jacobite crisis of 1745–6, revealed much about the political system, but was also atypical and, indeed, although very serious, did not define politics in those years. Opposition was only exceptionally expressed in rebellion, just as the government did not generally rely on force, and notably not in England. Indeed, there were few troops in England.

Instead, government drew on a broad public engagement. This engagement ensured that popular support for policy was mobilised in different ways from that on the Continent. This was the case both in terms of mechanisms, principally Parliament and the press, and in the content and ethos of politics and government. A belief in such difference was important to British self-identity, and thus to the narrative of the necessary development that was constructed. Mobilised can appear an unproblematic term unless it is appreciated that debate was inherent to the process, and not an add-on resulting from political failure or factionalism. This debate offered a definition and delimitation of support that brought political benefits.

In addition to these issues of political ideology, practice and process, the prime strength of the British political and governmental system was that it both

---

[32]   *Test*, 18 June 1757.

represented and brought together the principal social and economic interests in the country. The system did so successfully, and in a way that was seen, by most people, as legal and appropriate; thus reflecting, and also creating, a constitution that worked. These interests were historical and practical. Going back to the three Houses of Parliament – the Crown, the aristocracy, and the people or commoners – provided a pedigree in legal longevity. The *London Chronicle* of 7 May 1757 declared:

> The British government is neither a Monarchy, or the arbitrary government of one man, like that of France; nor an Aristocracy, or the government of the nobles, like that of Venice; nor a Democracy, or the government of the populace, like that of Holland ... It is a mixed legislature.

The governmental system drew on the different socio-economic interests of importance, and thus reflected the dynamism of the economy and the development of society. Moreover, the maintenance and adaptation of the political and governmental system created in the aftermath of the Glorious Revolution and the Act of Union with Scotland was a major achievement. As the failure of the Swedish Age of Liberty (1719–72) and the Orangeist overthrow of republican systems in Holland and Zeeland in 1747 demonstrated, the grounding of new constitutions in effective government was not inevitable.

The extent to which economic growth eased the political situation is unclear, but suggestive. Certainly, alongside criticism of government in the world of print, it is appropriate to note the range and extent of publications focused on ideas of improvement. Much of the latter did not have the political slant that some calls for renewal offered, but there was a degree of overlap in the sense that change was a key element. The title-page of Edward Weston's *New System of Agriculture: or, A Plain, Easy, and Demonstrative Method of Speedily Growing Rich* (1755) proclaimed that agriculture offered the 'only gentleman-like way of growing rich', while in 1756 appeared Thomas Hale's *A Complete Body of Husbandry. Containing Rules for Performing, in the Most Profitable Manner, the Whole Business of the Farmer, and Country Gentleman, in Cultivating, Planting, and Stocking of Land.* Those involved in agricultural improvement helped ensure that a rising population could be supported in Britain without significant difficulties other than in response to periodic harvest failures. The drive for improvement shadowed divisions in opinion and involved sociability and a related hierarchy of achievement in which aristocratic birth was not the key element.

However, in a pattern that also bears examination for politics, there were regional and local variations. For example, an agricultural improvement society was established in Norwich in 1755, and by mid-century, the Norfolk four-course rotation – of wheat, turnips, barley, and clover – was established on many farms. More fodder allowed heavier stocking of the land, while the animals were the source of manure in arable farming, besides providing meat, notably the 'roast beef of old England', and wool for cloth, much of it was exported. Nevertheless, there was far less agricultural progress in many areas. The controversy over grain exports in 1748 was linked to the liquidity of the agricultural economy. With the exception of the debate over grain exports, agriculture did not play a significant role in foreign policy.

Aside from quantitative and qualitative agricultural development, there was also a powerful and increasing comparative advantage for Britain in the shape of a growth in coal production that, in absolute and relative terms, was greater than that in any other country. As a result, Britain had a cheap energy economy, an economy provided from domestic sources and not related to foreign policy. By 1750, coal provided 61 per cent of all energy used in England.[33] By raising labour productivity, cheap energy made it easier to pay high wages, and thus to sustain demand.[34] The expansion of coal mining interacted with the transformation of the metallurgical industry, bringing to fruition the transfer from an essentially wooden age to a new iron age, one based on coal with its higher calorific value. The mutually sustaining nature of economic change was readily apparent.

Much of the headline-grabbing industrialisation occurred in Britain after 1760, but there was significant change earlier in the century. Aside from important growth at the national level, there was development in particular areas, such as central Scotland where, from the early 1750s, there was a build-up of forge and foundry establishments, especially around Glasgow. Moreover, in the 1750s, there was a rapid spread in the turnpike system, particularly in England. Already, by 1750, a sizeable network of new turnpikes had been created there. There was also a significant enhancement in the bridge system. Stone bridges replaced wooden ones and ferries, improving the capacity and reliability of the system. Bridges opened in the period included those at Westminster, Walton and Hampton Court, which underlined the significance of the Thames valley. Better transport routes helped further to integrate the country. It became easier to move between large hubs, while their status and significance were in part defined and maintained by these routes and services. From the 1750s, coach times improved on turnpike roads. Exeter to London journeys fell from three

---

[33]   E.A. Wrigley, *Energy and the English Industrial Revolution* (Cambridge, 2010), p. 94.

[34]   R.C. Allen, *The British Industrial Revolution in Global Perspective* (Cambridge, 2009).

days in the 1740s to two by 1750. Meanwhile, most goods services from London substituted more efficient stage wagons for packhorses and the greater ease of transport encouraged a convergence in prices. The centrality of London in the world of news and opinion was greatly enhanced by such developments.

By 1750, in a process that was important to the character of political culture, those employed in industry and commerce in Britain exceeded those who worked in agriculture which, in turn, was more productive than hitherto. The British economy had developed significant comparative advantages over European rivals. These advantages, which were to play a role in Britain's wartime capability helped, in the meanwhile, in the vital provision of credit. Bank-created currency added an elastic supply of finance to the relatively inelastic stock of coinage, although the latter itself rose from Britain's success as a trading power. The ready availability of working capital was crucial to economic activity, which explained the repeated vulnerability of the economy to reports of bad news from abroad. The national credit structure was vulnerable to challenges to financial credit, not least because most credit was short term. This credit structure greatly stimulated an interest in national and international politics and news.[35]

The fundamentals for sustained economic growth included a relatively stable political system, legal conventions that were favourable to the free application of capital, especially secure property and contracting rights, a social system that could accommodate the consequences of economic change, and an increasing and important degree of economic integration and interdependence. Although not always expressed in these terms, the significance of these factors was well understood by contemporaries. Secure property rights were the antithesis of the oppressive government decried by British commentators. Yet, these fundamentals were challenged, and, certainly, believed to be challenged, by a hostile international environment. That helped explain its significance. Newcastle suggested in 1753 that

> All rival nations may be glad to see the fleet of England, and the trade of this country, reduced and embarrassed; and the lesser powers may not be sorry to have a precedent for carrying on trade in time of war',[36]

and thus wrecking Britain's wartime commercial position.

---

[35]   J. Brewer, 'Commercialisation and Politics', in N. McKendrick, J. Brewer and J.H. Plumb (eds), *The Birth of a Consumer Society. The Commercialisation of Eighteenth-century England* (London, 1982), pp. 203–16, 229.

[36]   Newcastle to Yorke, 13 Feb. 1753, NA. SP. 84/462.

Without security, political stability and other fundamentals were threatened, a point that was very apparent at the time. However, although helpful, the presence of fundamentals for sustained economic growth did not guarantee political outcomes, let alone success in the highly competitive international arena. Yet, the eventual success of foreign policy was a key element in ensuring what was to become a transformative economic revolution, while, conversely, earlier failure posed a serious problem, notably in 1745–8 and 1754–7. This was more particularly the case as the fundamentals of the British system, both political and economic, were increasingly understood by the mid-1750s in trans-Atlantic terms, with the established emphasis on trade given a stronger additional colonial dimension.

The relationship between state and economy, success in the former and transformation in the latter, was two-way. States kept a close eye on the financial state of their rivals. Thus, British envoys reported on the condition of French credit. Financial strength was crucial to the ability of the British state to operate in war, to subsidise allies, and to offer a potent deterrent in peacetime. As a result, the financial viability of British policy was a key theme for commentators and one that ministers knew they had to refer to and demonstrate. Thus, in 1752, Frederick II sought to convince Louis XV that Britain was not in a state to sustain its allies,[37] while in 1755, Newcastle, who had been concerned in 1754 that Russia seemed to think the roads paved with gold, wanted to know if the Bank of England was willing to raise £1 million at 3 per cent interest. As a sign of his policy and attitude, all of the money was to be added to the National Debt; while 'the money can easily be got and the first offer was made to them, merely out of regard to the Bank'. In practice, most of the money was swiftly raised as the deposits for the subscription to a lottery.[38] Frederick's scepticism in 1755 about British fiscal strength was countered from London by his envoy, Michell, who observed no shortage of money.[39] Later in the year, as relations with Britain improved, Frederick noted that France was unable to borrow at 6 per cent or even 8 per cent at Europe's other major financial centre, Amsterdam, which limited its ability to sustain a conflict.[40] This was a convenient observation

---

[37]   Frederick to Louis, 9 Oct. 1752, *Polit. Corr.* IX, 235.

[38]   Perrone to Charles Emmanuel III, 9 May 1754, AST. LM. Ing. 58; Anon., 'Memo for the Bank', c. 27 Mar., J. West to Newcastle, 15 Apr. 1755, BL. Add. 32996 fols 65, 75; R. Browning, 'The Duke of Newcastle and the Financing of the Seven Years War', *Journal of Economic History*, 31 (1971), pp. 344–77.

[39]   Frederick to Michell, 2, 26 Aug. 1755, reply, 15 Aug., *Polit. Corr.* XI, 233, 276.

[40]   Frederick to Knyphausen, 23 Sept., 21 Oct. 1755, *Polit. Corr.* XI, 313, 347.

and reassurance given his move towards Britain, but was none the less accurate for that.

Interest rates were regarded as a key indicator of strength, and diplomats often commented on them. In 1755, Perrone confidently predicted an ability by the British government to borrow £6 million at 3½ per cent. He linked this to public attitudes, in the shape of support for defending the American colonies.[41] The French certainly focused on whether British merchants would lend to the government.[42] Meanwhile, an important structural change in Britain's favour was captured by a pamphleteer in 1755:

> The high sounding bugbear of eighty millions of debt, when stripped of the rags, with which disaffection and discontent had cloathed it, appeared less formidable than a debt of fifty millions was formerly; and that it was easier to pay the one at 3 per cent, than the other at 5.[43]

In policy terms, the ministry was confident in 1755 that it could afford naval and colonial operations, but not the cost of a war on the Continent. Newcastle took this tack when explaining policy to the leading ministers in Hanover.[44] It was similarly believed in 1755 that France could not afford war in Europe as well as further afield,[45] which proved true, although, significantly, only in the long term. France's financial weakness was certainly a factor for Rouillé.[46] This weakness played a role in the 1756 international crisis, but did not dictate a particular diplomatic alignment for France nor prevent effective military action by it. Unable to supply Russia with the necessary money for the mobilisation of military resources, Austria also feared that France could not pay for Russia.[47] Yet, these powers allied together.

The financial dimension of policy remained significant as the war developed; with, in particular, an increasing financial capability gap between Britain and

---

[41] Perrone to Charles Emmanuel III, 23 Jan. 1755, AST. LM. Ing. 59.

[42] Memorandum, 23 Mar. 1755, AE. MD. Ang. 41 fol. 12.

[43] Anon., *Reflections upon the Present State of Affairs* (London, 1755), p. 27.

[44] Newcastle to Münchhausen and Steinberg, 18 July 1755, BL. Eg. 3481 fol. 127.

[45] Maria Theresa to Starhemberg, 22 Nov. 1755, Batzel, 'Austria and the First Three Treaties', p. 101.

[46] Rouillé to Marshal Noailles, 21 July 1755, AE. CP. Ang. 439 fol. 265; J.C. Riley, *The Seven Years' War and the Old Regime in France: The Economic and Financial Toll* (Princeton, New Jersey, 1986).

[47] Maria Theresa to Starhemberg, 11 Aug. 1756, Batzel, 'Austria and the First Three Treaties', pp. 178–80.

France.[48] As important, this gap was perceived by contemporaries, and frequently so. While allied, Frederick had been dismayed by the state of France's finances.[49] In the early months of the war, there were concerns in Britain about the increase in the National Debt[50] and regarding difficulties in raising money.[51] However, interest rates remained lower than in France, and, as before the war, this was presented as a fundamental element in the relationship between the two powers. The *Con-Test* claimed on 2 April 1757:

> It is notorious to those who are conversant in public business that our enemies, the French, are at this time compelled to borrow money at 8 per cent ... While they are obliged to raise money at this exorbitant rate, what a mortification, what a discouragement, must it be to them, to find us so superior to them in public credit, as to be able to provide for the annual service in time of war, without any increase of interest. This is the most effectual means of reducing them to sue for peace. They cannot now depend on the load of our National Debt.

This situation became more apparent later in the year when Frederick was given a large subsidy at the same time that the war was pursued by Britain on a considerable scale in North America. Although the planned attack on Louisbourg did not materialise, the major force that was sent was a clear demonstration of power, purpose, and the ability to deploy resources. Britain's overseas trading system, a system underpinned by naval strength, contributed directly to its ability to act as a great power. The return of richly-laden merchant fleets encouraged the offer to the government of more loans than it wanted.[52] Underlining the financial theme, Newcastle boasted to British and foreign diplomats that he could raise large sums at 3½ per cent, whereas France could not do so even at nearly 11 per cent.[53] Diplomats reported France finding it difficult to raise funds, for example at Geneva[54], a major financial centre, and even seeking to borrow money in Britain.[55]

[48]   J. Pritchard, *Louis XV's Navy, 1748–1762* (Kingston, Canada, 1987).

[49]   Frederick to Lord Marshal, 1 Sept. 1753, *Polit. Corr.* X, 63–4.

[50]   Anon., *Observations on the Conduct of the Late Administration* (London, 1757), pp. 46–7.

[51]   Edward Weston to Edward Owen, 29 Mar. 1757, Weston Underwood.

[52]   Haslang to Wachtendonck, 18 Nov. 1757, Munich, Bayr. Ges., London 233.

[53]   Newcastle to Mitchell, 8 Dec. 1757, BL. Add. 6832 fol. 31; Haslang to Preysing and Wachtendonck, 9 Dec. 1757, Munich, Bayr. Ges., London 233.

[54]   Bristol to Pitt, 28 Dec. 1757, NA. SP. 92/65.

[55]   Alt to Landgrave of Hesse-Cassel, 6 Dec. 1757, Marburg, 4f England 261.

Conversely, more than structures were concerned. The unity of the British government was treated as important to its fiscal strength. At the same time, this fiscal success was seen as threatened by the failings of politics, which it indeed was in 1756–7, and sufficiently so to challenge the very nature of the British system, as well as its trajectory of success. Criticism came from a variety of directions, some stronger on hyperbole than analysis. Attacking the government in 1757, the anonymous author of the *Protest* suggested that Britain had become no better than France, indeed worse:

> the misery or slavery which the People are subjected to under the bad administration of those bad [Continental] governments, is often not so deplorable, destructive and tyrannical as what men may suffer under the best of governments in the hands of a bad administration ... for many years ... the losses we have suffered, and the disadvantages we now live under, while France is every day increasing her people and extending her influence, and undauntingly contending for those rights and liberties which we contend for indeed, but with more ostentation and show, than reality.[56]

In a parallel with comments about Britain, these dissensions in France were regarded as encouraging foreign powers, notably Britain, to press her hard on matters in dispute.[57] Criticisms of the British governmental system could rest on pragmatic grounds. There was, for example, the argument that British government was too open for war. Mitchell commented on the opposite situation with Frederick, 'a Prince, whose secret is known to no man; who executes before it is known that he has deliberated'.[58]

The commercial and financial significance of overseas links, links amply demonstrated in the early stages of the Seven Years' War, not least as British trade with the Continent was put under great pressure, contributed to a sense that Britain's interests, was well as the best way to ensure them, were changing. The growing redundancy of the views on British foreign policy that had become grounded as part of the Revolution Settlement was a theme of the 1750s, a theme anticipated in the public and ministerial debate earlier as opposition to interventionism was encouraged by differences with allies.[59] Nevertheless,

---

[56]   Anon, *The Protest* (London, 1757), pp. 30, 34.

[57]   Reporting view of Swedish envoy in The Hague, Bonnac to Saint-Contest, 8 Nov. 1753, AN. KK. 1400, p. 341; Frederick to Lord Marshal, 24 Nov. 1753, *Polit. Corr.* X, 161.

[58]   Mitchell to Holdernesse, 17 May 1757, NA. SP. 90/69.

[59]   C. Baudi Di Vesme, *La Politica Mediterranea Inglese. Nelle Relazioni degli Inviati Italiani a Londra..., 1741–1748* (Turin, 1952), pp. 86–8.

ignoring the alliance with France between 1716 and 1731, foreign policy had, in the 1740s and early 1750s, been conceptualised and implemented on the basis that France was 'the constant ... enemy of England' and 'the common enemy' of the Empire and, indeed, of the European system. From this background a pact between Austria and France could only be, as Holdernesse argued, a 'preposterous alliance'.[60] These assumptions, however, ignored the transformation in Austrian and Prussian ideas and did not capture the views of other states.[61]

This was a situation that had very obviously been the case more generally not only of British isolationists, but also for the interventionist strand of British foreign policy, and, most clearly, after the rise of Russian power-projection in the 1710s. In particular, the redundancy of his assumptions gripped Newcastle with anxiety and despair as he struggled to produce results from, indeed find logic in, the Old Alliance. Replacing his backing for the French alliance and his politically sensitive stance during the Whig Split of 1717–20,[62] the Old Alliance had become central to his account of his own history and significance. Such logic appeared to be offered by recruiting Russian support, as in 1748, 1753 and 1755.[63] However, failure was driven home when words turned to deeds from 1754 and Britain appreciated the need for its allies. Allies, difficult for many years,[64] were no longer prepared to match British suppositions.

Failure and anger were apparent in public attitudes as much as government policy. Indeed, Fox captured a link when he told Viry in July 1756 that, although it was likely that Austria would learn that it was the dupe of France, that would be too late, as the angry 'nation' would oblige the government for the future to adopt a peacetime system of avoiding the renewal of treaties with such allies. In response, Viry argued that the nation had benefited, notably in maintaining the balance of Europe, from its alliance with Austria and would surely wish to resume it when Austria changed policy (which would give Sardinia renewed freedom of manoeuvre), only to be greeted by Fox with sarcasm based on what Britain had gained from the money spent to help Austria.[65] In a process prefiguring that which was to be seen from 1762, as Britain under George III and Bute abandoned Continental interventionism and alliance with Prussia,

[60]   Holdernesse to Onslow Burrish, 18 Mar. 1757, NA. SP. 81/106.

[61]   For this being true of Britain and France, G. Lind, 'The Making of the Neutrality Convention of 1756. France and her Scandinavian allies', *Scandinavian Journal of History*, 8 (1983), p. 190.

[62]   *Protestor*, 21 July 1753.

[63]   Newcastle to Hardwicke, 21 Sept. 1753, BL. Add. 32732 fols 699–701.

[64]   Holdernesse to Burrish, 18 Mar. 1757, NA. SP. 81/106.

[65]   Viry to Charles Emmanuel III, 6 July 1756, AST. LM. Ing. 60.

one-time opposition satire had, by 1756, at least in the case of an angry Fox, become the view of ministers. Those arguing for Continental interventionism had to confront this response and legacy. On 23 April 1757, the *London Evening Post* felt able to claim:

> At present, surely all parties have ridded themselves of these Continent prejudices, and stand convinced that our only effectual barriers against France are a good navy and a national militia. With these, properly settled, we shall be always respected, our friendship courted by the powers on the Continent, and our resentment feared. We may then make what alliances are necessary for the sake of trade, without encumbering ourselves with foreign guaranties, or draining our almost exhausted treasure, in the payment of fruitless and foolish subsidies, paid to princes who will act with us, if it is their interest, without such subsidies.

The crisis, or rather crises, of 1755–7 not only caused a greater wariness about Continental interventionism but also a focusing of the relationship between domestic politics and foreign policy. Indeed, under the pressure of deteriorating relations with France as well as Austria's unwillingness to offer help, Newcastle felt able to write to Hardwicke in July 1755:

> I think both the King and my Lord Holdernesse very properly combine *our Home situation*, with the foreign one, and in order to support the one, His Majesty possibly might be brought to consent to whatever your Lordship and I should propose with regard to the other.

That, however, posed problems. Newcastle underlined the need first to consider 'what advice we shall give as to the support of the Continent'. Whether co-operation with Austria was viable was a key issue.[66] The two men agreed that 'His Majesty's views (as far as they relate to the Continent) should for the present be confined to the security of his own dominions there', a marked drawing in of commitments, although they were keen to pursue a subsidy treaty with Russia which was seen as a way to contribute 'to the preservation of the general peace'.[67] In fact, this policy was to fail totally.

---

[66]　Newcastle to Hardwicke, 6 July 1755, BL. Add. 35415 fols 3–4.

[67]　Newcastle to Holdernesse, 11 July 1755, BL. Add. 32857 fols 4–5; Newcastle to Gerlach Adolf von Münchhausen and Ernst von Steinberg, 18 July, Newcastle to Münchhausen, 25 July 1755, Hanover, Hannover 91, I 22 fols 10–13, 17–18.

Ultimately, Britain's international and strategic situation, its foreign policy, and the perceptions and politics closely linked to these, all changed considerably in, and as a result of, the mid-eighteenth-century crisis.[68] The consequences were to be important during its subsequent course as a great power.

[68]   S. Conway, 'War and National Identity in the Mid-eighteenth-century British Isles', *English Historical Review*, 116 (2001), pp. 863–93; M. Darnley and P. Speelman (eds), *The Seven Years War as a Global Conflict* (Leiden, 2012); E. Dziembowski, *La guerre de Sept Ans 1756–1763* (Paris, 2015).

Selected Further Reading

The range of primary sources available can be discerned through the footnotes of this book and those in this list. The list focuses on books published in recent years. Earlier works can be tracked down through the footnotes and bibliographies in these studies.

Anderson, F., *Crucible of War: The Seven Years' War and the Fate of Empire in British North America, 1754–1766* (2000).

Anderson, M.S., *The War of the Austrian Succession, 1740–1748* (1995).

Baugh, D., *The Global Seven Years War, 1754–1763* (2011).

Baxter, S.B. (ed.), *England's Rise to Greatness, 1660–1763* (1983).

Black, J., *America or Europe? British Foreign Policy, 1739–1763* (1998).

—— *Parliament and Foreign Policy in the Eighteenth Century* (2004).

—— *Continental Commitment. Britain, Hanover and Interventionism, 1714–1793* (2005).

—— *Trade, Empire and British Foreign Policy, 1669–1815* (2007).

—— *Debating Foreign Policy in Eighteenth-Century Britain* (2011).

—— *British Politics and Foreign Policy, 1727–44* (2014).

Borneman, W.R., *The French and Indian War: Deciding the Fate of North America* (2006).

Browning, R., *The Duke of Newcastle* (1975).

Cardwell, M.J., *Arts and Arms: Literature, Politics and Patriotism during the Seven Years War* (2004).

Clark, J.C.D., *The Dynamics of Change: the Crisis of the 1750s and English Party Systems* (1982).

Colley, L., *Britons: Forging the Nation, 1707–1837* (2nd edn, 2009).

Conway, S., *War, State and Society in Mid-eighteenth Century Britain and Ireland* (2006).

—— *Britain, Ireland, and Continental Europe in the Eighteenth Century; Similarities, Connections, Identities* (2011).

Dann., U., *Hanover and Great Britain 1740–1760* (1991).

Doran, P.F., *Andrew Mitchell and Anglo-Prussian Relations during the Seven Years' War* (1986).

Harding, R., *The Emergence of Britain's Global Naval Supremacy, The War of 1739–1748* (2010).

Harris, B., *A Patriot Press: National Politics and the London Press in the 1740s* (1993).

——— *Politics and the Nation: Britain in the Mid-eighteenth Century* (2002).

Horn, D.B., *Sir Charles Hanbury Williams and European Diplomacy 1747–58* (1930).

Lodge, R., *Studies in Eighteenth-century Diplomacy, 1740–1748* (1930).

McKelvey, J.L., *George III and Lord Bute: The Leicester House Years* (1973).

McLynn, F., *France and the Jacobite Rising of 1745* (1981).

Mapp, P.W., *The Elusive West and the Contest for Empire, 1713–1763* (2011).

Mimler, M., *Der Einfluss Kolonialer Interessen in Nordamerika auf die Strategie und Diplomatie Grossbritanniens während des Österreichischen Erbfolgekrieges, 1744–1748* (1983).

Mulligan, W. and Simms, B. (eds), *The Primacy of Foreign Policy in British History, 1660–2000* (2011).

Newman, G., *The Rise of English Nationalism: A Cultural History, 1740–1830* (1987).

Niedhart, G., *Handel und Krieg in der Britischen Weltpolitik 1738–1763* (1979).

Pares, R., *War and Trade in the West Indies, 1739–1763* (1963).

Peters, M., *Pitt and Popularity. The Patriot Minister and London Opinion during the Seven Years' War* (1980).

——— *The Elder Pitt* (1998).

Plank, G., *Rebellion and Savagery. The Jacobite Rising of 1745 and the British Empire* (2006).

Pritchard, J.S., *Louis XV's Navy, 1748–1762* (1987).

Rogers, N., *Whigs and Cities: Popular Politics in the Age of Walpole and Pitt* (1989).

Schilling, L., *Kaunitz und das Renversement des Alliances* (1994).

Schlenke, M., *England und das friderizianische Preussen, 1740–1763* (1963).

Schumann, M. and Schweizer, K.W., *The Seven Years War: A Transatlantic History* (2008).

Schweizer, K.W., *England, Prussia and the Seven Years' War* (1989).

——— *Frederick the Great, William Pitt and Lord Bute: The Anglo-Prussian Alliance, 1756–1765* (1991).

Scott, H.M., *The Emergence of the Eastern Powers, 1756–1775* (2001).

Simms, B., *Three Victories and a Defeat. The Rise and Fall of the First British Empire, 1714–1783* (2007).

Simms, B. and Riotte, T. (eds), *The Hanoverian Dimension in British History, 1714–1837* (2004).

Szabo, F.A., *The Seven Years' War in Europe* (2008).

Szechi, D., *The Jacobites: Britain and Europe, 1688–1788* (1994).

Thompson, A., *Britain, Hanover and the Protestant Interest, 1688–1756* (2006).

—— *George II* (2011).

Wilson, K., *The Sense of the People: Politics, Culture and Imperialism in England, 1715–1785* (1995).

Index

Printed in Great Britain
by Amazon